T0265626

DEGENERATIONS
of DEMOCRACY

DEGENERATIONS
of DEMOCRACY

Craig Calhoun

Dilip Parameshwar Gaonkar

Charles Taylor

HARVARD UNIVERSITY PRESS

Cambridge, Massachusetts

London, England

2022

FIRST PRINTING

Library of Congress Cataloging-in-Publication Data
Names: Calhoun, Craig J., 1952– author. | Gaonkar, Dilip Parameshwar,
1945– author. | Taylor, Charles, 1931– author.
Title: Degenerations of democracy / Craig Calhoun, Dilip Parameshwar Gaonkar,
Charles Taylor.
Description: Cambridge, Massachusetts : Harvard University Press, 2022. |
Includes bibliographical references and index.
Identifiers: LCCN 2021045367 | ISBN 9780674237582 (cloth)
Subjects: LCSH: Democracy. | Equality. | Political participation. |
Common good. | Solidarity.
Classification: LCC JC423 .C2444 2022 | DDC 321.8—dc23/eng/20211202
LC record available at https://lccn.loc.gov/2021045367

We dedicate this book to the Center for Transcultural Studies and its predecessor, the Center for Psychosocial Studies, which have enabled us to learn together for more than thirty years.

Contents

Introduction   *1*

1   Degenerations of Democracy   *18*

2   Contradictions and Double Movements   *48*

3   Compromises with Capitalism   *88*

4   Authenticity and Meritocracy   *129*

5   Making the Demos Safe for Democracy?   *159*

6   The Structure of Democratic Degenerations and the
     Imperative of Direct Action   *181*

7   What Is to Be Done?   *208*

Conclusion   *258*

Notes   *289*

Acknowledgments   *333*

Index   *337*

DEGENERATIONS
of DEMOCRACY

Introduction

The future of democracy seems increasingly dark. We want to say democracy can be renewed, that it can flourish, that it can be more inclusive, more egalitarian, and more empowering. Yet we have to admit this would be a reversal of the trends we see around us.

Americans could take heart in the remarkably high voter turnout in 2020. At least long-standing apathy had been reduced. But then the losing presidential candidate and millions of his followers refused to accept the results. There was even an invasion of the US Capitol amid widespread efforts to reverse the election. The extremity, malice, and even violence of partisan division remain alarming.

Nor are disunity and conflict limited to the United States. Democracy is under duress worldwide. Similar issues and emotions shaped Britain's 2016 Brexit vote and have bedeviled the country since. Anxieties about change, the power of citizens, and national identities are prominent in France, Germany, Poland, Hungary, and most European countries. Russia is officially but not practically democratic. Despite impressive resilience, the world's largest democracy in India is challenged by polarization and majoritarian nationalism. Democracy that seemed to be taking root is instead disintegrating in Ethiopia and becoming increasingly fraught in South Africa and much of Central America. China has long vacillated between long claiming to be building a kind of democracy, and contrasting its own model—variously termed Confucian, communist or just Chinese—to what it sees as the growing failures of Western democracies. As more liberal democracies suffered during the Covid pandemic, China became ever more authoritarian, yet boasted that it manifested "democracy that works."

In this book, our focus is not on troubled or halted transitions to democracy. It is on degenerations in what have long been considered strong democracies. Of course, there is a relationship. Degenerations of democracy in countries such as the United States make it look less promising to would-be democrats elsewhere. Ethnonationalist rule and increasing disregard for constitution and law make India less of a model.

There is no shortage of books and articles on the crisis and possible loss of democracy. This one is distinct in stressing both the long-term degeneration of democracy from within, as distinct from just external attacks and the depredations of bad leaders, and the importance of social and cultural foundations, not just narrowly political reforms, to renewing democracy.

To be sure, democracy *is* damaged by corrupt and self-serving leaders who promote social division as a tactic of power. It is weakened by manipulation of its rules, suppression of votes, gerrymandering, and attempts to discredit elections. But "saving" democracy requires more than just processual or technical repairs.

Renewal must address two kinds of foundations for democracy that are not entirely contained within political democracy as such: first, republican constitutions and norms of civic virtue, and second, social conditions for effective citizenship, including social solidarity and limits to inequality. Democracy cannot thrive without rebuilding these foundations.

The foundations are partly cultural and moral. Rebuilding must restore commitment to civic virtue and the public good; it must renew collective identity and reduce corruption. Constitutional protections for the rule of law, good government, and the rights of *all* citizens need not only be present on paper but also be understood and respected. Material factors are also crucial. Inequality has increased dramatically—in income, in wealth, even in the quality of health care during the coronavirus pandemic. This means that, in many countries, whole categories of citizens have sharply divergent experiences of policies and social changes; they literally are not "in it together." But inequality is not the whole story, either. At least as important is an erosion of social connections—communal and crosscutting—that knit citizens together across lines of difference. Social solidarity is not simply a sentiment; it is also a structure of social relations. It needs to be rebuilt at the scales of local communities, national institutions, and the many kinds of intermediate associations in between.[1]

Dimensions of Degeneration

In Chapter 1, Charles Taylor outlines three factors central to recent downward spirals of degeneration: disempowerment of citizens, failures of inclusion, and hyper-partisan and majoritarian pursuit of political victories at the expense of shared futures. These are not the only possible components to degeneration, but they are crucial, and we return to them repeatedly through this book.

Robust democracy is a way of empowering all citizens, both in politics and in the rest of their lives. Such empowerment encourages controversy and reveals tensions between public and private interests. It brings resistance from some elites. It also brings capacity for mobilization to solve common problems and keep improving common life. Liberty, equality, and solidarity are not mere abstractions. They are of practical importance in the lives of democratic citizens. But each can degenerate.

Democracy depends on the empowerment of citizens—and degenerates with disempowerment. This undercuts both having an effective voice in public affairs and efforts to meet personal challenges. Disempowerment comes not just through explicit blockages, such as voting restrictions, but from loss of social conditions for effective action. To benefit from democracy in routine ways, as well as to fight for more democracy, requires not just individual but social capacities. Citizens are empowered by communities and neighborhoods, organizations such as trade unions, networks formed in churches and synagogues, parent-teacher associations, youth sports leagues, and social service associations. Social movements empower those they mobilize, building on existing connections and developing new ones. They can be empowering even when they fail to achieve their explicit objectives.

Disempowerment is increased by extreme economic inequality, as well as by *political* inequality. Government is opaque and distant, inaccessible to ordinary people, and run by an apparently distinct political class. To say that the members of this class are privileged elites is not to say that they are the same privileged elites who dominate corporate and financial capitalism. They are different factions of the dominant class and not always completely aligned.[2] The so-called populist movements exemplified by Brexit in Britain and Trumpism in the United States, showed that even relatively well-off people can feel they lack political power. This is not just a matter of not being heard in Washington or Westminster; it is a matter of not being able to get garbage collected or neighborhood roads fixed.

Another dimension of democracy is political inclusion. Rather than having more or less power, this involves having a stronger or weaker sense of membership and participation. Democracy has often been limited by restrictions on formal political inclusion—as, for example, in the withholding in the United States of voting rights from slaves, women, and men without enough property. US democracy has advanced with wider voting rights, and it degenerates when efforts are made to curtail these—as happened after Reconstruction and is happening in many states today. And vote suppression is not limited to the United States.

But informal inclusion is also important. Do citizens recognize each other as common and equal members of the polity? Is formal recognition by the state matched by informal recognition among fellow citizens? Race, ethnicity, religion, immigration status, and other divisions can fragment and limit political inclusion. The issue is not just the rights of minorities; we need to ask how some people get recognized as the majority in relation to whom others are treated as minorities, or what happens when people who think they are the rightful majority confront the rising prominence of other groups. Majority status is a matter of cultural politics, not just numbers.[3]

A sizable fraction of US citizens resists redefining American identity to be inclusive of Blacks, American Indians, Latinos/as, Asians, and others. Some embrace an older idea of a white Christian nation.[4] They do not want to become the minority. Similar issues are at play as Canada seeks to put anglophone and francophone citizens on an equal footing, to give full citizenship and recognition to First Nations, and to integrate new immigrant populations. Anxious Englishness was basic to Brexit and undermines more inclusive British identity. Dominant ethnic groups seem obvious majorities—they are often described as constituting "legacy nations." Yet national majorities are always constructed—through material change as well as discourse—as much in France or Hungary as in more explicitly diverse countries such as Canada, the United States, and Britain.

When saying "We, the people," ceases to include the whole and expresses instead the hostility of a real or imagined majority to all minorities, the result is a distorted, pernicious expression of the genuine need for solidarity among democratic citizens. Solidarity is not conformity and seldom involves unanimity. Democracy is almost always contentious. Citizens pressing their different agendas are agonistic but not necessarily antagonistic. They want to win arguments, but not necessarily to win at each other's expense. This is different when extreme political polarization makes taking sides primary. Democracy degenerates when citizens ask first what do people in my camp believe or think or do—not what is good for the whole society.

Partisanship can be constructive, or at least manageable, when subordinated to concern for the public good. Advocates may clash over what is best for all. It is, however, a small step from seeking to win an argument to valuing victory more than pursuit of the public good. Unsurprisingly, partisans seek tactical advantages. Unfortunately, as Ezra Klein has argued, a variety of incentives routinely lead rational political actors to seek short-term advantage in ways that undermine good government and encourage polarization.[5] Extreme or hyper-partisans put winning ahead of all other considerations—and this is a problem. Extreme partisans do not merely find themselves in confrontations but seek them out and engineer them, seeing cooperation as betrayal of their factional cause. They stalemate effective government when they do not get their way, and they increase public rancor and frustration. They harness themselves to cultural divides so that the electoral interests of individual candidates align with the preferences of polarized voters. They demand complete adherence to extreme party positions, stopping elected officials from acting with any independence. Extreme partisanship can put a party at odds not just with other parties but with the preferences of most citizens—yet allow it to remain electorally effective in the near term. In short, extreme partisanship can be a major factor in democratic degeneration.

Extreme partisanship cannot be explained simply by the attitudes of individuals. It is encouraged by the careerism of politicians, but this is not an adequate explanation either. Extremes of partisanship reflect social divisions. They arise when social foundations for democracy are not shared. When connections among different social groups are weak, their members can more easily develop sharply different understandings of what is going on in society, clashing narratives of how things got this way, and strident attributions of blame for producing problems and blocking the way forward. And extremes of partisanship are typically reactive. They are not simply stable differences of views; they are movements stimulated by destabilizing changes—by great transformations.

The division of society into mutually uncomprehending factions is shaped by geography, by different positions in relation to economic change and security and to ethnicity and religion, and by politics. It overlaps the often-remarked echo chambers of different media networks. Siloed media reinforce social division. They make partisanship into an almost epistemological divergence when a primary criterion for truth is what those on my side believe. On each side, not only do people stick to their favorite channels or feeds; they also filter out discordant messages and evidence. Views of "reality" are distorted by emotional as well as intellectual effort to reduce cognitive dissonance. That is, people recognize those facts that fit with their established ways of thinking, feeling, and acting and resist or ignore those that don't.[6] For decades, highly mobile elites have looked at globalization and believed that "we are all becoming cosmopolitan." Nonelites have been more frustrated by changes and likely to believe in QAnon or other conspiracy theories. Different media spread and reinforce such beliefs but do not by themselves cause them.

Polarization is thus more than extreme differences of opinion; it is divergence in ways of seeing the world. It comes not just from tactical sacrifice of the public good, but from fundamentally different understandings of both the public and the public good. These different ways of seeing the world are grounded in different social positions with different material prospects as well as different ways of life. And these differences tend to be correlated with voting patterns: rural versus urban, more and less educated, professional and nonprofessional, actively religious and not, red states versus blue states.

Democracy is not solely a project of reasoned discourse. Emotions, identities, and interests all matter. Where democracy is robust, different identities are recognized and competing interests are negotiated. Sensing political exclusion and feeling impotent may sometimes lead to resignation and disengagement from politics. But at other times a sense of neglect, or exclusion, or being consistently on the short end of policy choices calls forth anger, resentment, and partisan efforts to find culprits to blame.

Frustrations rise when people experience disruption or deterioration in their lives and communities, when they feel they can't promise their children that things will be better in the future, when, in short, "the system" does not work well for them. Frustration is exacerbated when political elites fail to address popular pain or anger. Inequality affects experiences of globalization, of new technology, and of the role of finance, among other things. But political alignments are not simple, direct reflections of material interests or hardships.

Disempowerment, failed inclusion, and extreme polarization get their most visible public face when they come together in political movements claiming to give voice to the "real people" neglected by conventional politics. Commonly described as "populist," these movements are reactions to perceived (and perhaps real) neglect. Their motivation is less ideological than emotional, reflecting resentment and frustration. Driven by degenerations of democracy, such movements can bring further disruption, but also new participation to the democratic process.

Angry and resentful populists need not be socially marginal. Of course, some are direct victims of economic change. Many live outside the metropolitan areas that get most public attention. Some are genuinely neglected; some simply do not have their expectations met. They feel that they don't get their due, even when they live in upper-middle-class suburbs and send their children to private schools. Convinced that they are really *the* people, they chafe when "too many" opportunities go to immigrants or racial minorities. Some defend traditional gender roles. They are alarmed by social changes—even changes in intimate relationships—that make their countries seem unfamiliar or less fully theirs.

Taken by Surprise

For years, people who lived in the older liberal democracies simply assumed that these represented the future of humankind. To characterize those democracies as "liberal" means that they protected the rights of individuals, minorities, and open political dissent—as distinct from democracy understood as the pursuit of equality or other potential progress by authoritarian means. As we argue, especially in Chapter 2, complementing democracy with republicanism is what produces its liberal variant.

Sooner or later, the thinking went, everyone would come around to adopting this form of government. This belief is rooted in an optimistic reading of the history of modern democracy generally, as though it has been good and getting better since the Magna Carta or the American Revolution rather than proceeding in fits and starts and struggling to overcome significant limits. Americans, for example, told themselves (and taught schoolchildren) a story of a republic that was always democratic despite slavery and civil war, brutal treatment of American Indians, and long exclusion of women from voting rights.

The optimistic narrative was strengthened by the successive waves of democratization that occurred in the twentieth century: after World War I, after World War II, and after the fall of the Berlin Wall in 1989. The confidence survived even the failures and breakdowns of some of the new democracies that succeeded each wave. But it is shaky now.

Considering how extreme the crises of global depression, world war, and decolonization were, it is impressive that in their wakes so many people in different countries would think that democracy was almost inevitable. Democracy became a guiding project of Europe's separate countries and eventually the European Union, of all three North American countries, of Japan, Australia, and New Zealand. Postcolonial countries embraced democracy despite recognition that hypocritical colonizers had often been democratic at home and imperialist abroad. India stands out but is not alone. Quite remarkably, South Africa is a multiracial democracy, despite difficulties inherited from its apartheid past. After 1989, democracy came to Eastern Europe and some parts of the former Soviet Union. There was a brief wave of near euphoria—and, too often, complacency.

Optimists argued that democracy spoke directly to an innate human desire for freedom and to the obvious justice of equality. When people saw it in action, they would want it for themselves and their countries. This is not entirely false, but it is drastically oversimplified and misleading. Democracy is not simply a static, preestablished set of procedures that can be adopted like a new technology or the practice of wearing Western business suits and shaking hands at meetings. It is impoverishing to think of democracy as a set of formal procedures or minimum legal guarantees such as freedom of the press. It can be established only through processes of transformation. And once some package of democratic procedures is in place, change will necessarily continue. Democracy flourishes when approached as a project.

Democracy itself raises expectations that existing structures cannot meet. Citizens with some democracy will commonly want more and better democracy—and differ on what that means. As social and economic conditions keep changing, so, too, do the wants and desires of citizens, as well as their capacities for collective action. Both tendencies remind us that democracy is not simply on or off like a light switch, present or absent, or even more or less fully achieved on a linear rating scale.

Democracy, we argue, is necessarily a "telic" concept. It denotes not just a set of conditions but also commitments and aspirations; it is defined by purposes even if these are never perfectly met. Not only its routine operations but also its transformations are guided by ideals. To participate in democracy is to work for more and better democracy. In this sense, democracy is more than the most immediate expressions of popular will. The republican tradition is again important as a source of the idea that democracy can be better, but it is not the only one. Considering the well-being of future generations can be simply an enlargement of the democratic idea of the people. But for democracy to both endure and thrive, it is crucial that it be oriented to the future and open to evaluation and improvement.

And yet, insofar as democracy inherently raises expectations, it can also produce frustration with existing limits. Limits to democracy do not come simply from political mechanisms that incompletely realize its ideals (or the ideals of any particular democratic constitution). They come largely from economic and other social changes that democratic processes do not completely control, but to which they must respond—such as technological change, increases in scale, and the inequality and volatility of capitalism. There can be good aspects to these developments, including greater wealth and longer life-expectancy. But they also cause upheavals in communities and social institutions and at least temporary disempowerment of citizens. How democracies respond is crucial.

Karl Polanyi famously traced such a process of "great transformation" during the first 150 years of industrial capitalism. Enclosures restricted communal access to land, agricultural and craft work were devalued, novel property rights were absolutized, supports for the poor and unemployed were abolished. A new market society was built, bringing new wealth but distributing it unequally and always accompanied by great instability and insecurity.[7] After two world wars and a global depression, the "double movement" of disruption and reaction was tamed by active state intervention and the building of new institutions for public welfare.

We suggest that a new "great transformation" has been underway since the 1970s. It has brought financialization and globalization, successive crises and brutal austerity policies in response. It has made higher education more important than ever before, more expensive than ever before, and more unequal than ever before. It has been liberating for some and brought new respect for cultural diversity. But it has been sharply disempowering for members of the industrial working classes and created new challenges for many citizens. It has brought a populist response but not yet the needed rebuilding of institutions and communities.

Even while a political system remains formally democratic—conducts elections, for example, and has peaceful transfers of power—democracy can degenerate. Citizens can feel disempowered, and communities can lose capacity to organize collective life. Instead of progressively including a wider range of citizens in full participation, a democratic nation can embrace exclusion and hierarchy. Partisan polarization can fracture not just politics but ordinary social solidarity.

When social conditions change, democracies need to renew their political institutions. Too often, elites have instead stood aloof, deploring extreme problems, but also benefiting from changes that are disruptive or even destructive for others. Globalization is a prime example. It is an economic benefit for corporations, their shareholders, and their higher-level employees. It is a benefit for consumers who are offered new variety of products and competitive pressures to keep prices low. It is a tax benefit for those able to hide their wealth in foreign havens and shell companies. But it is not a benefit for workers who lose jobs or are forced to relocate, or for others who live in communities undercut by the loss of industrial employers. For decades, elites have enjoyed the benefits and been complacent about the losses. This has driven a weak policy response not just to globalization but to the transformations of globalization, financialization, new technologies, and new structures of corporate power.

Indeed, we can now see degenerations of democracy shaping responses not just to economic changes and disruptions, but to pressing global concerns, ranging from the coronavirus pandemic to climate change and migration. These challenges clearly cross borders. Response demands transnational collective action. Instead, we have seen renewal of competitive and sometimes belligerent nationalism. Citizens face these crises with little trust in government. Institutions are too often damaged or dysfunctional. The actual history of elite leadership inspires resentment more than confidence.

The coronavirus pandemic is a case in point. Hopes for recovery . . . have led many to speak of a return to "normal." This is misleading, not just because the pandemic is likely to last longer than many imagine, and its socioeconomic consequences to last still longer. More basically, recovery will not be a return to some imagined previous stable conditions. We will recover from the pandemic only with transformation. This will involve not just public health but systemic issues, from supply chains to restructured employment to global cooperation. Likewise, it is hard to conceptualize what might be meant by a return to normal in global migration. And it is at most a fantasy with regard to climate change.

To face these challenges without further degenerations of democracy, we need both to recover from degenerations of the last fifty years and to rebuild democracy's social foundations. It is vital to renew republican political norms and complement this with rebuilding structures of solidarity from communities to state institutions. And as we recover from each disruption, we will also face new challenges.

It will not be possible to save democratic freedoms, constitutional processes, and political cohesion without such transformation. This will require resuming historical struggles to deepen democracy; it will require commitment to new agendas.

In this book, we come at these challenges from two angles. Craig Calhoun and Charles Taylor focus mainly on the United States and other Western democracies that have grown wealthy through a compromise with capitalism. They examine deep problems and yet insist that these can be addressed and democracy can resume its telic improvements, albeit in nonlinear transformations. Dilip Gaonkar focuses on India, where an impressive democratic history has contended with massive inequality and deep heterogeneity. He offers a counterweight to Calhoun's and Taylor's determined optimism, pointing to the "politics of the street" in which popular will is expressed without being fully integrated into republican or other telic agendas for improvement. He recalls Greek arguments that democracy was necessarily unstable.

The cases are not diametrically opposed. India shows that republican institutions and telic pursuit of better democracy can take root outside the West and in a country contending with enormous poverty and division—even if the success of that achievement is now challenged. Conversely, the United States and Europe are not without a politics of the street, not without citizen mobilizations that express anger or resentment without clear agendas for improvement. And while Calhoun and Taylor stress the importance of more inclusive democracy, they recognize that it is a challenge and will be incomplete for the imaginable future. Gaonkar worries about a phase of "ugly democracy" but hopes renewal of republicanism and social solidarity can mitigate it.

Conventional stories and assumptions about democracy can be prone to illusions. For example, many Americans tell themselves stories of innocent origins that minimize the significance of exclusions and oppressions, not least of slavery. Or they acknowledge that there were problems but believe that these have been eliminated in a linear story of progress, forgetting the Civil War among other setbacks. And there are Indians who narrate a story in which the Mughal and British Empires brought distortions to an essentially Hindu country that would be a more thriving democracy and stronger nation if they were removed, forgetting both the need for struggles against inequality and their partial successes.

We should overcome these illusions, but not replace them with cynicism. It would be a mistake to see injustice and oppression as constants, to fail to recognize the extent to which democrats have not only fought for greater liberty, equality, and solidarity but sometimes achieved a great deal. Degenerations of democracy have undermined what these democratic struggles achieved, but attention to the past struggles shows that achievements are possible. Indeed, achievements have been remarkable. We will, for example, point to failures and difficulties in the social and political inclusion of migrants. This is a serious challenge. Even famous nations of immigrants such as the United States and Australia have recurrently been abusive. But the historical record is not one of unremitting failure. It is one of impressive achievement despite setbacks and obstacles. After long struggles, women did gain the right to vote. Inequality was reduced and opportunities for social mobility increased when universal public education was matched with expanding job markets and the support of trade unions. Now it seems to many that these possibilities are foreclosed. We do not agree.

Limits of Liberalism

For fifty years, dominant elites in the developed world have pursued broadly liberal agendas. These shared emphases on freedom and rights but with very different priorities. Classical liberalism, and then "neoliberalism," were grounded in "possessive individualism" and focused on giving maximal rights to the owners of property and minimizing government regulation and ownership. The other agenda has been an "expressive liberalism" seeking to expand the extent to which individuals can choose their own identities and goals and pursue them without obstacles.[8] Both have supported individual liberties, even if differently construed. They could converge in recognizing a similar right for different reasons—for example, to freedom of religion on the grounds that beliefs and conscience are forms of private property or because religion is a form of self-expression. But, as Calhoun and Taylor discuss in Chapter 4, emphasis on individual freedom can come at the expense of equality and social solidarity. In recent decades the two forms of liberalism have coincided to help upend the balance necessary to a viable democratic—and indeed, liberal—society.

Neoliberalism has shaped an economy with opportunities and rewards for entrepreneurs. Together with financialization, it has contributed to capital flows away from the richest countries and toward several historically underdeveloped but rapidly growing ones, and notably facilitated the rise of China. Domestically, it has brought dramatically increased inequality, disrupted communities, and damaged the environment. Expressive liberalism has brought important expansions of individual freedom. It has promoted rights for the previously underrepresented and disadvantaged—but only so long as these do not include economic reorganization or redistribution.[9] Too often, the inclusion has been more symbolic than material. Together, liberals of the two orientations have embraced cosmopolitanism but not community, technological change without enough care for those whose lives became more precarious.

In this context, right-wing populism flourished. However much it may have been manipulated from above or steered by financial contributions, it also expressed a popular reaction. First, populists reacted against fifty years of deindustrialization and neoliberal globalization, which had undermined communities, eliminated good jobs, deprived middle-aged workers of anticipated happy retirements, and brought devastating opioid addictions. Second, populists reacted against what they saw as disrespect from political elites and against the sense that less deserving minorities or immigrants or women were gaining at their expense. To an outside critic this might look like panic over potential loss of privilege but many experienced it as a threat to just entitlements. In the extreme, they feared that although they were the "real" citizens and "true" representatives of the legitimate nation, they were being replaced.

Initially informed more by anger, frustration, and resentment of elites than by ideology, these populist and grassroots mobilizations have been successfully claimed by demagogues and conspiracy theorists with the help of new media. Racism and hostility to immigrants are voiced in the name of "the people" and thus of democratic citizens even while they violate the democratic promise of inclusivity. Not least, at both national and international levels, new information and communication technologies join with corporations, markets, and finance to dramatically increase the scale of sociotechnical systems, embedding individuals in ever more indirect relationships that are hard to see, let alone manage. Citizens have faced all of these changes with too little social support from communities, intermediate associations, and institutions of the welfare state; many have experienced them as deeply disempowering. Collective identity, belonging, and well-being have suffered at the same time that economic capacity and political voice have declined.[10]

We can see examples in response to the coronavirus pandemic. Rich countries organized to produce vaccines, but not to deliver them throughout their societies—let alone the whole world. This undercut their effectiveness and opened paths for mutations and recurrent surges. Inequalities intensified by neoliberalism have manifested in different medical treatments and death rates for rich and poor. Stock and other asset markets have soared, making billionaires richer; millions of their fellow citizens have lost jobs or been forced to leave the labor force to become unpaid caregivers. Others have taken precarious employment as drivers, cleaners, and health aides. The call for "social distancing" has disguised the real social and economic distance between those able to readily adapt in comfortable homes and professional occupations and those forced by necessity to work in more problematic conditions. Response to the pandemic has been neither egalitarian nor unified.

Despite its wealth, the United States was initially unable to deliver needed protective equipment to health workers and ventilators to patients in intensive care. Public health professionals had warned of the risks for years, but planning and preparation did not keep pace. On the contrary, single-minded pursuit of efficiency in health care institutions has been the enemy of preparedness and resilience, since saving money by not keeping stock on hand brought reliance on long supply chains intended to deliver equipment "just in time"—supply chains that failed to perform. Not only have institutions been overstretched, but resistance to public health responses has been politicized. Leaders have exacerbated conflict when cohesion and common purpose have been needed. Citizens have felt helpless, unable to take charge of their own lives, shorn of influence over national policy or the global spread of disease. The United States has not been the only democracy unable to overcome regional, class, and occupational disparities—and political polarization. In Germany, for example, state governments have also rebelled against federal restrictions. In Britain and France, necessary public health efforts have been met with politicized opposition and rejection. Like many, India's government has vacillated between complacency and erratically imposed emergency measures that have weighed hardest on the poor.

An increasingly authoritarian China has suggested that Western (read liberal) democratic societies are too weak to deal with challenges such as Covid-19. This is trebly distorting. It ignores the part played in Covid's early rise by pathologies of China's authoritarian governance, not least of which was that local authorities hid crucial information for fear of what would happen if they shared it with higher authorities—let alone citizens. It ignores how well some democracies—New Zealand, for one—have done at managing Covid-19 and how democracies have led the world in developing vaccines. And it exaggerates the extent to which particular regimes, like Donald Trump's in the United States, represent failings of democracy as such, rather than degenerate forms. Still, the question of democratic capacity must be asked, as must questions about climate and other emergencies beyond the pandemic.

Amartya Sen famously argued that among the virtues of democracy was preventing famines.[11] Pestilence, floods, and crop failures have brought catastrophic reductions in food supply throughout history. But who starved depended not just on how much food there was but also on how it was distributed; entitlement to a share was basic to survival. In democracies, everyone had a claim on available food, and starvation was minimal, even among the poor and socially marginal.[12] One might have thought a similar commitment to the welfare—even just the survival—of all citizens would have kept fatalities low in democratic countries during the Covid-19 pandemic that started in late 2019. This has not been the case. The United States, Brazil, India, and several European democracies have been among the most affected. Democracy may be good at minimizing famine, but it has not proven equally good at preventing plagues—at least not in its degenerate forms.

How the consequences of the pandemic will play out is not entirely clear; there are still choices to be made. As Calhoun and Taylor argue in Chapter 7, a key question is how much they will be made on the basis of an egalitarian and unified pursuit of the public good. What is clear is that Covid-19 has made it impossible to ignore what was once called "the social question." During the Industrial Revolution, the term referred to challenges of poverty, unemployment, food shortages, toxic pollution, and inadequate housing. Now it has become apparent that the old evils have not vanished even from rich countries, let alone poorer ones.[13] Inequalities in vulnerability, vaccination, and care have become a new social question.

Democracies have faltered in handling the pandemic not so much because their governments lacked resources, power, or policy capacity as because they lacked social cohesion and commitment to the public good. The problem is not that democracy is necessarily weak. The problem is that democracy has degenerated.

Sources of Degeneration

The degeneration of democracy is caused not simply by poor political leaders, though too many are either puerile or corrupt, or by "technical" deficiencies of electoral systems. Nor does it stem entirely from external pressures, though these are real: massive economic upheaval, geopolitical shifts, destabilization of national institutions, failure of global cooperation, insidious manipulation of media and information systems, and intensification of inequality.

Democracy degenerates when ordinary people feel they are deprived of the ability to make good lives for themselves and their families. It degenerates when communities are not able democratically to shape their own futures, so fully are they determined by choices of distant powers and impersonal characteristics of capitalist markets or other large-scale systems. It degenerates when some citizens seek to marginalize others, not just blocking their votes but also restricting their access to public institutions and even public spaces. Democracy degenerates when citizens no longer treat each other with basic respect and recognition and when citizens refuse to accept that they really belong together.

Degenerations reflect erosion in the social foundations for democracy. Citizens have lost stable communities, supportive and enabling institutions, and political parties able to forge effective internal coalitions and external alliances to work for the common good. We are linked across communities by abstract and impersonal systems—most importantly markets. But we have too few occasions to forge more personal connections across the distances among us. Mass military participation did this for Americans in World War II. It achieved less solidarity in the ill-conceived and divisive Vietnam War. But in the wake of that conflict, the United States unfortunately replaced selective but compulsory military service not with a fair model of universal national service, but with "volunteer" recruitment that made participation a matter of class position, a caste-like continuity in families, and for some, a very politicized patriotism. Likewise, participation in religion can connect the local to wider networks, national denominations, international missions. But even in the United States, where religious participation long remained much higher than in most of the developed world, it has plummeted by more than a third in recent decades (and local church membership is less often integrated into national denominations).[14] Legacy media—newspapers, broadcast television—once supported public discourse partly by establishing such crosscutting connections and a common background of knowledge. But they have been undermined by the loss of their economic foundations in an era of new electronic media. New media have opened up democratic participation but not yet achieved adequate ways to stay oriented to truthful knowledge and cooperation, rather than deception and conflict.

Democracies have weathered deep crises before, but then again, they have also sometimes succumbed. The most famous instance is the end of Germany's Weimar Republic, as the National Socialists—the Nazis—came to power.[15] The end of Germany's democracy reflected degenerations of the kind we describe here, combined with economic crisis, adverse international relations, and an effective, organized, and ruthless movement to claim power. Democracy was reestablished only after Germany lost a catastrophic war, and only in one part of a newly divided country.

Still, democracy can survive and even thrive after degenerations—if they are countered by vigorous constructive action. We offer our account of degenerations of democracy in the hope that it can further such projects of renewal and regeneration. We hasten to add that these projects must involve more than mere repair or attempts to return to an old "normal." In Chapter 7, we outline some possibilities. What is crucial is to treat democracy as a project—to create stronger democracy and more generally a better future.

I

Degenerations of Democracy

CHARLES TAYLOR

Let's start off by repeating some very widely known things about the history of the word "democracy," because they help cast light on our present predicament.

"Democracy," as everyone knows, stopped being a pejorative term only two hundred years ago. The bad rap goes back to Aristotle. For Aristotle, democracy was the unchecked, as it were, uncontrolled, power of the *demos*—the demos being the nonelite of the society—over everyone else, including the elites, meaning aristocrats and those with money. Likewise, on the other side, oligarchy was unchecked control by the rich and noble. So, for Aristotle, the best society was what he called a *politeia,* a balance between the two, a balance of power.

Up until the eighteenth century, if you proposed democracy, including to the authors of the American Constitution, they would have said, "That's not what we want at all." They, too, thought in terms of balance, and they called their new polity a "republic," which is one possible translation of Aristotle's term: *politeia* is, after all, the original title of Plato's great work, which today we call *The Republic.* But democracy in the late eighteenth century was really bad news.

And then suddenly it becomes our word for the most desirable society. In other words, the term that was previously defined in contrast with a "polity" or "republic"—namely, "democracy"—suddenly usurps their prestige and legitimacy. It becomes our word for what we are fighting to make the world safe for, the highest form of political life.

But this shift leaves in its wake a certain ambiguity, which we can see in the double meaning of the words we use to translate *demos*—that is, *people, peuple, Volk, popolo,* and so on. They always have two senses. On one hand, they mean the whole population of the nation, or political entity, as when we speak of the French people or Dutch people being liberated from Nazi occupation in 1944–1945. But, on the other hand, we often use the term for what the Greeks called the *demos*—that is, the nonelites—just as early moderns distinguished "demotic" languages from Latin and the languages of often conquering elites, or as, today, when political leaders claim that the people are being tricked, exploited, or otherwise maltreated by the elites.

Democracy Is a Telic Concept

Double meaning is ineliminable, because it reflects the ambition behind the word "democracy." In the end, ideally, these two senses of the word would be fused: there would be a society ruled by the whole people, but without an elite that manages to put the rest in the shade and to operate to their disadvantage. In other terms, democracy would be a truly equal society. Democracy is a telic concept, necessarily a matter of purposes and ideals, not merely conditions or causal relations. It is defined by standards that can never be met.

So, we have different ways of identifying democracy: we say that some countries have a democracy because they have the rule of law, for example, or because they have elections in which all the people can participate. Universal suffrage is the key here, along with the requirement of "free and fair" elections, which in turn require that the media are free. But then we also frequently make another judgment about certain societies that pass the "free and fair" test, to the effect that they are very "undemocratic" because of inequalities—of income, wealth, education, class, or race—which are linked as both cause and effect with disproportionate elite power.

The electoral criterion is of an on / off kind: a country either passes the universal suffrage "free and fair" requirement, or it doesn't. (The world is, of course, much more fuzzy, but our judgments are categorical.) But the second notion of democracy is telic.

This is a concept of what the ideal should be, what democracy should integrally realize. This would be something like a condition of ideal equality, in which all classes and groups, elites and nonelites alike, would have power proportionate to their numbers to influence and determine outcomes.[1] But this defines a condition that we never fully attain—or maybe we do, for a short time, and then we slide away again. And that gives us the key to a very important dynamic in democracy, which is crucial to my first point, my first path to degeneration.

There are periods when we are moving toward democracy—liberation from foreign rule, liberation from dictatorial rule—the kind of thing that happened in 1989 in Eastern Europe, the kind of thing that seemed about to happen after Tahrir Square during the Arab Spring. And something analogous occurs when there is an assertion of the power of the demos in established democracies (those who meet the electoral criterion).

There's a great sense of enthusiasm, the sense we are moving in the right direction.

And then there are periods of lower morale, when we feel we are moving away. If you look at the two hundred years of what we now call "democracy in the West," you see that there were many movements that seemed to be steps forward; for example, the Jacksonian Revolution of the 1820s in the United States was a kind of democratic revolution against a class of elites, against powerful landed interests. But later in the nineteenth century, new and powerful interests asserted themselves—for instance, the "robber barons" in the Gilded Age, against whom the Progressives, and later Theodore Roosevelt, reacted with antitrust legislation.

Starting in some countries in the 1930s, and continuing after the Second World War, there was a further push against unchecked industrial power, with the creation of welfare states, the strengthening of workers' power, the adoption of policies of full employment, and other elements of social democracy. And then, since about 1975, we have been sliding in the other direction. It is this important feature—of first democratic encouragement, enthusiasm, and moving forward, and then democratic discouragement and sliding backward—to which I would like to call attention.

Part of what masks democratic degeneration is the hold of the first concept, the on / off one. It is widely associated with the renowned economist Joseph Schumpeter, for whom the people are made up of (at least theoretically) equal individuals. They all have the vote. Elites of experts and self-selected politicians actually rule.[2] But the people periodically vote, and these elections are free and fair. So there is a real possibility that the incumbents can be thrown out, and there is always an alternative elite ready to take over if the present rulers falter.

Let's call this the "contingency feature."

This feature also has other requirements. It demands free media, open fora of exchange, the right to organize, and so on. These contribute to free and fair elections; without them the contingency requirement fails to hold. And in some variants (for instance, the US Constitution) there is an attempt to balance unbridled and direct popular will (through, for example, an electoral college made up of local elites to elect the president.)

And today in liberal thinking in the West, there is also a requirement that all be treated equally and fairly. The demand here is for inclusion, even of people who are different from the majority, ethnically, culturally, religiously.

This inclusiveness is, of course, another telic concept, a standard we never fully meet, but may be at any given time approaching or sliding away from. But in this section, I'll be dealing with the standard directly encoded in the term "democracy": rule of the people, the demand that nonelites have a significant role in government. I take up the issue of inclusion in the next section.

Now, we have been tempted to believe that the system just described will eventually ensure the endorsement of at least most people. And this consensus will lead (and has in fact led in some cases) to an unprecedented stability in history. Such consensually generated stability is a great reversal from the classical period and even from the late eighteenth century, as I remarked above. The American founders were wary of democracy. They still held the view that goes back to Aristotle. Democracy is rule of the people, in the sense of nonelites. Such rule would bring dangerous instability, even the spoliation of people of property, on which prosperity and civilization depended.

But this anxiety disappears in the quasi-Schumpeterian view, along with the telic concept. And the perception that democracies are stable lies behind the optimistic prognosis of established liberal thought. On this view, the secret of democracy's appeal is that it offers the rule of law. People can live in security, because their rights are respected, and on the occasions when they aren't, they can obtain redress in the courts. At the same time, the holding of regular elections under universal suffrage ensures that the interests, at least of the majority, can't be totally ignored.

So, on this view, democracies can be stable in a way that other regimes can't. Moreover, these others are bound to come under steadily increasing pressure because of widespread features of our contemporary world. The idea here is that education, the spread of media, economic change, globalization, consumer capitalism, and so on, will break people loose from older allegiances to elite power. Authoritarian countries will eventually sail into seas of instability. The only way in which these can be calmed is by introducing democracy. Hence many predicted that even China will have one day to join the democratic club.

. There is *some* truth to this claim. People living under the rule of law do resist losing their rights, which does make democracy more stable. But history also shows that the lure of strong rule, or the temptation to "overcome disorder," or purge dangerous elements, can overcome the resistance.

This confident reliance on stability clearly underestimates the resources that authoritarian regimes can draw on: in particular, nationalism, a sense of historic grievance against formerly dominant Western colonial powers, a sense even of humiliation at their hands, and the feeling that these same Western powers are trying to weaken us by destroying the moral fabric of our society and its religion, fostering laxity, homosexuality, and so on. Putin is even trying to create a counter-liberal international on the basis of a common resistance to cultural-moral erosion.

What the optimistic prospect also neglects is the decay and regression within established democracies, which in turn intensifies their inability to respond to new challenges that they face. Overconfidence in the staying power of the rule of law suddenly looks rash in the age of Trump.

The Schumpeterian model seems to suppose that democracy has already irreversibly attained its highest form, so that the restrictive or class-based use of "people" can just be forgotten. Indeed, it is often claimed that it *ought* to be forgotten, and protagonists of egalitarian policies are often accused of waging "class war." But what we are now seeing are the ways in which forgetting the telos crucially weakens democracy in the face of certain sorts of authoritarian challenge.

The Decline of Citizen Efficacy

This brings me to my first path of degeneration: for a variety of reasons, democracies always have to remake their telic movement, their pursuit of specific purposes and goals. It may be because, when you move, let's say, from the early nineteenth century to the late nineteenth century, the sources of power have changed entirely. These sources of power have changed from landed property to industrial power, and power has shifted from landed gentry to large corporations; and then the sources and beneficiaries change again: finance has a tremendously important role to play in the way we live our lives.

Or the need to remake things may arise because of complacency or backsliding when democracy is at high tide, close to its telos.

But, in any case, it is clear that we in Western democracies have been sliding backward since about 1975. We could call it the "Great Downgrade." What has been progressively lost is a sense of citizen efficacy. I mean the sense that ordinary citizens can have in a democracy, that if they combine their efforts, they can influence government through elections, and thus redress grievances, and bring about tolerable conditions of life for themselves and their families.

The period I'm talking about saw a decline in actual citizen efficacy. And this decline translated into growing inequality; that's the fruit of it, but it's also the cause of it. That is why I talk about "slides," though they are not straight descents, but have more of a spiraling effect.

One such effect is this: the more people feel they don't have any real power in relation to the elites—that their fate is being decided elsewhere, such as by whether there is going to be employment in their area, or good and secure jobs, or affordable education for their children—the more they feel discouraged about their ability to influence these conditions and the less they vote. And, in fact, the last decades of the twentieth century saw a decline in the levels of participation in just about all Western democracies. Some started from a higher and some from a lower level of participation, but, generally speaking, the trend was downward. And, of course, that abstention increased the power of money and special interests, so the discouragement got deeper.

In the last couple of decades, electoral participation has been going up in many countries. In the United States, it reached an all-time peak in the 2020 presidential election. But this was because of the polarization that came about through what have been called "populist" challenges to liberal democracy. The challengers, such as Donald Trump, claimed to offer increased citizen efficacy, but in relation to the real grievances and inequality that nonelites suffered from, the offer was pure sham. In fact, the Trump presidency exacerbated inequality—for instance, with the tax cut of 2017—and chipped away at the Affordable Care Act.

There is a danger here for a spiraling downward—indeed, for various kinds of downward spirals, which feed on themselves.

The Decline of Equal Citizenship

It is worth pausing to look more closely at the changes in Western democracies since 1975, something Craig Calhoun will do in a more sustained discussion in Chapter 2. In the decades after the Second World War (in the United States starting with the New Deal), the political life of these democracies was frequently centered on a polarization between Left and Right, which brought about the development of welfare states, some nationalization and/or state economic planning, the extension of the rights and powers of organized labor, and so on. These were proposed and legislated for by parties of the Left, opposed or moderated by a main party of the Right. Political regimes were jointly created in the course of this competition/struggle. The dominant theme of these polities was a kind of tamed class struggle.

Much has changed in our societies since.

First, the tamed class struggle has been breaking down, or at least fragmenting—and for a host of reasons. One, which has in other ways been very beneficial, is the emergence of new issues that were sidelined in the old polarization, particularly those raised by the feminist movements, by environmentalists, by defenders of multiculturalism, and gay rights.

Then there is the coming of greater prosperity, which may make some people, even among nonelites, no longer feel class solidarity.

Then there is the growth of a new culture that is more individualist in certain respects. Consumerism is one aspect of this new culture; the ethic of authenticity, with its concern for identity, is another; and their effect, separately and together, is to heighten individualism.

And so, issues fragment. And the party system may also be transformed by these changes, as has happened with the rise of Green parties. The older "packages" of issues become looser, and in some cases new packages, linking lifestyle questions, come to the fore. But the change in model comes largely because people have lost faith in the first model, not just because the second has attractions.

The older sense of citizen efficacy is accordingly undermined; there is a loss of group solidarity around the original cluster, so I no longer have an obvious way of registering my goals politically and effectively. Support for the parties of the Left declines: successive age cohorts vote less for these parties, partly through lack of interest, partly through nonidentification with a party, partly through despair over one's inefficacy.

In the first part of our period (roughly up to the 2008 crash), the despair was intensified because voting abstention tilted the system toward entrenched privileges and the status quo. The vote, in fact, declined less among those who identified with entrenched interests:

- It declined less among rich than among poor.
- It declined less among educated than among uneducated.
- It declined less among people who have steady incomes and who own houses than among people living hand-to-mouth existences.
- It declined less among old than among young.
- Often, voting declined less among majority communities (class, ethnic, religious or other) than among minority communities.[3]

So, a sense of powerlessness in the face of bureaucrats, special interests, and elites grew. And this was intensified by the increase of economic globalization and latterly, of the power of finance to wreak havoc in our lives. All this increased the sense that our recourse, if any, was not the vote, but (perhaps) special-issue mobilization.

There are vicious circles here, downward spirals through which the sense of inefficacy decreases efficacy in fact, which in turn intensifies the sense. For example, despair over inefficacy leads to abstention and a decline in citizen participation, which as a result increases the power of money in politics. Politicians rely more heavily on expensive television because they lack a "ground game"; a fragmented society, with less mobilization, means that we need media more.

But the greater power of money, exercised through the oligopoly of media, makes the whole process less transparent, which in turn objectively reduces the efficacy of citizen action, which in turn increases despair—and the cycle starts again.

Then the gap between rich and poor widens. The middle class shrinks.[4] There are fewer steady jobs. And there don't seem to be mechanisms to reverse this trend.

The sense of equal citizenship, which is partly a matter of self-understanding, fades as the experience of acting together or even being in each other's presence becomes rarer. People in ghettos, on the one hand, and in gated communities, on the other, have trouble imagining themselves as partners in a democratic exercise.[5]

The power of the ideal of equal citizenship is then deflected by ideologies of unworthiness. The rich and successful come to believe that those drawing welfare, food stamps, and other subsidies don't really live up to the ethic of self-reliance so prominent in North America and therefore don't deserve to be full citizens along with them.[6] Hence the attempts by right-wing parties (US Republicans, Canadian Conservatives) to make it difficult to get to the polls.

These are self-feeding spirals. We are not only in an era of democratic regression, in which the telos recedes; but it seems that the decline is self-feeding. It is hard to see how to stop it.

Loss of Confidence

The spirals lead to a falling-off of confidence in the representative system as a vehicle for redress of the grievances of nonelites. This has set in motion various vicious circles of decline. I want to list them more tersely.

First, the fall in voter participation, mainly on the part of nonelites, and / or the declining support for parties of the Left has increased the influence of the better off, and also that of money in politics. I am thinking not only of voting, but also of citizen participation in campaigns. The less participation there is, the greater the importance of television, and hence the need for money.

Some of this is still (legally) above board, but today's condition approaches what the North and West sneeringly call "corruption," or "crony capitalism," when it appears in the East and South. And when nonelites begin to participate more, there are often efforts to restrict this.

Voter participation has been worsened by, second, a rise in inequality, the gap between rich and poor, which narrowed between the Gilded Age and what the French call *les trente glorieuses* and then began to draw apart again at an ever-accelerating rate. This has been due both to (a) globalization, or the lowering of trade barriers and the (b) attendant flight of manufacturing from high- to low-wage sites, and to the accelerating automation of many functions. The effects of both developments in the richer democracies have been aggravated by the blind ideological trust on the part of governments, even of the Left, in neoliberalism: the basic proposition that, if markets are free, the benefits of growth will always trickle down (a rising tide lifts all ships). Consequently, such attempts as were made to counteract the effects of globalization and automation through education, job retraining, adequate welfare provision, stimulus packages, and the like were inadequate. Lack of effective response by governments increased the sense among nonelites that they have no real say in the system, and hence lowered the vote further (at least until they had a charismatic champion to rally around).

Then, third, frustration takes the form of action altogether outside the representative system. Protest movements are often without effect, precisely because they have no impact on the vote (Occupy in Wall Street) or they propose to step outside the system altogether (5-star in Italy).

Then, fourth, the seeming incapacity of social-democratic parties to rectify the economic and employment condition of nonelites opens the way for a new definition of the drive toward the telos of democracy, in which the "people" is now defined culturally or religiously, and its target is the "other," but its political enemies are the liberal and multicultural elites. We see this dynamic virtually everywhere today in Western democracies. Of course, this is the basis of another downward spiral, because the programs of these populist movements can do nothing to remedy poverty and un-employment. They can only divide the demos, defined as the ensemble of disadvantaged nonelites.

Then, on top of these four spirals, there seems to be a "dumbing down" of electorates, in the sense that the grasp of the issues and of what is related to what declines among great swaths of the population. Am I wrong, dreaming of a past that never existed, when I say that previous cohorts of US voters in the postwar period would have laughed off the idea that stim-ulus packages won't increase employment, or (even crazier) that reducing taxes on the super-rich will automatically increase employment? How better to respond to the "voodoo economics" introduced by Reagan and echoed by Bush W., and Trump? This is paradoxical, because electorates in the West are by formal criteria better educated than ever before.

But in fact, it will prove more fruitful if we examine this phenomenon from the other direction and speak of the growing opacity of the represen-tative system.

In speaking of growing opacity, I am not assuming that total transpar-ency existed in some earlier period, such as immediately after the Second World War. The existence of waves of irrationality such as that of the Mc-Carthy era contradicts this assumption. But the term attempts to capture the phenomenon that certain matters that were relatively obvious to pre-vious generations have been lost from view—a forgetfulness that allowed some during the Tea Party campaign against the Affordable Care Act to say things like "Keep your government hands off my Medicare."[7]

But perhaps this increased opacity is an inevitable consequence of disengagement from the representative political system; what doesn't seem to work is not worth following closely. But even for those who don't turn away from the system, who would very much like to engage, but can't see how they can have an impact, the frustrating opacity of the system can make them vulnerable to savior figures who promise to restore (how is never specified) a better past.

I don't think that disengagement from the political system is the only cause here; I will return to this below. But to the extent that disengagement plays a part, it is both cause and effect of increasing opacity; hence we have a fifth spiral.

In many Western societies, this opacity leads to the surrender of mainstream political debate to the mythologies of neoliberalism, which of course further diminishes the ability of the system to help nonelites. This spiral number six is manifest in retrenchments of the social supports put in place to support nonelites when their interests were better represented in politics. As US president, for example, Bill Clinton proposed legislation to "end welfare as we have known it."[8] The Republican-dominated legislature passed the Personal Responsibility and Work Opportunity Act, which indeed dramatically eroded America's once-robust safety net. Despite Republican assertions that welfare recipients are major backers of the Democratic Party, in general, the "beneficiaries" of welfare (there ought to be a word "maleficiaries" for this situation) vote less often than the better off. Getting involved in politics would only drain energy from their daily struggles to find work and avoid hunger or eviction—and it didn't seem to promise much help.

Opacity

It is worth examining the motor behind spiral five above, what I've been calling the "increasing opacity" effect. What underlies this is a complex of causes. One of these is unquestionably the growing control of big money over media (Murdoch and Fox News) and their growing irresponsibility (lately illustrated by their treatment of Trump during the 2016 and 2020 presidential elections, which gave a great boost to circulation, but the media could also have helped point out when people were lying or saying absurd things).

At the same time there has also taken place a fragmentation of audiences, so that lots of people never encounter dissenting opinion. On one hand, we have seen a gradual movement apart of different media to constitute "echo chambers," so that older forms of confrontation of clashing ideas cease to take place. On the other, the rise of social media as sources of information and opinion intensify the creation of such echo chambers. The effects of all this are exacerbated by the inflow of fake news, which circulates in one echo chamber and is never confronted by the "truths" circulating in others. This effect has facilitated what appears to be an extraordinary spread of belief in wild and implausible conspiracy theories, such as QAnon.

Michael Warner, a theorist of the public sphere, points out a shift in the nature of the exchange flowing through social media, that it tilts toward the autobiographical, even the narcissistic: "Your political posts sit next to photos of your dog as presentations of self."[9] What are the cumulative effects of this tendency?

In addition to the factors mentioned above, opacity has partly been thickened by institutional changes, which have conspired to make our society less readable.[10] As pointed out above, if you have a big party on the Left and a big party on the Right, each with general programs, you have a pretty good idea that, if you vote this way, there is going to be more welfare, and if you vote that way, there's going to be less. But now there is much more fragmentation, with movements of various kinds—ecological, feminism, gay rights—so policy options and alternatives are less legible. And it is often less clear how one should vote if one seeks a certain outcome.

This greater opacity is certainly part of the reason for the decline in felt citizen efficacy, which leads on one hand to greater abstention and on the other to a diminished understanding of how our system works. And in this case, the misfortune and the irony is that it was partly brought about by the rise of social movements such as those just mentioned in the last paragraph, which represented for the most part a gain for democracy, in the sense that important causes and long-standing grievances began to count in a way they hadn't in the past, and the voices of LGBTQ people, women, the handicapped, and others at last began to have some impact.

But there is another reason for the decline in transparency, which is less benign, and that is the growing power over our institutions of the belief in unfettered markets as engines of a growth, which ultimately redound to the benefit of everybody. Since the late 1970s neoliberal ideas have steadily gained hegemony over many Western democracies, and even now when the follies of reduced regulation became plain in the crash of 2008, these illusions still have power.

It is only very recently, with the coming of the Covid pandemic in 2019, that the true costs of neoliberalism have been revealed—in underfunded health systems, inadequate provision for the elderly, glaring inequalities that have left certain groups much more vulnerable than others.

But the grip of this kind of fantasy is perhaps less surprising when we take into account a fundamental feature of modern democracy as against ancient democracy. In ancient Athens, when the *ecclesia* met it was dominated by the demos, and when it voted to do *x* or *y*, the outcome was the will of the people. And it may be that they thought afterward that it was a terrible thing that they had done, but it clearly had been their will. But in our rule-of-law, complex, representative systems, it is often very hard to be sure if the will of the people is being listened to or not. Intrinsically, there is a tendency for democratic decision-making to become more opaque as it becomes less open to the nonelites' participation. At the same time that the people don't vote, they also tune out, and they become less and less clear as to what is actually happening.

That means that they are very open to various kinds of appeal, which more knowledgeable people see as totally magic thinking—take "I'm going to make America great again," as an example. But that is another way in which the spiral can continue downward.

In any case, the neoliberal illusion has opened the road to certain policies that have done great damage to the livelihood of large segments of the population in Western democracies. One such policy has been the globalization of trade—that is, the lowering of trade barriers. This of itself has been of great benefit to developing countries and has helped to reduce world rates of poverty. But it ought to have been accompanied by national policies to ensure that its benefits were more widely and equally shared within the industrialized nations. The unthinking faith in the market helped to blind governments to the need for such policies (but fortunately, not universally so; some European, especially Scandinavian, social democracies have had greater success in this area). And so the chickens are now coming home to roost, as the populations of various "rust belts" and other neglected areas in the United States and Europe rise up and demand a reckoning.

If we look at the three factors mentioned here that have helped carry our Western democracies away from the pattern of politics of the postwar period (and there are obviously others)—namely, social movements, the spread of neoliberalism, and globalized trade—it becomes clear how fragile the gains of any such period of advance toward democracy's telos can be. They are always vulnerable to largely unpredictable changes in economy, culture, and shifting ideologies. No formula for a successful democracy can be forever valid.

Once a departure occurs from the positive equilibrium of social democracy, the various spirals mentioned above kick in and, in the absence of wise and effective remedial action, carry us even farther away from our telos and in fact strengthen elite hegemony. This is one way in which democracy is susceptible to a degeneration, to losing its nature. It would be different if departure from the telos automatically produced a move to rectify things, but on the contrary, the self-feeding spirals tend to aggravate the departure.

Nonparticipation and Deprivation

We should have no illusions: nonvoters may affect a kind of cynical indifference, but in fact, a great many of them feel cheated of their birthright. This feeling can be seen in the great power of slogans such as Obama's "Yes, we can" of 2008. (And we can note also that one of the parties that emerged from the Spanish Indignados movement is called "Podemos.") Many nonparticipants show themselves eager to take part anew if they see a chance to have an effect. Recent mobilizations in many Western democracies are a testament to this. New voters were important to Democratic success in the US midterm elections of 2018; they were important to record turnout for each side in the 2020 presidential election. New participants include the young—and teenagers are leading the way on climate change. But they are by no means limited to the young.

For many, the lack of citizen efficacy is felt as a deprivation; this is part of what it means to say that democracy, as it is imagined and lived by many in our civilization, is a telic concept.

In addition, the workings of our system have inflicted great losses on some sections of the population. In the context of more globalized trade, and also automation, advanced economies have suffered loss of regular, potentially full-time jobs; many can find only precarious and / or part-time jobs. For many workers this has meant a decline in living standards and for the societies concerned a growth in inequality. In the old days, right after the war, this would have led to an increase in the vote of the major left party or parties. But traditional left parties seem incapable of channeling this discontent. We see this in the United States, the United Kingdom, and France, among other countries. In the European case, the crisis of 2008 triggered off austerity policies in most member states of the European Union. Some were what orthodox budgeting required, given the debt crisis and the lack of room for maneuver for countries tied into the same (euro) currency. Some were voluntary and ideologically driven. Austerity measures have exacerbated the plight of the less well off, but social-democratic parties were either unable or unwilling to offer an alternative. Rather the discontent has led to the surge of populist votes, aided of course by the obfuscations promoted by Koch Brothers' funding, Sky News, and others.

Indeed, the power of neoliberal mythology, backed by the fear of trade competition from other societies, has inhibited the proposal and carrying through of the kind of program that would cope with the crisis of good jobs: more investment in retraining; better support for workers and their children in times of unemployment; stimulus packages building infrastructure; expansion of public services; including health, education, and care for the old (see Chapter 7). On the contrary, the emphasis has been on reducing taxes, or at least not raising them, on the grounds that this is the royal road to increasing employment; but then this policy has often led to an exaggerated insistence on austerity programs—see especially Europe after 2008.

So the West has seen a decline of "Fordist" industries, which had lifetime employees with benefits. From Fordist worker to precarious part-timer: this has been the fate of many workers or their children—a fate that amounts to a Great Downgrade of our time. This affects many people and some whole areas. These include the "rust belts," formerly the site of large-scale manufacturing, now in decline, as well as small towns and rural areas, which have also been left behind. Economic development in many Western societies in the last half-century has brought about a concentration of economic activities and job growth in a few large cities. Small centers have lost not only population, but many of their former institutions, among them frequently the local newspaper.[11] Many of the people living in these areas face the daunting prospect of downward social mobility for themselves and their children.

One might argue that we have gained something in compensation for our losses. I argued above that one of the reasons for the decline of the old left–right pattern of politics in the West was the rise of social movements such as feminism, LGBTQ rights, ecological responsibility, and the like. These have pushed us closer to what we recognize as another telos, or major objective, of liberal democracy—namely, the creation of a more equal and inclusive society, or, put negatively, the removal of certain serious and long-existing exclusions or inegalitarian hierarchical inclusions (such as that of women in patriarchal modes of life).

But we can't consider these two developments as an overall gain, or even a shift in which the losses are fully compensated by the gains. And that is because the responses to the Great Downgrade have very clearly and palpably called the gains of inclusion into question. This is one of the shocking conclusions that contemporary events force us to face. The "populist" revolts (we will soon have reason to question this term) have done great damage to nonhierarchical inclusion.

Let us turn now to these revolts and examine why democracies are susceptible to them. This is the subject of the next section.

Waves of Exclusion

The second path to degeneration I want to talk about is the move toward (or the power gained by) various movements of exclusion—that is, movements that say that certain members of the polis, certain members of the republic, aren't *really* members of the republic. This is another basic susceptibility of modern democracy that I think we need to look at more closely.

Democratic republics require a very definite sense of identity: Americans, Canadians, Québécois, German, French, and so on. Why? Well, because for several reasons, the very nature of democracy requires this strong commitment: it requires participation in voting, participation in paying taxes, participation in going to war, if there is conscription. If there is to be redistribution, there has to be a very profound solidarity to motivate transfers from the more to the less fortunate. Democracy therefore requires a strong common identity.

Finally, and very importantly, if we are in a deliberative community—we are talking together, deciding among ourselves, voting, and making decisions—we have to trust that the other members of the group are really concerned with our common good.

You see a situation arising where independentist movements start very easily—and I happen to know a case like that, coming from Quebec—in which the minority says, "Well when they're talking about the good of our society, they're not talking about us; they're talking just about them. We're not part of their horizon." When that kind of trust breaks down, democracy is in very big trouble. It can even end up splitting into two. So, we need a powerful common identity.[12]

But these powerful identities can slip very easily in a negative and exclusionary direction. A very good book by the Yale sociologist Jeff Alexander, *The Civic Sphere*,[13] makes this point: the common properties that make up this identity are very strongly morally charged; they're good. As a matter of fact, in most contemporary democratic societies, there are two aspects to this identity: one is defined by certain principles—that we believe in representative democracy, human rights, equality—but they also have a specific character: as a citizen, I am engaged in a particular historical project aimed at realizing these principles. Canadians, Americans, French, Germans—each of us believes in our national project, which is meant to embody these values. This is what the philosopher Jürgen Habermas is referring to with the term "constitutional patriotism."[14]

It's easy to see how this take on principles can generate exclusion. Recall the infamous speech by Mitt Romney in the 2012 US presidential election that helped bring his defeat at the hands of Obama. It contained the "47 percent" remark: 47 percent of the people are just passengers; they are being given what they need; they are not really producing; they are taking from the common stock, without adding to it. The underlying moral idea is that the *real* American is productive, enterprising, self-reliant. The allegation is that 47 percent of the people are not living up to the stringent requirement of this idea. So, these people are not behaving like real Americans.

A little reflection would show how false this particular moralization is: many of the people who receive state aid, welfare, say, or food stamps, are clearly doing their best to take care of themselves and their families; many of them are working, albeit at ill-paid jobs; while, on the other side, many of those whom this calculation includes in the other 53 percent owe their prosperity to luck or their parents or some form of inherited wealth.

This false moralization is not innocent. It provides the justification for a lot of measures in many settings—including efforts by Canadian Prime Minister Stephen Harper to roll back rights to free speech and media access, which, happily, were blocked by the public. False moralization is prominent on the American Right—for example in presenting voter suppression as the promotion of honesty, in ignoring the racial and other discriminations implicit in shifting demands for specific kinds of identification, and so on. Such false moralization could be a totally cynical move, but it is one that is probably justified by the sense that the people excluded fail to live up to the moral requirements of citizenship as we (good, upstanding, self-reliant citizens) define them.

Or you can get another kind of exclusion: in varying combinations, ethnicity and history provide the criteria. There are the people who really belong to the ethnicity that defines "our" identity, and then there are the people who came along later. There are the people who have always been here, in contrast to the immigrants who came later. What is operative here is basically an ethnic coding. And here, this slide to exclusion can occur.

Take Quebec: What's behind the identity expressed in "Je suis Québécois?" In one sense, there is a very powerful ethnic story behind that: seventy thousand French-speakers were left on the banks of the St. Lawrence when the British conquest occurred and was ratified by the Treaty of Paris in 1763. And then they built what is now this vibrant French-speaking society of 8 million. This is the result of a highly successful fight for survival. It's a very easy slide from a definition of "Québécois" as a citizen of Quebec today to a narrower concept, including only what we call Québécois *de souche*—old-stock Québécois. The memory of the struggle to survive, and the fears surrounding it, can encourage that narrowing. And as a matter of fact, it is not uncommon for long-established populations to react with fear when people of unfamiliar cultures and customs arrive. The reaction to the arrival of Sikhs and Muslims in Quebec was often the anxious question "Est-ce qu'ils vont nous changer?" "Will they change us?"

In our present epoch when human rights are taken for granted, this question is often asked in a new key: not only in fear, but also often with indignation. That's because the reason for discomfort that says simply "they make me uneasy" sounds too weak to justify measures of exclusion. One needs some serious moral reason. And so these days new arrivals are often labeled as threats to our basic principles. Thus xenophobic movements in many Western societies can suddenly take on new strength when they frame the outsiders as homophobic and antifeminist—as we saw for example in the Netherlands with the demonization of Muslim immigrants by Pym Fortuyn, a politician who used his gay identity to deflect accusations that he was part of the far Right. Fortuyn was assassinated, and his campaign taken up by Geert Wilders in a mounting series of wild exaggerations.[15]

Of course, it is true that the progress toward gay liberation and male–female equality that has been made in the Western world has not been matched in Islamic societies. Still, Islamophobic campaigns not only spread an essentialist view of Islam, but also affirm against the evidence that all Muslims share this view. Above all, they seriously misrepresent the outlook of Muslims in the Western world.

The calumnies both reflect fear and inflame it, and they offer a temptation that certain demagogues cannot resist. They produce a modernized xenophobia, one that is evident not only in the Netherlands, but also in
France. When Marine Le Pen wrested control of the Front National from
her anti-Semitic father, she renamed it *Rassemblement National* and aligned
it more with contemporary views on several subjects including gay rights.
Suspicion of outsiders, which used to be a mainstay of the Right, now gains
strength from some supporters of women's and gay rights, which used to
be the preserve of the liberal Left.

A similar kind of reversal has occurred in the social and economic sphere,
where "populist" demagogues claim to be the defenders of workers against
political elites, including parties of the center Left who used to act unchallenged in this role of defenders, on the grounds that these elites are favoring
outsiders over the real, native "people." This line has been exploited with
great success by Marine Le Pen in France and Donald Trump in the United
States, by the People's Party in Denmark, by Conservatives against Labour
in the United Kingdom, and by the Right in a host of other places.[16]

The main way that xenophobia can be overcome is through contact and
cooperation between immigrants and natives, at work, in schools, in
common projects. But it is precisely the fear, the stereotypes, on the part
of natives, in addition to the gestures, and even measures, of exclusion they
carry out, that can render this kind of transformative contact more and
more difficult. There may be a point of virtual nonreturn on this path. Contemporary France appears to be approaching it.

This fear of the other, intensified in a moral register, can reach a virtual
paroxysm in the nightmare fantasy that our ancestral culture may not survive, that we will be totally "replaced."[17]

But there are also cases in which those relegated to second-class citizenship are not immigrants, or recent arrivals, but long-standing members of
the society. They are victims of stranger, somewhat troubling notions of precedence. We see this in the United States, for instance. In a very interesting
book entitled *Strangers in Their Own Land*, Arlie Hochschild describes the
mentality. In the imaginary of certain "old-stock" populations, there is a
kind of order of precedence: the natives (but, of course, these don't include
the Indigenous populations, who are conveniently forgotten) come first,
the people who arrived later come second (as happens in many countries);
but, in an even more damaging version, precedence also holds between
groups who by any measure are long-standing residents, so that whites come

first, and Blacks, Latinos / as, and so on come after. Or, in virtually all "settler" societies, Aboriginal peoples' interests tend to have low priority, when they are not seen as total outsiders. These, rarely explicitly avowed, assumptions of precedence provide the basis for campaigns against "liberal" governments that are allegedly helping all these second-tier people at the expense of the first-tier people. That was a very powerful part of the Trump campaign. You get this slide from all Americans are equal, to some are more fully, really core Americans. The idea of precedence as a basis for greater entitlement becomes an exclusionary mechanism.[18]

Assumptions of precedence can cast light on phenomena such as the hostile reactions of many whites to Black Lives Matter campaigns. Across the United States and even globally there were inspiring reactions to the police murder of George Floyd. These show that these unstated hierarchical presumptions are not unchangeable. Arguably the pandemic encouraged recognition of some of the uglier and terribly dysfunctional side of our societies. But the inspiring wave of protests was relatively short-lived and there has been a partially successful right-wing campaign to demonize Black Lives Matter.

The slide to exclusion is a catastrophe for various reasons. It is a catastrophe because it deeply divides, hampers, and paralyzes democratic society, dividing us into first- and second-class citizens. It is also a catastrophe because it builds on the frustration caused by the first slide I discussed in the previous section, the Great Downgrade, as a result of which people feel that the system is stacked against them, that they can't affect it, and that their efficacy as citizens is virtually nonexistent. They are ready for a program that would liberate the demos or give the demos power again, against the elites.

Only the demos has now been redescribed, either in a moralist, or ethnic, or historical-precedent way that is by definition exclusionary, and this redescription has the double disadvantages that it deeply divides the society and that it does not at all meet the actual problems and challenges of the Downgrade. It's an open secret: Trump is not going to make America great again.

There is an element of quasi-magical thinking in the belief that real-world problems can be solved by blaming and scapegoating the allegedly undeserving minority from within. In fact, this kind of belief is part of the scapegoat mechanism—a continuing temptation for societies throughout the ages. We identify a group that is not *really* part of our society, whether it consists of external enemies or hidden internal foes, and see it as the cause of our misfortunes. This diagnosis is seductive, because it clears us, the *true* members of our society, of any responsibility for our misfortunes, and it offers what seems a simple remedy—namely, to expel, or cordon off, or neutralize the offending group.[19] Following this "remedy" will certainly lead to failure, and worse.

Such exclusionary practices call into question the consoling thought that our slide away from the definitional telos of democracy—that the demos really have a say in government—might be compensated by a move toward another telos—building an egalitarian society without discrimination or exclusion, which is the defining goal of modern liberal democracy. It is clear that this kind of society is not viable without a strong sense of solidarity and mutual help. Equality of respect, once one can paint it as bought at the expense of widespread neglect of important segments of the population, cannot be sustained.

Now, a word about the term "populism." There is more than one kind, with different political implications. Even in the 2016 election in the United States, the word was used to apply to two movements, represented by Bernie Sanders and by Donald Trump, respectively. One obvious meaning of the term applies when the "people," in the sense of the demos or nonelites, are mobilized to erupt into a system that has been run without considering them; they are breaking down the walls, breaking down the doors, disturbing business as usual, demanding redress of grievance. But there is a very big difference between the Bernie and the Donald version: the Bernie version is truly inclusive; it's not excluding anyone. One may not agree with the particular policies put forward; one may or may not be happy about this populist eruption. But Bernie Sanders's program does not embrace the notion that precedence gives some citizens greater rights than others. This exclusionary feature is basic and, I think, absolutely fatal to the populist appeals of Donald Trump, Marine Le Pen, and Geert Wilders. It is both deeply divisive and in programmatic terms a dead-end.

But the "bad," exclusionary populism also comes in a number of varieties today. The type I invoked above harnesses a justified sense of socioeconomic grievance to exclusionary feelings, or implicit understandings of precedence, which are widespread in the society. Trumpian Republicanism, Le Pen's *Rassemblement National,* and to some extent also the Brexit movement in Britain exemplify this.

That "we" are being neglected is a manifestation of what I refer to as our lack of citizen efficacy. This is closely linked in certain societies to a lack of efficacy in a wider sense. Citizens in a modern democratic state aspire not only to be heard by government, but also to be able to take care of themselves and their dependents; to make a living, either in a paid job, or in some gainful activity on their own initiative. It is when circumstances beyond their control make it impossible for them to do so that they expect to be helped by government. And when governments fail to provide this help, while offering (what is seen as) lavish support to those who are less deserving, or have lower priority, or belong to groups considered as "outsiders," that powerful anger at this perceived unfairness can be kindled. The sense of neglect will probably be less in societies that routinely offer various forms of support during such crises, which means societies with a more developed welfare state. Obviously, the outlier in this dimension in the Western world is the United States, and that has meant that the rise of "bad" populism in the United States has special features. Low levels of welfare provision have gone along with, and been conditioned by, a rather unrealistic ethic of self-reliance, which is often shared by the victims of neglect. People who have lost their jobs in rust belts often suffer the reproach that they haven't tried hard enough—Why didn't they move? Why didn't they acquire another skill?—even when these expectations are unreasonable.[20] Worse, this ethic is often at least half-shared by the targets of this criticism, which adds internal misery to external misfortune.[21] No wonder this unbearable situation should find relief in a wave of resentment against the "undeserving" beneficiaries of state aid and the "liberal elites" who give them preference. And no wonder, too, that this psychological and social predicament should blind those who share it to the responsibility of the "conservative" forces whose false moralization has denied them much needed help.

But elsewhere in Europe, we find mobilizations of nativism that seem to owe very little to socioeconomic deprivation. Germany might seem to be a case in point. Apart from the special case of the eastern region, the ex–German Democratic Republic, the economy is in relatively good shape, and unemployment is about half the rate that it is in France. But a closer study shows that among voters who ally themselves with the right-wing Alternative für Deutschland (AfD) a great number find their wages slipping in relation to the cost of living and that local infrastructure and services, such as local shops and transport, are suffering cutbacks. Here, too, there is a decline in the smaller centers that I noted above; these voters also fear downward social mobility and an uncertain retirement income. Even people who have long worked and lived alongside "Gastarbeiter"—the foreign migrants who participated in a guest worker program in Germany—and don't have fears for German culture, voted for the AfD out of a sense of relative neglect. When their needs are not being met by the political system, many ask, why so much attention and resources are showered on outsiders? In fact, the AfD started well before the current refugee crisis, in protest against the supposedly over-generous support the federal government wanted to accord the less fortunate EU economies that were victims of the 2008 crisis. (this ostensibly excessive German generosity was hardly perceptible in Greece, but this just underscores the narrow nationalism of the new party.)

The motif "Why them in preference to us?" is common to a great many "populist" movements.[22] And in this sense it echoes the notions of precedence that energized the Trump campaign in the United States, except that in the German case it can sometimes be shorn of the half-latent assumptions of racial and civilizational superiority that one finds in the United States (and also elsewhere in the West).

The motives for exclusion in Germany like other European countries certainly include the fear that the culture might be changed, that the majority would be forced to be different if too many immigrants arrived. This is partially analogous to the Québécois fear of being changed against their will. But the parallel is not to Quebec case, with its background of a long battle for survival as a francophone society, in a largely anglophone context. There are more similarities to recent Québécois anxieties about non-Western immigrants that threaten the relative homogeneity of their society and the achievements of their battles for linguistic autonomy. European fears also arise in confrontation with non-Western immigrants, starting with Germany's waves of Gastarbeiter, who began arriving in the 1960s. Hence the ominous invocations of German "Leitkultur" (leading culture) in the last decades. The geopolitical situation, the media saliency of jihadism, all have combined to create a situation where the temptation to exaggerate dangers and then to surf on them is just too strong for some politicians to resist. A clear example is how a massive refugee influx in 2015 led the Bavarian Christian Social Union to turn away from its traditional alliance with the Christian Democratic Union in anger at Angela Merkel's attempt to organize a positive reception for the newcomers.

So cultural fear, the sense of civilizational superiority, and resentment at being unjustly neglected by government in favor of outsiders all play a role in the upsurge of European exclusionary movements. There is no sharp line between different types of movement, but rather a sliding scale from those in which socioeconomic deprivation plays a major role, through those in which it is a minor part of the movement's appeal, to those in which it seems to play virtually no role at all and cultural fears and resentments dominate (for example, Austria, Denmark).

Despite what would seem to be antidemocratic tendencies, most European countries seem to have a firm intention to remain democracies and to seek to realize the definitional telos of giving the demos more serious say in government. They are all democracies in the on / off sense, by the "free and fair elections" criterion. Xenophobic parties would leave power if they lost an election. They retain the contingency feature, that there is no a priori limit to election results.

But the xenophobic movements in these European societies find themselves in collaboration with other ruling parties who govern societies that are no longer clearly democracies in this sense. Prominent examples are Hungary and Poland. There the consecrated national or "leading" culture has a quite distinct status. Its preeminence should never be challenged. So although many of the forms of democracy are present, the aim is to arrange things so that no government not dedicated to maintaining this culture's predominance can gain power.

These are not just "illiberal democracies," to use Viktor Orbán's expression, in the sense that they allow themselves to discriminate against minorities and against those whose morals are not in conformity with the supposed national culture; they are also "rigged democracies," because they are built with the intention of making an opposition takeover impossible.[23] Such a regime already exists in Hungary under Fidesz, and another is (perhaps) in the process of being constructed in Poland under the PiS.[24]

Rigged democracies seem to have become a major feature of the contemporary scene. They could include Russia, Turkey, and Iran. Xenophobic movements often strike liberals in the West as regressions to the 1930s, when totalitarian governments of the Right took over a series of European countries. But the present wave of rigged democracies do not seem to aspire to return to the model of, say, Fascist Italy or Nazi Germany. They are satisfied with something less, provided a real governmental overturn is ruled out.

Consequently, election results may make a serious difference—just not the crucial one of regime change. But the spectrum of opposition parties may change. Governments can even be defeated and changed, as occurred in Iran (in 1997, 2003, 2013, and 2017)—except that there, elections operate under the surveillance of the Guardian Council of Ayatollahs, who have the right and function of eliminating certain candidacies before the elections. Governments operate in the shadow of the irresponsible power of the Republican guards and armed forces, who pursue their own foreign and military policies, and do not have the ability to control the judicial system with its widespread abuses and use of torture. The central role of the Ayatollahs remains irremovable.

Good old-fashioned totalitarian rule seems mostly confined to East Asia: to China, North Korea, and the Indo-Chinese peninsula. Not that the Chinese model of "decisive action" may not attract followers in the coming decades, as Chinese economic and political influence expands. There are dictatorial regimes elsewhere, not least in Central Asia, but they have not—at least yet—institutionalized totalitarian rule for longer-term reproduction.

Contrary to our naive expectations in 1989, anti-democracies remain numerous and strong, with impressive recent recruits since 2010. Indeed, those who know twentieth-century history may have a sense of déjà vu in this respect: in face of the Great Depression of the 1930s many in Western societies had a sense of the powerlessness of representative democracies to master the crisis. Effective action seemed to be occurring only in dictatorships of the Left and the Right, in Soviet Russia, Nazi Germany, Fascist Italy.[25] The New Deal, as well as the aftermath of the Second World War and the victorious defeat of dictatorships, relegated this sense of powerlessness to an almost forgotten past. But in today's political scene, it is possible to wonder whether the challenge of global warming requires a response more like China's than those that our democratic regimes, especially that of the United States, are capable of developing.

Polarization

Now we come to the third axis of democracy's degeneration—the third great deviation from its telos—which is when it gets defined as "rule of the majority," where both "majority" and "minority" are given fixed definitions beforehand, without reference to any particular moment or decision. That means that those relegated to the "minority" cease to have the same legitimacy as their opponents; they are not really or fully part of the society. We cease to consider the whole republic as a deliberative community, in the sense defined by Hannah Arendt, a community that has to work things out together, respecting each other's opinions, listening to each other, finding some minimally divisive solution.[26] On the contrary, a certain segment of the people is excluded from this mutual respectful exchange.

The normal operation of a deliberative community in the above sense leads inevitably to changes in the constitution of the winning majority over time, whether we define a given majority in terms of the citizens who voted for its program, or in terms of the interests, policy convictions, and identities that were strongly represented in it. In the normal course of things, people can revise their view of their interests, modify their convictions about policy, change their understanding of their identity. And on top of all this, the issues that are salient at the moment shift over time. In short, it is normal for new constellations to arise.

Different senses of the term "majority" are relevant here. There is the operative majority, the one that confers power—such as the majority of seats in a legislative assembly or the majority of electoral votes in an American presidential election. But this majority does not necessarily correspond to the majority of votes cast, and the views of that voting majority may in turn be different from the opinions of the majority of citizens. Even if this last remains the same, differences in turn out, vote distribution between parties, the presence or absence of gerrymandering and the like can bring about different operative majorities.

The desire to make a given majority coalition the permanent victor is necessarily a threat to the normal operation of a deliberative community. Although one can understand a given party or political leadership wishing for permanence, being ready to use all and every means to bring it about is a danger to democracy itself. It is one of the pathologies that democracy can fall prey to.

This pathology can arise only where differences go very deep and are very acutely felt. Of course, this sense of radical opposition has to go beyond the leadership, if the attempt to ensure permanent victory is to succeed. Thus, a leadership that has decided on this course has to do everything in its power to keep the original coalition together. It has to create the sense that the opposition is somehow illegitimate, that including some elements of them in a new winning constellation is somehow a betrayal of the national identity.

Here is where the language and appeal of xenophobic populism can become virtually irresistible. Opponents are read out of the people, denied inclusion in the legitimate deliberative community—which, necessarily, will no longer operate as a normal deliberative community when it consists of only the "real" people. In contrast, a temporary majority in a normal deliberative community will begin to encounter differences, as its members revise their views on identity, policy, interests, and their sense of what the crucial questions are; and this will lead to a loosening of the original constellation.

Such a loosening is what a leadership aiming for permanent victory has to combat at all costs. Its interest therefore lies in whipping up the original differences of identity and stoking the resentments, the sense of grievance, of being belittled and neglected, which brought the original coalition together.

This strategy allows for, may even seem to demand, an authoritarian form of rule, particularly if a leader can be found who is on the same wave-length as the continuing and homogenous majority, now named the (real) "people" and can be counted on to keep the original, unifying grievances alive. The strategy does not require—it even excludes—intermediary bodies who need to be consulted or who relay proposals to the top, where they wouldn't otherwise reach.

And, above all, it has no room for what the French political theorist Pierre Rosanvallon calls "counter-powers" (*contre-pouvoirs*): these include various bodies that have to be consulted, but also courts that can invalidate decisions of the top authorities, be those decisions in the form of legislation or decree. And they also target media, another key constituent of "counter-powers," insofar as they are critical of the leadership.[27]

To enter on this path of attempting to ensure irreversible victory is a fateful step. Even if at first it shuns the methods of xenophobic populism, its logic can prepare the path for a demagogic xenophobe, as mainstream Republicanism in the United States opened the way for Trump. We enter on a terrain that resembles a civil war without guns (at least for the moment; sometimes this kind of division will end up bringing the guns out, too).

Where one side tries to make its temporary victory permanent, the normal rules of courtesy and civility are suspended, as are all those informal rules that are meant to assure that the debate can go on. When one party goes on this path, the chances are very strong that the other will eventually be induced to answer in kind, and then the bloodless (we hope) civil war starts.

Developments in the United States illustrate this development in a stark and worrying fashion. Since 2012, Republicans have been engaged in attempts to render their hegemony permanent and have used more and more extreme means to assure this: voter suppression, gerrymandering, the refusal of a Republican Senate to act on Obama's nominee for the Supreme Court, and other such actions.[28] Donald Trump's refusal to concede the election in 2020 is an extreme case based partly on his personal ambitions. But it is also a continuation of the pattern set by the Republican Party.

What kinds of division motivate this range of extreme, destructive behavior? Certain narrow interests—for instance, those of the rich and powerful—can play a role (think of the death of the Weimar Republic). But to create a broad enough movement that will back such extremism, an issue that will rally masses of people must be at stake. Usually, the crucial dispute turns on rival definitions of what we may call political identity. And this is certainly what is happening in the contemporary United States.

The battle over what the United States stands for is worth examining in greater detail. It is complex and (for this foreigner) rather bewildering: in particular American "conservatism" seems to combine elements such as guns, the Gospel, and a weakness for Ayn Rand that to outsiders seem incompatible. But the American case is too important to ignore, and we will come back to discuss it later in this book, when we consider what can be done to resolve the current crisis.

But for the moment, we can note that similar deep divisions over political identity shape other "populist" movements that attack their opponents as traitors and enemies of the "people." As noted already, examples range throughout Europe from Viktor Orbán *Fidesz* in Hungary to the French *Rassemblement National* and indeed throughout the world. In this kind of situation, the second and third degenerations—namely, the waves of exclusion and polarization—easily combine, and two segments of the population are declared to be outside the "people": the rejected outsiders (for instance, immigrants, or Muslims), on the one hand, and the "elites" who are supposedly favoring them over the "real" members of the nation, on the other.

Decline of citizen efficacy, waves of exclusion, and polarization: these three axes of degeneration go together today. They don't always go together, but they are occurring together now, and they mutually reinforce each other. Democracy is susceptible to each one. It's susceptible to sliding toward elite rule, and it's susceptible to various mechanisms that kick in and keep it spiraling downward. It's susceptible to falsely moralistic or "nativist" redefinition—to use this perhaps too-simple generic term for various forms of ethnic-historical exclusion. And these redefinitions also have a certain self-feeding property, because the divisions and exclusions they start or exacerbate tend to intensify. The cleavages and barriers they erect make it very hard to get the whole people back together again.

The exclusionary polarization also easily lends itself to a redefinition of democracy as the irreversible hegemony of today's winning party or tendency, "designated" by fiat as "majority rule" tout court.

The second two degenerations combine easily in the idea that there is one massive majority will and that it is being frustrated by the elite and the outsiders they are helping, and what democracy means is to establish *this* will, no discussion, no compromise, no respect. It's just rammed through.

Of course, even "good" (that is, nonexclusive) "populism" can be carried to extremes, so that all opponents are excluded from the "people." We saw this with Bolshevism, where those who stood in the way of the enforced remaking of Russian society—nobles, "kulaks," "deviationists"—were declared enemies of the people and ruthlessly eliminated. Something of this ruthless drive exists today in Xi Jinping's China, but this kind of politics has little attraction in today's democracies.

The slide of democracy into permanent "majority" rule is a disaster for any society. It introduces a ruthlessness into political life. It divides and poisons the public sphere. It renders society much less capable of dealing with the big common challenges that affect both sides of the division equally, challenges such as global warming and the negative effects of globalization and automation.

And it is this identification of democracy and irreversible majority rule that has helped to kill (full) democracy off in various very fragile contexts—I am thinking of Russia, Hungary, and Turkey as examples. Their moves to the "rigged" category have been built on the idea of who the real Russians, Hungarians, and Turks are—what culture and religious orthodoxy is being defended against Western liberal values or homosexuality. In the case of Turkey, the rigged democracy has been built on "pious Islam" and rejecting any compromise with the Kurds, who are demonized as "terrorists." This kind of move can actually destroy a functioning democracy. Even if these were not very stable democracies to begin with, you can still see where this kind of policy can lead.

And there are many democracies today that have not yet tipped over into the "rigged" category. Or where they have tipped, the result has not yet become institutionally stable. This is the case in Poland, where the struggle is still undecided. The "open" political identity, championed by Solidarnosc and John Paul II, rooted in the early modern Polish-Lithuanian Commonwealth (Rzeczpopolita), was reversed by a later, narrower, caricaturally integrist Catholicism, under the banner of the misleadingly named "Law and

Justice" Party. But 2020 protests against such narrowing of political identity show the game is not over. The party packed courts, as has recently been a widespread tactic of the Right. A constitutional tribunal, composed mostly of recently appointed judges, moved to curtail abortion rights. But this provoked a massive women's strike, which overlapped with broader antigovernment demonstrations.

Democracy is not what a majority at this moment or that happens to want. It is a project of greater empowerment and inclusion, liberty, equality, and solidarity for the future.

Our present parlous condition results from the combination of three serious paths of degeneration, which are, again, a decline of citizen efficacy, waves of exclusion, and polarization. We are unfortunate that they have occurred together. We could imagine worlds in which this destructive trio hadn't arrived in tandem. But they are not altogether without connections. The Great Downgrade and the decline of felt citizen efficacy prepared a fertile ground for demagogic attempts to target "outsiders" and for the more and more outrageous politics of discrimination, which has polarized us to a point that our democratic regimes are in danger—and some are already over the edge.

We have to tackle this crisis at its roots: the Great Downgrade and the galloping inequality and sense of citizen powerlessness which it engenders. And that means that we urgently need to create a new solidarity, across the divides that today paralyze us, and render us unable to address the challenges we face, and to define and carry through policies directed to the common good. We have to build the organizations and alliances that will do for us what social democracy did in the aftermath of the Second World War, laying the groundwork for the boom that is remembered today in France as *les trente glorieuses*. We can make comparable strides forward today.

2

Contradictions and Double Movements

CRAIG CALHOUN

Democracy is a project, not simply a condition. It is not switched on like a light and then safely ignored. Democracy is always a work in process, being built, being deepened, or being renewed. It requires a commitment to extend it into the future, to keep making democracy—not, for example, to try to use temporary advantage to foreclose opportunities for future democracy. When renewal and advancement stall, democracy degenerates.

This is so first and foremost because democracy is what Charles Taylor calls a telic concept. It is defined by ideals that can never be fully and finally realized. Liberty, equality, and solidarity are never perfected, for example, nor is the balance among them ever entirely stable. Yet they motivate as well as orient forward movement. Moreover, democracy is pursued not just for itself but for the public good, the well-being of citizens at large and their relations with each other, which self-rule is held to advance.

Second, democracies are not designed in utopian abstraction but built in specific historical contexts. They are durably shaped by their prehistories, by specific choices and compromises in their creation, and by generations of efforts to resolve or mitigate problems that sometimes create new ones. The United States has not yet transcended compromises over radical racial inequality, nor has Britain gotten past the legacies of monarchy, aristocracy, and empire. Canadian democracy has struggled with a divided colonial legacy, France with the ferocity of its commitment to *laïcité*, Germany with the terms of unification. Democracies must not only pursue their constitutive ideals but recurrently reform and improve their institutions and address contradictions in their constitutional structures.

Third, and crucially, democracy depends on social foundations. Citizens must be not only free and equal but well-connected to each other. Their capacity to participate effectively in politics, to organize themselves to pursue shared goods, and to exercise individual freedoms all depend on social resources and relations. Citizens are empowered by local communities, larger institutions, voluntary organizations, social movements, and communications media. These help a scattered or divided population cohere as a body politic—a *demos*—with an inclusive identity, social ties, and a sense of being in the same community of fate. They are both unified and divided by culture. Scale, complexity, and a powerful but contradictory relationship with capitalism are all challenges for modern democracies.

This chapter explores how democracy is shaped and reshaped in wrestling with these challenges. It begins by emphasizing the importance of republican ideas and ideals to the institutionalization of democracy—a theme crucial to the United States but important to democracy more widely. Advancement of democracy came within the republican framework, not without struggle, and often with advances for some and simultaneous setbacks for others. The ideas of the public and public good were crucial, but not to the exclusion of other dimensions of "peoplehood." These questions about the form and ideals of democracy played out in relation to expanding scale, new communications technologies, and shifting relations of local to metropolitan society. Transformations recurrently brought what the economic historian Karl Polanyi called the "disembedding" of citizens from older support systems, as well as "double movements" in which disruption occasioned reactions—including efforts to renew social institutions but also sharp contention.

A Republic with Incomplete Democracy

In the founding of the United States, democracy was a secondary but important theme. The stress fell on creating a republic. "The United States shall guarantee to every State in this Union a Republican Form of Government," says the Constitution. Democracy is not mentioned.

Constitutions are the most basic formulation of the rule of law, which is in turn the primary limit on unbridled individual power. Power is also "checked and balanced" by government bureaucracies with their established procedures. Republican constitutions also provide for public debate informed by public knowledge—notably through mechanisms such as a free press, public education, and transparency in government. This is crucial to ensuring that laws are indeed followed and that government is well-organized for the public good. Last and perhaps hardest to ensure is the virtue of citizens: republican government depends on honesty, refusal of corruption, and commitment to the public good.

Most countries we call democracies are formally constituted as republics.[1] France is officially the French Republic (in fact, it is today the Fifth Republic since every revolution or major structural change legally inaugurated a new state). We can add the People's Republic of China, the Republic of India, the Federal Republic of Germany, and so on. American schoolchildren pledge allegiance to the country's "flag and to the *republic* for which is stands."[2]

From the time of Aristotle, a republic (*politeia*) meant "mixed government." Instead of the cycle of monarchy, aristocracy, and democracy succeeding each other in more or less traumatic transitions, republicanism promised to combine elements of each. The Roman Republic offered the preeminent example, lasting five hundred years from the overthrow of the Roman Kingdom to the establishment of the Roman Empire.

The US founders were steeped in this morality tale.[3] Among its themes were problems with achieving peace or power at the expense of liberty, the corrupting influence of wealth and luxury, and how destabilizing a thirst for power could be.[4] The founders sought to prevent any president from behaving as a dictator, king, or emperor. They balanced the power of the presidency with that of Congress, including its more aristocratic Senate and more democratic House of Representatives. They made it subject to review by an independent but powerful judiciary. The difference from France's more integral state power was clear even to contemporaries.[5]

But while the Constitution spoke to the design of laws and political institutions for the new republic, it had less to say about the social conditions also basic to the success and survival of a republic. The nearly contemporary French Revolution put these more clearly on the agenda. One of its great slogans was "Liberté, Egalité, Fraternité." Not only was equality on a plane with liberty, but in the French formulation solidarity (or as the original had it, *fraternité*) was seen as a necessary complement.[6] By this we can understand both mutuality as a dimension of interpersonal relations and cohesion as a feature of society as a whole. Solidarity is a crucial consideration for both republicanism and democracy. It evokes the importance for citizens of feeling that we are really joined to each other and "in it together."

Liberty is sometimes imagined as freedom from all interference. This idea of freedom is especially popular in the United States. It is a product of experience as well as intellectual traditions. Life as a small farmer, shop owner, or independent craft producer meant having an intuitive understanding of freedom as noninterference, which in turn informed thinking about political rights.[7]

The contemporary republican philosopher Philip Pettit has suggested that noninterference is too extreme a standard, and we should understand republican liberty as freedom from domination.[8] This makes sense. Indeed, the notion that no one dominates is important to ideals of community as well as individualism (though to be sure many people have accepted patriarchal domination as normal to family). And the notion of freedom as noninterference is deeply implausible given the necessary interdependence of modern social relations. But Pettit's proposal is still more negative than positive, and misses the extent to which republican thought seeks to harness liberty to virtue, civic participation, and pursuit of the public good. The republican idea of liberty was not just about freedom, indeed, because it was embedded in norms for being a good elite.

Citizen empowerment is not just a matter of freedom *from* interference or even domination; it is more a matter of the capacity *to* pursue freely chosen goods.[9] These are not just objects of utilitarian desire, as though democratic freedom inhered only in greater choices of consumer goods. Free citizens also pursue higher goods such as justice, beauty, or a sustainable future, which help to orient their judgments of what is really worthy. Their freedom lies partly in the opportunity to discern these higher goods by their own lights.[10] The radical unfreedom of enslavement is a sharp contrast; it is "social death," in the phrase Orlando Patterson adapted from Franz Fanon. Freedom is the opposite—a positive fullness of life choices.[11]

The US Constitution accepted slavery, failed to give women the right to vote, and allowed property restrictions on the rights of men. This was sharply at odds with the ringing pronouncements of the earlier Declaration of Independence that "all men are created equal" and endowed by their Creator with unalienable rights. Even the more freedom-oriented Declaration left women out and failed to address the issue of slavery.[12] But it did evoke ideals more strongly. The later Constitution was, perhaps necessarily, shaped more by instrumental compromises and in any case focused more on tangible mechanisms of government than on aspirations. It made history by embracing democracy, but was at least as clear about limiting it.

Still, partly because it provided for its own revision, the same Constitution paved the way for the United States to become more and more democratic. Revision started almost immediately with the ten amendments known as the Bill of Rights. These protected basic liberties, notably of religion, press, assembly, and petitioning government. Yet these protected the liberty of some at the expense of others. The Second Amendment, protecting the right of the people to keep and bear arms, is a case in point. It was passed in part to ensure that white property owners had the capacity to quell any rebellions of those they enslaved. It coexisted with prohibitions on Black ownership of weapons.[13]

Enslavement was a more radical exclusion than denying women or men with little property the vote. It meant not just domination rather than liberty, but complete exclusion from the polity and the very right to have rights.[14] When the United States was founded, Black Americans, including those freed from slavery, were not fully included in contemporary understandings of "the people." In 1857, in the infamous Dred Scott case, the US Supreme Court affirmed this with brutal clarity:

> The question is simply this: Can a negro, whose ancestors were imported into this country, and sold as slaves, become a member of the political community formed and brought into existence by the constitution of the United States, and as such become entitled to all the rights, and privileges, and immunities, guaranteed by that instrument to the citizen? . . .
>
> We think they are not, and that they are not included, and were not intended to be included, under the word "citizen" in the Constitution, and can therefore claim none of the rights and privileges which that instrument provides for and secures to citizens of the United States.[15]

The Court ruled that even in states that made slave-owning illegal—as a result of democratic action—the formerly enslaved and their descendants could not be citizens.

Change was not just hard; it took a devastating Civil War. But the Thirteenth and Fourteenth Amendments to the Constitution abolished slavery and guaranteed citizenship to all born or naturalized in the United States. Trying to implement this citizenship was a central theme of postwar Reconstruction; trying to limit it was at the heart of the Jim Crow era that followed that. And so it has been since, steps toward greater democracy and steps back, emphatically up to the present moment (discussed further in Chapter 7).

The contradictions between slavery's reality and the country's professed ideals shaped perhaps the biggest challenge American democracy would face. Enslavement could not exist without racism, and racism remained a force after the slave system was abolished. Bias is still built into laws and institutions. Racism still motivates actions that undermine democracy.[16] And racism is not the only contradiction embedded in American democracy.

Yet contradictions are not "fatal flaws" and do not mean that there can be no improvements in the quality and extent of democracy. They do mean that such improvements seldom follow a straight path of incremental progress. Contradictions are fundamental oppositions between different elements of a social formation—such as enslavement and freedom, or racism and equality. Changing them requires transformation of the whole structure of relationships of which they are a part. A contradiction cannot be eliminated with everything else untouched. It is good, thus, for individuals to try to be less racist at a personal level. And individual changes can add up. But overcoming contradictions requires deeper structural change, creating a social order no longer shaped by antagonism among its defining internal features.

In the US case, the country's republican Constitution has been paradoxically both crucial and a problem. It embodied and helped reproduce fundamental contradictions. Yet it also aided the struggle to overcome those contradictions, providing levers for fundamental change. So too around the world. The importance of republican constitutions is paradoxically both to stabilize democracy—which entails constraining it—and to provide mechanisms to recognize needed basic changes.

In the United States, removing restrictions on full citizenship has been a long story and is sadly not finished. A movement for women's rights grew throughout the early nineteenth century, though it was not until 1920 that the Nineteenth Amendment guaranteed American women the right to vote. By the 1820s and 1830s, property qualifications were removed for nearly all white male voters; the country's first major populist movement was a result, bringing Andrew Jackson to power in 1828. Of course, workers' organizations were violently suppressed for another century after this; formal political enfranchisement was not enough to guarantee full citizenship rights. Not only laws but administrative procedures, cultural norms, and social capacities may all differentiate among citizens—even on so basic a matter as voting. Ending slavery took a civil war, and bringing effective voting rights to Black Americans is an ongoing struggle.

The United States is not the only republic to have excluded many people resident in and contributing to the country from the status of citizens. Nor is it the only one to have made formally equal citizenship unequal in practice. Just take the right to vote. In France, the Revolution of 1789 made radical steps toward democracy. Universal male suffrage between 1792 and 1795 put it ahead of the United States. But France degenerated into empire under Napoleon. A succession of nineteenth-century revolutions brought experiments with democracy only to have the gains repeatedly reversed— all the way into the twentieth century. French women only gained the right to vote in 1944–1945 as France regained its independence from Germany near the end of WWII. In the UK, the Reform Acts of 1832 and 1867 brought voting rights to only two million of England's seven million men. Property restrictions were not abolished until 1918, when women over 30 also gained the right to vote; rights for younger women had to wait another ten years. Switzerland did not allow women the right to vote until 1971.

Between the founding of the country and its devastating Civil War there were multiple instances of democracy advancing for some and being withheld from others. The same populist Andrew Jackson who helped increase electoral participation of white Americans signed the infamous Indian Removal Act that brutally forced the relocation of Eastern American tribes from their traditional homes to reservations in the West.

The US Civil War itself resulted both from problems built into the Constitution and from social changes that exacerbated divisions. Economic transformation and religious revival, westward expansion and immigration all posed challenges to the constitutional order and practical political problem solving. Democracy sometimes degenerated by failing to move forward toward greater citizen empowerment and a more inclusive polity. Sometimes partisanship degenerated into unbridgeable enmity. In the 1850s, a South Carolina congressman beat the abolitionist Senator Charles Sumner nearly to death on the floor of the Senate Chamber.[17]

The Civil War killed a million and a half Americans—and expanded American democracy. After the Civil War, greater democracy was imposed on the South by the victorious Union. Dubbed "Reconstruction," this period brought voting rights and other protections to the formerly enslaved and their descendants. One of its peaks was the Civil Rights Act of 1875, the last legislation advancing civil rights—for African Americans or others—until the Civil Rights Act of 1957.[18]

Two Steps Forward, One Step Back

Late in the Civil War, Abraham Lincoln offered one of the most enduring renderings of the idea of democracy. The war itself had followed from the most severe degeneration American democracy has ever seen. Yet, said Lincoln, its successful conclusion meant that "government of the people, by the people, and for the people . . . shall not perish from the earth."[19]

The line is embedded in Lincoln's brilliant speech at the dedication of the national cemetery after the Civil War's bloodiest battle. At 272 words, Lincoln's Gettysburg Address was short enough that inspired citizens or diligent schoolchildren could commit it to memory—as I did at age eleven or so. That generations of schoolchildren did the same was long part of the recurrent renewal of the American polis—and perhaps still is, though I think it is less common. Faith in American democracy—and indeed a sense of American identity—was kept alive by continual reweaving in which such threads of rhetorical continuity joined with new inspirations, historical commemorations, cultural contexts, material achievements, and memories.[20]

This was not simply the happy history of settled democracy, though sometimes commemorations verged into self-congratulation. Nor was progress toward more democracy always assured. Civil war made a mockery of that. So did later reversals of gains for Black Americans. So did the defeat of the great American populist movement in the 1890s, which elites partly coopted and partly undermined by fomenting racist divisions. So did government collusion in employers' violent suppression of labor unions. Still, temptations to see history as linear and progressive often overrode remembrance of degeneration and disruption.

Lincoln's phrase was recurrently quoted, sometimes as an aspirational ideal, sometimes as though it could mask the tensions and limits of actual democracy. I memorized the address around 1963, in the midst of the vaunted "postwar boom," or what the French call *les trente glorieuses*. The United States, like Europe, made enormous forward strides in the middle of the twentieth century. Equality grew, education was expanded, the economy provided new opportunities. A range of institutions and policies provided support and security to an unprecedented part of the population. Some of these had roots as far back as the Progressive Era; more were grounded in the New Deal of the 1930s; and some built on wartime experiences.

But not all was glorious. America was both divided and inspired by the Civil Rights movement. Nineteen sixty-three was the year of Martin Luther King's "I Have a Dream" speech during the March on Washington. It was also the year President John F. Kennedy was assassinated. The deeply divisive Vietnam War was getting underway. So was the American Indian Movement, which attempted to reverse the violation of treaties and theft of lands that was not just old history but active government policy during the postwar boom. The high ideals of Lincoln's phrase were not met then and have never been fully met since.[21]

Yet democracy demands ideals; even conceptualizing what might be an advance requires an evaluative framework. Lincoln's speech harked back to ideals articulated in the Declaration of Independence and the Constitution. In 1863, it was not necessary to stress failures to live up to them as much as it was to look to hopes for a better future. Still, we also need clear-eyed examination of the reality that limits or sometimes contradicts our ideals.

Struggles to realize the ideals of Lincoln or the American founders, of liberty, equality, and solidarity, or of Martin Luther King's dream have had to contend from the start with the limits and contradictions built into the US Constitution. But advances in democracy have also depended on the very same republican constitution with its procedures for interpretation and amendment. Not least, the rights the Constitution protected empowered citizens. Equally, though, empowerment comes from the ways social and economic life is organized, the extent to which citizens can depend on each other, and the institutions created to support both their individual and their collective lives.[22]

Large and rapidly growing, the United States could depend less than any previous republic on face-to-face relationships and an established sense of belonging to the whole. It had to build new forms of social organization and indeed new infrastructures of transportation and communication to be a cohesive country. It has struggled to link personal relationships and place-based communities with larger scales, with institutions and bureaucratic organizations, with far-flung connections through markets or media.[23] From the outset, immigration added challenges. The country became increasingly diverse geographically—and economically—as it expanded.

Democracies constantly narrate their forward and backward steps. The narratives can be contentious, fraught with condemnations, and bitter. They can be excessively celebratory—as many invocations of Lincoln and the end of slavery have been. Like Northern and Southern narratives of the Civil War (or for some in the South, "the War of Yankee Aggression"), they can keep oppositions alive. In that case, the Northern narrative has collapsed into half-memory and mere celebration. The more bitter Southern narrative remains alive in contemporary discussion. But both are also altered by new themes—by the World Wars in which the United States fought "for democracy," or the decline of the rust belt and rise of the sun belt. It is in such narratives that citizens both claim pasts and try to work out what counts as advance, defeat, or frustration.

Forward steps come largely through struggle in social movements. But they come also through lonelier struggles of individuals trying to "do the right thing" in their lives, through members of communities trying to achieve local fairness and solidarity, through legal cases, through incremental improvements in government policies, and through cultural shifts pushed forward by artists, entertainers, conversations around dinner tables, and sharper arguments about what is fair.

Often, two steps forward are followed by at least step one backward. Gains on one dimension are matched by losses on another. More basically, the very mechanisms of progress on some dimensions often block progress or even bring regressions on others. This pattern of contradictions echoes throughout American history, from long before the Civil War to the present day. It is embedded in the Constitution, but it is also embedded in social change and how we respond to it.

The GI Bill after World War II is a case in point.[24] Government funding for veterans facilitated a dramatic transformation in who could attend universities and aspire to middle-class jobs linked to graduation. It brought extraordinary new opportunities, and it contributed to the country's postwar economic growth. It stands along with other New Deal and postwar policies as dramatic evidence of the positive effect government social programs can have.

As it was implemented, however, most of the GI Bill's opportunities were denied to Black veterans. Had the law been applied fairly as written, at least a million more Black Americans would have had a chance to attend college.[25] Likewise, because of the gender structure of who had been in the military, the GI Bill favored men. It actually increased the gap between men and women in higher education.[26]

In other ways, too, policies that helped white men after the war did less for women and minorities. During the war, women had moved successfully into a variety of jobs—Rosie the Riveter is the pop culture example. After the war they were mostly removed from jobs they had done well. The late 1940s and 1950s did not just return to the ideology that jobs should go to male breadwinners and women should take care of the home; they intensified it. Women were laid off from the auto industry and other sectors regardless of seniority and often without much defense from their unions.[27]

Black veterans returned from military service to segregated communities and discriminatory hiring practices. Only a few men found jobs that paid "living wages" that could fully support their families.[28] Black women were more likely than white women to work outside the home—that is, outside their own homes, since many took care of the homes and children of white women. The sexist ideology that women should be home to take care of their families was racist in application. It took the Civil Rights movement to start a process of change. Alas, progress stalled, and the earnings gap between Black and white workers remains as great today as it was in 1968.[29] When deindustrialization and globalization eliminated working-class jobs starting in the 1970s, whites more often had other opportunities, and fewer Blacks had the chance to go to college.

These social and economic factors all have implications for democracy—and its degenerations. For many Americans the social programs and new institutions of the postwar era were empowering. For others they were less so or not at all. Biases limited the inclusion of all citizens in the democratic polity. And while, overall, the United States proved itself open to change in the direction of wider empowerment and inclusion, this was not without resistance. Beneficiaries of existing arrangements sought to make their dominance permanent—be it racial, male, Christian, or all of these. And new arrangements had their own beneficiaries—owners of investible assets, highly educated meritocrats, and cosmopolitan elites best prepared to benefit from globalization.

The People, the Public, and the Public Good

The American Declaration of Independence does not refer simply to the thirteen colonies or potentially independent states, or to the action of a majority. It does refer to the "United Colonies," but crucially it also refers to a "people."[30] When Lincoln emphasized government of the people, by the people, and for the people, he echoed the declaration. This is not some people, nor all the people as individuals. The reference is to *the* people as a body.

There are many dimensions to how any "people" is cohesive. Common culture, ethnicity, and ways of life, cohesion in social networks and institutions, or subjection to external domination may all be important.[31] But republicanism emphasizes one additional dimension: mutual engagement in public reason and will formation.[32] Engagement in public is not just a way to make decisions. It is a way to *achieve* cohesion, to make something new, not simply find it or inherit it. The philosopher Hannah Arendt, who had fled Nazi Germany in 1933 and eventually made her way to the United States, famously celebrated this image of citizens forming a new society together, literally *constituting* it, as part of the American Revolution.[33]

When the Declaration of Independence declared that all people have certain self-evident and unalienable rights, including "life, liberty, and the pursuit of happiness," it began to articulate a notion of the public good. It did not simply assert that people were alive, free, and engaged in the pursuit of their own happiness. It suggested that the new country would be organized to secure those rights for all. This was the goal of government design—constitution-writing and legislation. It was also an obligation for each citizen—a demand for public virtue.

It is easy to say "public good" without stopping to think what it really means. Individualism and preoccupations with material gains and losses encourage us to think the public good must be what a majority wants or the immediate material benefit of as many individuals as possible (the utilitarian "greatest good of the greatest number"). But the public good is more. Consider four distinctions: The public good can be long-term, such as the sustainability of society in the face of war or climate change. It can include not just aggregate goods—the gross national product—but also fair and equitable distribution of these goods. The public for which it is good is not necessarily a community or category of essentially similar people; it is a public because it includes members of multiple communities and different categories—such as different religions. Not least, the public good can include moral standards such as rejection of corruption.

A key republican ideal is for public reason to identify the public good and shape the will to achieve it. This suggests we can consciously choose how to knit our lives together. But solidarity can never be achieved by reason or rational-critical debate alone. Even when they are not democracies, republics also depend on other dimensions of solidarity among their citizens, though republican theory is less articulate about these.[34]

Communicative engagement in public life includes poetry and stories as well as debate, entertainment TV as well as news, music as well as words. Citizens are knit together in private as well as public relationships, in communities, voluntary societies, businesses, and market transactions. All these go into making a people. Not least of all, the constitution of a people depends on shared identity, the distinction of *this* people from others.

Bringing democracy into the constitution of a republic places an especially strong demand on common peoplehood. This is the demos from which the word "democracy" derives. Democracies depend on citizens being able to say with confidence "We the People," feeling and believing that they *belong* to the demos and thus with each other. There is tension—but not contradiction—between the communal dimensions of peoplehood and public respect for the diversity and independence of citizens.

The Declaration of Independence begins precisely by articulating the extent to which the American people has grown apart from the British: "When in the Course of human events, it becomes necessary for one people to dissolve the political bands which have connected them with another . . ." By implication peoplehood is more than only a matter of political bands. But for there to be "self-rule" requires some understanding of just what the self is.

The Declaration certainly does not assert that all Americans are the same. Political identity does not require cultural uniformity or even any single common denominator such as language. Nor does resolving political issues require unanimity. It may be a matter of negotiation between people who see the issue and options differently and even hold different values. Parties can help to bring divergent interests into negotiation.[35] Sharing a polity does not forbid partisanship, but it does require that loyalty to the larger republic come before partisan interests.

It remains a question, whether and when the particular loyalties of family and community are, like partisan interests, in tension with the republic, and when and how much they are crucial to achieving the social integration of a people able to be either the subject of democracy or the object of republican pursuit of the public good. Democracy degenerates and republicanism fails when citizens fail to recognize each other as members of an inclusive polity.

The Declaration does not spend much time on what makes the people a cohesive body. But it is significant that near the end the representatives who signed it on behalf of their different former colonies "mutually pledge to each other" their lives, fortune, and sacred honor. Republican self-rule—including democracy—depends on explicit or implicit commitments citizens make to each other.[36]

Among these commitments is to prioritize the public good. "Ask not what your country can do for you, ask what you can do for your country," as President John F. Kennedy put it (channeling an old republican theme). This does not mean that citizens will not act on separate, private interests in many aspects of their lives. They will legitimately have personal agendas when they choose spouses or sign business contracts. Of course, there is a public dimension to even a private contract; this is what makes it enforceable through the courts. And at least traditionally, marriage involved not only an agreement between spouses but the performance of that agreement before an assembled community or public that was enjoined to support the marriage. Being a good citizen need not mean sacrificing all these private dimensions of our lives but rather finding a good balance. It does mean making space in our lives and our attention for public, shared concerns. And it means using our public engagements to advance the public good, not just pursue private ends.

The public good is more than the sum of what citizens happen to want at any moment. It is also an aspiration and an extension into the future. While votes and majorities are valuable mechanisms for making decisions, they are not the final definition of either the public good or identity of the polity. As James Madison wrote to James Monroe (his successor as president), "There is no maxim in my opinion which is more liable to be misapplied and which therefore needs more elucidation than the current one that the interest of the majority is the political standard of right and wrong."[37]

The interest of the majority is short-term and shifting. It easily neglects the public good. And it leaves out the interests of minority members of the political community. Add to this the problems of distinguishing "true"—or more basic, longer-term, and reflectively considered—interests from the immediate thoughts of the members of a temporary majority about what they want.[38]

Having opened the door to an unprecedented level of democracy, Madison and other US founders were acutely concerned about unbridled and immediate expressions of popular will. When they worried about democracy, it was largely direct democracy they had in mind—efforts of citizens to govern themselves without the mediating selection of representatives.

They worried that this arrangement couldn't scale up, that it was vulnerable to crowd psychology and demagoguery, and that it would be too easy for an assembled crowd to think it obviously was a majority—or even the people as such—without taking the step of actually checking the views of those not assembled. For democratic government to be effective, fair and stable demanded combining it with republican institutions—which was the task of the Constitution.[39]

The French Revolution offered a frightening example as temporary majorities sent not just the king but a succession of the revolution's own leaders to the guillotine. Many founders of the United States grew increasingly concerned that their democratic experiment would be short-lived.[40] Indeed, the radical republic of the French Revolution *was* extremely short-lived. This is a reminder that social stability has a positive value; change, even idealistic change, is not the only good. But it can be crucial, even to saving what we value when it is under pressure.

Simple majoritarianism is a degenerate form of democracy and a problem for republican ideals. And as Charles Taylor suggests in Chapter 1, it is a still bigger problem when parties try to make temporary majorities into permanent structures of domination. Yet this is what happens over and again, in large ways and small. It is, for example, central to the efforts at voter suppression that are so strong in American history, as we discuss in Chapter 7.

According to the Declaration, citizens do not just express the individual urge to personal freedom but also choose a society in which everyone is free.[41] They choose to share that society. The choices of equality and solidarity are equally shared. Absent the sharing—and the limits it brings—democratic freedom can be corrosive and self-undermining.

How much we get of "life, liberty, and the pursuit of happiness" depends on both social conditions and political freedoms. These relevant rights may be "self-evident" but they are not intrinsically self-realizing. Life depends on food, obviously, and on clean rather than contaminated drinking water, health care (especially during a pandemic), and in the long run, reversing or coping with climate change. Citizens are empowered very unequally to pursue happiness. They may have more or less money and better or worse schools; they may or may not face sexual harassment and gender-based discrimination and brutal policing. And they are affected by broad social conditions, such as factory closings and the destruction of communities or, in the United States, incarceration of huge numbers of Black men.

These are matters of both "public goods" and *the* public good. First, some *goods*—such as clean air, national security, equality, or solidarity—are hard to enjoy without sharing them. No one can enjoy them without others also participating (and indeed, no one gets less of them because others get more).[42] Provision and access to public goods has been under attack in the United States and most capitalist democracies in the last fifty years of neoliberalism. Strengthening provision is important to both empowerment and equality. It is also basic to facing challenges such as the ongoing Covid-19 pandemic and accelerating climate change (as we discuss in Chapter 7).

Second the public *good*—singular—is an ideal for the overall constitution of a people, not simply a class of goods. As John Adams wrote, "The public Good, the *salus Populi* is the professed End of all Government."[43] It is not a matter of consumer benefits—as though wanting a country free from corruption was much the same as wanting a fancier car. The public good is a higher value than such private goods. It is a matter of virtue and moral obligation in a way that personal benefits are not. There is obviously self-interest to wanting a better car, but that is not a matter of virtue. Wanting a better country—one that lives up to its highest ideals or potential—is different. One might even sacrifice personal benefits for such a higher good—as for example do soldiers.

Of course, in elections people often vote based on what they perceive to be their short-term material interests. They vote based on what they think one party or another will do for jobs, or housing prices, or old-age benefits. This is not unreasonable, though too often we are actually taught—both in schools and by experience—that selfishness is rewarded, even that "greed is good" (as the 1987 movie *Wall Street* put it). Adding up expressions of private interests is not the same as identifying the public good.

Still, many people do vote for one party or another because they think it will be better for their country—or even the world. Some vote for better schools even if they don't have children, or they vote to keep the national debt down, or they vote for peace. There are still many examples of civic or public virtue (thank goodness). It has not vanished, but it does seem to have eroded.

Scale, Communication, and Surveillance

Classical and Renaissance republican thought focused on small societies in which all citizens could be known to each other. Both concern for their reputations and ability to see the consequences of their actions would promote virtue. But this was unlikely to work as well at large scale. This meant that both the design of the republic and the project of democracy confronted different challenges from those of smaller, mostly face-to-face societies.

It is worth pausing to emphasize the transformation in scale. At its founding, the United States had nearly four million people. Ancient Athens included perhaps 250,000 at its height. Renaissance Florence peaked at perhaps 60,000 in the early fifteenth century. In 1900, the US Census made news by reporting that the population had grown 21 percent in the preceding decade to reach the total of 76,212,168. In 2000, the Census measured the population at 281,421,906. Today, just twenty years later, it exceeds 330 million, of whom 93 percent are citizens, with 250 million old enough to vote. There are on average 750,000 people in each district electing a member to the US House of Representatives. The number stipulated in the original US Constitution was one representative per thirty thousand. And the United States is small by comparison to the world's largest, if also struggling, democracy: India. More than 600 million people voted in India's most recent election, out of some 900 million eligible. The population exceeds 1.4 billion.

The nineteenth-century French analyst of American democracy, Alexis de Tocqueville, sought to discern how civic virtue could be cultivated not just in a narrow elite, but among the wider range of citizens. Political associations, he argued, provided "great free schools for democracy."[44] In other words, citizens can learn to do democracy better. And they learn by doing. What they learn is not only how to manage the procedures of democracy—say, using Robert's *Rules of Order* (or "Martha's" more communitarian rules) to run a meeting or the appreciating virtues and limits of different voting procedures. They learn the spirit of democracy that encourages them to improvise as democrats in new contexts.

In a thin sense, public virtue involves a variety of kinds of "good behavior"—such as not littering or wearing masks to prevent spreading infections during a pandemic. Many of these can be taught, made into habits, or enforced by laws. They reflect good government (or good upbringing) in general. Democracy can become a way of life. But democracy also demands a stronger sense of public virtue. It insists that mere compliance is not enough, that public virtue requires conscious participation in public life and commitment to making choices for the public good. The boundary is fuzzy, because citizens may form good habits as well as reach good decisions through public debates.

Madison famously worried that large scale and complexity limited the effectiveness of civic virtue; he demanded the use of laws and policies to ensure individual and group interests also supported the public good.[45] These were to address not only scale but a rapidly growing and increasingly complex market economy (which today we might call "capitalist"). The individual autonomy dear to the liberal tradition could be transformed either into a kind of naked economic egoism or, as Tocqueville hoped, into a "self-interest, rightly understood" that could complement civic virtue and religious morality.[46] What the political theorist Michael Sandel has called "the formative project of Republican citizenship" helped nurture good citizens.[47] This was not all prior preparation; it included "on-the-job learning." Participation was itself a school for better participation.

Seeking balance among liberty, equality, and solidarity, Tocqueville stressed the importance of associations.[48] Churches, fraternal societies, mutual benefit societies, civic organizations, both labor unions and businesses, political parties, charities, social movements, and clubs were all basic to American society. These knit society together at levels between individuals and the centralized state. Americans, he said, were by character and culture "joiners," and this was a good thing. Social affiliations were an antidote to excesses of individualism, which among other things could paradoxically lead to overdependence on the central government and degeneration of democracy into calls for government to remedy citizens' deficiencies. It is precisely this rich web of voluntary, intermediate associations that Robert Putnam, the analyst of social capital, argued America was losing at the end of the twentieth century and beginning of the twenty-first. The seemingly mundane example he made famous was the decline of bowling leagues.[49] His point, like Tocqueville's, was not that the associations were directly political but that educated citizens in the basic practices of democracy nurtured solidarity and encouraged public virtue. This, he thought, was good both for individuals and for the country.

In the early twentieth century, John Dewey influentially held that democracy must be a process of education.[50] It was not enough that citizens be educated *in order* to participate; it was also crucial that they be educated *by* participating. A good election campaign was one in which citizens could learn more about issues and policies. For them to do so required both honesty and clear explanations of the views on the part of candidates. But it also depended on open, reflective debate. At the time Dewey wrote, participation and education were both being transformed—and rendered problematic—by the growing scale of society.[51] The old image of a town hall holding the citizens who needed to gather for debate was superseded even in towns, let alone large cities or the whole country. Debate and the public education of citizens were transformed.

Tocqueville saw newspapers as central to informing this debate and indeed simply carrying it out at necessary scales. Newspapers not only educate citizens and enable them to express opinions (and learn the opinions of others). They also gather the dispersed citizenry into a democratic public rather than atomistic individuals. "Nothing but a newspaper," he wrote, "can drop the same thought into a thousand minds at the same time."[52] Of course, he didn't live to hear radio, see TV, or become addicted to social media.

In the late eighteenth century, newspapers were commonly the projects of individuals, often printers writing articles even as they set type. But newspapers grew with democracy. By Tocqueville's time, they had come to be closely linked to associations. In his words: "newspapers make associations, and associations make newspapers."[53] But through the nineteenth century newspapers grew as businesses, commonly local. By the mid-twentieth century, they became large organizations (supported by others such as Reuters, United Press International, the Associated Press, and other "wire services" for long-distance information-sharing). Newspapers persisted as broadcast media grew, though profits came under pressure. A wave of consolidation followed as chains bought up the previously local papers and organized them into national structures.[54] Of course broadcast media provided for journalism as well as entertainment. And journalism became a profession with strong (though variable) norms of objective and fair reporting, reproduced in part by professional education.

Educative, informative public debate depends not only on media, but also on transparent governance. Citizens need to be able to know what laws or policies are under consideration, what information politicians have about them, and what data guide government implementation. Progress in this came with measures such as publishing congressional debates—or now, putting them on TV. There are requirements that many governance meetings must be open to all citizens. But in fact national government seems distant and relatively opaque to most citizens. This is partly an effect of its scale and complexity; it has relatively little to do with trying to keep secrets except in a few key areas.

Participating in public life can give citizens an enlarged view of what is possible and preferable; it can change our standards of evaluation. Better understanding of the public good may even be linked to better understanding of ourselves. Tocqueville and the range of republican thinkers after him saw public virtue not just as self-sacrifice but as a way to benefit from the many goods that were available only when shared. So both the actual sharing and seeing the public benefit were important.

Of course, some participants in public life may seek only power or gratification of their immediate desires. We do not rely simply on moral exhortations to try to limit this. One traditional republican notion was that citizens would be concerned about their reputations. They would want to be seen as virtuous when observed by others. When governance was undertaken by a small elite or in a small polity, observation could be fairly direct. In larger countries, publicity about politicians plays something of the same role. Within communities some people may be praised as public spirited or criticized for shirking obligations.

Direct observation among citizens works less well in very large-scale societies. Indirect mechanisms of observation and evaluation have become ubiquitous. States monitor social media to prevent terrorism or repress dissent. Companies monitor credit card usage to manage risks and target advertising. Applicants for loans are not assessed by a local banker with awareness of their personal circumstances or an ability to look them in the eye or shake hands; they are assessed by algorithms. And media audiences are also active participants, generating their own messages or reposting and commenting on those of others. This interactivity is crucial to how social media have transformed older print and broadcast media, but it has the effect of generating far more data about each individual.

More and more data are collected about each of us, not just by intentional surveillance but as a byproduct of all the routine transactions that are recorded—from making purchases to browsing websites to watching TV. Take a seemingly innocent survey on Facebook—about health, say, or where it is good to live—and you provide data to a vast marketing operation. Both real and artificially constructed "news" stories about a particular disease will start popping up. Search "healthy weight" on Google, and you will start receiving ads for diet programs. The ad companies and the social media platforms make money by competing for consumers' attention.[55] These vast amounts of personal data are explored by artificial intelligence programs designed to construct profiles, identify patterns, and make predictions. This process tracks much with remarkable accuracy, but also introduces a variety of errors, including racial bias.[56]

In addition, we are lured into a ubiquitous ratings culture, for consumer goods, yes, but also for political speech. Ratings are yet another source of data about each individual's views and preferences and are used to sell not just cars or cosmetics but politicians and policies. In the West this is mostly operationalized through business enterprises.[57] China has recently introduced computerized monitoring systems aided by artificial intelligence to produce "social credit" ratings.[58]

Ubiquitous surveillance, whether capitalist or statist, has all but eliminated privacy. This is frustrating for individuals and linked to material risks such as identity theft. But it is also a challenge to democracy, which is rooted in the notion that both individuals and groups can engage in "interior" reflections and debates that are not completely subject to external gaze or control. A citizen can have an interior dialog about how to weigh different interests and values, how to estimate the risks of different actions—including expressions of political opinion. But privacy also allows, crucially, for apolitical engagements—for love, friendship, family, music, sports, dance, and literary pleasures. Subjecting everything to political control or judgment is as basic a feature of totalitarianism as repressing political dissent. Both are fatal enemies of democracy, which requires both public and private empowerment of citizens and webs of social relationships that connect the two.

Neither capitalist nor statist surveillance is a matter of citizens' direct observation of each other. It is an asymmetrical monitoring. It takes place in ways we cannot even see, let alone control. Even more than privacy is at stake. Opaque or covert technologies are used to shape our identities, allegiances, and preferences. This introduces a tension with the core republican idea that individuals free from domination should choose the conditions of their lives together through reasoned discussion. It is a challenge to the idea of democratic will-formation.

It is also simply a shock and disorientation. New technologies have transformed infrastructure and communications for centuries. Printing presses were once new and basic to the rise of modern democracy. Telegraphs joined with railroads to knit together whole countries. Telephones allowed maintenance of interpersonal linkages across distance. First radio then television allowed broadcast messages to reach "masses." Such media rewove the fabric of life. They both contributed to the rise of an urban society and helped to connect even the remotest rural areas into large-scale information flows. The recent wave of new technologies have (including but not limited to social media) continued some trends and transformed others, notably by enabling many more people to be "senders" of messages potentially received at long distance and by large populations but also by fragmenting publics.

The new media technologies have come as part of a package with ubiquitous monitoring, such as with watches tracking heart rates. They bring economic transformation alongside workplace automation and the rise of computer-enabled logistics businesses such as Amazon and Uber. The ways they could transform warfare are alarming. The frequency of actual cyber-attacks and system failures makes for a pervasive anxiety.

The very fact of the new technologies creates a sense of risk at least equal to any sense of new empowerment, and sometimes greater. It has upset routines and expectations. But the response cannot be to eliminate the computer-based technologies. Rather, we must find good institutional structures to help us use them well, regulate them where necessary, and provide new replacements for the support old media gave to democracy.

The Local and the Metropolitan

The American founders rebelled against imperial Britain, and they did not choose to create another empire. They created a republic. They saw its citizens as "a" people (even if, at the outset, most had loyalties to their states at least as strong as their loyalties to the new country).

Indeed, the founders were in many ways localists. Despite his happy years in France, Thomas Jefferson recurrently retreated to his farm at Monticello. He imagined American democracy rooted in small towns and farming villages. He thought these would nurture greater virtue among citizens and restrain tendencies to reinstate aristocracy. This was a matter of principle as well as taste, for like others in the classical republican tradition, he worried that large scale and especially empire was intrinsically an enemy of virtue, encouraging excessive luxury and pomp, intrigue and conspiracy, arrogance among leaders and servility among the rest. He worried about expensive government and a standing army.

Yet Jefferson also presided over the Louisiana Purchase. This doubled the territory of the country. It also made the United States de facto an imperial power as it contended for control of the new territory with a range of American Indian nations.[59]

Despite the tension with the republican ideas of the founders, the United States kept growing. It expanded westward and eventually annexed Hawaii and Alaska. In all these territories it ruled over Native peoples as subject populations. The expansion was achieved not just by purchases or by accession of states formed by settlers. It was a product of conquest and war with Spain and Mexico as well as American Indian nations. And in the world wars, the United States acquired overseas territories such as the Philippines. It occupied Haiti, the Dominican Republic, and the Panama Canal Zone. Cherishing the idea that it was a republic, the United States became an imperial power without using the word "empire." This remains an unresolved issue—notably with regard to Puerto Rico, with the American Indian nations, and with the District of Columbia which is a majority-Black territory ruled by the US federal government without the rights of a state.

Growth also meant immigration and, especially, cities. Today less than 20 percent of the US population lives in even somewhat rural areas, and less than a tenth of those more or less rural Americans are actually farmers. There is vastly more wealth and luxury in the United States today than at its founding. The American democratic project has been transformed by industrialization, urbanization, expansion of the country itself, and development of an infrastructure to integrate it. Versions of this story have played out around the world. The "internal colonialism" of England against Scotland, Wales, and Ireland is one example—and again, still fraught today. European countries sought to be republics (and nation-states) at home, even while being empires abroad. They live with complex consequences.[60]

In the United States, farmers formed the backbone of the great Populist movement of the late nineteenth century.[61] They struggled not least against the burden of debt; they borrowed for equipment and seed; deflationary national fiscal policies made it harder to pay even when the harvest was good. In 1896, William Jennings Bryan gave one of the most famous speeches in American political history, culminating in the cry "You shall not crucify mankind on a cross of gold." The issue was whether more silver coins might be minted, increasing the money supply (much as the Federal Reserve might lower interest rates to counter recession today). This would help farmers, but not banks. Government sided with the bankers. Many family farms were lost.

At the same time as the great farmers' movements of the late nineteenth century, the United States saw a major increase in immigration. The population of the United States more than doubled between 1860 and 1900 despite the loss of life in the Civil War. Sadly, there was never an effective political alliance between the Populist farmers and the largely immigrant industrial and mine workers. Along with Black Americans, immigrants became scapegoats attacked by politicians seeking to mobilize the votes of farmers and other rural producers. Then as now, immigration is a vital force for economic growth. But divide and conquer is a recurrent strategy for political elites seeking power against the threat of more unified democracy.

The late nineteenth century anticipated our own era in many ways. Mark Twain and Charles Dudley Warner dubbed it "the Gilded Age," lampooning the greed and corruption that were rampant.[62] This was the era when "robber barons" amassed great fortunes from investments in railroads, oil, and, indeed, debt. Inequality was extreme. Eventually efforts were made to try to control it. With legislation such as the Sherman Act of 1880, the government tried to restrict cartels and other collusion in restraint of trade. This became the basis for antitrust law and efforts to break up monopolies. There were also new efforts to provide for shared welfare, which recognized that many Americans lived in precarious economic circumstances and without much community support. The formation of unions was an effort by workers to provide for collective security and build new community institutions to sustain life in cities and factory towns. Industrial relations were fraught and often violent as owners and managers tried to stop workers from forming unions. Pensions were first established for the widows and children of Civil War veterans, later for workers in some companies. Settlement houses tried to help immigrants. Support was modest until another shock, the Great Depression of the 1930s, generated enough pressure for major government action.

Yet the consolidation of farms continued, soon under corporate control. Farmers loved the land and tried to keep their farms going despite the economic pressures. In 1985, Willie Nelson, Neil Young, and John Mellencamp organized the first Farm Aid concert to raise money to help farm families manage debt and stay on the land. The project continues, though farmers have dwindled to just a little over 1 percent of the American population from 40 percent in 1900. Agriculture has not ceased, of course; it has just been taken over by large corporations.

Rural and small-town life still has an outsize grip on American self-understanding. It is particularly the felt past and wished-for present of white Americans. It is not entirely foreign to Black Americans but much more problematic. The myth and desire have less purchase among more recent immigrant populations who have known the country mainly through its cities. Still, immigrants—from Latin America, especially—sometimes bring sensibilities that connect to the social vision if not the specific history of the rural United States.

That social vision is one of individual self-reliance and autonomy coupled with strong family ties and a sense of security. It is largely mythical but not less powerful for that. It is no more mythical than the notion that urbanites are all cosmopolitan devotees of diversity, attending the theater rather than watching TV, or engaged in political discussion at cafés. These are not accurate descriptions, but they are meaningful myths.

The decline of rural districts and the rise of industrial cities are both part of transformation in the very scale of social life. And both are echoed around the developed world. Few modern states tried as hard to protect rural life as France did. Yet, a French version of this story made headlines in 2019 thanks to protestors wearing yellow vests. The vests simultaneously referenced a fuel tax that nonurbanites thought fell unfairly on them, a claim to widely shared French identity, since every car owner is required to have a vest, and a sense of urgency, since the vests are designed precisely to attract attention in emergencies. Their protests were classically "populist," challenging a technocratic prime minister for an out-of-touch style and policies serving the rich more than the masses. Claimed both by the right-wing National Front and by the Left Party, the Yellow Vest protests were at least as much about the fate of communities and livelihoods in nonmetropolitan France as about any specific political ideology.[63]

All through the twentieth century, France sought to avoid so complete a transition in livelihoods as the United States experienced. It adopted a range of price subsidies and other policies to try to protect both the rural villages thought central to *la France profonde* and the foods thought integral to a proper French way of life. Industry still developed, and overall France enjoyed a high standard of living. It built one of the strongest welfare state systems in the world. And, for a long time, it sustained agricultural prosperity, with at least 350 distinct types of cheeses and fresh bread produced daily.

Nonetheless, by the 2020s, French rural livelihoods have been deeply and painfully disrupted. What France achieved was to slow—but not altogether stop—the decline of rural areas and small towns. Slower can mean less disruptive and more humane. But now, partly because of government policy shifting in a neoliberal direction, France is facing rural decline and deindustrialization at the same time. In the 1950s and 1960s, demographic shifts accompanied growing employment in industry. New jobs were relatively well paid, and workers were empowered by high rates of unionization. Now those industrial jobs are being disrupted or destroyed.

Today, jobs are most plentiful in the service sector, but generally not for former farmers or former industrial workers. This is partly because of gender biases—not only against men in traditionally female occupations, but also among men against those occupations. And not all of the service sector is thriving. Bakeries and cheese shops are closing in the face of convenient supermarkets and two-career families. Moreover, the costs of the French welfare state are facing resistance from middle- and upper-class taxpayers. This transformation has become integral to both political challenges from the populist Right and protests that unite parts of the Left and Right in opposition to technocratic liberal reforms designed to advance French economic competitiveness as a whole in the context of European integration and globalization.

Transformations of rural and nonmetropolitan life do not mean that either Jefferson's vision of a village and small-town United States or the prioritization of *la France profonde* was wrong. It does mean that without amendment neither is adequate to contemporary conditions. That low-density areas voted for populist politicians reveals important facts about how people in those areas feel and how they believe they have been treated. It does not indicate that populist demagogues had actual solutions to their problems or ways of reconciling local futures with growth of a large-scale economy.

This is not just an agricultural story. It is a story of sharp disruption to the social conditions for democracy. It has been equally important in England's industrial Midlands.[64] This region was central to the nineteenth-century Industrial Revolution and to a mining and factory economy—and way of life—that thrived after. But, by the late twentieth century, most of that was gone. While Birmingham remained a major city, small towns throughout the region declined. The East Midlands airport is symbolic: it is an all-cargo facility because warehousing and shipping for the new logistical economy have replaced older modes of production. It brought jobs, though, in a familiar pattern: not unionized and not as well-paid as those lost. Though the region remains the geographical heart of England, it is ironically peripheral to the newer economic circuits of global commerce and technology.[65]

The growth of large-scale integration has undermined place-based, local communities. It has enabled employers to weaken unions by increasing competition among workers, escaping from localities where workers organize, and sometimes simply moving whole sites of employment to places where workers have less power. Early in twentieth-century in the United States this meant relocating textile factories from New England to the South. But from the 1970s the relocations became increasingly international. Long supply chains made the logistical economy intrinsically nonlocal.

The very systems that connected nation-states into the global economy pulled nation-states apart internally. Blows could be as dramatic as the closing of a factory that had been the mainstay of a town's economy. They could come in increments, such as the incursion of big-box stores and mail-order shopping, which undermined a downtown business district. Centralization of services could exacerbate the loss; consolidation of school districts undermined the identity and cohesion of towns; local hospitals and doctors' offices closed in favor of larger regional centers. An early symptom was often the loss of young people when the town couldn't provide strong economic opportunities.

While unionized industry flourished, leaving home could bring attractive working-class careers elsewhere, as for example teenagers from Kentucky looked to Michigan, Ohio, and the auto industry for opportunities or, more ambitiously, to California and aerospace.[66] But even after the good factory jobs disappeared, they kept leaving the small towns of Kentucky—and West Virginia, and Eastern Ohio—because there was no viable future there. Steadily rising average ages and often shrinking school enrollments measured the loss.[67]

Disembedding

The economist, historian, and anthropologist Karl Polanyi saw a similar tension between locality and large-scale organization in the Industrial Revolution. He described it as a process of "disembedding." In prior social formations, market actors were bound to each other in a host of different ways including traditional obligations of the prosperous to the poor.

The Industrial Revolution disrupted both such reciprocity and local community. Over time, new social support systems were developed; community was rebuilt in new forms. People went to an overlapping range of churches, their children went to the same schools, their customers were neighbors, their creditors were local. But local community could not provide all the support needed in a large-scale and volatile society. Schools and churches connected the local to the larger scale. Social support also came from larger institutions. The state institutions built after World War II were crucial, but so were other institutions from agricultural extension programs to trade unions.

For elites and the upwardly mobile, disembedding commonly came with opportunities. Moving to an urban area could bring higher education, jobs, access to museums and performing arts. Cities might be less "communal" but relative anonymity brought advantages.[68] An urbanite could move more easily among contexts, experiencing greater freedom because these over-lapped less. Women could live free from paternalistic families; lifestyles could vary more fluidly. There is a reason gay culture flourished in San Francisco and New York before most smaller, nonmetropolitan towns.

It has seemed through much of modernity that the individually ambitious were always moving out. They went away to university if they could. They joined the military and didn't return. They took off for the bright lights of the big city. These efforts didn't always work out. Sometimes the formerly ambitious returned chagrined (a common theme of country music songs). But the dominant story was seeking opportunity *elsewhere.* This made it easy to think of those still embedded in smaller, place-based com-munities as somehow backward. It also obscured the possibility of moving up without moving out, by strengthening local communities and devel-oping *their* economic and other potentials.

Disembedding was not just a lifestyle choice for elites. It was a necessity for millions of workers who faced declining opportunities in older agri-cultural economies and craft production. More than 70 percent of Ameri-cans worked in agriculture in the 1840s; less than 2 percent do today. Four million farms disappeared between the end of World War II and 2015. The demography of the United States was reorganized in favor of cities and suburbs. But if mobility opened opportunities, it also made it harder to have close-knit community. It wasn't just that cities were less communal, it was that moving itself was disembedding. This was a trade-off many were prepared to accept, but it could be a loss even for those who chose it consciously.

The great Black migration from the rural South to cities such as Detroit and Chicago in the industrial north was a great disembedding. So was in-ternational migration from the Irish, Italian, and indeed Mexican coun-tryside, Jewish *shtetls* in Russia, and rural regions of China, albeit by way of coastal cities. Those who migrated often did find economic opportunity.

But their success depended significantly on "re-embedding." They built new communities and organizations to replace those they lost. Trade unions were important to make the most of hard economic conditions. Synagogues and churches helped rebuild community as well as sustain faith. Recovery was possible, but disembedding was a cost. And it was one thing for those whose economic or professional fortunes did improve, another for those who never found the promised opportunities.

Polanyi's account of disembedding incorporates three distinct ideas. Easily confused, all are useful for understanding what has happened to Western democracies—and what is to be done.[69]

First, Polanyi sees a one-way historical process leading through most of modernity to ever-more disembedded markets. Agricultural produce is a prime example, marketed to ever more distant consumers, with an ever more complex chain of intermediaries. But consider also capital markets. The capital to start a new business can be raised locally, from friends, family, and already successful local businesspeople. Bill Gates and Donald Trump both got the money to launch their business careers from their fathers; having rich parents helps. Such local support is crucial to many entrepreneurs, including immigrants setting up street corner groceries or nail salons. But through the course of modern economic development this local support has mattered less and less because larger-scale capital markets have evolved. Sometimes religious and kinship networks helped at long distances. But today young entrepreneurs also pitch their ideas to venture capitalists to whom they have no personal connection. They borrow money from banks rather than their parents-in-law. Depersonalization has some attractions, but it is still a transformation. And the pattern applies long after entrepreneurial founding of new businesses, as firms raise capital in equity and financial markets.

Second, Polanyi rightly points out but does not emphasize equally that there are continual processes of re-embedding markets in new and different webs of social relations. For most of modernity those who migrated from rural areas and small towns to industrial cities built new webs of social relations into which markets were incorporated. Whether the new cities were better or worse than the older small towns could be debated, but throughout modern history the social fabric surrounding and supporting markets has been rewoven. This involved a mixture of multipurpose relationships similar to those that characterized smaller, more traditional market towns and new, often bureaucratic structures. It meant creating consumer protection agencies, for example, and web-based ratings, which present the gossip of strangers as an impersonal information about what are good restaurants, or cars, or even universities. In principle, there can be new supports not only for large-scale consumer markets, but for workers. Unions are the preeminent example. During the last forty to fifty years, however, the reweaving of social embeddedness has lagged severely behind disruption. This is central to the current moment.

Third, Polanyi points out that markets are never as disembedded as they may seem. Leaving behind roots in a local town doesn't mean going *nowhere;* it means entering a wider set of organizational relations. Markets that have lost ties to localities and even traditional flows of goods have become "metatopical"—they operate across specific spaces. But it is not true that these are anchored in no webs of social relations at all, only that the relations look radically different. They are typically indirect relations, not directly interpersonal. They situate the market in relation to corporations and other formal organizations including governments and in relation to abstract categories of people such as investors and customers.[70] It is important that we see that these are still social relations, even though not directly interpersonal. And of course, directly interpersonal relations still matter in some contexts, even if they don't organize as much as they once did. Business leaders may come together in person for Wednesday prayer breakfasts. When Warren Buffet calls, a CEO answers the phone personally.

Still, when we inhabit a town, we inhabit a landscape, buildings, and indeed located memories as well as webs of social relationships. Systemic threats such as climate change become compelling in relation to place: it is *this* river that floods; it is *that* farm that may fail. We value familiar locales—say, a New York City street—even when our social contacts are with strangers or those with whom we share only limited relationships.[71] We also inhabit places at different scales—not only a town but also a country, for example, not only a neighborhood but a city. And on the other side of the contrast, locality confronts not just one system but a multiplicity of systems. Large organizations such as business corporations and government that are central to that systemic world.[72] These disrupt the potentially level playing field of equivalent and comparably empowered citizens. In both markets and politics, corporations are actors of a fundamentally different kind, with asymmetric powers.

Corporations play a huge role in large-scale social integration both nationally and globally. They are central to capital accumulation, of course, but they are also central to connectivity. It is not just that they have market power; it is that they expand markets. Communication, for example, has been transformed by computers, cell phones, the internet, social media, and a range of other technologies grounded in microelectronics. The underlying research and development were largely funded by the government, but deployment at scale has come through for-profit corporations.[73] Many employ tens or even hundreds of thousands of people in dozens of countries. This at once extends certain connections to the large scale and undermines the dense and multiplex connections of local community. Firms may create some level of community among their employees, though the trend has been toward contingency and volatility rather than stable long-term careers.

Further, the indirect relations that knit together large-scale societies are at least partially automated. I mean this not only in the sense of technologies working with little or no human participation. There are also standard procedures and workflows that reduce choice even where humans remain involved. And not least there are complex adaptive systems the organize activity and generate effects through feedback mechanisms of cause and effect rather than choice. There may be choice in their design, but at large scale they seldom have a single moment of design but rather emerge from millions of separate actions—such as the buying and selling that constitute markets. They can only be observed and managed with the aid of statistics about their operations, not direct observation. The notion that systems are "objective" disconnects them from deliberation over the public good. Markets are imagined, for example, to provide material outputs in response to economic supply and demand. Government comes too easily to be a matter of caring for such systems—markets, infrastructures, bureaucracies—rather than demanding that they provide for the welfare of citizens.

Markets once had been particular places open on particular days of the week. As Adam Smith recognized in the late eighteenth century, they were becoming systems; they worked as though by "an invisible hand." They were (or could be) at least in part self-organizing and self-regulating. They became national and then extended to, and by, global relations of supply and demand, buyers and sellers, and complex, increasingly electronic record-keeping. Logistical systems of increasing sophistication now fulfill orders from almost everywhere with products from almost anywhere (but especially Asia). Yet, though they may have become despatialized and opaque, markets are still a basic dimension of human connection.

Much economic ideology, including neoliberalism, obscures this. It focuses on individuals, their property, and their decisions in relation to scarcity and opportunity. Even otherwise strong academic economics emphasizes the choices of individual actors aggregated into relationships among more or less abstract variables—say, supply and demand. At best, this describes the systemic operation of "the economy." But it does not make clear that the economy is also a web of connections among human beings. Moreover, it commonly exaggerates the extent to which all such relationships are shaped not just by natural scarcity or spontaneous aggregation of individual choices. In fact, these basic economic relations are organized importantly by power. Power may be wielded directly in the way corporations work. It may be wielded indirectly as businesses lobby legislators (and fund their campaigns) to that ensure laws and regulations are written in ways they find acceptable. It appears internationally as countries support domestically based firms and block others. It is basic to when tax evasion is prosecuted as a crime or not.

Of course, inequality is also basic. But what makes markets disempowering for *citizens,* as distinct from consumers, is not only lack of money. It is inability to change their organization—to steer investment to make diseases of women as high a priority as those of men, to end profiteering on life-saving vaccines, to stop the destruction of local community, or to respond effectively to climate change.

Citizens can use market mechanisms to assert leverage. They can organize campaigns against corporations that market the products of sweatshops or against universities that invest their endowments in fossil fuel companies. But overall, citizens tend to confront markets as systems that operate by autonomous relations of cause and effect over which they have little control. Their primary recourse is demanding that state policy regulate or even reshape markets. This is discouraged by economic ideology that exaggerates the autonomy of markets and the extent to which they should be judged only by internal "efficiency."

Ideology presents markets and government as sharply separate, at least ideally, rather than interdependent and mutually shaping. It encourages the view that markets should be left untouched and treated as autonomous constraints in pursuit of the public good. This narrows the scope of democratic decision-making. While markets do provide a realm of partial freedom, they operate only within severe constraints of inequality and powerful organizational structures. Neither buying consumer goods nor selling labor to employers is really analogous to voting for the best approach to the public good.

None of this means that markets are bad or that states should attempt control so complete that it blocks market mechanisms. Markets have contributed enormously to both the generation and the distribution of wealth in modern societies. But they are not just neutral aggregators of individual decisions. Markets are socially organized systems, shaped not only by inequality but by the exercise of power, not least by large corporations, hedge funds, and venture capitalists. They are facilitated and shaped by government actions: issuing currency and guaranteeing credit, insuring bank deposits and making massive purchases for defense or health care, providing police to defend private property and courts to adjudicate contract disputes, and entering into international agreements to manage infrastructure such as air travel, shipping, and the internet. So government engagement in the economy is not some illegitimate innovation, but a normal and constitutive feature of capitalist markets. However, government itself can feel as distant and almost as abstract as markets.

The growth of distant, systemic organization of social life helps to explain why citizens feel a lack of efficacy. It's not just that their political clout may seem puny by comparison with the money and power wielded by a corporation. It's that distant systemic factors keep impinging on local life: providing or eliminating jobs; polluting, perhaps cleaning up but often not; opening or closing stores; selling products that may be dangerous; advertising medical treatments that are expensive and mysteriously may or may not be covered by insurance and then may or may not help; creating a sense of insecurity. And indeed, when systems don't work well—as, for example during the coronavirus pandemic, it is not only the poor who suffer. Many relatively well-off citizens may feel disempowered.[74]

The "state" has become more impersonal and distant. Legislation and regulation are enormously complex. Policy is administered by bureaucracies full of trained specialists—and specialized technical knowledge is necessary. In most of the developed democracies there has been a process of centralization. Political choices and power struggles shape this. But centralization is also a product of the growth of large-scale sociotechnical systems. Air transport involves local facilities, for example, but it depends on nationally and internationally organized management of air traffic. National defense is a matter of global logistics not just militias keeping guns handy. Businesses depend on the ability to procure and sell goods across long distances and in different local jurisdictions. Long histories of cumulative changes add up to a level of centralization and distance that no one precisely chose. This cannot be reversed without a radical transformation of human life, but it can be counterbalanced with stronger local relations and intermediate associations.

Societies of millions of people necessarily depend on indirect linkages among citizens, often mediated by technology as well as government bureaucracy and private companies. In modern democracies, citizens do not know each other directly except in pockets or as images in media. Keeping millions of citizens connected to each other is a basic challenge for both democracy and republicanism. And, as Abraham Lincoln said, so is maintaining "the *attachment* of the People" to their government and its laws.[75]

Scale not only makes political and economic power structures less transparent and government institutions more distant; it makes the importance of civic virtue more obscure. Reliance on technical experts is necessary but makes it harder for citizens to feel well-informed about crucial decisions. It is also harder for citizens to see the positive results of their public-spirited actions.

But when large-scale systems don't work for the well-off, they have opportunities not available to others. They can use their money to buy other kinds of support. They can send their children to private schools. They can buy houses behind gates and pay for private security services. They can bypass public health care and use private doctors and hospitals. They can shop at different stores. Material resources enable the middle and upper class to escape problems that plague provision of support to their fellow citizens. Most citizens depend much more than the well-off on some combination of local, community support and public institutions. It's not that they are not mobile. They migrate, permanently or shorter term for jobs. They join the Navy. They drive trucks. But their mobility is less cushioned.

Elite mobility helps to underwrite a global ideology and self-understanding that I have dubbed "the class consciousness of frequent flyers."[76] Typical especially of those who fly business class and frequent members-only clubs and lounges, this includes the illusion that one can embrace the world as a whole without embracing particular places in it.[77] One result is an uncritical cosmopolitanism that among other things neglects how much the easy mobility of the frequent flyers depends on passports from certain countries, credit cards, and often white skin. Forgetting the material foundations of their own relationship to the world, such cosmopolitans imagine that those who do not share their views just have bad attitudes or need education. It is easy for them to conflate a moral stance on the unity and value of the world as a whole with a style based on well-heeled consumption of consumer goods sourced from all over.

During the Covid-19 pandemic, frequent travelers have been annoyed at being grounded. Their frustrations are real, but they are mostly those of people confined in large and attractive homes, working online with no disruption to their income, easily able to order in what they need, but nostalgic for cafés. Others, of course, have either lost jobs or had to bear high risks to work.

Cosmopolitans commonly think of the local as backward, limited by cultural particularity. They think of themselves as escaping this into a world of reason, competent and informed analysis, and universalism. It does not occur to them that the culture of those who read the *Financial Times* and knowledgeably discuss the politics of a dozen countries is still culture and still has blind spots. The notion of "flyover country" points to one.[78] Cosmopolitans and the global cities in which they live are much better connected to each other than to the rest of their own countries. Such cosmopolitan frequent travelers figure prominently among the "liberal elites" that so annoy today's populist rebels against globalization.

Disruption and Double Movement

Covid-19 and restrictions imposed to protect public health are of course massive disruptions to contemporary life. Wars, floods and droughts, famines and forest fires are all disruptions. Climate change may be increasing their frequency and severity. But the most relentless driver of disruption remains capitalism, with its imperative of growth and innovation and its tendency to crises. To those likely to benefit, innovations all look good. But it is important to remember that for most citizens security is a paramount value and hard to achieve.

As Karl Marx and Friedrich Engels wrote: "The bourgeoisie cannot exist without constantly revolutionizing the instruments of production, and thereby the relations of production, and with them the whole relations of society."[79] Or in a phrase popular in Silicon Valley, it's good to "move fast and break things."[80]

Without becoming Marxists, more recent fans of entrepreneurial capitalism have become enthusiasts for disruption. From the point of view of those making money from economic transformations, disruption could look good, like rapid progress. Out with the old and in with the new. Clayton Christensen of the Harvard Business School famously urged his readers to "catch the wave" of "disruptive technologies."[81] Silicon Valley is full of venture capitalists and entrepreneurs trying to identify and profit from the next big technological disruption.

The TED talks of business gurus reveal an attitude as old as the Industrial Revolution. In the nineteenth century, capitalism disrupted—quite radically—older ways of life centered on local communities, crafts, churches, and reciprocity between property owners and those who labored. There was human suffering, but a great deal of money was made.[82]

Perhaps the most famous case of disruption and displacement involved the "Luddites," who smashed machines in England in 1811, at the dawn of the industrial age. They have been mocked as simply backward-looking and are often cited today by those who argue that resisting technological transformations is futile. But they were not opponents of all technology. They were workers who grew relatively prosperous using one generation of new technology (framework knitting) and then were displaced by another—more completely mechanized and eventually power-driven looms.[83] The Luddites were angry, but not just about new technology. They were angry that it was introduced by capitalists in ways they considered deceitful and manipulative, to get around previously standard and mutually agreed practices of labor and payment. They were angry because they were offered no good opportunities in the new industrial production process. They were angry that the government protected the capital businessmen invested in machines but not the human capital craft workers had invested in acquiring skills. They were not even allowed to form unions to make their case together, to bargain for retraining or other opportunities.

Framework knitting was not one of the great old crafts with long artisanal traditions like those of the goldsmiths, wheelwrights, or printers. The prosperity of handloom weavers was relatively recent. A niche was created by a temporary bottleneck in technological development. Spinning mechanized ahead of weaving. We can see in retrospect that it was a transitional occupation, not unlike becoming a driver for Uber or Lyft. Computerized communications could take over dispatch of cars, and the new car services have themselves displaced or undermined older taxis. But this is not an industry for the long-term. Human drivers will be dispatched by computer only until driverless cars make them obsolete. In the meantime, oversupply of drivers (and corporate domination) drives down earnings.

During the Industrial Revolution, defenders of progress insisted that in the long run the British economy would be larger, the whole country richer. Indeed, this happened. But as John Maynard Keynes famously said, "In the long run we shall all be dead."[84] Keynes was not saying that the future doesn't matter. He was saying that neglect of current suffering is not justified by eventual economic recovery or even improvement.[85]

It was a hundred years before the descendants of the Luddites could expect to earn factory wages comparable to what their artisan ancestors had lost—and then largely because they had finally won the right to organize unions.[86] Even when incomes recovered, this didn't restore local communities and the networks on which they depended for security and solidarity. Whole communities—like those of the framework knitters—saw their ways of life destroyed.[87]

The factory and the assembly line were disruptive technologies in their day, bringing first steps on the path toward industrial automation. Railroads were disruptive, changing, for example, the way farm products were brought to market and in the process making possible a once-disruptive technology of consumerism, the supermarket.[88] Rail systems brought huge benefits to cities and towns with stations—and left others to languish. So simple an apparent progress as replacing coal fuel with diesel meant not just that trains could go longer distances without refueling, but also "death by dieselization" when trains no longer stopped in once-thriving communities.[89] This was not just a matter of self-regulating markets or technological progress. Railroad lines came with railroad companies—powerful corporate structures—and new forms of finance with their own robber barons.[90]

It was not just new technologies that produced unemployment. So did relocations of industry—whether within countries or internationally. So did every economic downturn. During the Industrial Revolution, England was beset by liberal economic theorists who joined with industrialists to argue against more than the minimal help for those who suffered. They were afraid more support would undermine workers' desire to take the jobs on offer or encourage them to seek higher pay.[91] The same arguments were repeated by neoliberals during late twentieth-century deindustrialization. They helped drive "welfare reform" under President Clinton. In the context of the Covid-19 pandemic, Republican senators have argued on similar bases against extension of unemployment benefits.

Disruption is not just market opportunity. It is derailment of life-plans, stressed marriages, parents struggling to support their children. It is upheaval in social relations as people relocate to find work, damage to important institutions as schools and hospitals close. The costs of disruption include loss of the implicit social security systems offered by local communities. And as Polanyi showed in his classic *The Great Transformation,* it is not just the scale of social change that matters but the speed.

Friedrich Engels pointed to the long time lag between the destruction of old ways of life and attaining prosperity in new ones. The economic historian Robert Allen calls it Engels's "pause."[92] Engels's point was that this was a good time for revolution. In fact, political revolution didn't come in the way Marx and Engels had anticipated, but Engels's pause is still significant. During the long period between the destructive phase of early industrial capitalism and the achievement of more "mature" industrial societies in the postwar boom, workers built the movements that made possible both the development of welfare states and the achievement of industrial relations compromises that provided workers with significant benefits. Instead of making revolutions, workers in rich and relatively liberal societies demanded social democracy.

Writing in the wake of the Great Depression and in the midst of war, Polanyi described this as part of a "double movement."[93] Disruption was the first movement. Response was the second. This was inevitable—action and reaction—but response could take different forms. Without organization or care, it was likely to bring riots, crime, or support for fascism. Populism, whether of the Left or the Right, has been among the most common political responses. Liberals often touted frugality and self-reliance, but this could succeed only for better-off workers and not those whose whole communities were devastated.

Too often, workers were literally displaced—whether from agriculture, craft work, or smaller-scale industry. These displacements swelled both international and internal migration. Eventually, new jobs replaced old, but eventually is a long time. Commonly the disappearing old jobs took with them support systems that at best took a long time to rebuild.

Faced with new economic challenges and the loss of old support systems, workers relied on family, community members, and churches. They bartered in informal economies when few had cash. They also organized for mutual aid. Many major insurance companies still have "mutual" in their name because they grew out of subscription-based shared-benefit societies. Communities could be rebuilt. But the pattern was—and almost always is—for each displacement to encourage expansion of cities rather than full recovery of old localities. Formal institutions help, but do not replace the webs of interpersonal relations.

Perhaps most importantly, workers founded unions, which were organizations for mutual support as well as bargaining. These new solidarities were often marked by old patterns of exclusion. In the United States lines of race and hostility to immigrants were the basic division. For a time, there were similar issues about Irish workers in England. This made it easier for powerful interests to divide and dominate.

Still, it was possible to build social movements. The labor and socialist movements were forged as part of this "second movement" response. So were movements of Christian reform. So were campaigns of local community-building. As "Engels's pause" suggests, it took a long time to form unions, to form the Labor Party and its cousins in other countries, to press adequately for the transformation of working conditions and wages. All involved a huge amount of institutional development—regulation of occupational safety and health, for example, of industrial production of food to prevent its contamination. Beyond regulation, governments had to develop new capacities: for unemployment insurance, for pensions, for health care.

Reactions to disruption were chaotic and open-ended. Possibilities ranged from the terrible—fascism, say—to the promising—social democracy, for one. The struggle for democracy was integrated with struggles to build new kinds of societies. The double movement took too long and too many people suffered enormous losses before governments built successful programs to address unemployment, retirement, health care, schooling, housing, and more. It took two world wars before there was relatively stable resolution.[94] The welfare states built after the Second World War were not perfect. Still, *les trente glorieuses* showed that democracy could flourish in a compromise with capitalism and that governments could build new institutions to meet changing social needs.

This underpinned an era of prosperity and relative equality, though not a permanent escape from upheaval. After the disastrous Great Depression and Second World War, society was reorganized and stabilized on the basis of new institutions. Citizens benefited enormously from large-scale government structures—old-age pensions, health care, education—though citizen well-being still relied on mutual support in communities and associations.

The relative stability of the postwar era—*les trente glorieuses*—confronted its own disruption from the end of the 1960s and early 1970s. Transformation in industry and infrastructure was again rapid. Steel mills and factories closed. Once-great cities in the US "rust belt," Britain North and Midlands, and "peripheral France" went into decline. The manifest culprits were globalization, new technologies, and overinvestment in older lines of production that lost out either to business cycles or to changing consumer demand. A new wave of giant corporations emerged to capitalize on and shape new computational and communications technologies.

In short, there was not just one great transformation and double movement. We can recognize double movements throughout the modern era. The transformation of societies by capitalism, technology, and growing scale has continued throughout the modern era. In part it has been built into patterns of gradual growth. But capitalism recurrently brings disruption. This often includes sharp dispossession as workers secure under older conditions lose livelihoods and institutions of mutual support. Response can be populist anger from the Right or the Left, often stronger in voicing grievances than finding solutions. Commonly it is an effort to defend the ways of life being destroyed. Sometimes there is an agenda for building new ones. Democracy can degenerate; it can be renewed.

3

Compromises with Capitalism

CRAIG CALHOUN

After World War II, democracy came with surprising rapidity to seem normal in much of the world and a widespread aspiration elsewhere. Europe played a central role, as it had in the war. But the impact was global.

Democracy was joined with the building of strong institutions for social welfare in the project of reconstruction after the war's devastation. Labor and social democratic parties came to the forefront as advocates simultaneously for political rights and socioeconomic inclusion. Communists were prominent in politics and unions, but usually hesitant about pursuing democracy as such in still-capitalist societies.[1] Crucially, conservative parties throughout Europe accepted democracy and even welfare state institutions. The common experiences of devastating war and depression before that both played a role. Had the Right remained resolutely in opposition, much less could have been done.[2] A kind of compromise was forged between democracy and capitalism.

Such a compromise had already been developing in the United States, advanced by the New Deal, and in Britain, though Labour's biggest successes still lay ahead. Democracy was built in ways that facilitated rather than threatened capitalism, but capitalism was subjected to regulation and reform. Contrary to far-left arguments that nothing significant could be achieved by democratic reform in capitalist societies, there were remarkable improvements in many of the social conditions for democracy—in the United States, Canada, and other relatively rich countries as well as in Europe.

While tax rates were high, the foundation of industry on private property was not challenged. Of course, compromise is a limit as well as an achievement. There were struggles to try to improve its terms and balance. The Cold War, political repression—and indeed repression more generally—all curtailed freedom. But the accomplishments of the era stand as demonstrations that concerted action can strengthen the foundations of democracy.

State institutions played a central role in this. They provided citizens with greater security—a stronger safety net against unemployment, poverty in old age, and less predictable misfortunes than workers and their families had previously known. They provided direct support for health care, the quality and supply of food, and sanitation. They supported scientific research and dramatically expanded access to education and otherwise elite culture. They built roads, extended the electrical grid to rural areas, insisted that the post needed to reach all towns and that trains needed to stop at a range of local stations not just metropolitan hubs. They also worked to end poverty and reduce inequality, but as the list above suggests this hardly exhausts the notion of "welfare."

Central though state institutions were, building democratic society meant more than strengthening the democratic state. Associational life was crucial. Trade unions secured not just higher wages but job security, pensions, and health insurance for their members (whether through market provision in the United States or national health care elsewhere). An enormous range of organizations proliferated in civil society, complementing what state institutions offered. From Boy Scouts and Girl Scouts to churches and philanthropic campaigns for medical research, private action was collectively organized for the public good; local communities were largely self-organized.[3] This played a proportionately larger role in some countries than in others but was nowhere absent.

This chapter begins by examining the consolidation of democracy—and social conditions for democracy—in the first decades after World War II. There were always limits and tensions, of course, but the achievements are instructive. In many ways, they represented a positive culmination to the great transformation inaugurated during the Industrial Revolution (at least for the global North).[4] As we saw in the last chapter, that transformation brought both dramatic expansion of productive capacities and massive disruption to the lives and livelihoods of working people. Older communities and coping mechanisms were undermined. Replacements were slow to develop and often actively resisted by those with capital and power. State policy was informed by a "liberal" commitment to the freedom of property at the expense of equality or solidarity, which blocked support for those displaced and sometimes actively made things worse.

The resultant disorder brought a chaotic mix of large-scale displacements and migrations, crime, the Great Depression of the 1930s, the rise of fascism and the war itself. More constructive responses to this disorder and disruption came from charities, churches, trade unions, and social movements, Crucially, social democracy sought to extend earlier, limited political democracy and at the same time directly improve economic and social conditions. We understand this broadly to include American mobilization for the New Deal and civil rights, democratic socialism, and other mobilizations that informed the building of "welfare states" from the 1930s through the postwar boom.

We begin with the boom years. These did not perfect political democracy; bring perfect economic equality; or sustain solidarity enough to include minorities, respond to social movements, or weather dramatic cultural and technological changes. But they did bring forward movement. The second part of this chapter examines how that movement was blocked and partially reversed and how a new political economy shaped the degenerations of democracy that followed.

Les Trente Glorieuses

Looking back from recession and slower growth in the 1970s, a French author labeled the postwar years *les trente glorieuses*.[5] The term caught on. Like the counterpart term "postwar boom," this pointed above all to rapid economic growth. We use the French term in this book to emphasize a wider experience of social improvement underpinned by that growth, as well as by public policy.

Growth was especially dramatic by comparison with the previous decades of war and depression. As important to democracy, however, was the relatively wide sharing of wealth and income, the opening of new opportunities, and the building of new institutions. Pension schemes, unemployment benefits, and health insurance brought a new sense of security. Fundamental improvements in public health show how this extended beyond the narrowly economic. Maternal mortality, for example, had long been an almost commonplace tragedy. Over thirty years it became rare in the world's richer countries.[6]

The American economist John Kenneth Galbraith suggested that growth was bringing a long-term transition to "the affluent society."[7] The middle classes flourished, and there were relatively widespread chances not only to move from the working to the middle classes, but also to enjoy better standards of living as workers. Rising consumerism was variously loved or criticized, but cars, refrigerators, and televisions all became increasingly standard—along with processed food and pre-prepared meals. So did higher levels of education. During *les trente glorieuses,* the proportion of American children enrolled in school went from just over half to 90 percent. The proportion of adults who had finished secondary school doubled.[8]

The 1950s are often remembered as a culturally stifling era from which the 1960s were a release. Though not without an element of truth, this caricature is misleading. During the 1950s, the United States did see more than a little conformity, including the rise of the grey-suited "organization man." There was also the Red Scare, a mass panic over communism promoted by the populist senator Joseph McCarthy and the House Un-American Activities Committee (whose very name signals repression of diversity). In Germany, Chancellor Konrad Adenauer balanced "deNazification" with protecting the careers of former Nazis and curtailing public debate and dissent. In France, Charles de Gaulle reigned in the name of conservative nationalism. But eventually there was growing freedom in politics and in personal life, as well. It is partly because of the growth in cultural and personal experimentation that the 1950s are remembered as repressive: they produced innovation that some would try to stifle.[9]

The 1950s saw a flowering of modern art and expansion of museums, galleries, media, and education to open up wider access to "high" culture.[10] There was excitement in literature and expansion of the reading public. Both schools and museums became more accessible, especially to the growing middle classes.

The Harlem Renaissance may have ended in the Great Depression, for example, but jazz music continued to flourish. Indeed, jazz was both multiracial and international, linking the United States to Brazil, Japan, South Africa, and Ethiopia. Rock music was even more alarming to the cultural stiflers.

There was a utopian dimension to the Western postwar project. Societies devastated by war and those that had languished underdeveloped (or dominated by colonialism) were to be rebuilt in the context of new transnational structures that would ensure peace and human rights as well as economic prosperity. The United Nations was established in 1945 and the

Universal Declaration on Human Rights adopted in 1948. The Bretton Woods institutions (the World Bank and the International Monetary Fund) preceded the United Nations by a year, perhaps signaling the primacy of economics in the new global order. Here too Western democracies were ambitious, envisioning a process of "modernization" that would bring economic advancement by extending capitalism while also promoting democracy.[11]

Retrospectively, the Western Allies declared that saving democracy had been the purpose of the war. They demanded democratic constitutions for Japan, Italy and West Germany. East Germany, of course, joined other communist countries in claiming the mantle of democracy for a political system that put material equality ahead of political freedom (yet in the long run failed to deliver comparable prosperity). Throughout the ensuing Cold War, the West fought for a "freedom" that combined democracy and capitalism.

In the often insular and isolationist United States, and alongside campaigns for Americanism, there was an unusually high level of interest in the rest of the world. There was a surge in foreign language education, and academic area studies flourished—and it is noteworthy that both declined precisely during the era of so-called globalization that began in the 1970s. Americans became tourists and foreign travelers and flocked to "world fairs" (as they had at the end of the nineteenth century). The United States understood itself as the leader of the "free world" and confidently expected modernization to bring both unprecedented prosperity and democracy.

As evidence of their leadership, Americans could point to the Marshall Plan. This was somewhat self-interested and not quite utopian, but still generous in its combination of assistance for European recovery and investment in a growing capitalist market. A similar effort helped renew the Japanese economy and create a strong long-term relationship with the United States. And there is no denying the utopianism of projects such as the Peace Corps.[12]

The call of utopia was strong as Western Europe embarked on an agenda of integrated economic development. This started with postwar material reconstruction but always incorporated the goals of ensuring peace and providing the basis for democracy. The European Coal and Steel Community, established in 1951, became the basis for the European Economic Community with its "common market" in 1958, and then the European Union from 1993. Economic goals dominated, though articulated in terms of freedoms— free movement for goods, services, people, and money. Political integration increased over time, though accompanied by sharp debate over just how democratic the EU itself was. Whatever the "democratic deficit" of the consolidated structure, only democracies were admitted as members. This was a key basis for inclusion of Greece, Spain, and Portugal in the 1980s and of Eastern European countries starting in 2004.[13]

Disturbingly, leaders of the Western Alliance seemed to feel little contradiction in declaring themselves the tribunes of democracy while denying it to the colonies over which they ruled. France fought a brutal war to resist Algerian independence; Belgium was murderous in its effort to hold onto the Congo. Indonesia struggled for four years for independence from the Netherlands; former World War II allies at first supported the Dutch but then switched to applied pressure for recognition of the new state. And, of course, the heritage of settler colonialism was felt in apartheid South Africa (and in treatment of indigenous populations in many countries). Even the United States, with no formal colonies, resisted calls for democracy in Puerto Rico and intervened against democracy throughout the Americas and Caribbean. It also, of course, intervened in a Vietnamese civil war with roots in an earlier defeat of French colonial rule.

Still, whether the glass was half empty or half full, there were also successes of decolonization. Greatest among them, perhaps, after long struggle with Britain, India was democratic from its independence in 1949. The Philippine Republic gained independence in 1946, though the United States retained substantial influence.[14] Korea gained independence from Japan only to fall into Cold War division, but democracy gained strength in the South. Ghana led a succession of African countries to independence and democracy in 1957.[15] Haiti had led the way to independence for Caribbean countries already in the eighteenth century, but in 1962 Jamaica and Trinidad and Tobago started a new wave of independence and democratic transitions in former British colonies.

Postwar international optimism was never complete. There was fear of nuclear war in the wake of Hiroshima and Nagasaki; this informed campaigns for nuclear disarmament that already in the late 1950s helped to shape the rise of the New Left. Cold War suspicions and anxieties were pervasive. "Losing" China was disturbing to Western and especially US policy elites and was followed by full-fledged war in Korea. There was near-panic in the Cuban Missile Crisis and post-*Sputnik* mobilization for the space race. But even these alarms were channeled into a more positive story of accomplishments. Sadly, the same optimism informed the United States' growing war in Vietnam, which would help to end the postwar era.

In short, this was an era of contradictions: continued repression and renewed struggles for liberty. This was not just true internationally. Was the American civil rights movement an optimistic sign of change or evidence that resistance to full democracy continued? Certainly, as discussed in the previous chapter, it was only one phase in a very long American struggle with the heritage of slavery and continuing racism. It was inspiring, but was it more than two steps forward and one step back? Or less?

The civil rights agenda could be construed narrowly and negatively as ensuring that Black Americans were not legally disadvantaged compared to whites. This would require removing racial restrictions on voting, housing, jobs, and education. Or the agenda could be understood more broadly and positively as a call for all Americans to enjoy the unalienable rights of life, liberty, and pursuit of happiness articulated in the Declaration of Independence. This would require not just that Blacks should be no worse off than whites, but that they should enjoy better lives, together with whites, in a freer, more equal, and more unified society. Interpreted this way, achieving civil rights required social transformation. Martin Luther King Jr. articulated this social democratic (or democratic socialist) agenda as he called for a Poor People's Campaign and endorsed the Freedom Budget that Bayard Rustin developed for it:

> The long journey ahead requires that we emphasize the needs of all America's poor, for there is no way merely to find work, or adequate housing, or quality integrated schools for Negroes alone. We shall eliminate slums for Negroes when we destroy ghettos and build new cities for *all.* We shall eliminate unemployment for Negroes when we demand full and fair employment for *all.* We shall produce an educated and skilled Negro mass when we achieve a twentieth-century educational system for *all.*[16]

The Poor People's Campaign climaxed in 1968 but ultimately failed to achieve traction. King was murdered. The civil rights movement he had led was challenged not only from the Right but by advocates for Black Power. Republicans made electoral gains. Vietnam became a dominant issue. And by the 1970s, the long postwar growth wave was coming to an end. Still, the civil rights movement remains a striking example not just of progress long-deferred, but of the optimistic, even utopian, dimension of *les trente glorieuses.*

The vision was not fully realized, but major strides were made. Despite racial divisions that were strong and enduring, Congress passed major legislation to advance voting rights and racial equality. It should not be forgotten that support was bipartisan; Republicans made up for the resistance of Southern Democrats. The Johnson administration was able to introduce Medicare, Medicaid, major antipoverty and economic opportunity programs, support for both public transportation and motor vehicle safety, dramatic federal support for education, cities, and consumers, and such new organizations as the National Endowment for the Arts and Humanities and the Corporation for Public Broadcasting.[17] Public investments during *les trente glorieuses* provided specific services, but also sought to knit society together. Providing access to education served both goals. But perhaps the clearest demonstration of the second came in building infrastructure. In Europe, the project of rebuilding after the damage of World War II ensured that trains, postal delivery, and the electrical grid reach all (or nearly all) citizens. Nationalizing railroads was a central policy.

The United States also took on building new, better, and more democratically distributed infrastructure. Electrification was extended throughout the countryside by building on the New Deal success story of the Tennessee Valley Authority and supporting cooperative rather than only for-profit utilities. But the United States chose road building rather than strengthening its railroad system.

The Interstate Highway System, launched by President Dwight Eisenhower in 1956, joined all the continental states (and I am sure mine was not the only family in the 1950s and 1960s to pack the kids into the station wagon every summer and set out eventually to visit all those states so the children would know their country). Road travel was supported by voluntary associations, such as auto clubs, and boosted motels, fast-food franchises, and similar businesses. It was complemented by an increase in the number of national parks—a system launched during the westward expansion that followed the Civil War. Public investment in roads and parks encouraged private investment in motels, gas stations, and above all cars. Connecting a large and geographically diverse country, it also encouraged a sense of public solidarity, as middle- and working-class Americans flocked to enjoy the different parts of the country. Of course, the sense of solidarity was grounded in compromise that helped to set up later crises. Cars brought dependence on fossil fuels that contributed to climate change, vulnerability to oil shocks, and indeed future wars and terrorism. Enriched by the auto boom, car and tire makers and oil companies lobbied against public transit systems. When rail transport was reorganized, it was into a disastrously bad system that left passenger rail perpetually underfunded, not least because it was separated from profitable freight services.

During the decades after the Second World War, both European and North American countries succeeded in providing dramatically improved housing to majorities of their populations (though substandard housing remained a mark of poverty). In Europe, the trend was for public housing and state support for private rental construction. In the United States, it was for private home purchases made possible by state-subsidized or guaranteed low-interest loans. Rental prices were controlled in some urban areas, but public housing remained exceptional, and mainly for the urban poor. White anxieties about racial integration exerted a strong influence.

Individual home ownership—which spread people out and made them dependent on cars—was a popular choice more than a policy imposed against resistance. Still, it was steered not just by zoning but by finance and government investment. US housing was organized into suburbs accessible mainly by cars, while in Europe, residential communities were better served by trains and buses. Policy choices blended with personal preferences and a culture prizing individual autonomy. In the United States, cars were at the center of the postwar boom.

The separation of residential from commercial areas was a mixed blessing from the point of view of sociability.[18] Tracts of houses were developed to sell within narrow price ranges, maximizing homogeneity of circumstances. Many carried explicit prohibitions on selling to Blacks, Jews, and other excluded groups. The Supreme Court ruled against these in 1948 but provided no enforcement. This came only with the Fair Housing Act of 1968. Among other things, the act required removing racially restrictive covenants from deeds (a task I performed as part of a high school job in a title insurance company).

Suburbanization brought gains for individuals understood as consumers, though with environmental costs and reinforcement of social divisions. Increased geographic mobility reduced connection to local communities—more rapidly in America than Europe, but widely. Growing numbers of young people who went away to college didn't return to their hometowns. Corporate executives were transferred among multiple locations. Economic opportunities beckoned people to urban and industrial areas. Even family changed. Fewer people lived in extended family groups, more in nuclear families of just parents and children. As more moved in search of economic opportunity, fewer lived near their relatives, though telephones allowed them to keep in touch. The average number of children in each family declined. The length of time parents lived without their children increased. And the nuclear family of the era came with a strong ideology of men working and women at home. As men worked away from home, often commuting some distance, women were increasingly isolated.

In short, even real gains had downsides. And some of the gains were slower or more limited than many hoped. Still, *les trente glorieuses* saw sustained growth, relative peace, and improved standards of living.

Social Democracy and Organized Capitalism

The compromise between capitalism and democracy also meant a compromise between pragmatism and possibilities for more radical improvement. Even in the Nordic countries that incorporated the most socialism into their compromises between democracy and capitalism, there was more focus on incremental improvement than sweeping change. Everywhere there was a compromise between maintaining established and inherited privilege and introducing more equality.

This new regime came only after the Great Depression, thirty years of world war, and a shift from British to American hegemony.[19] It grew out of reconstruction after disaster. Still, it was a remarkable change. It was born of a meeting point among campaigns to improve society, business efforts to combine growth with stability, and governments committed to active pursuit of an enlarged conception of the public good. Growth helped make possible expanding welfare states, agreements between unions and employers, and better working conditions in a range of businesses. Newly inclusive politics brought wider participation in elections and pressure to use government to improve conditions throughout society. Parties explicitly representing workers played an increasingly central role. They campaigned not only for material benefits for workers but for broader political improvements and building of government institutions. In the United States, the Civil Rights Act of 1964 and the Voting Rights Act of 1965 signified something similar. Culminating achievements of the New Deal, as well as of the civil rights movement, they could not have been passed without trade union support. This combined pursuit of economic justice and empowerment with democracy represented an American version of what Europeans called social democracy.

In many ways, *les trente glorieuses* was the great era of social democracy—not simply of parties with that name but of the project of pursuing political democracy and a better society together against the background of relative capitalist prosperity. But this depended also on receptivity in business and on the political right. Social democracy was mirrored by what has been called "organized capitalism."[20] This centered on the advantages to business of a close relationship with government and a more stable working relationship with labor. Workers in the advanced industrial societies were also central to expansion of consumerism.

Businesses were themselves settings for social relations as well as jobs and profits. Employment also brought a variety of secondary benefits including a sense of dignity and security to plan for the future. Industrial capitalism concentrated workers in cities and towns, and many companies supported the communities where their facilities were located. Companies were the distributors of benefits such as health care—not just voluntarily but as a result of labor negotiations. This is why later deindustrialization and radical emphasis on private property had such a brutal and destabilizing effect.

What I have just called "organized capitalism" is also sometimes called "Fordism" after the leading role the Ford Motor Company had played in the maturation of industrial society.[21] Ford pioneered not just assembly lines and mass production, but vertical integration—bringing as many different parts of the production process as possible under the control of one company instead of leaving them all to different smaller businesses. Ford owned iron-ore mines and rubber plantations, freighter ships and a railroad; it made its own glass for car windows. This strategy enhanced Ford's control and reduced its vulnerability to market competition.

At the societal level, Fordism meant a regime of cooperation among capital (companies, but also their investors and creditors), labor (represented by unions), and government. Capitalism continued to generate wealth—indeed, to grow it. The rich got richer. They just didn't get richer as fast as they did in the early twentieth century or have since the 1970s, or quite as much at the expense of working and middle classes. Nor were there as many of the super-rich in proportion to the just pretty rich. This meant that the gap between the rich and other citizens could be reduced—which was good for democracy.

As part of the postwar compromise, governments invested directly in capitalist growth. They built infrastructure, educated skilled workers, and funded research crucial to the new high-tech industries and transformations of health care that took off from the 1970s. These brought wide consumer benefit and also a massive windfall for corporations and their financial backers. Government economic engagement was actually good for business. Government regulation helped stabilize capitalism itself. Regulations on lending practices, capital requirements for banks, and requirements that publicly traded companies honestly disclose their financial accounts were correctives to the kind of recklessness that had led to the Great Depression. Governments also acted to support business by providing insurance for banks and for mortgage lending. Regulations benefited workers by setting working hours and minimum wages. They also benefited consumers by setting product safety standards in areas such as food and drugs—and insisting that sleep wear for babies not be made of highly flammable materials, as it once had been.

This social democratic compromise included transfer payments from government and thus taxpayers to those judged needy. Children and the elderly were prime beneficiaries (and support for young children changed their whole lives). Transfer payments significantly reduced poverty, but they were not the center of the welfare state: this was provision of services like education or health care. Nor were they as important to reducing inequality as expanding opportunities for employment and social mobility. They were, however, crucial to security and stability.

So were policies and private sector agreements such as contracts between unions and employers, which brought workers (including middle-class office workers and professionals) a greater share of national income. Bargains between workers and employers produced other key elements of the larger compromise—safer working conditions, for example, an end to child labor, and limits on the working day—some of which were then reinforced by laws and regulations. These bargains derived from union strength. Unions were successful because after a century of looking the other way when employers blocked the formation of unions or had striking workers beaten and shot, governments eventually passed laws guaranteeing the right to organize and to fair conditions for bargaining. As important as specific material benefits or greater equality was the rich range of intermediate organizations to which workers and other citizens belonged.

Solidarity and social organization were not only benefits *of* social democracy, thus, but also crucial resources *for* achieving it. A social contract more beneficial to ordinary citizens was rooted partly in the solidarity forged in the war itself. Greater equality and a sense that government institutions must provide for the well-being of all citizens were ideas advanced in long struggles from the English Civil War to the American and French Revolutions through the growth of trade unions, labor and social democratic parties, the socialist movement, and Christian movements for social reform. Broader democratic participation was rooted in 150 years of campaigns for women's rights, for religious freedom and inclusion, and for public health. And each of these social movements forged solidarity in addition to re-shaping culture and thought and pursuing instrumental objectives.

Social democracy and organized capitalism brought a relatively good but temporary resolution to the double movement Karl Polanyi had described. They stabilized the chaotic dynamic of action and reaction initiated by dis-ruption and dispossession during the Industrial Revolution. Social demo-cratic compromises brought a combination of stability with growth, wide-spread prosperity, and care for those most in need. As noted at the start of Chapter 2, some were left out, and some were even pushed backward as others advanced. Nonetheless, equality and opportunity grew, and there was an increasingly optimistic sense of the future.[22] Solidarity or social cohesion was also important and was grounded in a combination of local communi-ties, states or provinces, and national institutions; in strong trade unions, civil society organizations, and the expansion of the middle class. Solidarity was as important as individual economic incentives to securing majority support for building tax-based public institutions to provide health care, education, old-age pensions, even high-quality television. It was important that citizens regarded these as provisions in which the whole society shared and that they regarded their fellow citizens as full members of that society.

The middle class grew in every developed country. The share of total na-tional income that went to the richest 1 percent declined from the Great Depression and World War II until the late 1970s—when it started a rapid increase.[23] Indeed, unionized manual workers often enjoyed sufficiently high wages and benefits that the boundary between "working class" and "middle class" became fuzzy. Not only could workers earn enough to sup-port their families, but they enjoyed high levels of job security and could plan for their own old age and their children's educations.

Of course, just as political inclusion of women, Black Americans, and immigrants took many decades and remained incomplete, so economic in-clusion was unequal. Employers were biased, but even social democrats focused most on the needs of a relatively privileged subset of workers— mainly male, white, and national (that is, nonimmigrant but sometimes not even the children of immigrants). Others experienced less job security, lower wages, and often less dignity at work.[24] The very idea of a "family wage" presumed male breadwinners—and idealized a kind of nuclear family that was more prevalent in the 1950s than today, but hardly universal. And, as discussed briefly in Chapter 2, opportunities such as the American GI Bill were often structured specifically for white men.

Greater fairness for racial and ethnic minorities, women, and others came slowly and was constantly resisted. Fatefully, this meant that some groups were durably excluded from full participation in the overall advance. Black Americans and women are the prime examples, but there were also other pockets of relative exclusion—famously Appalachia but also significant parts of the rural South.[25] While many international immigrants found impressive opportunity in the United States, racial and ethnic bias was significant. Exploitation of migrant workers, notably Mexican farm laborers, was extreme.

Social democracy—considered a radical project before World War II— became a mainstream effort to use democratic governments to deliver more equal economic and social benefits. In Europe, specific political parties bore the name—such as the Social Democratic Party in Germany. But a much wider range of citizens took on the project of simultaneously extending democracy and building institutions that would sustain it. National health care, pension, childcare, and educational systems all produced wider sharing in the benefits of capitalist growth. They also supported greater participation in pursuit of the public good. And they were supported by Christian Democrats and even some Conservatives as well as parties officially called Social Democrats or indeed Socialists.

In the United States fear of the Left was stronger. Few spoke explicitly of social democracy (let alone socialism). Still, some of the kinds of institutions social democrats built in Europe were built in the United States with support from Democrats and sometimes liberal Republicans. The United States even led in some areas, such as education—though not in others, such as public health. The US version of social democracy relied on corporations to deliver many benefits, from health insurance to pensions. This meant that such benefits were not universal, as they were in Europe, and the role of political mobilization in securing them was less evident. Still, for a time, it did mean that there was growing security for most American workers. But reliance on corporations set up a crisis that would grow from the 1970s as employment in secure jobs with benefits declined sharply. Workers in the United States lost benefits faster than those in Europe.

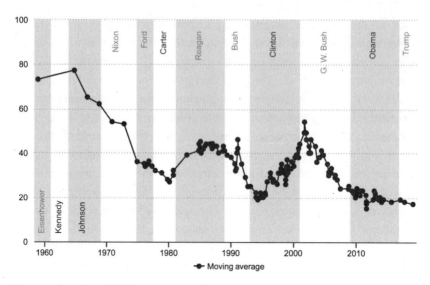

Figure 1. Americans' declining trust in their government: percentage who trust the government in Washington all or most of the time
Pew Research Center, "Public Trust in Government: 1958–2021," May 17, 2021.

The postwar achievement was to make the wellbeing of at least most citizens the object of government policies and institutions and to support this by more equitable sharing of costs and at least tacit but sometimes active business embrace of a more equal society. This was neither automatic nor just the result of top-down decisions by government leaders. It was the result of protracted struggle. Eventual cooperation was shaped both by recognition of social change and by a sense among the powerful that because of consumer markets and growth generally, higher pay and greater social benefits did not have to come directly at the expense of owners and managers. Before the postwar boom ended, however, confidence that it was delivering all it should began to erode. This is in many ways the story of the increasingly questioning 1960s. Did schools really bring opportunity to everyone? Did the benefits of government programs outweigh the frustrations of bureaucracy? Did churches deliver salvation or promote complacency? Was racial integration working? Our trust in each other and in institutions declined. Declining public confidence in government set in during the 1960s and has continued into the present. (See Figure 1, which presents a moving average of multiple polls.)[26] Both twenty-first-century Trumpian anti-intellectualism and Britain's secession from the EU in Brexit reflect disappointed optimism, but it is important to remember the hope and promise.

Three Catches

Democracy is always in part a promissory note from all citizens to each, offering assurance that everyone's interests will matter in collective decisions. Not surprisingly, the glass of progress is seldom more than half full.

Perhaps paradoxically, the protests of the late 1960s grew from the very optimism of *les trente glorieuses,* the belief that a better society could and should be built. But they grew also from the discovery that some of the promises of the era were false or at least exaggerated. Western countries were still imperialist. Expansion of educational opportunities had not ended inherited inequality. Public debate remained constricted despite formal democracy. Prosperity alone did not make life satisfying.

These advances came with three catches that made the achievements of the welfare states feel less liberating by the 1960s and 1970s. We can name them after great social theorists who focused attention on the complexities and even paradoxes of democratic extension of state benefits in capitalist societies.

The first catch is the reliance of the welfare state on bureaucratic structures and the rationalization of social life. Let's call this the Weber catch, after the German scholar Max Weber, who was clear a hundred years ago about the significance of scale (discussed in the previous chapter): "bureaucracy inevitably accompanies modern mass democracy, in contrast to the democratic self-government of small homogeneous units."[27] In all national versions, those who built welfare institutions as "second movement" responses to what had been disrupted by capitalist industrialization bet more on formal organizations and expertise than on decentralization and community engagement.

Genuinely important public benefits became sources of frustration when access to them was governed by bureaucracies that seemed too complex, too impersonal, too obsessed with rules, and too often ready to deny the benefits to those who made errors in their applications. From issuing drivers' licenses to getting health care or pensions or paying taxes, bureaucracies gave government an unattractive face. Schools often seemed more about rules and compliance than about education. Hospitals seemed to have more forms than medicines. Of course, corporations could be bureaucratic, too, but bureaucracies came to dominate citizens' experience of government.[28]

The second catch is that the delivery mechanisms of the welfare state turned out to be disciplinary. It's not just in prisons, the military, or traffic control that modern states demand adherence to detailed rules and punish deviation. The state becomes disciplinary in regard to health, sexuality, and education. States offer welfare benefits only in exchange for participation in disciplinary regimes.[29] Social workers visit homes to check up on recipients of benefits; even well-intentioned advice may carry an implication of criticism and may implicitly seek to discipline recipients into conformity with the cultural values of the bureaucrats.

Schooling focuses not just on manifest fields of knowledge, but also on a "hidden curriculum" of learning to arrive on time, sit still, turn in assignments promptly and neatly. These are all dimensions of discipline that correspond to demands of employers, especially in the growing sector of office work.[30] Schools discipline children into conformity with gender roles. This has changed, but only recently and partially. In the 1950s, girls were commonly taught cooking and domestic skills—and boys were not. Even extracurricular activities such as sports or dances were settings for disciplined training in dominant binary gender role expectations.

Discipline remains implicit in many of the recent efforts of behavioral economists and policymakers to "nudge" citizens toward better health, more saving, or compliance with regulations.[31] The nudge can easily shade into surveillance and control, not least as "big data" are mobilized to shape all manner of human behavior.[32] Already in the 1960s, protesters at Berkeley repurposed the instruction "do not fold, spindle, or mutilate" into a protest against being reduced to a component of a bureaucratic system.[33] We can call this the Foucault catch, after the French social and cultural historian and theorist, Michel Foucault.

The third catch is the tendency to perpetuate inequality in new and disguised forms. Let's call this the Bourdieu catch, after the French sociologist Pierre Bourdieu, who demonstrated how inequality could be reproduced in cultural distinctions and resources (cultural capital) that yielded the effect of inheritance even in nominally meritocratic or egalitarian societies.

Take education as an example. Before the 1930s, the chance to complete secondary school was rare even in the most developed countries, and college or university was available only to a tiny elite. Starting with responses to global depression in the 1930s and dramatically expanding in the 1950s and

1960s, access became much more widespread. This was good, but less egalitarian than it seemed. Students of different classes and races were educated in schools of very different quality and ambition. Differences in what
families could offer their children in preparation for school and supplemen-
tary activities were enormous. These meant the playing field wasn't level.
But standardized tests and formally equivalent credentials disguised inequality. All universities granted bachelor's degrees, for example, but these
did not have the same meaning in job markets or social status. At the same
time, the amount of formal education required for work at a given level of
the economy increased. Jobs previously available to high school dropouts
began to require university degrees. With this focus on more and more credentials, education became increasingly a sorting mechanism.[34] Not least,
the apparently equal access made it seem as though failure to get enough
or good enough education was entirely a personal failing rather than of
family resources or how the system worked.[35]

The Bourdieu catch is thus more than simply the fact of continuing inequality. It is the covert way in which social transformations, even mostly
good ones, are constrained by reproduction of enduring inequalities. It is
the enlistment of individuals in seemingly fair and shared projects for which
they are very unequally prepared. This makes winners more sure they deserve
rewards—and less humbly grateful—and leads others to blame themselves or
be angry at institutions for lack of success (see Chapter 4). Not least, it is a
sense of false promises. Even progressive social transformations that bring
forward movement on some dimensions withhold it on others; steps forward for some come with blockages or disadvantages for others.

These three catches shaped discontents with welfare states that came to a
head in the 1960s. Initially, the first two catches seemed more central. In the
neoliberal era that followed the postwar boom, the third became more and
more striking. The three catches were not inevitable. They motivated political
efforts to deepen and improve democracy, protests to end specific abuses or
problems, and a counterculture that for a time flourished in opposition to
unequal, rationalized, and disciplinary society. This brought some lasting
changes—notably in gender roles. Overall, though, the issues did not go away;
many became more severe as inequality deepened after the 1970s. Pursuit
of authenticity and personal expressive freedom dovetailed with an ideology
of meritocracy that purported to make inequality fair. (See Chapter 4.)

All three catches to *les trente glorieuses* kept their force after that more
optimistic era ended, and indeed were intensified in the new neoliberal era

of massive privatization and loss of confidence in government. The 1960s and early 1970s were transitional. If *les trente glorieuses* failed to achieve as much equality as they promised, the neoliberal era that came after radically deepened inequality. It did so in part by saying "greed is glorious" but also by denigrating the public institutions leading efforts to ensure equality. Neoliberal reforms of government did not make it less bureaucratic, but they did sometimes starve institutions of resources, which, in turn, made bureaucracy all the more frustrating. Welfare reforms made at least parts of the system even more disciplinary, demanding work and policing of private life from those receiving social support. Meritocratic ideology intensified the Bourdieu catch (see Chapter 4).

Crisis

During the 1960s and early 1970s, a variety of social movements challenged the legitimacy of the institutional arrangements that had reconciled capitalism, democracy, and the Cold War in wealthy Western countries. From civil rights to labor to peace and the environment, activists held that democracies could do better. Efforts to expand participation in democratic politics grew increasingly prominent. Public support for international conflicts, and the Cold War and imperialism behind them, began to fade. The conflicts symbolized by the year 1968 combined calls for peace with demands for greater equality, refusal of capitalist demands for growth, and rebellion against cultural conformity. Institutionally structured compromises crucial to *les trente glorieuses* came under pressure across a range of scales from personal psychology through national politics to global political economy.

As often, crisis came with a perfect storm of causes, many internally related. Some were cultural, even "countercultural," as students and others at once challenged some of the ideals of postwar culture and demanded that societies do a better job of living up to their professed ideals. There was rejection of tacit limits to the vaunted freedoms of democratic society. There were demands to overcome the blockages on opportunities for Black Americans, American Indians, women, and others.[36] There was growing recognition of the environmental damage brought by the commitment to economic growth that underpinned the postwar compromise between democracy and capitalism.

As important as the cultural and political movements of the 1960s were, it was in 1973–1975 that *les trente glorieuses* came to an end with a jolt. Rebuilding after World War II, government investment, and commercialization of new technologies had underwritten a massive secular boom. In the 1970s, this long period of stable growth abruptly gave way.

Acting on the promises of equality and opportunity, workers demanded higher wages and benefits; women and minorities demanded inclusion. Memories of the Great Depression and World War faded while taxes remained high and profits at best stable. Expansion of markets ceased to compensate for declines in profit rates. At the same time, new technologies began to challenge established industries. The tacit bargain between capitalism and social democracy grew increasingly stressed.

In 1971, President Richard Nixon responded to growing inflation by freezing wages, placing surcharges on imports, and unilaterally canceling the international convertibility of the US dollar to gold. From a US perspective, European and Japanese economies had grown from clients into increasingly effective competitors. Expansion in the "developing" world confronted increasing pressure from governments and movements seeking a greater share in the proceeds. There were revolutions, failed revolutions, and national independence movements. At the same time, the Vietnam War grew more expensive—partly because it expanded, contrary to leaders' recurrent promises that it was nearly at an end, and partly because of deployment of more expensive weapons. As it became more controversial, the government shifted from ground to air combat and also to financing the war by bond issues rather than taxes.

Then, in 1973, Israel defeated neighboring Arab states in the Yom Kippur War. In response, Arab leaders turned the Organization of Petroleum Exporting Countries (OPEC) from a sleeping talking shop into a formidable cartel. They restricted production and drove up prices. Ordinary motorists faced gas shortages in Europe and especially the United States; heating fuel was in short supply as a cold winter came on. Industry either slowed or paid much more for energy. All this brought the deepest economic recession between the Great Depression and the financial crisis of 2008–2009.

If the 1960s were years of exaggerated voluntarism when a counterculture imagined reshaped the world by almost unilaterally remaking culture, the 1970s brought home the message that choices were limited. The crisis was among other things a demonstration of the power of a larger "system" in which finance, oil supply, job markets, and inflation were all connected. It produced a fundamental shift of direction for the developed democracies. At its center were (a) a new ideology claiming that private property was sacred, public alternatives were illegitimate, and market efficiency should be the goal of all economic activity, (b) a restructuring of capitalism that gave less centrality to the production of material goods and dramatically more to finance and global trade, and (c) a dramatic reminder of the dependence of the developed democracies on fossil fuel and the countries that exported it.

Neoliberalism

The most influential economic ideology of the last fifty years, neoliberalism, has given its name to the whole period and policy approach. Its roots lay in the 1930s, and it had been gaining followers for decades. But it got a jump start by shaping policy in Chile after the military staged a coup against the democratically elected socialist government of Salvador Allende. The general who took charge, Augusto Pinochet, relied heavily on a group of economists trained under leading neoliberals at the University of Chicago (and they on their old professors). By 1979, Margaret Thatcher was elected Prime Minister of the UK on a neoliberal platform, and as president of the United States from 1980, Ronald Reagan helped make neoliberalism dominant, rather than only an aspect of economic policy.

We should recognize that the term "neoliberal" masks complexity.[37] Not all neoliberals thought exactly the same things—though they had a formidable apparatus for developing and maintaining a party line. Neoliberal ideals shifted and developed over time and were given different emphases in different practical contexts. Both adherents and critics often reduced neoliberalism to a caricature; more than once some said it was over and some that it had never existed.[38]

Much of the reasoning core to neoliberalism was shared with a wider range of economists, though some features were given special emphasis (especially those linked to individual freedom and private property) and some lines of thought were anathema (especially those dubbed "collectivist"). The rise of neoliberalism came partly because economics moved to center stage, and economic considerations dominated public policy from the 1970s until at least the financial crisis of 2008.[39] Though grounded in economics and political philosophy, neoliberalism was equally a political movement.

Neoliberalism signaled basic commitments to private property and minimalist government. This dovetailed with a long-standing conservative objection that big government was expensive. But it placed much more central emphasis on the fear that any government beyond the most minimal was a threat to liberty. This is the theme of Friedrich Hayek's foundational book, *The Road to Serfdom* (1944), composed with Nazism an especially looming presence but focused on the threat of socialism. The UK and United States, Hayek suggested, seemed to be abandoning "that freedom in economic affairs without which personal and political freedom has never existed in the past."[40]

Neoliberalism was literally liberal, not conservative in the traditional sense. It was not about saving the best of an old order, but about a radical conviction that private property is the necessary basis of liberty as well as wealth. This made it compatible with considerable social liberalism. Many neoliberals even thought of themselves as libertarian. They favored legalization of marijuana and ending restrictions on homosexuals. It became common to say, "I am socially liberal but economically conservative." But where "conservatism" meant neoliberalism and its market fundamentalism, it lost touch with older conservative traditions. It supported capitalism and private property, but not the longtime conservative goal of saving communities.

Believing that markets would always produce the most just and freedom-promoting outcomes, neoliberals opposed restrictions. Most recognized that some minimal collective needs, such as national security, might be provided on nonmarket bases. Otherwise, they were "market fundamentalists." They supported privatization and marketization of health care, education, old-age care, the building and operation of infrastructure, and nearly everything else. Though Hayek himself argued that it made sense to pursue universal health care even by means of government action, later neoliberals, especially in the United States, did not follow his lead. The more extreme among them opposed minimum wage laws and the existence of a government agency to protect the environment. Many even believed that the government should play little or no role in setting standards for food purity, say, or pharmaceutical safety.[41]

Market fundamentalism also made neoliberals oppose restrictions on capital flows, tariffs, and attempts to protect national economies from international market competition. They were avid proponents of free trade. With Margaret Thatcher, they said "there is no alternative" to global competition. Thatcher repeated the phrase and its acronym, "TINA," over and again. Her statement was close to a paraphrase of Herbert Spencer and echoed a long history of insisting that much of economic policy should be seen as a matter of necessity rather than choice. This invited the rejoinder "another world is possible." It also amounted to excluding democracy from the realm of economics.

Underpinning the specific political and economic claims of neoliberalism was the notion that government should not take on "substantive" agendas such as improving society. Instead it should defend the "process" rooted in markets and private property. Hayek argued this centrally on the basis of maximizing individual freedom; to pursue the collective good, government would have to take property from individuals, reducing their freedom to use it. In addition, Hayek and later neoliberals argued that markets based on private property would do a better job of securing the good than planned action by governments. Markets would be more efficient. Even a democratic government should not interfere with market self-governance.

Hayek and most neoliberal economists did recognize that there would be some "market failures"—occasions when rational individual choices would not add up to rational collective outcomes. But they contended that markets were by far the best mechanisms for discovering inefficiencies—and that removing these inefficiencies was the best path to improvement. The neoliberal presumption is that in most cases, government intervention to solve market failures will actually produce worse outcomes—because of bureaucracy, values in conflict with efficiency, or inadequate foresight. The preferred neoliberal solution is almost always to let competitive markets work. Barriers to competition—such as tariffs or subsidies—must be removed. It is on this basis that politicians influenced by neoliberalism have sought since the 1970s to reduce government provision of housing, welfare payments, or postal services. They have seen these only as restrictions on free market competition.

More extreme neoliberals objected even to minimum wage laws—which offer something of an index of what the neoliberal era has meant for workers. The federal minimum wage was launched as part of the New Deal. Periodically adjusted, its value peaked in 1968. Since then, it has risen more slowly than the cost of living, the average wage, or economic productivity. If it had in fact tracked productivity, it would be $24 as of 2021.[42] By this standard, President Joe Biden's 2021 proposal to raise the minimum wage to $15 was moderate, and the prevailing reality of $7.25 per hour was shockingly low. Of course, many factors besides just productivity go into determining wages. And while there has been inflation in many components of the cost of living, there has been deflation in a few, and even low-wage workers today benefit from goods that were nonexistent in 1968—for instance, cell phones. But the point here is not to debate precisely what the minimum wage should be, but to show how neoliberal thought translated into practical policies.[43] These favored returns to assets over compensation for work.

Neoliberals regarded workers as simply a special interest and thus treated labor unions as restraints on free markets. Ironically—or perhaps simply contradictorily—most neoliberals did not see either corporations or concentrations of wealth in investment funds as comparable problems for free-market competition. Their abstract models of the economy simply assumed individuals as the basic actors.

Corporations

Neoliberals claimed Adam Smith as an iconic forebear and embraced the notion of a *laissez-faire* approach to the economy. Smith, however, saw relative equality as a condition for the "invisible hand" to work by conditioning the behavior of all market participants. For this reason, he objected to "combinations" of capital—that is, modern corporations—as well as of labor.[44] Neoliberals followed only half their great ancestor's prescription. For the most part, they ignored the asymmetry between modern corporations and human individuals.[45]

While the importance of corporations to contemporary economic and social organization is hard to miss, it is unclear both in theory and broader public discussion just what a corporation is. One long-standing legal theory sees corporations as created by delegation of power from states, as suggested historically by the governmental grants of corporate "charters"—not least to the companies that established the British North American colonies that became the United States.[46]

Neoliberals, by contrast, more often regarded corporations as a form of property structured by contract among individual owners. But this form of property is itself dependent on law for its structure and economic viability. Investors in corporations are protected by limited liability for any actions the corporation may take. This allows more or less impersonal large-scale markets in shares—by contrast to partnerships among investors known to each other. Limited liability establishes the corporation as a special sort of being. In a pivotal US Supreme Court opinion in 1819, Justice Marshall described a corporation as "an artificial being, invisible, intangible, and existing only in contemplation of law . . . with no soul to damn or body to kick."[47] Building on this, corporations are sometimes treated as a kind of person. In the 2010 *Citizens United* case, the Supreme Court held that corporations enjoyed First Amendment rights like those of human citizens—in that case, the right to make political donations as a matter of free speech.

Delegation of power is the perspective of a state; formation by contract is the founders' view of a corporation. To an investor, limited liability is crucial. This is basically the guarantee that investors can't lose more money than they invest. It is a legal provision that the contract of shared ownership does not extend to shared responsibility for damage the corporation may do. If the firm creates unsafe working conditions or harmful products, the investors (usually) cannot be sued. To a manager, a corporation is a hierarchical organization with rules, a power structure, and perhaps even a culture.

Whichever rationale is claimed, there is a basic asymmetry between corporations and "natural" human beings—since, among other things, corporations don't have natural life spans and can be much larger, more powerful, and wealthier than humans.[48] As I suggested in Chapter 2, this asymmetry (along with quasi-automated systems) is a major challenge to the condition of equality among discrete individuals presumed by Adam Smith and carried forward into neoliberal thinking.

As long as corporations are seen merely as devices for exercise of the powers of their owners, they fit well into the mainstream of neoliberal thought. But when it is recognized that they are organized to wield power, not just to pursue market efficiency, the alignment comes undone. Corporations are bureaucracies and hierarchies internally, and they take advantage of their asymmetrical clout to influence and often dominate other stakeholders, from employees to communities to suppliers and customers. But, by and large, neoliberals have embraced corporations, even lacking a fully coherent account of just what corporations are and why they are legitimate.

Milton Friedman took an extreme view. Corporations were created to manage the investments of shareholders, he wrote, and therefore should be run solely to enhance "shareholder value"—not to serve other stakeholders such as employees, customers, or the communities where they worked. "There is one and only one social responsibility of business—to use its resources and engage in activities designed to increase its profits."[49] If they wanted, investors could use their shares of these profits for charity or to make a better society, but neither the corporation nor the government should make that decision for them. They should be allowed to choose only private benefit and ignore public good.

Friedman did not see inequality as an economic problem; in fact, he saw some level of inequality as desirable, mostly for motivational reasons. He argued in favor of poverty reduction, calling for a negative income tax as a way to provide basic resources to the poor. But he suggested this on the basis of compassion, not because he thought inequality was wrong.[50] The basic economic principle for the distribution of incomes should be "to each according to what he and the instruments he owns produces."[51]

In the context of deindustrialization, neoliberal doctrines suggested that states should not help workers. That would mean taxing wealth to pursue a "substantive" agenda. Even if this agenda involved the public good, that should not be a government choice, but a choice of the private beneficiaries of corporate profits (who alas did not step up much). Likewise, beyond what was necessary for smooth business transitions, corporations should not help workers who lose their jobs because this would be a misappropriation of the property of investors.

Moreover, neoliberal arguments suggested that helping fellow citizens was less likely to produce the public good than simply letting market forces work. Help to workers in the places where they lived might, for example, discourage them from moving elsewhere to find work. The situation from the 1970s to today has basically followed neoliberal lines: fading state action and reluctant corporate action at best. This did not stem just from neoliberal ideology, of course, but also from the pressures of financial markets. Action to help workers make decent transitions would appear as a cost on corporate balance sheets.

Other ways to think about corporate responsibility are possible. There has recently been a renewal, for example, of arguments for "stakeholder capitalism." The notion is simply that firms should be responsible to multiple stakeholders. Investors are one class, but also important are workers; counterpart firms such as suppliers, clients, and financial institutions; and the communities (and countries) in which firms operate. Some argue that humanity at large or even the planet should be on the stakeholder list in the face of climate change and similar threats. In settings such as the World Economic Forum in Davos, Switzerland, arguments are made that this amounts to enlightened self-interest for corporations: is the morally right way to think and also economically wise because otherwise the door will be opened to less desirable forms of government intervention.[52]

Whether for self-interest or the public good, it is clearly good for firms to respect the interests of other stakeholders beyond shareholders. This is important because corporations are central institutions in the contemporary world. They shape economies too much, employ too many people, and deploy too much wealth to be left on the sidelines by theories of democracy. It is vital to find ways to make them positive contributors to the public good. Indeed, there is great variation in the extent to which corporations work in positive ways. This suggests that it is a mistake simply to condemn corporations wholesale and that it is important to find ways to improve them and their impact.

Corporate social responsibility is sometimes conceptualized mainly as charity, as using some share of profits for public purposes. It can be good to support orchestras or schools in this way. But much more fundamentally, corporate responsibility involves the ways in which corporations do business. Do they operate with honesty and transparency, with care for the environment and good wages for their employees, with commitment to the communities in which they work? Or do they hide their finances, allow corrupt practices, try by any means to block unions, pollute when it is convenient, and seek to dodge taxes by questionable accounting or manipulating international reporting? Do they use outsourcing simply to avoid paying workers better? Is chasing cheaper labor abroad simply a way to avoid paying fairer wages "at home"? Do they seek suppliers that also work with high ethical standards? Are they willing to buy goods produced by forced labor, even imprisoned populations of ethnic minorities such as the Uighur in China?

Indeed, to what extent do corporations recognize that they have homes? They work in local communities and in countries. But they also devise a variety of ways not to be bound by membership in either. The *Citizens United* case in which the US Supreme Court affirmed that corporations enjoyed First Amendment rights was curious not only for treating them as persons but for treating them simplistically as citizens—thus ignoring the extent to which they operate transnationally, avoiding taxes and laws that constrain human citizens much more.

Voluntary actions based on stakeholder capitalism can bring improvements on every dimension. But the extent of improvements is likely to be limited. Managers will often choose what is expedient. Managers make choices faced with competition from other firms. They can't simply increase their costs relative to competitors and easily stay in business. As basic are pressures from financial equity markets with very short time horizons. Voluntary action cannot substitute for government failure to regulate.

It is far from obvious that protecting or nurturing the social conditions of democracy should be left to the beneficence of investors or corporate managers. Government has a key responsibility and a distinctive capacity to ensure conditions for democracy. It can shape whether and how much corporations contribute to the public good. Taxation and redistribution are important. Corporations could, for example, pay for a greater share of the schools that educate their future workers. Laws and enforcement could prevent tax avoidance. Regulations are vital, whether to ensure fair labor practices or appropriate management of social media abuses. Regulations can, in fact, help companies that want to contribute to the public good by ensuring that they are not undercut by competitors who do not share their public values.

The last fifty years are rightly called the neoliberal era partly because they are marked by government retreat from regulating economic activity. In the United States especially, but not only in the United States, laws that had long ensured greater stability, honesty, and transparency in business practices have been repealed without real replacement. This has enabled firms to generate more wealth for investors (their sole purpose, according to neoliberalism). Sometimes as a happy byproduct they have contributed to general prosperity, but more basically their flourishing has accompanied a division between skyrocketing stock prices and a much more troubled real economy. Bankruptcies have also skyrocketed.

There are three issues here. First, deregulation and finance-led wealth creation have made economies more volatile and risky. From the New Deal through postwar organized capitalism, stability had been an important goal alongside growth. This was an important condition for democracy. It gave citizens more chance to organize their own lives, both individually and in communities. It allowed participation in government agendas focused on improvement rather than emergency management.

Second, the wealth corporations created has been appropriated mainly by investors and a few highly compensated managers. For most workers, wages have remained stagnant, as shown in Figure 2.

Neoliberalism has produced an economic system in which profits have been shared much less widely than had been the case during the organized capitalism of the postwar era. But democracy depends not just on total amounts of wealth, but how it is distributed.

Third, neoliberal capitalism has created not just enormous wealth but massive "illth."[53] Statistics such as gross national product (GNP) or gross domestic product (GDP) measure how much value is added in an economy.

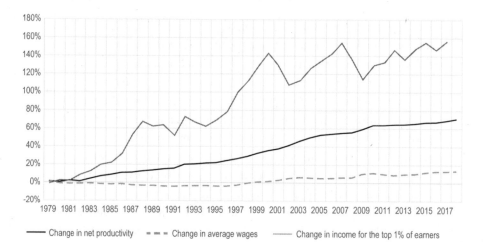

Figure 2. Change in productivity and income since 1979
Data sources: Lawrence Mishel and Julia Wolfe, "Top 1.0 Percent Reaches Highest Wages Ever—Up 157 Percent since 1979," Economic Policy Institute, October 18, 2018; Josh Bivens, Ellis Gould, Lawrence Mishel, and Heidi Shierholz, "Raising America's Pay," Economic Policy Institute, June 4, 2014, updated May 2021 as "The Productivity–Pay Gap."

They do not measure the damage to the environment, death and disease from unsafe consumer products or breathing polluted air, or displacement of workers without adequate compensation. Illth is, in short, the negative side of wealth, the bad stuff created by the same economic activity. In the neoliberal era, wealth has been accumulated by an ever-narrower and more exclusive upper class—call it the top 1 percent. But illth has been more widely shared. Illth has created costs for governments as they tried, for example, to clean up environmental problems. Illth has been a problem for citizens at large and communities everywhere. But the burden of illth has been greatest for those who live nearest to the bad stuff or have jobs in the least healthy workplaces. In the United States, the human cost has been born especially by Black Americans, American Indians, Hispanic populations and immigrants, and by those in some specific regions who could not avoid the stench of meat-processing plants or the cancers linked to toxic waste. This is a basic challenge to democratic equality.

Externalities

From the point of view of individual businesses, these ill effects are all "externalities." That is, they do not appear on the balance sheets of firms—

unless governments intervene to demand that firms pay, for example, for the cleanup of environmental damage. One of the basic features of modern capitalism, especially pronounced in the neoliberal era, has been that firms have enormous capacity to externalize the damages they cause.

Externalization of costs—both financial and human—has been basic to the deindustrialization and broader economic transformations of the neoliberal era. When factories close, neoliberals oppose public subsidies to maintain services. When communities collapse, they say to let them go. If workers need jobs, they should just move to wherever the jobs were even if it means starting over with few resources. And if there aren't any good jobs, unemployment benefits should be kept to a minimum (perhaps the minimum for subsistence, perhaps the minimum necessary to avoid social unrest) so that workers will take whatever jobs are offered at whatever wages employers wanted to pay.

The overwhelming neoliberal focus on property rights has severely devalued community and social relations. It aligns with a view that individuals should be compensated for their work to the extent that the market values it and no more. All other economic rights belong to investable capital, against the claims of workers for better treatment or the right to form unions, claims for the environment or racial justice, or more generally to balance the freedom of property against other understandings of the good. In effect, neoliberalism defines the public good as maximal freedom combined with maximal capital appreciation. Placing no value on social cohesion or association, except insofar as it advances the interests of property owners, neoliberalism has undermined the solidarity on which democracy depends.

Like classical conservatives, neoliberals favor a minimal state. But the conservative tradition since its great pioneer Edmund Burke was not simply individualistic; it insisted that community and social institutions were crucial. Devaluing these, neoliberalism has left only markets. But markets are a weak basis for mutual commitment among citizens. Indeed, since market fundamentalism has dovetailed with the pursuit of frictionless globalization, it has offered no basis for citizens to value their country or their fellow citizens in particular.

Because neoliberals do not believe in a broader idea of the public good, they see promoting and securing economic liberty to be the fundamental purpose of politics. Most have rejected the previously dominant Keynesian view that strong governments should exercise their power to guide the economy and achieve social welfare. Of course, neoliberal economists vary in where they see legitimate exceptions to that rule. Some have even joined in efforts to design better government policies—say, to protect the environment. But more orthodox neoliberal ideology has been very influential (and helped to legitimate policy commitments that derived less from economics than from the self-interests of various business and political actors). Because of its overwhelming emphasis on private property and hostility to collective action, neoliberalism is not simply the radical defense of freedom its backers claim it to be.

Though neoliberal ideology calls for less government, neoliberal policies have been largely implemented by governments. They included selling off state assets such as railroads (not always in ways that preserved ideals of public service, and often at prices that gave investors bargains), charging user fees for access to public parks that were previously available free, and making educational policies that favor private schools over public. Despite individualistic rhetoric, the main beneficiaries have been large corporations and investors.

Moreover, while neoliberalism seeks less regulation, it has actually created new demands on government. Corporations have pressed governments to use the right of eminent domain, for example, to take land for highways and airports. They have not left this to the market alone for that would have increased the costs of the projects they favored. More generally, capitalist firms have depended on government picking up many of the costs they have treated as externalities.

Financialization

The mid-1970s crises were not resolved within the terms of the compromise that had governed capitalist democracies for the previous thirty years. In place of the Fordist pursuit of an institutionally organized, managed capitalism, "neoliberalism" brought attacks on taxes, regulation, government programs, and unions—all in the name of greater individual freedom.[54] It also helped bring a dramatic shift from emphasizing industry to emphasizing finance.[55]

The change was in a sense announced in policy responses to the "stagflation" the followed the 1973–1975 economic crisis. Workers and capitalists agreed that a stagnant economy was a problem. But they differed on whether to prioritize fighting inflation or protecting jobs. The Federal Reserve Bank took a clear stand. It put all its effort into bringing inflation down, even though this meant employment and wage levels would suffer as they did for years after.[56] The bank sided with capital not labor. But it sided especially with finance capital.[57] Industrialists, after all, needed to make and sell goods—and in the course of that created jobs. Those bothered most by inflation were those who owned debt.

This issue had been prominent before. It motivated the great farmers' movements of the 1890s. Banks not only insisted that farmers repay debts during hard times, rather than supporting them to continue until weather and markets improved; they also insisted that payment be made in hard currency, gold-backed US dollars. They blocked the US Mint from printing more silver coins. They said inflation was worse than throwing farmers off their land (partly because they could then buy the land cheap). In 1896, this led the populist leader William Jennings Bryan to give one of the most famous speeches in American political history, culminating in the cry "You shall not crucify mankind on a cross of gold."

By the 1970s and after, the role of finance—essentially, tradable debt—was even more extreme. This became an era of bond traders who thought they were "masters of the universe," of the rise of investment banks and hedge funds, and the decline in American manufacturing.[58] Over the next forty years, the proportion of wealth held in the form of physical assets—factories, for example—went from 75 percent to 25 percent. The proportion in financial instruments went from 25 percent to 75 percent.[59]

At the same time, what had been the prosperous middle and working classes of *les trente glorieuses* faced increasing pressure. A long-term decline set in from the mid-1970s. Deindustrialization brought closures and lost jobs to one industry after another. Unions were undermined by changing government policies as well as opposed by employers. White-collar jobs grew in number, but fewer and fewer brought "middle-class" levels of pay, job security, or opportunities for career advancement. It commonly took two incomes to support a family as well as one income had done before. Savings rates declined as people spent all they had on current costs. Indeed, consumers borrowed more and more—for houses, cars, and college for their children. Their parents' generation would have called this living beyond their means, and indeed, it helped set the stage for the massive financial crisis of 2008–2009.

Domination by finance also brought an increasingly short-term orientation. Companies had to generate quarterly results to please stock markets and investors.[60] To do so, they began to cut employee health care and siphon resources away from pensions. The result was an increasingly disorganized capitalism, rising inequality, and weakened support for citizens and democracy.[61] Not least, finance separated the interests of investors and those managing their investments from other citizens and the rest of the economy. Stock markets were never fully aligned with the "real economy." But it is striking that during the first months of the Covid-19 pandemic in 2020, while millions of ordinary workers lost their jobs and as many as a fifth of American businesses closed, the wealth of billionaires increased by 27 percent.[62]

Financial institutions themselves were revolutionized. Banks used to be local and bankers commonly cautious and conservative. The Glass-Steagall Act was put in place during the Great Depression to encourage prudence and discourage speculation and turning local banks into national conglomerates. It was effectively neutered in 1999. Local banks that knew their customers and were committed to their communities were bought up or merged into Citigroup, Chase, Bank of America, and Wells Fargo. The Big Four now control of most of the total banking business of the United States.[63] The same thing happened to insurance, which is also a financial industry. The mortgage and loan industry was similarly transformed. Increasingly loans came from new companies that employed salespeople on commission rather than prudent bankers and quickly offloaded the mortgages they issued in the form of securities that bundled bad with good.[64]

Deregulation brought ever higher risks, high velocity, and more opaque investments—and fantastic rewards. Wall Street and the City of London became almost synonymous with wild excess—$500 bottles of champagne to celebrate multi-billion-dollar share offerings that enriched innovators, investors, and bankers at one stroke. Investment banking became dominant over commercial banking and traders over the bosses and compliance officers of investment banking. Thousands of the "best and brightest" young people aspired to careers in "financial engineering."[65] Banks became as risky as hedge funds (which specialize in risky investments made without transparent reporting or regulation). There were recurrent crises—the failure of a third of US savings and loan associations in the 1980s and 1990s, for example. These brought huge pain to clients and ordinary investors, though some big players made millions through fraud and at the very best risky dealing. To make a long story short, finance led the global economy into deep disaster from 2008 to 2011.[66]

The crash was a direct result of financialization without regulation. But this was more than just poor individual judgment or a culture of excess. It was the transition to a new form of society in which debt was an increasingly integral part of capitalism. Not just consumers but corporations took on more debt. Debt financed mergers and acquisitions. Financialization accelerated globalization, making relocation of industrial production much easier. East and Southeast Asia were prime beneficiaries.[67]

Despite ample evidence of wrongdoing, hardly any senior officials of investment banks or hedge funds, hardly any of the out-of-control traders, hardly any of the paid pundits who lied in their public advice were ever prosecuted. Financial crimes undermined both trust and citizen efficacy.

Impunity for those who made the financial crisis undermined social trust. It came on top of impunity for all those who benefited from fifty years of deindustrialization, intensified inequality, and destruction of social support systems in America.

Transition to postindustrial society was shaped by finance as much as new technology. It was hard to move a factory from Ohio to Malaysia. It was easy to withdraw funding from a factory in Ohio and invest in Malaysia. To invest in better equipment to meet international competition, American industry would have needed money. But they faced the same problem as the farmers in the 1890s. Financial institutions and investors didn't want to help and indeed found ways to benefit by buying up assets at fire-sale prices.

The rise of finance did not just support flows of investments overseas. It encouraged flows from older industries into new high-tech firms. Indeed, it is no accident that Apple and Microsoft both date from the 1970s. Both grew by commercializing technological advances paid for largely by American taxpayers and funded by the Department of Defense and other government agencies during the era of organized capitalism.[68] Google, Amazon, Facebook, and a range of other new technology companies followed close behind, likewise benefiting from taxpayer investments they didn't repay. These new giant corporations have brought enormous convenience and other attractions to consumers. But they have become yet another challenge to the social foundations of democracy.

Capital flowing into high tech has not created jobs at rates comparable to those of older industries. There were new manufacturing jobs at the factories built in Asia, though as these have become automated, wages have been kept low. Those calling for bringing lost jobs back to the United States keep overlooking the automation and deskilling of large-scale manufacturing. This doesn't mean more manufacturing wouldn't be good for the United States. But it does mean new factories won't bring back the good jobs of the past. Where creativity flourishes, it is mostly on a smaller scale.

With globalization, the decline of manufacturing, and investment in more technology, jobs have grown fastest in the service sector. Typically, jobs in the service sector pay less than those in manufacturing.[69] Employees are much more likely to be women, racial or ethnic minorities, and immigrants. Fewer are unionized, though this could change.

The idea of a service sector is very broad. It includes teachers and tax accountants, the staffs of restaurants and nursing homes. Growth in service sector employment is shaped by several trends. More care work is demanded by an aging population, working parents, smaller families living at a distance from each other. Much service work provides amenities for beneficiaries of the new economy who can afford them: financial planners, fancy restaurants, massage therapists. And a large and growing "subsector" is logistics: the combination of warehousing, delivery, and computerized control systems typified by Amazon. But importantly, the places where service sector jobs have grown most are not those that lost factory jobs.

Deindustrialization would have been painful enough had new sources of employment and economic vitality been found, but in fact many communities have been left in long-term decline. They have lost population as those who could move went where jobs might be; they have lost their young. They have lost their downtown shopping streets. They have lost their schools. In the United States, many have fallen victim to the opiate epidemic, itself produced partly by fraudulent corporations deceiving both doctors and patients.[70] As if to dramatize the undermining of citizen efficacy, those who fought to help their communities have confronted neglect from public officials and forceful resistance from corporations.[71]

New technologies and reorganization of work have brought greater productivity to work in the United States. But what the nineteenth-century Luddites (discussed in the previous chapter) experienced has been repeated. The workers who lost good old jobs have not shared in the new benefits. Indeed, as Figure 2 shows, almost all the proceeds of rising productivity have gone to the rich. We are once again living through an example of Engels's pause.

The problem with inequality is not just that some people don't have enough, though that is certainly true. Two further problems are also crucial. One is that money confers power, and those with more of it can exert influence rivaling a democratically elected government. The other is that social solidarity is undermined. Citizens stop sharing the similar-enough life experiences for membership in the country (or the local community) to mean the same for all. And both government policies and broader economic trends such as property inflation have very different implications for those at different income levels.

Since the 1970s, as we have noted, there has been catastrophic upheaval and often loss for the working class, and there has been substantial erosion for the middle class. During the same period, the very rich have gotten dramatically richer, and the top 20 percent of the population has also fared well. This upper-middle class has gained from rising house prices more than it lost, been able to afford high college tuitions, benefited from global trade and finance, and often even made money during crises. During the financial crisis of 2008–2009 and the economic crisis linked to Covid-19 in 2020–2021, the upper-middle class made money, and the upper class made a lot more. Both in those crises and in throughout the last fifty years, the working class and the rest of the middle class lost ground.

The split in the middle class is of basic importance. Educated, mostly urban professionals prospered while the rest of the middle class lost ground alongside workers. Those benefiting constituted themselves as elites by embracing cultural distinction and claiming meritocratic justification for their privilege. Resentment helps to explain recent anti-elitist politics. But anti-elitism also masks the distinction between the well-off but even more culturally distinct upper middle-class and the very rich.

Even more basic than income differences, are shares of wealth. Some wealth takes the form of luxury goods, of course—of fancy cars, emerald necklaces, and condos at ski resorts. But much more wealth consists of investable assets—capital. More than three-quarters of all wealth is controlled by the top 10 percent, 40 percent by the top 1 percent. These very rich households holds fifteen times more wealth than all the bottom 50 percent combined.[72] But if the share of the top 1 percent is alarming, even more stunning is the rate of growth in proportion of wealth controlled by the top 0.00001 percent, as shown in Figure 3.

There are more than six hundred billionaires in the United States. Just three of them—Jeff Bezos, Bill Gates, and Warren Buffett—together own more than the bottom half of Americans.[73] The fifty richest Americans have more assets than the poorest 165 million.[74] And the share of the very richest among them is growing.

One reason why the very rich can accumulate so much wealth is that they pay very little tax. In principle, the US tax code is "progressive," which means that those who make more pay a higher percentage of their income. This holds true up to about $5 million in annual income—a lot compared

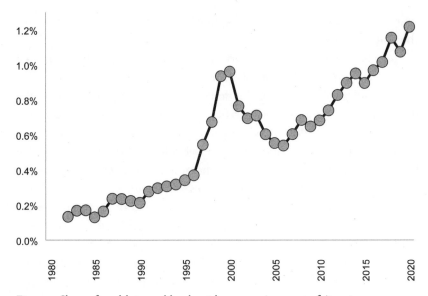

Figure 3. Share of wealth owned by the richest .00001 percent of Americans (about 3,300 people)

Reformatted from Edward Saez and Gabriel Zucman, "The Rise of Income and Wealth Inequality in America," *Journal of Economic Perspectives* **34:4 (2020), 3–26, Fig. 1, supplemented with data from https://gabriel-zucman.eu/files/SaezZucman2020JEP.pdf. With permission of the authors.**

to ordinary Americans, but nowhere near the Bezos and Zuckerberg level. Americans who earn between $2 million and $5 million a year pay an average tax of 27.5 percent, the highest of any income level. Those who make hundreds of millions a year pay less. In many years, Jeff Bezos, Elon Musk, and other billionaires pay no income tax at all.

One reason is a complicated web of deductions, credits, and exemptions—combined with lawyers and accountants to manipulate them. Another reason is that more of their income comes from returns on their investments—wealth—and the US federal government taxes this at a much lower level than income earned in a job. But so far we have just been discussing the failure of the government to collect a fair share of taxes on the income the rich admit they have.[75] A further issue is the massive use of shell corporations, tax shelters, tax havens, and other devices to hide income or avoid declaring it in the countries where the rich actually live.[76]

Some of the very rich have actually called for more taxation. Warren Buffett has repeatedly argued that the United States should have an estate tax—collecting more of the wealth of citizens who die—in order for the rich to pay their fair share and the ordinary working people to pay less. So have George Soros and Mark Benioff (founder of the company Salesforce and one of the hundred richest Americans).[77] Their argument is basically that the public good—the fate of the country—requires reduced inequality and fairer taxation. They do not want, in the phrase of sociologist Richard Lachman, to be first class passengers on a sinking ship.[78] Of course, not all of the very rich join them—not Bezos or Musk for example. This may be partly because they feel they can distance their own experience and that of their families from the fate of the United States or any other country.

As Figure 4 shows, the gap between the rich and the rest grew smaller from the Great Depression and World War II through the years of organized capitalism and into until the late 1970s. It has since increased dramatically. Such extreme inequality, passed through inheritance, undermines citizens freedom, empowerment, equality and solidarity, and thus democracy.

Beyond the radical inequality between the billionaire class and the rest, relative wealth still shapes life chances profoundly. For example, some young adults have parents who can give them the money to buy their first houses,

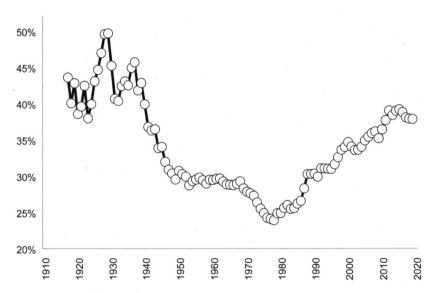

Figure 4. Top 1 percent's wealth share in the United States

Reformatted from Edward Saez and Gabriel Zucman, "The Rise of Income and Wealth Inequality in America," *Journal of Economic Perspectives* **34:4 (2020), 3–26, Fig. XA, supplemented with data from https://gabriel-zucman.eu/files/SaezZucman2020JEP.pdf. With permission of the authors.**

even in fancy areas. Some have parents who can give them enough for down payments. More some have parents who can't help financially because they don't have the wealth.

The same goes for paying for university. College costs have increased dramatically. Richer parents can guarantee their children's opportunities. College costs can be a hardship for middle-class parents, and their children commonly graduate with large debts. But the majority of the poor don't even go to college. Children of wealth are also much more likely to attend elite institutions that reinforce their advantages over others. At many of these highly selective schools, more students come from the richest 1 percent than from the bottom 60 percent.[79] For-profit schools offer the least educational advantage and have the most poor students.[80]

Wealth locks in inequality even among those with comparable wage and salary incomes. Not having it means having to borrow to buy a house or go to college; continuing to have to pay off those loans means not having money to invest in getting greater wealth. The gap keeps growing, because having wealth—inheritances, say, or parents' gifts—means getting to keep more of what you earn.

And who is it who most lacks wealth? Race and ethnicity are big factors. Whites have much more wealth than others, including Blacks (who own less of the United States' total wealth than 150 years ago), American Indians, Latinos and Latinas.[81] Women (especially single parents) have less wealth than men.[82] And residents of regions that have suffered deindustrialization or even long-term neglect have else wealth than the rest of the county—and this gap has been growing not just in the United States but throughout the wealthier democracies.[83]

Lack of wealth contributes to a more "liquid" life. Flow may sound attractive, especially to young people who think they will have many opportunities. But lack of property does not always mean freedom. It means not owning a house and being subject to forced relocation. This often goes along with precarity in work. And importantly, it can affect not just the very poor but people from different class backgrounds.[84]

Social support is not just a benefit for individuals and their families. It is crucial to democracy. The disempowerment of citizens, failures of inclusion, and majoritarian hyper-partisanship all reflect erosion or upheaval in democracy's social foundations. Citizen disempowerment reflects not just media manipulation or the role of money in politics, but the destructions of local community and social institutions that have accompanied deindustrialization, unbridled capitalism, and finance-led globalization. Problems of inclusion reflect waves of immigration, intensified inequality, and racial divisions. Hyperpolarized politics reflect broken political parties and encourage insidious campaign strategies and voter suppression. But they also draw sustenance from combative responses to rapid cultural change, divisions in social geography, and blocked social mobility.

This was another example of what Karl Polanyi called a "double movement."[85] There is no action without reaction. As happened before, so once again capitalism, new ideologies and government policies have disrupted the lives of workers and local communities. This is a first movement. But what will be the second movement in response? It could be crime or armed rebellion or a rising suicide rate. It could be political rebellion expressing anger and frustration but no clear choice of means to change the frustrating conditions. Or it could be the building of better social institutions to advance the public good.

The example of *les trente glorieuses* demonstrates that social foundations for democracy can be rebuilt—even after depression and war. Democracy can be expanded again. This depends in part on directly political choices—such as refusing the various strategies of voter suppression by which those temporarily in the majority seek to make their power last. But it depends equally on renewing the social foundations of democracy.

This is, in part, what happened during *les trente glorieuses*. After thirty years of spectacular instability—two world wars and a great depression—new stability was achieved. It was far from perfect, and it came at a cost, but stability itself has a value for those trying to make the most of "life, liberty, and the pursuit of happiness." *Les trente glorieuses* brought not just stability but rising standards of housing, transportation, education, and health care. They furthered the New Deal and earlier efforts to overcome inequalities that had been built into the foundations of democracies. And they showed that republican institutions providing a necessary framework for democracy had not been destroyed, though they had been shaken.

Precisely in this context of relative stability social movements took shape to try to do better. In the United States, the civil rights movement, the women's movement, the American Indian Movement, and the gay movement have all sought to address long-standing repressions and discriminations. The peace movement responded to a particular (and particularly painful and pointless) war, but it has also sought to address imperialist tendencies at odds with the higher values of the American republic. The environmental movement has addressed a range of issues from pollution, to extinctions, to degradation of the land, and increasingly to climate change. These were all in tension with some of the dominant politics of the era, but they drew from its institutions: labor unions, churches, universities. All of these pursued democracy in its telic character, defined not just by institutional arrangements and procedures but also by ideals: Liberty, Equality, Fraternity; Government of the People, by the People, and for the People; the Public Good.

The neoliberal era that followed has seen lots of activism and many articulations of grievances. There have been successes in efforts to advance democratic inclusion. New freedoms have been achieved, as has new recognition of the legitimacy of different identities. But to a very large extent cultural freedoms and calls for recognition have been advanced precisely insofar as they did not call for basic change in political economy. Workers have lost trade union representation while structures of employment have been transformed asymmetrically in favor of employers. Inequality has increased. Debt has increased. The capacities of local communities have eroded; national institutions have not compensated, and some that once built greater equality have become organizers of inequality. In short, citizens have been disempowered and solidarity undercut. Populism has been one response, though it neither a driver itself, nor able to stem the degeneration. Political polarization grounded in social change has become increasingly debilitating. The demos on which democracy depends has lost cohesion.

The mid-twentieth-century solutions to social disruption were not perfect and cannot in any case be restored. But they demonstrate that it is possible to take effective action to achieve greater equality and solidarity. The fifty years since have seen the degeneration that gives this book its title. The era has not seen the broad-based social movements that might reverse the trend, though there are hints. In words ascribed to the pioneering African American judge and civil rights leader William Hastie, "Democracy is a process, not a static condition. It is becoming rather than being. It can be easily lost, but never is fully won. Its essence is eternal struggle."[86]

4

Authenticity and Meritocracy

CRAIG CALHOUN AND CHARLES TAYLOR

Freedom, equality, and solidarity are all basic for democracy. Omission of any, or excessive tilt toward one, can be fatal.

Freedom is often a greedy concept—or passion—seizing attention that should be shared with equality and solidarity. Too often it is seen as the "essence" of democracy. We speak of the free world, for example. The most prominent index of democracy is published by Freedom House. But important as it is, freedom is only one of democracy's ideals and part of its story.

It is crucial that freedom be pursued as the equal freedom of *all,* not the privilege of a few. To be sure, the definition of "all" the people has everywhere required expansion over time. Two hundred years ago, many "semi-democrats" convinced themselves it was legitimate to exclude women and people without property—and even to condone slavery.

Inclusion involves not just equality and freedom but also solidarity: full membership in the body politic depends on integration into cohesive social relations. No combination of freedom and equality can substitute for solidarity—or even be stable without it. Of course, conversely, solidarity—community, social cohesion—cannot substitute for freedom or equality. We need all three, and must work to keep them in balance as interdependent goods.

Since the 1960s, two projects of liberal freedom have powerfully reshaped most democracies, bringing new levels of inequality and undermining solidarity. *Authenticity* has become a powerful ideal of self-definition and identity. It is part of a tradition of expressive liberalism focused on freedom as self-realization but also prone to essentialism. *Meritocracy* is an ideal of justice as fairness, commonly harnessed to distributing rather than reducing inequality and shaped by neoliberalism with its emphasis on more instrumental action and especially the rights and independence of property owners.

The two ideals are distinct, but both are complicit in legitimating enormous inequality and deteriorating solidarity. Inequality and declining solidarity are products of a new "great transformation" linking globalization, financialization, and technological innovation. Jobs have shifted away from manufacturing to services and logistics. Towns and whole regions have lost their economic basis.

Democracies have broadly failed to address adequately the disruptions and inequalities of this new "great transformation." It is important to ask why. What have the citizens and policy-makers of the world's democracies been thinking about when they could have been thinking about equality?

Obviously, many have been thinking about money. This has been an era when even the leader of Communist China declared, "To get rich is glorious." Or as the American movie *Wall Street* (1987) put it, "Greed is good." But even those who are not rich have had monetary concerns: paying their mortgages, sending children to "good" colleges, and struggling to save for retirement. And more and more even of the previously well-off have had to cope with loss of jobs, declining incomes, and downward mobility. If getting rich captured the imagination of many, trying to avoid becoming poor has become a daily struggle for others.

But material pressures and possibilities have not been not the whole story. Social policies have shifted. Powerful ideologies—ways of thinking, structures of feeling—have distracted citizens from the problems of inequality and the importance of the public good and distorted how they understand the relations among liberty, equality, and solidarity. This chapter is about two of these ideologies: authenticity and meritocracy.

Authenticity and meritocracy are seductive because each was important in previous struggles that actually advanced equality. The idea of authenticity shaped a new understanding that saw capacities for citizenship in every individual. The idea of meritocracy helped challenge systems of inherited privilege, such as aristocracy. But in recent decades, each has been taken to extremes. Each has also been distorted by an exaggerated view of the autonomy and self-sufficiency of individuals.

Authenticity, Recognition, and Solidarity

When we look back at our Western democracies in the postwar period, we are struck by the legislation they passed to dramatically improve the condition of their people. In some cases (for example, the United States and Sweden), this continued a trend that started or resumed in the 1930s. Elsewhere, it represented a new departure, and everywhere a dramatic increase in extent.[1] These measures included the building or marked extension of welfare states, provisions to maintain full employment, legislation favorable to trade unions, increase of minimum wages, economic planning (in France), *Mitbestimmung* (worker participation in governance of firms, in Germany), and an even greater extension of social democracy in Scandinavia. These measures were obviously the expression of, and the sustaining force behind, a high degree of solidarity across the whole of society and embracing all classes.

The contrast is striking with the state of affairs in these same societies in the aftermath of the financial crisis of 2008. The response in most of these countries to a sudden decline in the standard of living of many of their citizens—lost jobs, mortgages foreclosed—was surprisingly stingy. The American Congress called for "fiscal responsibility." Throughout the EU and especially in soon-to-exit Britain, governments demanded austerity from citizens. These were ill-advised policies. Economic benefits were debatable. But in moral and political terms they amount to forcing citizens to pay for a crisis caused by profiteering financial elites. They have contributed to the rise of belligerent populism. But these policies are continuous with the dominant neoliberalism of the immediately preceding decades. They represent a striking loss of the solidarity that so strongly marked the postwar period.

What brought about this change? An important part of the background lies in the great social and economic transformations of the last half-century, described in Chapter 3. Institutional changes—the decline in many countries of trade unions, the shrinking of social democratic parties—reflect and intensify the socioeconomic changes. We have traced the rise and spread of the most important ideological justification: neoliberalism, starting from the work of Friedrich Hayek. But what is still missing, or at least greatly underdeveloped, in our account, is an adequate portrait of the great changes in culture and outlook on life chances that have taken place in the West over the last three-quarters of a century since 1945.

The Ethic of Authenticity

One way to conceive the loss of solidarity is to see it from the other side, as it were, as a rise of various forms of individualism. And one of the important forms of individualism that has come to prominence in Western culture in this period is what has been called "the ethic of authenticity." This ethic flows from the core idea that each person has their own way of being human. Taken seriously, it lays on each individual the responsibility to find their way and realize it against social or familial pressures to conform. And it lays on others the obligation to respect this choice and facilitate, or at least not hinder, it. To show a person respect is to respect their path, or, as this has come to be described, their "identity."

Of course, the ethic of authenticity is often seen as a new form of individualism. The individualism of personal responsibility called on us to choose certain crucial life commitments—first of all in the domain of religion: it was in a sense initiated by the Reformation. But then came the instrumental individualism of the agent seeking personal advantage, including the "possessive individualism" identified by Brough Macpherson (and later prominent in neoliberalism).[2] But another form, which is often called "expressive individualism," comes with the Romantic turn at the end of the eighteenth century. At first, it was an ethic confined to elites, in particular to artists and poets. In keeping with this, originality came to be seen as a key component of truly creative art.

It was in the period after the Second World War that this ethic became widespread in many Western societies. This complemented growing freedom from immediate material necessity, more consumer choice, and greater opportunities for social mobility. Smaller families, new emphasis on childhood development, and longer adolescence with extended education all mattered. So did the idea of freedom itself. As the 1950s gave way to the 1960s and 1970s, "Do your own thing" was one of the slogans of the day.

The widespread adoption of an ethic of authenticity in the postwar period changed the framework in which many long-standing forms of discrimination and inequality were understood. We can illustrate this shift from the attitude toward homosexuals. Homosexuality was long seen as a deviant form of sexual life. Many authorities sought to forbid and punish it; negative views were embedded in families and local communities, causing enormous pain. With increasing momentum from the 1960s, this changed. For the most part, being gay is now treated as an "identity," a direction in life integral to and given legitimacy by individual personhood. Sanctioning it or depreciating it has moved from standard practice to an act of illegitimate discrimination. Issues remain, such as the insistence of some religious groups that their members should not be obliged to follow antidiscrimination laws. But by the early twenty-first century, the legalization of gay marriage moved forward with relatively little controversy.

The same can be said about the removal of obstacles to new career paths for women or the lifting of the stigma surrounding certain disabilities. Barriers and prejudices remain, but they retain less and less force. It now seems obvious nonsense for a person who can walk easily to feel that accommodating wheelchair users with curb cuts or lower elevator buttons is a restriction of their freedom or a violation rather than an achievement of equality. But is the equality achieved simply fair distribution of private goods to different individuals or categories of individuals? Or is it an advance in the public good, a desirable way of life to share?

If we look at the ethic of authenticity as a novel form of individualism, then the suggestion is unavoidable that this is partly responsible for the weakening of solidarity that is plainly one of the great negative developments of the last forty years.

If this is really so, then it looks as though the demands of nondiscrimination, and in this sense of equality, are in conflict with the kind of solidarity that we need to ensure a decent life for those whose standard of living has suffered devastation from the march of globalization, automation, and geographic concentration that has dominated recent decades, and will continue to do so. Since these are two of our basic values—or if you like, two facets of our basic value of equality—this conflict would be tragic. We have to find a way beyond it.

But examined more closely, demands for recognition based on authentic identity are not in conflict with solidarity as such. On the contrary, they always calls on a form of solidarity, at least among the group suffering from discrimination—of homosexuals behind gay marriage, of women in the #MeToo movement—and of their supporters. Does this have to be at the expense of a wider solidarity across the whole society? That it can work that way is undeniable. But does it have to?

Solidarity

In a democratic polity, we are motivated to accept differences—sometimes very sharp differences—with our fellow citizens not simply as a matter of tolerance for different views and statements or cultures and identities, but because we recognize citizenship, shared belonging, being "one of us." Not least, solidarity sustains commitment to a common future even among those who lose an election or who are still struggling for full rights.

Solidarity can be achieved without freedom and equality, but democracy requires all three. Families, churches, communities, craft guilds, small businesses, and military platoons can be close-knit with a strong sense of common identity and purpose. But such cohesion becomes democratic only when it can (in principle) be freely chosen in equal proportion by all and when its benefits are shared equally by all.

Solidarity can be achieved in ways that are repressive rather than supportive of individual creativity, distinction, and expression. What looks to some like a close-knit family can feel to others like an organization of patriarchal domination. Conflict may arise when living out a particular identity puts a person at odds with their local community, or even with their family; and then this alienation may be deepened and hardened when the person affected feels they have to move away. And since there are more and more reasons to move in a modern society—to get an education, to find a congenial job—this way of resolving or rendering tolerable family or community conflict is more and more frequently resorted to in the contemporary world. And this, in turn, yields the pattern we're all too familiar with, wherein the (frequently small) home community maintains its prejudices all the more fiercely and condemns the "permissive" culture of the larger cities that are the refuge of "deviants" in general.

At larger scale, the social psychology of mass nationalism involves a celebration (and enforcement) of complete unity. This is very different from a strong, shared identity combined with freedom and equality. The ethic of authenticity has been a powerful driver of the liberal pursuit of freedom and recognition. But self-declared liberals have too often assumed the declarations of equal freedom could be adequate without material equality. This produced a fuzzy mood of benign optimism among elites and growing frustration among others.

We need both equal recognition of each other, in our differences, and recognition of each other and ourselves as members of a common polity. It is easy to lose balance between respect for freedom or rights and promotion of equality. Communist societies, for example, encouraged fears that pursuit of equality would require domination. Conversely, one-sided emphasis on freedom has been inimical to both equality and solidarity. The outlook we call neoliberalism justifies the most appalling lack of solidarity in the comfortable assurance that the globalized market unleashes a rising tide that will somehow lift all boats. It is like a "prosperity gospel" that urges Christians to pray for personal favors, one at a time and separately, rather than for community or justice. "Oh Lord, won't you buy me a Mercedes-Benz . . ."[3]

The combination of freedom or rights with equality does not by itself provide for mutual commitment among the citizens of a democracy. Whatever its sources—and these are contested—solidarity is required for building institutions and countries, for undertaking projects such as reducing inequality, and for movements to strengthen and deepen democracy. It is basic to sharing communities, sharing countries, and indeed, to sharing the world.

David Goodhart, discussing mainly the British scene, notes a growing rift between two kinds of people, to whom he gives the names "Anywheres" and "Somewheres."[4] The latter term designates people who remain in and attached to their communities of birth; the former applies to people for whom career fulfilment is the major value and who are willing to leave home, and indeed, change their residence many times to attain this end. The conditions of success in the professional and managerial occupations more and more demand that one become an Anywhere. First, these careers require tertiary education; this often requires going away to college (though this varies among countries). And then living the career requires that one stay in or move between major centers. This is just another facet of the process described in Chapters 1 and 2, whereby smaller towns find themselves drained of life and activity in favor of a few large cities. The small town no longer has a newspaper, no longer contains the headquarters of an important firm, cannot offer the more lucrative reaches of a career in law, and so on. You have to go away—or since you may already be off somewhere else at college, you have to stay away—if you want to succeed.

Seen from the perspective of one's Somewhere relatives and high school friends, this is the inexorable process of community decline, and often downward mobility, as well-paying, secure jobs become less and less available. It is lived as a process of being Left Behind, not only left by your high-flying relative, now living in London, or New York, or even Singapore, but also abandoned by the globalizing society and economy you belong to.

It is this sense of neglect and abandonment by the governing elites that has helped produce a feeling of powerless, or declining citizen efficacy, which is at the heart of our first degeneration.

Goodhart shows evidence, at least for the United Kingdom, of a deep split in values between his two types. Obviously, there is a difference in their understanding of the good life, between career fulfilment far from your roots and community life among the people you belong to. But he notes also other differences in values that correlate with two career patterns.

Anywheres place a high value on autonomy, mobility, and novelty and a lower value on group identities, tradition—what he calls "local / national social contracts (faith, flag, family)." With Somewheres, the reverse is true. Anywheres are comfortable with immigration, European integration, and the spread of human rights; Somewheres are "socially conservative and communitarian, and moderately nationalistic; less comfortable with mass immigration and fluid gender roles."[5]

For Goodhart, the vote of the people who feel left behind put Brexit over the top: 56 percent of "self-described have-nots" voted for Brexit.[6] But a finding that is more important for the issue addressed here concerns the "liberalism" of the Anywheres. Goodhart breaks this too broad concept into more subcategories and singles out one associated with rights and equality and another one associated with "the market revolution of the 1980s that we call economic liberalism." This latter is close to what we are calling "neo-liberalism." His finding is that Anywheres tend to accept a too-easy merger of the two and generally approve of this "double liberalism," which "has dominated British society since the early 1990s and strongly overlaps with Anywhere progressive individualism."[7]

In the light of Goodhart's findings, we can see how the commitment of the professional and managerial strata to "double liberalism" has exacerbated the social polarization that bad populism feeds on. If it is true, as he argues, that the people left behind by globalization and automation are anchored in communities that have been slower and more resistant to adopting the more open stance to newly recognized identities, then how much greater will the resentment be if the main proponents of rights liberalism show a sublime lack of interest in the great downgrade that their less fortunate compatriots are experiencing? Think of the firing up of revolutionary zeal in Paris in the wake of Marie Antionette's (alleged) remark, when told that the people lacked bread: "Qu'ils mangent de la brioche" ("Let them eat cake"). There is a public danger in the fact that so many of our high-flyers are living in a beautiful Versailles of the mind.

A Silicon Valley (A)Morality Tale

The new Versailles may be less a monarchical palace than a corporate head-quarters. The pursuits of authenticity and meritocracy converged to dramatic effect in the high-tech world of Silicon Valley. Early Silicon Valley culture was Romantic and embraced expressive individualism as it over-lapped the countercultural pursuit of freedom and creativity in 1960s Northern California.[8] Individualism still reigns ideologically; Silicon Valley politics are largely libertarian. Apple, Google, and countless startups try to look and feel cool, not bureaucratic.[9]

At the same time, the sense among the industry's elite of being a technological vanguard, trained at top universities, and able to work with tools outsiders simply cannot understand, encouraged a sense of being the smartest kids around. Hugely empowered by their educations, grants from the US Defense Department, and investments of venture capital, many of these young men (for they were almost all men and indeed almost all white) focused instead on a sense of their own personal achievement. Declaring themselves the best and the brightest, many genuinely brilliant and creative scientists, engineers, and entrepreneurs also declared themselves entitled to lead (as well as to accrue great fortunes). They believed this to be fair as a matter of meritocracy.

Meritocracy told those on the losing end that, in essence, they didn't have what it takes. This could be internalized, diverting those it frustrated from blaming the actual sources of inequality. But it could also breed new discontents. In the nineteenth century, Alexis de Tocqueville argued that in ages of aristocracy people saw their statuses as fixed and immutable, but in democracies they believed they should be able to change them. They could rebel, but they seldom did because they had weak class solidarity. They responded as individuals. Richard Sennett and Jonathan Cobb summarize: "People still remained restless unto death, forever seeking to find some manner of living in which they felt authentic, worthy of being respected, dignified."[10]

Anxiety and self-doubt reflect a tension between the pursuit of authenticity and what was in Chapter 1, termed "a lack of citizen efficacy": to feel that your needs are not being met, that your standard of living is declining, that your children may not have the chances you have had; and all along to see this decline as the working of an opaque political system, which seems to offer no insight into the inner workings of cause and effect within it, and hence no levers for change that you can set in motion.

Inequality has been justified by the notions that the economy would always grow and that citizens have equal opportunities to get the new goods. President Joe Biden articulated a version of this American dream in a tweet shortly after being elected:

> I've always believed we can define America in one word: Possibilities. We're going to build an America where everyone has the opportunity to go as far as their dreams and God-given ability will take them.[11]

It is appealing to hope that equality of opportunity might adequately take the place of material equality. This would, for example, eliminate the need to decide between redistribution of wealth and continued, perhaps growing, inequality. This was never quite as feasible as the hopeful suggested. But there was more reality to open opportunity for most of American history than for the last fifty years. It was a country of social mobility, punctuated by crises such as the Great Depression, but resumed in the postwar boom. Social mobility has been almost completely blocked in the neoliberal era.

For neoliberals, private property is the nearly sacred basis of freedom. Taking money away from the rich to provide more opportunities for the poor seems to many (especially the rich) like a fundamental violation of freedom. But is life "free" when being born safely, sent to school, protected from violence, and provided with medical care all cost money? Is it meaningful to say everyone is "free" to drink wine that costs $20 or $200 or even $2,000 a bottle or send their children to a school that costs $100,000 a year? Inequalities of wealth and income make some people freer than others. We probably don't worry very much when the consequence is only more freedom to be a wine snob. But we do—and we should—when the result is lack of education, or good health, or other conditions basic to exercising the freedom a democratic society offers.

Neoliberalism celebrates inequality. Its ascendancy since the 1970s has produced innumerable top-ten lists, rankings of the best phones or cameras or business class seats on airlines. Special issues of magazines claim to help consumers find the best physicians or cars or cities in which to live (though most are only one step removed from simple advertisements). The world's numerous university rankings date from the neoliberal era and reflect reconceptualization of higher education from public good to private investment. In the United States, where there is no state regulation of university prices, they track those of luxury goods.

Not only have luxury goods proliferated in the neoliberal age; they are themselves hierarchically differentiated. A ten-year-old Scotch whiskey used to be special; then norms shifted to twelve and fifteen years, eighteen and twenty-one. Just in one product range black labels trumped red, then were in turn trumped by green, gold, and blue. And even the fanciest of these can't touch the upper end of single malt prices. Not to be left out of the profits, distributors of bourbon and rye have followed suit with their own high-priced, distinction-conferring bottles.

London's *Financial Times,* a business-oriented newspaper, took to publishing a special monthly supplement catering to the rich under the title "How to Spend It." The rich seem to need not only ideas of what to do with their money but intelligence on how other people are spending theirs, what will confer the most cultural capital. The market for watches has long since ceased to be about telling the time. Nor are yachts mainly about transport or vintage wines about refreshment.

"How to Spend It" basically tracked the obsession with hierarchy and the growth of discretionary income among the rich. It was launched as a one-page feature in 1967, became a magazine in 1994, and gained an online version in 2009 at the height of the financial crisis. It promoted properties for £10 million and up, £1 million paintings, £100,000 motor cars, £10,000 skin treatments, and classes in vegan cooking. There is perhaps no clearer demonstration of how little pain the financial crisis caused the very rich: During the Covid-19 pandemic, "How to Spend It" reported on obtaining the fanciest possible meals—"all-encapsulating evening" events—by delivery.[12]

Can this unfortunate fusion of authenticity and the neglect of the less fortunate be broken? Citizens cannot be political equals if they are divided by too much inequality. How much is "too much" can of course be debated. Certainly not so much that it takes tyranny to achieve and maintain it, or even the use of state power to limit democracy. A short answer could be that enough citizens are confident they are not dominated by others, that the opportunities of others do not deprive them of their own chances to pursue happiness, and that all citizens share in both the public good and public risks. In any case, there must be substantial actual equality, not just "fair" distribution of inequality.

Identities and Recognition

A politics of recognition follows naturally from the ethics of authenticity.[13] In a sense, this is integral to democracy itself. Authenticity helped produce a strong notion of the individual that informed demands to be recognized with democratic citizenship. In both aristocratic and republican forms, elite rule was not just a material injury—oppression—but also an insult to the dignity of individuals.

It took a very long time for women to be recognized as citizens fully equal to men—and there are limits to full recognition today—for example, whenever government policy facilities a gender-based gap in pay. It took a civil war for Black Americans to gain equal recognition—and it has taken a century and a half of struggle after that for formal recognition to be matched by full respect for their equal rights. The same issue is on the table when marriage is restricted to heterosexuals or when planning of the country's infrastructure fails to provide for citizens with disabilities.

In other words, identity politics is not something new that rose in the wake of the 1960s, as critics often allege. But from the 1960s on, renewed focus on authenticity and self-expression did contribute to a dramatically increased politics of recognition—both legal and cultural. Previously marginalized or excluded citizens claimed the right to be seen, accepted, and valued equally with others. This was a double expansion of the pursuit—and achievement—of equality.

First, it moved beyond the issues of economic class that had been basic to social democracy and democratic socialism. Inequality and blocked freedoms and aspirations come in many dimensions. Indeed, members of the middle classes became increasingly important advocates for the new sorts of egalitarianism—on lines of gender, sexuality, race, and ability. Unfortunately, they often abandoned or relegated to low priority the older concern for economic equality that had been central to trade unions and the "old Left." The genuine gains of cultural recognition appeared to come at the expense of material equality.

Second, the new politics of recognition challenged an older idea of political equality based on disregarding differences of identity to achieve impartiality. Too often the "impartiality" achieved actually embodied an affirmation of the status quo. It relegated important dimensions of the public good to treatment (or neglect) as merely private, or sectional concerns. But "the personal is political," as the feminist slogan had it fifty years ago. A key achievement of the new politics of recognition was to put issues associated with the previously excluded or marginalized on the political agenda. There was often, however, a failure to address these as matters of the public good rather than only a fairer distribution of private goods. We should want good childcare, for example, not just to benefit women but to benefit society. University admission is access to education as a public good, not only credentialing for individual career advantage.

Full, equal recognition is hard to achieve, but important. Not least, it requires citizens (and their government) to overcome historical and institutional biases so deeply entrenched and taken for granted that it is sometimes hard for those not directly affected to see them. This is part of what is meant by institutional racism or sexism, though both also include rules put in place with a conscious intent to discriminate.

Indeed, the very visibility—or, rather, invisibility—of our fellow citizens is an issue. The middle and upper classes may know about poverty in the abstract, but seldom see it personally, let alone experience it. In a host of other ways, those of us who are relatively well off insulate ourselves from disagreeable aspects of society that are all too familiar to other citizens.

Indeed, an issue of recognition is part of what aggravates many followers of Donald Trump and analogues in other countries. The issue is that their fellow citizens—especially members of the political and professional elites—seem not to see *them* or regard their grievances as legitimate.[14] Of course, this is exactly how others denied recognition have felt—including women, racial and sexual minorities, and the disabled.

It is not just elites who have distorted views of social reality. Citizens much more widely failed to fully see pervasive sexual aggression and violence until celebrities and a social movement call it out. Men often simply denied the reality. But the name of the #MeToo movement makes clear that part of the challenge is overcoming silence or repression of the speech of women. Absent public recognition, too many women will think this only happens to "other people," that it is rare, or that victims must share in the blame.

The importance of public recognition is also basic to calls to *say the names* of the victims of police killings: Breanna Taylor, George Floyd, Daunte Wright, and the still growing list of others.[15] White citizens don't see racism until more and more shocking videos of police violence and the Black Lives Matter Movement make it hard to ignore. Even then, whites don't see Black people. This is one of the enabling conditions of systemic racism. We not only fail to perceive the racism; we literally do not see Black people. This is partly the result of pervasive segregation in housing, schools, and workplaces. It is also deeply reinforced by the media.

A glaring example in the United States is the extent to which the white elite of Hollywood have minimized Black roles (and indeed Black writers and directors). This was not a market-based decision. Pervasive racial bias actually cost Hollywood a lot of money—as much as $10 billion in annual revenues according to a 2021 study by the corporate consultants McKinsey & Company.[16] Indeed, film production is the least racially integrated of all industries in the United States, and this has a consequence for how Americans see their country and the world.

Integration itself is a vexed issue. Does equality demand blindness to color and equal presence of Blacks everywhere? Or does it demand Black-owned production companies (and other businesses)" Should every community reflect the national or state proportions of Black and white? Or should there be some thriving mostly Black communities? Is there a role for Historically Black colleges and universities that even well-integrated mostly white universities cannot play?

There are no easy or clear-cut answers. Intermarriage means that many families incorporate multiple races and ethnicities. Part of the significance of mixed-race identity is that some people feel *both* Black and white (or Black and Asian or American Indian or other combinations). This is not simply a matter of different technical definitions. It is partly a matter of continual redefinition. Sayings like "America is becoming majority minority" are too often repeated without critical reflection on the extent to which the majority itself is continually redefined.[17] Indeed, self-definition is a basic right of citizens. Equal recognition requires that citizens be able to shape their own lives—to pursue happiness and, indeed, life and liberty—in their own ways.

Meritocracy: Choosing Inequality

Equality was long a basic democratic goal. We saw that Alexis de Tocqueville viewed it as central to democracy's definition. The project of greater equality is what made the United States stand out compared with European countries. It was not just a matter of wealth and political rights but also of culture, relations between children, even terms of address. Americans stood less on ceremony.

Europe was stuck, thought Tocqueville, but equality would come to Europe, too. Indeed, it did, with revolutions and social movements that tried to close the gaps between working and middle classes as well as between both and aristocrats. By contrast, Americans more often convinced themselves that inequality was ok so long as it was fair. (In this, as much else, Britain and to some extent Canada were placed between Europe and the United States.) Americans were more apt to see the rich as successful businessmen made wealthy by their own achievements. Instead of trying to close gaps between classes, they sought to create opportunities for individuals to move up in the social hierarchy (without dwelling much on the converse potential for downward mobility).[18]

Deserving and Earning Inequality

Reluctant to embrace equality in general, elites and perhaps especially the growing middle classes drew a distinction between the "deserving" and the "undeserving" poor. The deserving demonstrated their merit by working hard, displaying customary morality, and refusing political insurgency. The dustman Alfred Doolittle in George Bernard Shaw's *Pygmalion* offers an exposition:

> What am I? I'm one of the undeserving poor: that's what I am. Think of what that means to a man. It means that he's up agen middle class morality all the time. If there's anything going, and I put in for a bit of it, it's always the same story: "You're undeserving; so you can't have it." . . . Well, they charge me just the same for everything as they charge the deserving. What is middle class morality? Just an excuse for never giving me anything.[19]

There is a seed here of what would become meritocracy—the notion that justice could be achieved in an unequal society so long as social advancement was based on "merit." Merit was defined largely as a combination of native ability, self-discipline, and hard work.

Late in the postwar boom, the English sociologist and Labour politician Michael Young gave the name "meritocracy" to this combination of aspiration, policy, and social change. An egalitarian social activist, Young had been one of the architects of the British welfare state. He founded England's Open University, National Consumer Council, and Social Science Research Council. He contributed enormously to opening up access to education and political opportunity. And he saw that this might not work out entirely as he hoped.[20]

Meritocracy is the idea that being part of the ruling class (or the elite or the "rich and powerful") should be based on merit. It is opposed to aristocracy and the idea that the right to rule—or to have access to wealth and education—should be based on inherited social positions. It embraced both opening up opportunities—on the basis of merit—and fairness in rewarding talent and hard work.

Ending aristocratic inheritance had obvious resonance with democracy. Greater openness of opportunity did facilitate growth of the middle class. It did remove obstacles that previously prevented people from different backgrounds becoming wealthy and powerful. Selecting officeholders based on their ability and performance also promised improvements in government (and other) institutions. Wouldn't armies work better if generals and all officers were chosen on the basis of how well they could do their jobs rather than whether their parents were aristocrats? And aren't there good reasons why publicly held corporations choose top managers based on ability? Of course.

But meritocracy is not democracy. The Mandarin elite of imperial China was chosen on the basis of examinations, but was not in the least democratic. A ruling class based on merit would still be a ruling class.

For the middle class, meritocracy was an empowering ideology. It was not just what distinguished deserving from underserving poor, but what accounted for their own relative prosperity. It also underwrote their attack on aristocratic privilege. Opportunity should be more equal, they argued. Middle-class children who demonstrate more merit should get into Oxford or Cambridge (or Harvard or Yale) ahead of the offspring of dukes and earls. Access to land should be open to farmers—or developers—who would show merit by "improving" it, not restricted to aristocrats who would try just to keep it beautiful. Jobs in the civil service should be awarded on merit, not used to provide sinecures for younger children of the elite. Political participation should be opened up to those of merit. The public should judge the merit of candidates for office. The judging public should itself be open—at least to those citizens who could read and write and perhaps owned a little property.

As so often, however, those seeking greater opportunity for themselves saw reasons to deny it to others—or even saw restrictions so natural that they didn't need to offer reasons. In Britain and sometimes in the United States, Protestants thought Catholics demonstrated less merit. The English thought the Irish underserving; Americans have recurrently thought immigrants undeserving. In many contexts whites have thought Blacks lacked merit. Almost everywhere men saw women as less deserving.

Still, the ideological commitment to merit and fairness was powerful in loosening restrictions on opportunity. The working and middle classes shared aspirations to move up and therefore made demands for more open and fair access to the conditions of advancement. They were at least partially successful with regard to education, credit to start a business, the chance to work as a civil servant, and the opportunity to be a military officer.

Hidden Inheritance

Education is central to the ideology of meritocracy. Those who succeed in school are deemed to have demonstrated their merit. So, if one relies on educational credentials (and further examinations and performance reviews) for positions of power, one is in principle creating a new system of rule based on merit, not just privilege.

There is a variety of problems with this. To start with, of course, meritocracy may be a sham. Exams may be biased. Universities that claim to admit students only on the basis of academic merit in fact give preference to the children of earlier alumni or wealthy donors. This has been far less controversial than policies of "affirmative action," which use multiple standards to assess academic merit in order to achieve racial diversity.[21] The first policy—of perpetuating privilege—also shapes the racial composition of student bodies, but it more often remains hidden. And what is true of university admissions is also true in practices of hiring and promotion. There are many ways in which those who have benefitted from past inequality can perpetuate those benefits and pass them on to their children. They can move to the "right" neighborhoods, for example, and hire tutors.

So, it can be an illusion that there really is a free and open competition based on merit. There are biases in the seemingly objective tests and other forms of evaluation. There are parental investments that give students with more family resources an advantage. And putting the "objective" measures in the foreground also diverts attention from the frequency with which institutions make exceptions. We are encouraged to forget this by the fact that we all participate in examinations so often that we take them for granted. But the result is that access and promotion on the basis of apparent merit disguises and legitimates inequality. This is the Bourdieu catch described in Chapter 3, a limit to the otherwise great achievements of *les trente glorieuses*.

Bourdieu famously analyzed the ways family background and cultural privilege allowed some to succeed at the expense of others in the supposedly meritocratic postwar educational system.[22] But he made clear that this was an indictment of covert bias and inequality, not of more widespread education. He pointed out that though he was the son of a village postman and grandson of a sharecropper in one of France's poorest regions, he was enabled by scholarships to go to top schools and eventually to become one of the most celebrated intellectuals in France. But he stressed that his case was an exception that proved the rule, not a demonstration that opportunity was completely open in France.

Pointing to exceptions as though they were much more common than they really are is one of the ways people are convinced to misrecognize the reality in which they live. Rags to riches stories obscure the more common paths of some riches to more riches or simply staying stuck without riches.

Young was on the same page with Bourdieu. They both saw expansion of educational opportunities as a great achievement. It was basic to the empowerment of democratic citizens. Young campaigned all his life for greater educational opportunity. But he genuinely wanted equality and solidarity, too. He championed better schooling for everyone at every stage, not just opportunities for more people to be part of the narrow elite selected to attend the "best" schools.

But Young was not happy about the rise of meritocracy and predicted a bad end. The ideas of merit and fairness were being made into rationalizations for inequality and lack of solidarity. Indeed, during the last forty-some years, the term he introduced as a critique has been claimed as a virtue. It is used to celebrate inequality by claiming it has a fair basis. Business, financial, and technological elites imagine they are the smartest people and therefore the most entitled to rule. This is taken to an extreme among the ostensibly self-actualizing elites of Silicon Valley and investment banking. To Young's enormous disappointment, the Labour Party under Tony Blair explicitly claimed to be meritocratic.[23]

In the United States, the educational system long discriminated openly on the bases of race, gender, and property (not unlike the original US Constitution of 1789). Eventually explicit barriers were lowered but covert ones remained. Even today, admission of a few Black or immigrant students to Harvard gives them great opportunities and appears to demonstrate that educational (and career) access is really open when in fact it remains sharply biased by race and class.

New kinds of inheritance are not as openly visible as the old. When there is a formal division between aristocrats and common people, the role of inheritance is clear. When inequalities are matters of prices and only some have enough to pay, the disadvantaged are usually well aware that their problem lies with lack of wealth or income—not merit. But when they are embedded in different levels of preparation and support for the same apparently objective selection processes, the sources of inequality are obscured.

Invidious Comparison and Artificial Scarcity

Even honest efforts at meritocracy narrow the idea of merit and neglect other virtues besides intelligence or even hard work. There is merit to honesty, care for others, and considering the public good alongside one's selfish interests. As Michael Sandel suggests, "The more we think of ourselves as self-made and self-sufficient, the harder it is to learn gratitude and humility. And without these sentiments, it is hard to care for the common good."[24]

Merit is too easily equated with worth. Are those who demonstrate "merit" in certain kinds of performance—tests, for example—in fact worth more? Do they deserve more investment in their futures? This is what placing them in better-funded schools or honors programs with smaller classes amounts to. And indeed, almost all modern democracies are limited by the extent to which they focus more resources on those already destined to do well. And the rewards of seemingly meritocratic competition include honor, recognition, and respect as well as money and power.

Students who succeed in admission and exams keep being promoted. Why shouldn't they think they are simply more deserving? This dovetails with the ascendant rhetoric of authenticity: "smarter" becomes one more important feature of personal identity deserving recognition.

Starting down that path, it is easy to lose sight of notions such as the moral worth and dignity of all human beings or that every citizen has equal rights. This was more or less explicit in the eugenics movement of the early twentieth century. Seeking to "improve" the population—at large, or of a country, or a race—eugenicists defined certain individuals as lacking merit, often on the basis of alleged mental deficiency or criminal tendencies. Some were sterilized. But this ostensibly meritocratic project was also shaped by ideologies of racial purity. In the United States, the eugenicists were typically white and privileged. They exercised power against Black Americans, immigrants, and the poor. In Nazi Germany, eugenics was a justification for genocide.[25]

Stressing unequal talents naturalizes inequality. Meritocracy insidiously harnesses individual-level experience to justify systemic inequality. Some kids do better on tests, or in football, or at playing the piano. Variations can feel obviously natural and no doubt are *partly* natural.[26] Building on this naturalization, middle- and upper-class parents call for public schools to offer special tracks and programs for the "gifted." Implicitly, these parents are also asking the public schools to consecrate inequalities at least partially grounded in private wealth.

In the face of ubiquitous competition, it is not surprising that parents work hard to give their kids advantages. During *les trente glorieuses,* buying an encyclopedia was an exemplary investment in children's future. During the neoliberal era more and more investments have been demanded: computers, expensive achievement-oriented summer camps, music lessons, and tutoring. Of course, richer parents have more to invest.

An ideology of meritocracy may actually encourage inequality. As those who win at games like to play more of them, those who get sorted into the top rungs of social inequality seek further gradations in which they can be ranked highly.

If it is good to make distinctions, isn't it better to make more distinctions? Perhaps distinguishing among A, A–, and B+ is too crude. Do we need more fine-tuned (often quantitative) evaluations? For those who score well, tests are like a drug that offers more chances for the high of success. But addiction to test success (and meeting other challenges) can be the enemy of finding satisfaction in human relationships—including even with members of one's own family— as well as recognizing others with equal respect.[27]

Meritocracy encourages invidious comparisons among individuals and groups, distracting from broader democratic struggles for greater public good. It emphasizes rewards to individuals rather than improving the situation of whole communities, or classes, or racial categories. Take the example of New York City high schools: these are not equal. The city funds a small number of elite schools for especially talented students, as measured by standardized tests and sometimes interviews. There are only nine, in a system with 542 high schools. This distribution of opportunities puts the focus on fairness in selection but not fairness in overall availability. This shortchanges the public good. In short, New York City could choose to have more good schools instead of more unequal ones.

Ambitious parents call for more magnet schools and honors programs; they want public institutions to give talented children advantages otherwise available only on the basis of wealth. But these run into two problems. If members of some ethnic groups—say, Jews or Asians—do better on tests and gain more and more of the places, other members of the middle class— especially whites—get upset. Not all are rich enough to escape competition by buying their children a path to privilege through private schools (and some invest poorly in academically inferior private schools).

The key issue is artificial scarcity of high-quality public schools. This is the product of government policy. There could be better funding for all high schools. If there is a need for high schools organized particularly for the most talented students, there could be more of them. There is also a further layer of inequality because the vast majority of all elite secondary schools are in metropolitan areas, especially those already better off than other localities.

As hierarchy increases—as there are more rungs in the social ladder— there are fewer places at the "top." Perhaps 1 percent of students attend super-elite, extremely selective colleges and universities—those that admit fewer than one out of ten undergraduate applicants and confer enormous prestige. As many as 10 percent get degrees from a wider group of excellent and still selective colleges and universities. The remaining 89 percent or so attend minimally selective universities. Some are helpful. Some are scams. But none conveys the prestige of the elite.

Admission to a highly selective institution confers as much prestige, as what students learn there. Consider the cachet of Harvard dropouts in the tech industry. They are understood to have proved themselves by getting admitted in the first place and then to have proved themselves again by not needing further teaching. This doesn't mean a Harvard degree can't reflect wonderful education. It means the allocation of prestige is based as much on admission as on education. So is introduction into the social networks that link the admitted elite to each other.

There is no educational reason for this radically skewed system. It is like an economy with a rung of billionaires, another rung of millionaires, and then everyone else trying to stay afloat and meet their mortgage payments. Of course, that is the economy we have.

The inequality of the higher education system is one key to this socio-economic reality. Instead of creating equal opportunity, it has created a massive and expensive college admissions apparatus for managing and perpetuating inequality. This is really most of all about exclusion—which students should be turned away from the most elite schools. Students' chances are influenced by the neighborhoods in which they grow up, their accents, the schools they attend, how much their parents read to them, and whether their families can afford music lessons. As one critic has put it, which looks better on an elite college application, being captain of the lacrosse team or working twenty hours a week at a fast-food restaurant?[28]

Public Good or Private Right

Focusing on personal success also obscures the public good. It encourages people always to think the key question is who gets the reward—or even the opportunity. But if that matters at all, it should follow from more basic questions about what we are trying to accomplish together. We might, for example, be trying to make our society healthier. It is one thing to say communities needed the best possible doctors and another to say certain kids are entitled to all the public investments that go into to training doctors. There is a slide from preferring selection on the basis of talent because it advances the public good to seeing it as a personal right.

Support for greater overall health could mean investing in truly more equal opportunities—such as good schools and free universities for all. Individual differences in ability or effort could still matter in matching students to courses and eventually jobs. But the public good—health, in the example just given—would be the point, not individual success.

The idea that performance makes selection for success a right encourages beneficiaries to think they are entitled to keep all the proceeds—fighting fair taxes and failing to give back to society. At the same time that meritocracy makes the dominant feel naturally entitled, it disempowers the rest. It literally leaves them out of the opportunities of democratic society. It often makes them feel personally inadequate, for they internalize negative sorting and test results while others internalize success. Members of the elite feel encouraged to see nonelites as less deserving, probably less intelligent or hardworking. Those are people who didn't make the grade. Some elites will make their contempt manifest in ways that add insult to the injury of lower incomes and lesser life chances.

Elites continuously identify new ways to demonstrate their superiority. Consumer goods are the obvious example, as Thorstein Veblen argued in his theory of conspicuous consumption.[29] But investing in fancy universities can be at least as satisfying as investing in fancy clothes and more helpful for reproducing status across generations. Symbolic success is as important for reassuring the winners of competitions as for lording it over the losers.

Making hierarchical distinctions is hard to avoid. It is even implicit in many efforts to contest established hierarchies and distinctions. Consider how often arcane, abstract, and polysyllabic words are used to articulate concern for justice. In many cases the terms have clear meaning in academic theories, and they genuinely focus on ways in which dominant cultural and social categories can be unfair. Heteronormativity really is pervasive in the United States. Terms such as "cisgender" and "postbinary" can both clarify and offer liberatory insight to those who take them up. There is good reason to seek an inclusive category—say, "Latinx"—and to avoid genderings embedded in ordinary language. But it is almost inescapably the case that such terms do as much to make high-status education manifest as to advance social justice.[30] We repeat: this doesn't mean the terms or uses are wrong—any more than wearing well-tailored clothes is wrong. It means that their use is at least implicitly and sometimes consciously a manifestation of meritocratic distinction from the less well-educated—who by implication have not only inferior understandings of justice but also inferior vocabularies.[31]

Encouraged to take pride in their own successes, the winners in social competitions forget what the public paid for and too often underestimate the parts played by specific other people. The reality, though, is that each is a beneficiary of both public and private support. Even at high-tuition private universities, student fees do not pay the whole cost. Private gifts are important but encouraged and supplemented by tax deductions at public expense. As the British philosopher Harry Brighouse put it, "We tend to equate merit and achievement, but no one who is meritorious gets to achieve anything unless someone invests in them."[32]

Failing to appreciate the contributions others make to one's own life is both a personal failing and evidence of weak social solidarity. As importantly, the exaggerated focus on individual success and the correlated social sorting directly undermine solidarity. There are fewer shared experiences establishing social bonds among people headed in different directions and to different levels of success. Mass military service, as in the Second World War, meant that army platoons brought together soldiers with great and mediocre school records, soldiers from the working and middle classes (even if the latter were more often selected to be officers). Scout troops, churches, sports teams, and summer jobs have all done the same thing—and do it less today than in the past.

Nothing is perfect. In the United States, old-fashioned community-level public schools mixed students of different talents, aptitudes, backgrounds, and ambitions in the same classes. This was not always matched by creative pedagogy for encouraging collaborative learning. Schools were often racially segregated or at least reflected the communities in which they were located.[33] Mixing wasn't always a brilliant success; schools are full of cliques that intensify social differences. But it did foster greater connections across class and other social boundaries than the hyper-sorted schooling of the neoliberal and ostensibly meritocratic era.

As successful people move to new levels—and often new locations—they leave families and communities behind. Rock stars and neurosurgeons once married to high school sweethearts find that their old partners just don't fit into their new lives or that they have "earned" new trophy spouses. We are veering here into the themes of sentimental movies, but for good reason. Meritocracy may actually bring corruption to the character of those it rewards and privileges. They may think success is everything, which is a constricted outlook. Personal relationships are undermined by exaggerated meritocratic sorting. So is the solidarity that is basic to democracy.

Hierarchical Incorporation

The only way to be part of a highly unequal society is to be incorporated into its hierarchies of value and distinction. One can fight to change the system, but one cannot escape. The logic of membership is inextricably also one of hierarchical incorporation.

Higher education provides the paradigmatic example. It is on offer only through colleges and universities that stand in a hierarchical relationship to each other, conferring different amounts of prestige and shaping different life chances.[34] To get a degree is precisely to get a place in the hierarchy. It may still be a good investment, and you may learn a lot; you may work hard to better than most with your degree, but you must buy into inequality. This is like buying a house. It comes with a neighborhood that has more or less prestige and better or worse resale prospects, as well as potentially nice neighbors and commuting convenience. You can say this isn't important to you, but you can't entirely avoid it.

During the postwar boom public investment made possible dramatic expansions in education at all levels. In the rich democracies, literacy became nearly universal. Secondary school completion followed. And if access to universities did not become universal, still it increased substantially. This was a democratic and egalitarian project, aimed at overcoming class-based blockages on "life, liberty, and the pursuit of happiness."

The United States led the way. The GI Bill (discussed in Chapter 2) enabled nearly eight million veterans to attend college or university. Public universities expanded remarkably in almost every state. Expanding educational opportunity was part of the social democratic bargain in Europe and indeed in many countries around the world.

In Michael Young's Britain, the number of graduates each year rose from 22,426 in 1960 to 51,189 by 1970.[35] This did not come without opposition. For one thing, the beneficiaries of aristocratic privilege were not eager to give it up. For another, those with new wealth wanted the benefit of expanded education more for their own children than for "the masses." Indeed, there was even a prominent argument that there simply weren't enough intelligent young people to benefit from expansion.[36]

As the number of universities expanded, so did hierarchy among them. A flatter hierarchy with a broader pool of graduates from respected (but not necessarily super-elite) institutions would be better for almost every educational or public purpose. It could achieve a wider geographic distribution of opportunities, counterbalancing domination by the coasts in the United States, by London and nearby counties in Britain, and by Paris in France.[37] It would leave fewer first-generation graduates frustrated and resentful because they worked hard and went to university only to find the degrees they earned are less valuable in job markets because they are not from elite schools. Unfortunately, schooling was increased much more than equality in job markets.

Steeper hierarchy creates artificial scarcity. It serves the interests of institutions that claim bragging rights, but not of the whole system, the whole pool of potential students, or indeed democracy. But universities themselves have made competing for status a major focus of their efforts (pushed of course by students and alumni wanting market advantage, by those who do rankings, and in general by the whole of neoliberalism). This has driven up costs. In this competition, universities have become more and more like other luxury goods, priced at whatever level the rich will pay and discounted for the rest where subsidies are available or where it is necessary to fill empty places. To complete the picture of a vicious circle, costs have gone up largely because the fees students pay are used to support the competition for rankings—for example, by attracting star faculty—and for more students—for example, by building fancy facilities.

Corruption

Great inequality and selectivity have, not surprisingly, encouraged corruption. This was made public in a laughable (but also sad) 2019 scandal that revealed abuses in admissions to elite US universities. It was found, for example, that sports programs at elite private universities were, for a fee, happy to offer places to children who never fenced, or rowed, or ran competitively. This corruption was driven mainly by wealthy white Americans—like the actress Lori Loughlin and her fashion-designer husband. They paid an "admissions counselling service" to find loopholes to get their children into selective universities that in principle selected on merit.

Indeed, one of the beneficiaries of corruption, in this case an international student, explained the ideology of merit even while her parents subverted it. The family of Stanford student Yusi Zhao (since expelled) paid $6.5 million to help her get in. This attracted special attention because Ms. Zhao had posted videos to her blog advising prospective students to follow her example. The key to success, she said, was just hard work. "Some people think, 'Did you get into Stanford because your family is rich?' No, the admissions officers basically do not know who you are," she explained in a video she posted online. "You just need to have a clear goal and work as hard as you can toward it."[38]

The salacious side of scandal focuses attention on the unusual elements, the apparent bribe and the ill-considered video. But we might want attention to fall on the condition that made the corruption desirable, such as the displacement of educational goals for status, the hierarchy in which only a few schools could seem really valuable, the existence of an entirely legal market for college preparation and placement services, or the fact that Stanford costs $60,000 a year before living expenses. Most potential students couldn't begin to afford Stanford and aren't in life circumstances that would make them even consider it. It really is about families being rich. The supposedly meritocratic competition is largely about which rich children get into which elite universities.

Less rich students are not simply kept out of higher education. They are admitted, but at a disadvantage: the less rich have less chance to get into the very top schools; they have less support to finish degrees. Some do make it; some are even supported by scholarships. But this does more to make the competition seem fair than to produce actually equal opportunities.

Even more pernicious, students from middle- and working-class backgrounds end up financing higher education with loans. Borrowing to pay university costs has risen dramatically. While fees in France and Germany remain relatively low, in the UK a single policy change brought them from £1,000 to £9,000 in 2010. Most students finance their studies with loans. This is a more extreme issue in the United States, where public university fees are close to British levels but fees at many private universities exceeded $60,000 by 2019 (not counting living costs). Total student debt passed $1.5 trillion in 2018. Heavily indebted students graduate with reduced freedom in their career and life choices because of the loan payments they face. They are inhibited from choosing jobs in which they might help their fellow citizens—as teachers, say, or health care workers. It's not just that the finance sector pays more; it's that public service jobs often don't pay enough to live and also pay off loans.[39]

Student debt is a disaster regardless of what colleges or universities students attend. It is a particular disaster where students accumulate debt to attend schools that do not greatly advance their life chances. This is part of the scandal of the for-profit institutions promoted by former US education secretary Betsy DeVos. Companies made their profits by getting students to borrow money in government loan programs. But students graduated with more debt than success in the job market. They were sold a dream of higher education and opportunity. They received what Tressie McMillan Cottom has called "lower ed," and it has kept them locked into subordinate social positions.[40]

Opting out of higher education is not always a realistic choice. Hierarchical incorporation is the only form of opportunity available. Education remains necessary for learning skills, even though hierarchies of universities are more about status. Indeed, the hierarchies may even get in the way of education since a university's status is elevated more by being highly selective—excluding most students who apply—than by offering good classes. Rankings accentuate the difference between the top, the next, and the rest. In higher education, there is only modest difference in the quality of what the highest ranked universities offer students and what the many just below offer. Indeed, the biggest effect of the hierarchy may be not on what kind of education students get, but on whom they get to have in their network of classmates: other anointed winners. And of course, status has a big influence on who gets what job, how much they get paid, and how quickly they advance.

Making Exclusion Fairer

Tools such as standardized examinations purport to make exclusionary effort fairer. It might be better to reduce exclusion. In addition, the process selects in ways based on different levels of social support and "cultural capital."[41] The UK and France use national examinations of students' achievement. The United States places even greater emphasis on the illusory notion of natural differences in talent. The Scholastic Aptitude Test (SAT) ostensibly evaluates students' natural ability and suitability for university as such, rather than through testing specific learning. Though supposedly neutral, it has been shown by substantial research to be seriously biased.

Even more in the era of neoliberalism than in the postwar boom, elites see their power, privilege, and wealth as justified by their educational success, by their brains or other talents, and by the success of risky investments they made. Few ask whether there is any good reason for the whole system to be so unequal. Instead of extreme hierarchy with scholarships for a few less well-off students to attend the top universities, public funds could have gone to create a more equal educational system open to a wider range of students.

The possibility of social mobility was perhaps the most important legitimating promise of the compromise between capitalism and social democracy, not least during *les trente glorieuses*. Children were to have a chance at better jobs than their parents, at owning homes, at living longer. Opportunity was real, if not as great as announced. But mobility was sometimes bittersweet; upwardly mobile children had to leave their families and communities behind. This was one factor in the growth of cities and suburbs. Equality of opportunity was offered to individuals. Actual equality would have benefited whole communities.

Still, genuine mobility made it look like the system was fair (even if statistical analyses showed continued bias). At least children seemed to have a clear path to being better off than their parents. But this hope has pretty much ended. Young people today will not have higher incomes than their parents. Social mobility has become pervasively blocked. In a blow to the famous American dream, it may even have become more blocked in the United States than in Europe.[42] For the first time, a whole generation is reaching adulthood with weaker economic prospects than its parents. This is one of the most jarring features of the last fifty years, deeply undermining citizen efficacy and democracy.

Meritocracy is a profoundly antidemocratic ideology. In place of democratic recognition of the equal worth of all citizens, meritocracy suggests that some are more worthy than others. It is self-serving for the elites, who think their positions and accumulated wealth simply reflect their merits. It is disempowering for others. It disguises the differences of starting points and support on the way that help account for success stories. Seemingly neutral assessment of individual merit not only obscures biases and differential investments; it also obscures the policy decision behind the hierarchies—the creation of artificial scarcity. It discourages solidarity with those less well off, implying that they deserve their fate. Perhaps most perniciously, it suggests to everyone else that their own lower position must be their fault.[43]

Of course, as Young's novel predicted, this breeds resentment. Michael Sandel sums up: "Like the triumph of Brexit in the United Kingdom, the election of Donald Trump in 2016 was an angry verdict on decades of rising inequality and a version of globalization that benefits those at the top but leaves ordinary citizens feeling disempowered. It was also a rebuke for a technocratic approach to politics that is tone-deaf to the resentments of people who feel the economy and the culture have left them behind."[44]

Resentments of those not selected for the ostensibly meritocratic elite are exacerbated by what Pierre Bourdieu called "symbolic violence."[45] They not only don't get the benefits of selection; they are implicitly told that this is because of their own inferiority and often that they belong to a category they cannot change. They hear contempt in the ways they are discussed by highly educated professionals—famously in Hillary Clinton's reference to supporters of Donald Trump as "deplorables."[46] For many, frustration is compounded by the sense that others with less merit than themselves receive benefits at their expense. Why are the needs or wants of those in other categories privileged, they ask, while their own are neglected or even insulted? Critics of welfare insist it rewards those who don't work or have too many children or otherwise demonstrate lack of merit. They complain that their own genuine merits are overlooked. The tyranny of merit turns out to be not only about who has it and deserves to be part of the elite, but also who doesn't and deserves abjection.

Young introduced the idea of meritocracy in a satirical novel that described first the ascendancy of this elite so confident of their own merit and then a revolt against them by resentful masses on whom the elite looked down. *The Rise of the Meritocracy* gave what we now call "populist" revolt the fictional date of 2033. The real revolt came even sooner.

5

Making the Demos Safe for Democracy?

DILIP PARAMESHWAR GAONKAR

The idea that democracies have good days and bad days, or more accurately, good decades and bad decades, is not new.[1] This is true of all democracies, ancient and modern alike. Their rises and falls, their comings and goings, and their eruptions and suspensions have been variously theorized and historicized. Democracy often emerges unexpectedly amid hierarchically structured authoritarian political and cultural formations. While the coming of democracy is invariably deemed "untimely" by its detractors, the manifestations of its historically and culturally variable shape and substance, in a given arrangement of institutions and through a repertoire of forms and practices, surprise even its champions. Democracy comes in many versions. While adhering to a set of core doctrines, commitments, and practices, which come under question and contestation periodically, democracy takes multiple forms and trajectories. How democracies emerge, evolve, mature, flourish, decline, and decay varies according to the differing national and cultural spaces in which they are embedded. Democracy does not stand alone. As Craig Calhoun argues, it is grounded in shifting societal formations, aligned with and attuned to the perils and possibilities of those formations. Such is the contingency and novelty of democracy and its other republican variants.

The rhythm and tempo of how democracies emerge, rise, decline, and fall are also historically variable. They may emerge slowly, mature gradually, become dominant, and then begin to decline due to internal decay as well as external pressure, and thus fade and sometimes disappear altogether, as with the ancient democracies in Greece and their republican counterpart in Rome. The rhythm and tempo can be swifter and more violent in modern times, especially for those democracies that emerge from the womb of revolutionary unrest and ferment, as with England in the seventeenth century and the United States and France in the eighteenth. As they have proliferated over the last three-and-a-half centuries, the career of these modern democracies is substantially different from their ancient counterparts (including their more proximate predecessors among the Italian city-states).

The most important difference is simply that modern democracies, once born, don't seem to die. They may break down, retract, and recede, but they always come back. The idea of the sovereign demos, once planted, cannot be fully eradicated from the political imaginary of a people who have glimpsed and experienced it and claimed it as their collective right. In some countries, especially in Great Britain and the United States, democracy, while periodically shaken, has remained hegemonic and unchallenged. Democracy is not pure, however, in its composition. In those two countries—both of which are often regarded as paradigmatic cases of successful modern democracies—it has endured while harboring palpably undemocratic institutions and practices for extended periods of time: slavery in the United States and the colonial subjection and exploitation of the British Empire. Even today, despite all the triumphal progressive narratives, democracy in those countries is by no means perfect. In fact, perfectibility is not one of the possible or even desirable ends of democracy. This is what Charles Taylor means when he calls democracy a "telic" project. It has no final destination; it always fails in some respects while succeeding and living up to its promise on other fronts. It is a historical enterprise, enabled and embattled by the time and place of its people and their traditions, values, resources, aspirations, and spirit. The career and fortune of modern democracy in other countries has been less stable and more discontinuous (including in France during earlier republics). This should not be surprising. The coming of democracy is rarely peaceful because it involves a significant reconfiguration of political society and power. The predecessor regimes are unlikely to yield to their democratic successors without a prolonged, often violent, struggle. Such oligarchic resistances, which never fully disappear, leave scars on the body politic. Moreover, the few, the elites (worthy or unworthy), continue to dominate newly emergent democracies with their wealth, talent, ideological control, and rhetorical power.[2] This imbalance makes the demos, the nonelites, anxious and suspicious. The fear of being dominated, ignored, and dispossessed lingers with different degrees of intensity and manifests in unexpected ways. It is an affective reservoir, what German philosopher Peter Sloterdijk calls an "anger bank," always available to visionaries and demagogues alike to tap into and rattle the status quo.[3]

These anxieties, tensions, and vulnerabilities mean that, for a variety of reasons, democracies tend to break down and revert to nondemocratic modes of governance. The reversion, however, is never permanent. As Taylor notes, democracies are always susceptible to internal decay and degeneration and, when weakened and irresolute, can be overthrown internally by an oligarchic coup d'état, often led by the military but invariably endorsed by the dominant economic groups and business elites (as has happened so often in Asia, Africa, and Latin America throughout the twentieth century). The tension and mutual suspicion between the elites and the masses never fully disappear. As I argue below, neither elite nor mass is a stable, homogeneous category, especially when placed within a comparative historical / cultural perspective. And yet, the rhetorical force and hermeneutic legibility of that distinction in practical—especially electoral—democratic politics is inescapable. To dismiss the tension and conflict between the elites and the masses as sociologically vague or as a distorting myth engendered by reckless demagogic populist rhetoric is itself a sign of an elitist bias, rooted in a deep and abiding anxiety about mass democracy and mass politics that afflicts a vast number of liberal democratic theorists today.[4]

Democracies can also be overwhelmed by militarily superior foreign powers, bent on regime change, sometimes motivated by an alternative ideology, as in the case of the Soviet Union overpowering Eastern European countries after the Second World War, and sometimes driven by sheer economic interests, as when the United States covertly intervened in Iran to overthrow the democratically elected government of Prime Minister Mohammad Mosaddegh in 1953. These often violent reversals tear apart the social fabric in a manner not easy to mend. Hence, intimations of danger and fratricidal conflict invariably accompany the rise, the decline and decay, and the fall of democracies. In modern times, despite these breakdowns, reversals, and setbacks, precipitated from within as well as without, once the spirit and project of democracy have touched and resided among a given people, they rarely ever fully dissipate or disappear, even under the most severe repression. They subsist in the shadows awaiting recall and restitution. Renewing democracy by recalling and remaking the demos is an ineliminable, ever present possibility. This volume is committed to exploring that very possibility under the current state of democratic degenerations.

After the Third Wave

Influential American political scientist and democratic theorist Samuel P. Huntington characterized the pattern of democracy's comings and goings as "waves": when democracy comes and goes, it tends to do so in clusters of countries—within a geographical region or among countries with a shared historical experience (such as that of colonialism or the Soviet satellite states)—in quick succession rather than disparately in single countries. In his much cited "three waves" schema, the "first wave" of democratization in modern times endured for almost a century, from 1828 to 1926. Huntington's "first wave" includes transitions from nondemocratic to democratic regimes in thirty-three countries, all of them located in Europe, the Americas, and the overseas English dominions.[5] It was followed by the "first reverse wave" of democratic breakdowns, which lasted from 1922 to 1942 and led to the reestablishment of some form of authoritarian or totalitarian regime in twenty-two countries. The "second wave," covering the period from 1943 to 1962, witnessed the establishment or reestablishment of democratic regimes in forty countries and included, among others, the newly independent postcolonial nation states. It, in turn, was followed by the "second reverse wave" of democratic breakdowns between 1958 and 1975, which resulted in the return of nondemocratic regimes in twenty-two countries.

The "third wave" began in 1974 with the retreat of authoritarian governments in southern Europe (Portugal, Spain, and Greece) and Latin America. It includes the recuperation and restoration of democracies that had withered and broken down in the post-colony and culminates in the democratization of Eastern Europe and the Soviet successor states after the collapse of the Soviet Union. This wave added thirty-three countries to the democratic column, bringing the grand total to sixty-two (out of the seventy-one countries on Huntington's list). There was already some erosion as three countries had relapsed back into some form of authoritarian governance by 1991, when Huntington's book was published. There have been additional bursts and reversals since that date. While the third wave persists, according to political sociologist Larry Diamond, an admirer of Huntington's schema, we are now well into the third democratic recessionary phase.[6] The most stunning democratic upsurge and swift collapse was the fabled Arab

Spring, which, instead of spreading across the whole of the Arab world as it had initially seemed to promise, has not only withered in the countries where it had once bloomed—especially Egypt—but has also precipitated civil war in Syria and unending civil strife in Libya and elsewhere.

Among those who are concerned about the current phase of democratic recessions, however, the primary focus of liberal anxiety, public concern, and scholarly analysis is not on the rapid and dramatic failure of the Arab Spring; nor is it overly preoccupied with the endless travails of struggling democracies in the poor and developing countries of Africa and Asia, which are mired in corruption and violence. Rather, the focus is on the mature democracies of Europe and the United States and on those non-Western countries where democracy appeared to have successfully, if fitfully, passed through its transitional phase and entered a state of relative consolidation—as in Mexico, Turkey, South Africa, the Philippines, and especially India. Moreover, it is misleading to characterize what is happening in these regions and countries (as well as in Russia and the other Soviet successor states) as simple "democratic reversals or recessions" engineered by an oligarchic coup d'état spearheaded by the military. What is going on is more complicated and more troubling as democracy is being hollowed out and undermined from within.

Since the Second World War, the classic model of how democracies meet their sudden, if not unexpected, end, has been with military tanks rumbling through the streets of the capital city in an early morning coup. For Steven Levitsky and Daniel Ziblatt, the authors of the much-discussed and provocatively titled *How Democracies Die* (2018), the paradigm case of how democracies used to die spectacularly during the second reverse wave is the Chilean military coup d'état. On September 11, 1973, General Augusto Pinochet launched his final assault on Santiago's presidential palace and Chile's democratically elected socialist president, Salvador Allende:

> This is how we tend to think of democracies dying: at the hands of men with guns. During the Cold War, coups d'état accounted for nearly three out of every four democratic breakdowns. Democracies in Argentina, Brazil, the Dominican Republic, Ghana, Greece, Guatemala, Nigeria, Pakistan, Peru, Thailand, Turkey, and Uruguay all died this way. More recently, military coups toppled Egyptian President Mohamed Morsi in 2013 and Thai Prime Minister Yingluck Shinawatra in 2014. In all these cases, democracy dissolved in spectacular fashion, through military power and coercion.[7]

But no more. Notwithstanding what has happened in Egypt and Thailand, democracies no longer die with a bang—they simply wither. They may be stymied, but they are never fully suspended. Yet the discourse on the death of democracy is rife among Western political theorists and comparative political scientists alike. Alongside *How Democracies Die,* we now have a spate of recently published books, both scholarly and popular, that grimly announce the coming death of democracy: *How Democracy Ends, Ill Winds, The Road to Unfreedom, Democracy May Not Exist, but We'll Miss It When It's Gone,* and so on.[8] It seems we are keeping a vigil. The anxiety is palpable; the mood, bitter and foreboding. For once, normative theorists and empirical comparative scholars are fighting the same battle, side by side.

The Coming of Ugly Democracy

Paradoxically, the trope of the death of democracy coexists with a proposition that came into vogue in the early 1990s, around the same time that Mikhail Gorbachev and George H. W. Bush declared a "new world order" in which "democracy is the only legitimate form of government." And that historical conjuncture was anointed with a liberal democratic destiny by Francis Fukuyama with his "end of history" thesis in 1989 / 1992.[9] For Fukuyama, the long twentieth century was a period of trial, testing, and, eventually, triumph for liberal democracy, which thus closed, once and for all, the ideological debate over the political future of earthlings. Liberal democracy had met the dual ideological challenges of fascism and communism. It had survived two massively destructive world wars, followed by a long Cold War. It had endured a series of economic crises, including the Great Depression. Liberal democracy now stood triumphant and fully committed to promoting its brand of free-market economics worldwide.

While the thesis that "democracy is the only legitimate form of government" has lost some of its luster since the 1990s, it is by no means out of fashion. Mostly among technophiles, there is some positive chatter about the "China Model" and its emphasis on paternalistic "good governance" (benevolently administered by the mandarin party elite) over popular "self-governance"—the latter, in many parts of the world, dismissed as appallingly corrupt, dysfunctional, and disorderly.[10] It is unclear how the appeal of the "China Model," based largely on its spectacular economic success, will play out in the long run. The luster of that model has significantly eroded in recent years as the Communist Party apparatus continues to concentrate and centralize administrative power in its hands, thus stifling the vitality of civil society institutions. More than anything else, the massive deployment of surveillance technology to closely monitor its entire civilian population has disclosed how far the Chinese government will go to suppress and silence all dissent and criticism. In the meantime, democracy remains the most viable machine or method for garnering political legitimacy, however fleeting and fragile that legitimacy might be.

How can these two seemingly contradictory claims about democracy—the reports about its impending death and the need for its continued existence for garnering legitimacy—plausibly coexist and hold currency in today's political thinking and discourse? For liberal political thinkers, especially those, like Michael Ignatieff, who are chastened by the recent resurgence of authoritarian populism in Europe and the United States, this is a case of legitimate democracy versus illegitimate democracy.[11] This kind of opposition does little to clarify modern democracy's contradicting claims. Today, there are at least two, possibly three, types of democracy: the good, the bad, and the ugly. The good is being hollowed out and disfigured, if not eliminated, by the bad and the ugly. Moreover, this hollowing out is realized by the selective deployment of certain well-established and venerable democratic protocols, procedures, and practices, as in Viktor Orbán's Hungary. To seize the reins of government, the key targets of the attack are elections and the electoral process. As Levitsky and Ziblatt put it: "Democratic backsliding today begins at the ballot box."[12] Given that democracy is being undermined from within by some of its own distinctive and constitutive features, it might be more accurate to characterize such democracies as "ugly" rather than "bad."

Liberal democratic theorists tend to distinguish the good and the ugly in accordance with the Anna Karenina principle: all good democracies (like all happy families) are alike, and each ugly democracy (like each unhappy family) is ugly in its own way.[13] All good democracies are wedded to a liberal package with some "republican" (as in France) and some "social democratic" (as in the Nordic countries) variations: constitutionally guaranteed individual rights; the separation of powers (especially an independent judiciary); the rule of law; majority rule balanced with minority rights; an autonomous civil society; a vibrant public sphere; a functioning party system; and stable protocols for the peaceful transition of power through fair, free, and regular elections.

While each ugly democracy is ugly in its own unique way, the challenge is to decipher what common features they might collectively share. They come in different forms and under different names: authoritarian democracy, majoritarian democracy, populist democracy, illiberal democracy, pseudo-democracy, and so on. In accordance with the diverse nomenclature bestowed on them by their liberal critics, ugly democracies display a rich variety of stylistic and performative differences ranging from electioneering to governing. It is not easy to compare and catalog all of the strategies and tactics these political leaders and their parties—Viktor Orbán and Fidesz in Hungary; Hugo Chávez, Nicolás Maduro, and the United Socialist Party of Venezuela (PSUV) in Venezuela; Recep Tayyip Erdogan and the Justice and Development Party (AKP) in Turkey; Narendra Modi and the Bharatiya Janata Party (BJP) in India; Vladimir Putin and the Union of the Russian People (SRN) in Russia; Jarosław Kaczyński and Law and Justice (PiS) in Poland; Rodrigo Duterte and the Philippine Democratic Party–People's Power (PDP–Laban) in the Philippines; Jair Bolsonaro and the Social Liberal Party (PSL) in Brazil—deploy to subvert democracy from within. While most of these leaders and parties are characterized as nationalist and populist, they represent a wide spectrum of ideological positions from left to right. Their ideologies tend to be "thin" and "flexible," constantly adapting to claims and demands, conjunctural moods and sentiments that can be local and / or national. Hence, to decipher what is common among ugly democracies and their practitioners, one has to pay close attention to their tactics rather than to their ideological positioning, to what they do and how they operate rather than to what they say, let alone to what they believe.

Fortunately, some useful work has been done along these lines, and there appears to be an emerging consensus among political theorists and comparative political studies scholars as to how ugly democracy is undermining and devouring good democracy from within.[14] That consensus might be summarized as follows.

Ugly democracies come into power through elections. For them, elections are not a deliberative pedagogical process to discover who should be entrusted with defining and securing the common good for the electors, but a vehicle for capturing power and arrogating the spoils of power to the elected. Elections are not rhetorical situations in which one might persuade the undecided, the independents, and maybe even one's opponents, but sites and targets for mobilization. Steve Bannon, the US-based ethnonational strategist, puts it starkly: "This is not an era of persuasion, it's an era of mobilization. People now move in tribes. Persuasion is highly overrated."[15]

Ugly democracies retain power by undermining democratic institutions. Once elected, ugly democrats proceed swiftly and systematically to undermine constitutional norms and institutional guardrails to establish an authoritarian, majoritarian, and exclusionary mode of governance with a democratic facade.

Ugly democracies consolidate power by undermining democratic culture. They seek to ensure long-term control of the state by permanently disabling and disempowering opposition, by intimidating or coopting the media, and by colonizing the civil service, the judiciary, and the university with their own party cadre.

Before I proceed to draw out the implications of this emerging consensus, a comment on Bannon's distinction between persuasion and mobilization is in order. While this distinction is a bit murky, he is on target. Yes, one wins by mobilization. But mobilization runs on a dual track: rhetoric *and* logistics. One must persuade as well as organize. On the persuasive track, ugly democrats mobilize by deploying polarizing, scapegoating, and exclusionary rhetoric and by disseminating misinformation (not just the "Big Lie" but a daily tide of little lies). The organizational track is more complex. It is much more than what Americans call the "ground game"—the campaigning body that is put together by candidates and parties prior to elections and often dismantled soon after they are over. This is precisely what the Barack Obama campaigns did, as they effectively combined rhetoric and logistics, especially during the election of 2008. Obama's soaring eloquence—"Yes, we can"—was matched and augmented by the organizational genius of a team that incorporated resources from newly emerging social media into the traditional arsenal of mobilization. The traces of Obama's rhetoric haunt our public culture and memory, but the electoral machine that was assembled (it was much more than a coalition) during his campaigns disappeared with him. Neither Hillary Clinton nor anyone else inherited it. The point here is to recognize that, as the Obama case attests, the option of strategically conjoining persuasion and mobilization is available to good as well as ugly democrats. In fact, it is more than an option; it is an imperative required of any candidate, party, or movement, representing the good or the ugly, that seeks to successfully navigate electoral politics. But one must mobilize on a permanent basis. Good democrats used to rely on the organizational apparatus of their respective parties to mobilize, as they continue to do today, but ineffectively. Ugly democrats, on the other hand, are building electoral machines that mobilize on a permanent basis. Having been long marginalized and dismissed politically as illiberal "fringe" groups given to shrill and divisive rhetoric, they have learned the hard lesson. By the sheer will to organize and mobilize and without significantly altering their ideology or their rhetoric, they have successfully attenuated, if not fully erased, the force of that negative characterization. Mobilization on a permanent footing has rendered their rhetoric respectable by repetition and acclamation.[16]

Fear of Elections

Let us be clear about what this emerging consensus entails. What does it mean to view elections and the electoral process as democracy's Achilles' heel? We are no longer talking about fake elections (sometimes in the guise of referendums) with predetermined outcomes, as when Hosni Mubarak won by 90 percent of votes cast in Egypt in 1981. Nor are these closely contested, but rigged elections (as in the case of Ferdinand Marcos's election as the president of the Philippines in 1986, the Kenyan general election of 2007, Robert Mugabe's reelection as the president of Zimbabwe for his seventh term in 2013, and numerous others), the outcomes of which having little claim to legitimacy. Instead, we are now confronted with the relatively, if not perfectly, free and fair elections that brought Orban, Chavez, Erdogan, Modi, Duterte, and Bolsonaro to power. When they came into power electorally, they were not part of the incumbent party or coalition. They took control of the reins of government through a "peaceful transition of power," another coveted protocol, deemed indispensable for nurturing a healthy democratic tradition and culture since 1800, when Thomas Jefferson was elected president of the United States and peacefully assumed his office.[17] To be sure, corruption, criminality, intimidation, and violence mar these democracies and make them ugly. That is not in dispute. But focusing on these features blinds us to the deeper and irredeemable anxieties that liberals harbor about democracy or, more precisely, about mass democracy in the age of the people empowered with universal adult suffrage.

This liberal anxiety revolves around elections, not just around the corruption of elections. In the United States, one might find some consolation in the belief that Donald Trump was elected by the corruption of the electoral process (Russian meddling or the undemocratic electoral college).

One might further believe that, with proper resolve and vigilance, these issues can be fixed and integrity be restored both to the electoral process and to the political system as a whole. For liberals in India today, however, there is no such consolation available in the wake of Modi and BJP's recent resounding victory in the federal parliamentary elections. In India today, liberals face the challenges posed by a duly elected majoritarian democracy that will continue to strain and undermine constitutional constraints and institutional guardrails, sometimes with stealth and sometimes with impunity. Three short months before the federal elections, Modi and BJP had lost "state elections" in three Hindi-speaking states, regions usually seen as BJP strongholds. This had raised the hopes of the opposition, including liberals, who had hailed the defeat as yet another indication of the infinite wisdom of the Indian electorate, voters who routinely punish transgressing and arrogant incumbents, the most famous instance being the electoral loss of Prime Minister Indira Gandhi after "the Emergency" period.[18] Although there are the usual complaints about procedural irregularities, Modi and BJP's victory in the federal election was such that a different outcome is unimaginable, even if every one of those irregularities were to be corrected and reversed. The electoral victory was simply overwhelming. In short, the election system in India, while not perfect, is working fine *and* producing "undesirable" results.[19] Universal suffrage was once regarded as a great democratic achievement and the incarnation of popular sovereignty. Today, the fear is that universal suffrage, not as the citizen's individual political right but in the collective register, could lead to majoritarianism.

Such liberal fear of democratic elections calls into question what was, only a decade or two ago, the most dominant conception of democracy among comparative democracy scholars. As opposed to a "classical" conception of democracy that privileges the source of authority (the will of the people) and / or the very purpose of governing (the common good), a "realistic" conception saw democracy's core as its "method." The *democratic method*, according to the celebrated economist and political theorist Joseph Schumpeter, "is that institutional arrangement for arriving at political decisions in which individuals acquire the power to decide by means of a competitive struggle for the people's vote."[20] The *electoral method*, in turn, "implies the existence of those civil and political freedoms to speak, publish, assemble, and organize that are necessary to political debate and the conduct of electoral campaigns."[21] Thus, the electoral method merged with the liberal theory of "rights" to generate a realistic conception of democracy.

Huntington reiterated the centrality of elections, emphatically claiming: "Elections, open, free, and fair are the essence of democracy, the inescapable sine qua non. Governments produced by elections may be inefficient, corrupt, short-sighted, irresponsible, dominated by special interests, and incapable of adopting policies demanded by the public good. These qualities may make such governments undesirable but they do not make them undemocratic."[22] Similarly, Robert Dahl, the foundational theorist of democratic pluralism, privileged elections because they provided, among other things, a mechanism for controlling the "leaders by non-leaders," and enabled ordinary citizens to exert "a relatively high degree of control over leaders."[23] For Dahl, as the incisive critic of liberal democracy Carole Pateman rightly notes, "political equality" does not refer to "equality of political control or power." Rather, it refers to universal suffrage and, "more importantly, to the fact of equality of opportunity of access to influence over decision makers through inter-electoral processes by which different groups in the electorate make their demand heard."[24] What is more, paradoxically such salutary control is exerted with a moderate or even minimal amount of active participation by the citizenry. Schumpeter, Dahl, and Huntington all believed this low standard of participation to be a key benefit of the political equality that universal suffrage afforded. There is a palpable anxiety over mass democratic participation running through this line of thinking.[25] Writing in the shadow of totalitarianism and impressed by the stability of Western democracies with low electoral participation, especially the United States, these scholars looked on increased participation by the lower economic groups with trepidation because they were believed to be largely unschooled in democratic norms and more inclined to possess "authoritarian" personalities.[26]

Origins of Liberal Anxiety

This anxiety about the collective agency of the people is not new. We find it expressed loudly and repeatedly by democracy's critics, both ancient and modern. For the intellectual critics of Athenian democracy, the target of their critique was political equality, especially as it was embodied in *isegoria*, the equal right to speak and proffer advice and to render judgment on a proposal before the assembly. Plato, as well as Thucydides, Aristophanes, and many others, regarded the practice of *isegoria* and everything it represented as the fundamental flaw of democracy.[27] It is important to note here that what was being attacked was not what we moderns think of as the freedom of speech, a key component of civil liberties. Nor was it the right to question and criticize the government, its leaders, or its policies. Instead, what was being criticized was the very right to political participation on equal footing, be it speaking, advocating, advising, casting a vote, or holding office.

In effect, Plato has two enduring, if narrowly focused, critiques of political equality. The first is a critique of an individual citizen's capacity to learn the art of politics, and the second, a critique of deliberation and action when the political subject is not an individual but a collective. These critiques can be disassociated from his idealized hierarchical vision of a well-ordered human community made up of different classes of people, each occupying their proper stations and discharging their assigned duties in accordance with their natural endowments ranging variably across their respective physical aptitudes, intellectual abilities, and moral rectitude. In fact, Plato's critiques of political equality presuppose a *society of equals,* like the one operative in the Athens of his time. This is a society of a privileged and exclusive class of citizens, who, in Aristotle's later formulation, alternate being "the rulers and the ruled." It is precisely for this reason that Plato's critique has a real bite.[28]

Plato's first critique of political equality is that one cannot entrust every single individual citizen with the task of political deliberation and decision-making on matters pertaining to the common good. For Plato, it was inconceivable that all citizens, simply by virtue of being born into citizenship, would have an equal natural aptitude and talent for the political art. In every art, be it medicine, architecture, or marine navigation, there are masters under whom apprentices train. In any of these domains, Athenians turn to experts rather than rely on their fellow citizens for advice and guidance. Why then, in passing legislation and dispensing justice—two components of the political art so vital for ensuring the health of the city—would Athenians accept the untutored judgment of their fellow citizens? For Plato, therefore, the celebrated Athenian right of *isegoria* that entitles every citizen to speak freely, proffer political advice, and cast his vote in the assembly makes no sense. While Plato speaks bluntly, his view was shared by many other intellectual critics of democracy and popular rule. It is an aristocratic critique that continues to attract adherents in modern times, both conservative and radical.[29]

There are various ways in which Plato's first critique is addressed, modified, and dismissed. Plato himself provides one of the most compelling rebuttals in *Protagoras*. In this dialogue's great speech, the sophist Protagoras gives a mythical account of how Zeus, fearing the extinction of the human race, sent Hermes to impart to men the qualities of *dike* (justice) and *aidos* (reverence), the constituent elements of *politike techne*.[30] Conversely, Prometheus's gift, *empyros techne* (technology based on fire), was given only to a few specialists. Zeus's gift of *politike techne* is given to all men because, as Zeus explains, cities cannot survive if only a few partake in justice and reverence. He commands Hermes to lay down as "law that if anyone is incapable of acquiring his share of these two virtues he shall be put to death as a plague to the city."[31] In political art, one can be superior to others by talent, practice, and theoretical reflection, but everyone has a basic, untutored proficiency. Just as one learns language by growing up in a community of speakers, one learns politics, justice, and reverence by growing up among others. And, like language, the basic capacity for political art can be strengthened through education.

The belief that the natural human capacity for the political art of living together in cities and nations can be improved upon runs more or less uninterrupted from *Protagoras* to John Dewey. This is the venerable tradition of democratic education, whose task changes as we move from the ancient polity to modern nation-states of varying size and shape, from a relatively simple traditional society to modern complex societies with large-scale integration. But this tradition is not without its sceptics. Dewey and Lippmann debated whether individual citizens are capable of rendering sound political judgment in complex modern societies.[32] Pateman's thesis that political participation itself sharpens and deepens the average citizen's political competence and judgment is met with doubt not on the ground of philosophical anthropology, but in terms of sociohistorical formations by scholars such as Michael Walzer, who reluctantly concede that the modern democratic subject does not consider citizenship as their preeminent identity as the Athenian did once upon a time.[33] These perennial questions remain open and unresolved.

While the rebuttal of Plato's critique is not conclusive, the critique has been largely neutralized and, for various reasons, faded into the background. To put it differently, Plato's first critique may be rejected not only on anthropological grounds—unlike other capacities, all citizens receive the gifts of justice and reverence—but also on practical grounds. Since political legitimacy is indispensable for governing and since it can be garnered only by incorporating the demos in some sort of agential capacity, of which the equal right to vote and everything it implies is the constitutive sign, the real question is not whether there is any merit to the critique, but instead whether its negative consequences can be managed and domesticated by constitutional and institutional strategies.

In his second and more enduring critique, Plato leaves behind the individual citizen and takes aim at the political capacities of democratic collectivities: in an assembly, or in any other public forum, when a group of citizens is called upon to deliberate and make decisions collectively, the situation deteriorates and becomes dangerous. The argument is based on the idea that, when assembled, each individual citizen's deficiency in the art of politics gets compounded by the deficiencies of other citizens. Collectively, the stage is set for flawed deliberation, compromised judgment, and perilous outcomes. Those who seek to steer and lead such an assembly of citizens, the demos incarnate, find themselves standing before a great wild beast given to radical mood swings and desires rather than before a group of prudent individuals with common interests and concerns. This "great beast" image of the demos sets in motion a powerful tradition of a deep and abiding anxiety about the collective political agency of the people in Western social and political discourse.[34] The rhetor (the oratorically gifted political actor) and the great Sophists (who promised to train the rhetor in political art) mistakenly believed that they could manipulate, mobilize, and manage the beast in service of their own ends. According to Plato, irrespective of whether the ends sought by rhetors are those of personal aggrandizement or of a common good (often confused in the minds of actors such as Alcibiades), they are doomed to fail because, in the long run, the direction of influence is reversed—the manipulator becomes the manipulated; the seducer is seduced. Ideally, Plato would prefer to exclude the people as a collective political agent altogether.

Aristotle was not exercised by the questions Plato repeatedly debated with the Sophists: Are the demos educable? Is political *arete* (political excellence or virtue) teachable? Instead, he had a different approach. For Aristotle, the popular classes, who were indispensable to the defense of the polis that was so often at war, were also the primary source of political legitimacy.[35] Thus, he posed a different question: Can the demos be bridled and controlled? Ultimately, his answer was "yes." Aristotle's conceptual and institutional mechanism for bridling and controlling the demos was a mixed constitutional government, the *politeia*. First and foremost, this meant acknowledging an endemic and ineliminable tension between the rich and the poor, the aristoi and the demos, the elite and the mass. This is what Taylor is referring to when he says that democracy can succeed only if it can "tame" class struggle. He does not say *eliminate* class struggle. Unlike Marx, he does not foresee an end to class struggle with the triumph of the proletariat. In fact, Taylor's struggling classes are not strictly classes in the Marxist lexicon. He is referring to the struggle between the elites and the nonelites, or the popular classes. Mixed government and everything that comes with it in modern times—the separation of powers; checks and balances; minority rights that are refined, elaborated, and constitutionally grounded—are not primarily mechanisms for preparing individual citizens for the privilege of standing on equal footing in the political assembly or at the ballot box. Instead, they are deterrents to the collective agency of citizens qua demos. Bias toward an elitist model of democracy is built into both the ideology of "mixed government" and the operations of a "representative" system. The real challenge facing elites in modern democracies is how to tame and manage the multitude in an age progressively committed to the doctrine of popular sovereignty, which would lead, sooner or later, to the granting of universal adult franchise.

Taming the Demos: An Elite Project in Disarray

Aristotle's mixed government is only one way of balancing the belief that the demos are the primary source of political legitimacy with the imperative that they must be controlled. The unassailability of our commitment to universal suffrage has much to do with the dynamic of political legitimacy. No government, according to Aristotle, can garner and sustain legitimacy without acknowledging and giving due consideration to the democratic element, its claims and demands.[36] We are far from the doctrine of popular sovereignty here. As the legitimacy criterion shifts, however, from the practical matters of effective and inclusionary governance to a theoretical justification, it gets drawn into the gravitational field of popular sovereignty, an onto-theological doctrine, from which its extraction becomes ever more difficult.[37]

This basic legitimacy requirement becomes compounded in modern times in two ways. First, in *Democracy in America,* Tocqueville notes that a constitutive feature of modernity is a sociohistorical drive toward equality in all spheres of life. Hence, modern democracies have had to contend with the inexorable march of equality.[38] When pressed to widen and deepen political equality, modern democracies have responded positively by granting nonelites the political right to vote, to run for office, and to assemble and organize as collective entities, ranging from farmers' cooperatives and labor unions to political parties. The formal, if not substantive, terminus of this drive for political equality is universal adult suffrage without the restrictive qualifications of things like a minimum education, ownership of property, and exclusions on the grounds of gender or race. The slow, steady, and seemingly irreversible inclusion of nonelites in every walk of political life, however, has always been accompanied by a palpable anxiety among the ruling and nonruling elites about the misuse and demagogic manipulation of the equal rights to voice, vote, and stand. Second, after the great revolutions of the late eighteenth century, the challenge of conceptually and institutionally bridling and controlling the demos was further complicated by the near universal acceptance of the doctrine of popular sovereignty. As soon as this doctrine was embraced and the people became the ultimate source of legitimate political authority, a vexing question arose: Who are the people? However indispensable, universal adult franchise is not a satisfactory practical or performative embodiment of the "people," even to the populists. Fiction, myth, or empty signifier, the "people" is an essentially contested concept.[39]

Across democracy's long history, the "people" is usually understood in two basic ways. Aristotle's class-inflected idea of the demos as the "poor," for one, has had a long and enduring career.[40] Over the course of the twentieth century, but especially since the 1970s, however, it has lost some of its specificity and appellative force in Western societies now under the ideological spell of two related developments: meritocratically driven contentious affluence and the quest for authenticity and identitarian recognition (as discussed in Chapter 4). As the idea of the people mutates from the "poor," to the "subaltern," to the "uncounted," to the "marginal," and to the "other" dispersed in multiple registers, it oscillates between calls for a politics of "redistribution" and a politics of "recognition." In all these iterative mutations and oscillations, it becomes aligned with an "agitational" model of rhetoric that makes claims on behalf of all groups and movements that seek redress for grievances "in the name of the people." This is one version of a part standing in and speaking for the whole, a part claiming to incarnate the whole.[41]

Second, the unified idea of the national people as embodied in "We, the people," points to a different historical trajectory for how, in modern times, the democratic project has become deeply embedded in the national form, the "imagined community."[42] This idea of a "whole people" is a distinctly modern idea. One could not have explained this to Aristotle or Cicero: there was no word for it in Greek or Latin—not *demos,* not *plebs,* not even *populus,* as in *Senatus populusque romanus.* While this invention of the "whole people" within a national frame strategically erases class differentiation, stratification, status, and the social question, it also makes the underlying juridical logic of "constitutive exclusion" explicit: Who counts as a citizen within a national community and who does not?[43] This exclusionary unity in difference might be experienced positively, especially when conveyed in soaring nationalist rhetoric during anti-imperialist and anticolonial struggles. The effervescent moments of unity in difference that unexpectedly surface during such struggles, what Hannah Arendt calls the moments of "public happiness," become iconized in the public memory of a given people and serve as invaluable resources for emancipatory projects of tolerance and understanding in darker times of polarization and suspicion.[44] Martin Luther King Jr.'s "I Have a Dream" speech delivered during the March on Washington for Jobs and Freedom on August 28, 1963, is a paradigmatic instance of the performative enactment of such a "unity in difference." Thus, one needs to acknowledge that the exclusionary unity of a national people contains within it the seeds of potential concord and solidarity.

The idea of a national people also has a dark side, however, or a dark twin. As has happened time and again during periods of civil strife, this exclusionary unity can also turn against itself, devouring its own children of seemingly "lesser origins." Turning inward under conditions of duress and disharmony, this exclusionary strand invokes the principles of precedence and priority and thus posits a dark and polarizing alternative understanding of the "people." In this vein, a noticeable drift toward a "primordial" ethnonational pole begins, and the "real people" pit themselves against the "not so real people." The former designate themselves "heartlanders," "sons and daughters of the soil," and the "real people," while painting the latter as immigrants (legal and illegal), resident aliens, guest workers, refugees, and so on. This schism, once introduced, is difficult to bridge and heal, especially when it gets caught up in an electoral politics susceptible to the temptations of exclusionary rhetoric.

As the pragmatics of legitimacy and the onto-theology of sovereignty converge across these two contested notions, the elite project of taming the "people" becomes ever more difficult and urgent. It also complicates the challenge of managing the endemic conflict between elites and nonelites that flares up in times of significant social transformations, as is the case today. The unifying project of a national "We, the people," can succeed only if it can fend off and neutralize the divisive politics from both ends: the "agitational" rhetoric of the aggrieved (mostly from the nonelites) and the "exclusionary" rhetoric of the "heartlanders." While one can analytically distinguish these two rhetorics, they can mix and mingle in the course of practical politics to give rise to a volatile, sometimes toxic, polarization. Thus, within the liberal calculus, instituting, deepening, and widening democracy runs parallel to the project of taming democracy by bridling the democratic subject. The overt objective of this taming is geared first to protect private property and second to protect bourgeois human rights, understood as the rights of individuals. But covertly, and using different strategies, it is a method by which the elites as well as some governing nonelites exercise governmental, ideological, and cultural control.

Today, what we conceive of as a full or mature democracy is a product of two strands of struggle to deepen and widen democracy: the struggle to secure universal adult suffrage and the struggle to secure individual rights (against arbitrary rule) and minority rights (against majority transgressions). One of the most effective taming strategies has been to play universal suffrage and individual rights against one another. By disaggregating the people into discrete, rights-bearing individuals, citizens come to view their rights as individual and inalienable possessions, even though they were historically secured through collective struggle. Here it is assumed that the *telos* of a people as a collective entity is to become rights-bearing individual citizens. Once such a citizen is judicially constituted and objectified, their grounding in peoplehood is effaced and let go as a fiction. In the economic realm, this would lead to what the political scientist C. B. Macpherson calls "possessive individualism."[45]

A second strategy might be called the constitutional-institutional strategy, which, among other things, seeks to build and secure "counter-majoritarian" institutions such as the court (independent judiciary), the church, and the free press, as well as the independent institutions of the public sphere (the university, scientific communities devoted to the pursuit of knowledge, the associational life of civil society). The record of these "counter-majoritarian" institutions in curbing the will of the majority or of the prevailing hegemonic ideology is quite murky. These institutions have a stellar record when it comes to upholding the sacred right of private property and a reasonable record in defending bourgeois human rights against state transgressions.

But, when it comes to injustices against minorities and marginalized communities, they are generally aligned with the status quo and prevailing public opinion. In the United States, during the antislavery struggle and then up until *Brown v. Board of Education* during the civil rights movement, despite all the efforts of the National Association for the Advancement of Colored People (NAACP) (and notwithstanding the customary rhetoric of seeking redress for grievances through the judicial route), the Supreme Court was generally a step behind the progressive curve.[46] It is only after the aggrieved take to the streets or squares or resort to some other form of direct action to seek redress for their grievances that they catch the attention, and in due course command the support, of counter-majoritarian institutions.

Making the Demos Safe for Democracy

We need to resist the temptation to attribute the primary cause of today's political crisis to the electoral capture of the democratic state by ugly democrats, bent on disfiguring, if not destroying, democracy from within. As I pointed out earlier, this way of thinking is characteristic of a number of comparative political scientists who once touted "free, fair, and regular elections" as democracy's litmus test but now vehemently denounce the so-called electoral fallacy and resolutely distance themselves from the idea of democracy as a "method."[47] This liberal backtracking has other features.

Invoking the political wisdom of John Adams, both classical liberals and republicans alike were accustomed to saying that "it is not the rule of men, but rule of laws and institutions" that secures the ramparts of democracy.[48] Consequently, they placed a great deal of emphasis on constitution making and institution building. When democracies fell in the post-colony during the second recessionary phase, Western political scientists routinely explained those failures in terms of weak institutions and cultural formations inhospitable to the cultivation of democratic subjectivity—especially patriarchy. Now that the ugly democrats are using the tools and procedures of democracy itself to undermine constitutional and institutional guardrails from within, the contemporary liberals are once again shifting their focus. Writing in the context of the Trump presidency, Levitsky and Ziblatt aver: "Institutions alone are not enough to rein in elected autocrats. Constitutions must be defended—by political parties and organized citizens, but also by democratic norms. Without robust norms, constitutional checks and balances do not serve as the bulwarks of democracy we imagine them to be."[49] This is fine, but one might inquire: From where do these unwritten norms come? Are they grounded in the political traditions, experiences, and practices of a given people or in some vaguely prepolitical collective ethos? Larry Diamond, also writing with the Trump presidency in mind, posits: "The ultimate defense of liberal democracy lies not in the constitution but in the culture—in free, informed, and principled citizens who will not tolerate the abuse of their democracy or their rights."[50] This too is fine, but one might ask: Over the last two hundred years of democratic struggle and governance—including a devastating civil war that nearly ruined the Union—has not the United States developed a democratic tradition and culture, rich and resilient, capable of withstanding the mayhem that a Trump might wreak in four years? Much of this talk about norms and cultures as an enabling and sustaining layer, something that precedes constitution making and institution building, is vague and circular. It strikes me as a project geared toward hailing a specific type of political subject into existence—namely, the citizen who doubles as ruler and ruled and who has internalized liberal norms. Are we not back to square one, calling for rule by men and women, albeit the right type of men and women? Facing the current challenge of numerous majoritarian and authoritarian regimes, duly elected by the hitherto accepted and respected method of regular elections based on universal suffrage, such a call, however high-minded, is neither credible nor adequate.

Under present conditions, any emancipatory project associated with democratic politics would have to awaken the sleeping giant, the nonvoter, not simply to vote but to engage. The terms of engagement may vary across time, place, and people, but not to engage (or to not engage beyond voting) is no longer an option if the goal is to deter the ugly democrats and their designs.

In this context, one must recognize and address a galling and vexatious fact about the electoral system at large: almost all majoritarian regimes, even those with a huge and commanding legislative majority—as BJP has in India, for instance—have ascended to power without ever winning more than 50 percent of all eligible votes. This is not all due to "voter suppression" by the bad and ugly democrats. For much too long, the hegemonic liberal ideology, while ritually extolling the virtues of voter participation, has viewed anything significantly higher than the expected voter turnout as potentially dangerous and destabilizing. This has, in turn, enabled and and encouraged a culture of disavowing and avoiding democratic politics.

According to Taylor, the primary cause of such distancing is that awful feeling of steady diminution and loss of efficacy among a vast number of citizens. It is time to restore and enhance citizen efficacy. This can be achieved only through engagement and participation. How citizens engage and participate and to what effect and consequence cannot be foretold. It is time to awaken and mobilize the disaffected and discouraged nonvoters and not fear that they may not be suitable liberal subjects. It is their choice, as it should be. That is one of the paradoxes of political freedom among equals and of democracy. It is time to relinquish the exhausted project of taming the demos.

6

The Structure of Democratic Degenerations and the Imperative of Direct Action

DILIP PARAMESHWAR GAONKAR

Charles Taylor has identified three vulnerabilities "internal" to the democratic project that, under certain sociohistorical conditions, can trigger a series of degenerative ideas and ideologies, dispositions and behaviors, mobilizations and movements detrimental to liberal and cosmopolitan values and constitutional norms.[1] These vulnerabilities are rooted in what is constitutive of, and hence unavoidable in, modern democratic politics: the contentious relationship between elites and nonelites; the exclusionary temptation and rhetoric built into the very idea of "We, the people"; and the dangers of "winner-take-all" majoritarian rule facilitated by an electoral system based on universal adult suffrage. Along with its legitimacy, dynamism, and appeal, democracy, imagined and conceived by the Athenians as a form of "popular" self-rule of the people—and enshrined for modern times in Lincoln's succinct formulation "government of the people, by the people, for the people"—is recurrently susceptible to degenerations. According to Taylor, these three vulnerabilities are converging today into a perfect storm and jeopardizing democracies across the world.

Craig Calhoun complements Taylor's thesis by showing how democracy is a societally embedded historical project: democracy does not control its destiny. Calhoun provides us with a short but compelling historical account of how the fate of democracy, time and again, turns on the shifting social formations within which it is embedded. To put it differently, Calhoun's account alerts us to Machiavelli's profound insight that politics, especially republican politics, is eternally held hostage by the passage of time.[2] For democracy, there are good times and bad times; there are hospitable social formations that allow it to flourish and inhospitable ones that destabilize and endanger it. Democratic societies cannot always anticipate these shifts. Forced to contend with the consequences of expanding capitalism over the last two hundred years, democracy has struggled to adapt. Every core social formation and institution—from family, neighborhood, and school to work, leisure, and religion—critical to the cultivation of democratic norms and civic virtues has been subjected to accelerating, often disfiguring, transformations wrought by capitalism and its market logic. This is amply illustrated in Calhoun's account of Karl Polanyi's two movements, the first marking the great societal transformation triggered by industrial capitalism and the second marking the delayed political response to the derangements and negative externalities of the first. Calhoun masterfully describes how the long hiatus between the two movements—"Engels's pause"—challenged, strained, and diminished the very ideas of a common good and a shared future, both essential to democracy's flourishing (see Chapter 2). Given the dynamism of capitalism today, "Engels's pause" keeps recurring, and democracy is placed under duress, time and again.

The Structure of Three Degenerations

In the first part of this chapter, I try to decipher and specify the underlying structure of the three degenerative vulnerabilities intrinsic to the democratic project and explain why they can, at best, be managed, but not eliminated. In the second part, I make a case as to why "direct action" mobilization is and should be a necessary element to reanimating the democratic project now in disrepair.

First Degeneration and Taming Class Struggle

Taylor's first degeneration is triggered by a generalized feeling of diminished political efficacy and agency among the vast majority of citizens, especially the nonelites. While Taylor identifies multiple causes that have contributed to the loss of citizen efficacy in mature Western democracies in recent years, he singles out what he calls the breakdown of "tamed class struggle." This is an interesting formulation. This means that the health and stability of democracy is predicated on keeping class struggle under check, taming it ideologically and institutionally to ensure that it does not spin out of control. Here, Taylor is not using the phrase "class struggle" in any Marxist sense. Instead, he is referring to a proposition with a long and complex lineage—namely, that all known settled (non-nomadic) communities are marked by and contend with an enduring conflict between an elite (a small numerical minority) and a nonelite. While the intensity of conflict varies according to time and place, it is always present and ineliminable. This conflict turns chiefly on the asymmetrical and inequitable distribution of wealth, status, and resources within a given community.

The idea that socioeconomic inequality is constitutive of any and every political community, both ancient and modern, whether governed democratically or otherwise, is commonly accepted by thinkers of every persuasion—liberal, radical, conservative, and even reactionary.[3] There are many explanations of how social inequalities arise (anthropological, structural, and causal) and justifications (economic, normative, and theological) of why they are unavoidable, and even necessary. Much of this is beyond the purview of this chapter. However, the historical experience of socioeconomic inequality accompanies and haunts the democratic project like a spectral shadow, and poses a question: What is to be done about it? Responses to this question (which has exercised the minds of many great thinkers from Plato and Rousseau to Marx and John Rawls) range widely, from how to organize and manage social inequality, both normatively and practically, to how to eliminate it altogether, as in a utopia. In all these speculations and analyses, there is one constant consensus: whatever its causes, explanations, and justifications, social inequality becomes dysfunctional, dangerous, and destructive once it crosses a certain point. Where that threshold lies is not easy to specify. Culturally and historically, it is elastic and variable, but within the social imaginary of any given people, it becomes legible, palpable, and obdurate. When Taylor says that "tamed class struggle" has broken down, he is suggesting that the degree of social inequality in today's "Western democracies" has crossed the threshold and become dangerous. For Calhoun, the roots of the threshold breach are historical and reside in the steady dismantling of democracy's social foundations since the 1970s (in short, the welfare state and its network of social provisions), under the so-called neoliberal dispensation.

Both Taylor and Calhoun regard the postwar *trente glorieuses* as an admirable period of "tamed class struggle," a period of civil harmony across the various tiers of social stratification in Western democracies. Calhoun is relatively unambiguous about how one might address the current crisis. We need to rebuild social foundations to soften the impact of growing economic inequality and stem the corresponding tide of public anger and distress swelling among the nonelite. The statistical data on income and wealth disparity among the different quintiles of the US population are simply horrendous.[4] The statistical data also alert one to the fact that categories of elite and nonelite are not homogeneous. There is a great deal of internal variation and differentiation in each category, not only in terms of economic resources, but in terms of social status, cultural values, religious beliefs, and ideological leanings. Modern Western societies are highly complex and stratified. Nevertheless, the distinction between the elite and the nonelite resonates loudly across all these layers of stratified differences and in the realms of political perception, public discourse, and folk understanding.[5]

Calhoun is also clear that "rebuilding" the social foundations of democracy is not a simple matter of reinstating dismantled welfare state provisions and returning to the good old days of *les trente glorieuses*. We are now in a different sociohistorical conjuncture, but one that is once again propelled by the ever-expanding and changing modes of capitalist production and reproduction that shape our lives. We are faced with new modes of production and distribution, new modes of communication and circulation, new modes of wealth creation, new labor regimes (what some call the "international division of labor"), and new modes of precarity.[6] These formations directly affect and shape the vexed relations between the elite and the nonelites. They call for different and novel strategies for "taming class struggle," new visions of the common good and a shared future, and new ways of building and strengthening bands of solidarity.

Looking forward, Taylor and Calhoun also insist that expanding existing social provisions will not be sufficient to resuscitate citizen efficacy. Citizen efficacy, as Alexis de Tocqueville noted in the nineteenth century, runs on dual tracks.[7] Obviously, democracy won't work for you if you feel that your voice is ignored, your welfare neglected, and your interests systemically disregarded. The functional complexity and technical opacity of modern societies might also deeply undermine and erode one's sense of civic and political efficacy. However, the modern citizen, reconciled to living under a representative system, is not primarily concerned with the exercise of something equivalent to the ancient right and practice of *isegoria* (the equal right of every citizen to speak freely). In fact, the most generalized sense of loss of citizen efficacy occurs elsewhere, well before it surfaces in the political sphere. First and foremost, citizen efficacy is rooted in a person's ability to provide for themselves and their dependents. For a vast majority of people in our time, that means having a steady, decently paying job. In this regard, state-sponsored social provisions such as health care, public schools, old-age pensions, and job training programs serve as infrastructural support and furnish necessary aid, allowing citizens to take care of themselves and their dependents. Second, there are other forms of incapacitating inequalities and discriminations based on race, gender, sexual preference, religion, and ethnicity that also contribute to and compound this generalized sense of loss of citizen efficacy. There are multiple ways in which one is made to feel marginalized and abandoned. Hence, restoring a semblance of citizen efficacy and agency requires more than simply reinstating the recently diminished or dismantled social provisions of a welfare state. It calls for renewing the demos and charting a course toward becoming a more egalitarian and culturally inclusive society.

Calhoun's historical account of how democracy copes with the relatively regular disruptions wrought by capitalist acceleration provides a structural insight about the conflict and tension between the elites and the nonelites. If the struggle for reducing or stabilizing social inequality is directly related to "taming class struggle" and augmenting citizen efficacy, and if every attempt to reduce and stabilize social inequality gets disrupted by the technoeconomic logic of capitalism, then class conflict in a generalized sense cannot be eliminated. The struggle to reduce or stabilize social inequality discloses a palpable structure, one of oscillation. It is not directional. The intensity and magnitude of social inequality fluctuate over time but class conflict does not get progressively better or worse.

This structural insight yields two additional claims regarding how social transformations destabilize the already contentious relationship between the elites and nonelites. First, the negative externalities of periodic sociohistorical transformations affect the lives of elites and nonelites in different ways. As a rule, the disruptions and instabilities that accompany these transformations pose significantly greater economic risk for nonelites than they do for elites, as evident from the differential impact of the financial crisis of 2008 on these two groups.

Second, when a government does respond to the deepening crisis and institutes social programs and provisions to remedy the situation, its impact is compromised by what Calhoun calls the "Bourdieu catch." That is, instead of providing relief for those left behind by the unfolding social transformations, the benefits of new social programs and provisions are captured largely by the more highly educated and better positioned social strata. All of this is intuitively grasped by the nonelites as they begin to notice how utterly the "system" is rigged against them.

Unlike struggles for civil and political liberties, the struggle against socioeconomic inequality is neither directional nor progressive. It does not have a clear telos, a set of final "ends." There are no grand emancipatory narratives in which it takes center stage. Except for those who had once succumbed to the utopian lures of a classless society, those engaged in this struggle rarely entertain the prospect of radically leveling income and wealth. This is a highly variable and contextual struggle, shaped by the history and culture of a given people. It is imagined and fought within the frame of the possible, the feasible, and the negotiable. It involves back and forth movement within a horizontal spread. What is gained can be lost or diminished. To be sure, some gains, such as that of the eight-hour movement, have been permanent and irreversible, but even these provide little solace when job security, health care, pension benefits, and much else are in constant flux. The resultant volatility of socioeconomic inequality makes the conflict between the elites and the nonelites impossible to eradicate and limits the degree to which class struggle might be tamed. This does not mean that in the long history of democracy, the intensity of class conflict and its propensity to produce political discord has remained the same. *Les trente glorieuses* alludes to a time when class conflict was less intense, but never absent. Perhaps, it was already smoldering beneath the surface, not visible to untrained eyes.

Second Degeneration and Neutralizing Ethnonationalism

The idea of conceiving democracy as a telic project, as Taylor does, requires one to think of the project as unfolding on dual tracks: first, democracy unfolds *normatively,* motivated by different, often conflicting, visions and versions of human flourishing; second, it unfolds *narratively,* as a sociohistorical account of who we are, where we came from, and where we are going—a self-hermeneutics of an unfixable "We, the people." One can find such powerful and imaginative narratives, often tinged with myth, in texts as diverse as Walt Whitman's *Democratic Vistas* (1871) and Jawaharlal Nehru's *The Discovery of India* (1946).[8] It is more productive to historicize democracy's checkered career than to posit a refined or perfectible normative model. Such historicization calls forth competing narratives of "We, the people," from which ethnocultural identity (however fictitious) and its disturbing claims to priority can never be fully expunged. Thus, the contested play between the normative and the narrative manifests itself in the guise of a crisis, both structural and historical.

What does it mean to say, as Taylor does, that there are degenerative tendencies intrinsic to the very idea of "We, the people"? Since democracy is an ongoing telic project and struggle, as we have claimed, its agential substance—"We, the people"—can never be permanently ascertained, fixed, or certified. This does not mean that the idea of "the people" has no referent. It is not only an empty signifier, as political theorists Claude Lafort and Ernesto Laclau claim, nor is it a necessary fiction of statecraft, as historian Edmund Morgan insists.[9] On the contrary, it is a sociohistorically sedimented and essentially contested concept whose referent is both elusive and evolving. Hence, there is always a rhetorical and ideological struggle over the meaning of the phrase "We, the people."

This raises the question: What is the underlying structure of the struggle over the meaning of "the people"? In my opinion, there is a similar structured movement to the one we detected in the case of the struggle against socioeconomic inequality. The phrase "We, the people," oscillates between two poles: the "primordial" and the "constitutional" without ever settling at one end of the spectrum. The primordial pole stresses ethnonational and monocultural roots, real or imagined, of a given people. It often invokes an autochthony of the "first people," of the "people of the soil," and of the "heartlanders."[10] It calls for solidarity based on shared language, history, and religion and it looks backward to a golden age of imagined pristine unity unsullied by the differences and divisions afflicting the present. It fears that unity and solidarity are being contaminated by differences from within (minorities) and threatened by differences from without (immigrants). By contrast, the constitutional pole stresses the conscious political will of a self-made people and endorses multicultural difference as well as the myriad world-making lifestyles of their constituents (be they individuals or groups). It celebrates multiplicity, mingling, and hybridity. It proposes to enrich and strengthen unity in and through difference and to cultivate "constitutional patriotism."[11] Each pole has its characteristic bias or belief. The proponents of the primordial pole insist that the core meaning of "We, the people," has a legitimate, verifiable historical basis. Although rhetorically potent, this kind of claim is always of dubious empirical validity. The error haunting the constitutional pole is not an obsession with fixing the meaning of the people, but of ascertaining its directionality. Its proponents claim that "We, the people," is not a static given, but the dynamic "self-making" project of a collective agent capable of progressively undermining claims of ethnonational primordiality and priority. Those taking this position hope and believe that the trajectory of history would favor their side, as in the case of historian David Hollinger's call for a "postethnic America."[12]

It is not easy, however, to dispel, let alone eliminate, ethnonational claims or to annul the popular appeals and resonances they elicit. Both Calhoun and Taylor note that democracy requires strong solidarities to bridge cultural differences as well as socioeconomic divisions and intergenerational discord. Since the great revolutions of the eighteenth century, the democratic project has been closely aligned with the nation-state, its viability and durability dependent on the solidarities the latter facilitates. In modern times, nationalism has been and continues to be the most potent solidarity-building engine.[13] But just as readily as nationalism unifies people, it can also divide and fracture them. Being so closely aligned with the nation-state, democracy can easily become embroiled in exclusionary politics. Democratic institutions, forms, and practices associated with elections and party systems are especially prone to polarization. During the heat of electoral campaigns, ethnonational majorities have a tendency to target minorities with exclusionary rhetoric and read them out of the body politic.

This struggle between the two poles is not an abstract one. It unfolds differently in different national and cultural contexts and has a history that shapes its scope and intensity. It would be inaccurate to pretend that the ethnonational's pull and the constitutional's push are of a uniform force across, say, the United States, Iran, and India. History, culture, and often religion can play crucial roles in mediating the tension between the two poles. To presume that the pull of the ethnonational has been attenuated and quelled in the mature and affluent Western democracies is no less an error than to forsake the constitutional struggle to protect and promote pluralism under the theocratically contained Iranian democracy. India today represents an excellent example of an ongoing struggle in which the two poles are more evenly matched. To be sure, under the Bharatiya Janata Party (BJP) government and its avowed Hindu nationalist majoritarian agenda, the constitutional pole is very much under duress. It is, however, by no means or measure lost or abandoned. The struggle over the meaning of "We, the people," in India, amid all of the country's ethnic, religious, linguistic, and geographic diversity, is fully engaged, as it should be. Democracy is not a guarantee, but a promise of solidarity that "We, the people," must fight to keep amid all our differences. While the fate and the trajectory of a given democracy are not foretold, there are intimations of the things to come, of the challenges to be met so that the struggle may continue.

In short, the ethnonational strand, with all its rhetorical appeal and potency, cannot be abolished. It may go dormant, but only for a time, awaiting the conditions that inevitably invite its resurgence. This does not mean that the primordial pole's claims to validity and priority are legitimate. Instead of hoping that ethnonationalism will run its course and vanish, one should pose a series of constructive questions: Why does the specter of ethnonationalism continue to haunt the democratic project? Under what conditions does this specter erupt, suddenly dominating the political horizon? Why is this eruption named "populism," time and again? Since what stirs and galvanizes ethnonationalism is rooted in nationalism itself, are there strategies for controlling its consequences—perhaps strategies analogous to James Madison's institutional designs to curb and deflect the dangers of unencumbered factionalism?[14] Distinguishing between "good nationalism" and "bad nationalism" is no longer productive, if it ever was. Nationalism is what it is. Evaluating nationalism from a cosmopolitan perspective ignores too much.

Third Degeneration and the Challenge of Majoritarianism

Taylor's third democratic degeneration pertains to the dangers of unchecked "winner-take-all majoritarianism" facilitated by an electoral system based on universal adult suffrage. It is not easy for us to detach the democratic project from a representative form of government based on the principle of majority rule. Today, elections, universal adult suffrage, and majority rule are the basic mechanics of representative democracy. In the liberal imaginary, these basic mechanisms are embedded in, aligned with, and buttressed by a wide range of cultural forms, constitutional norms, and institutional practices, chief among them being the rule of law (especially an independent judiciary), free media, and a well-functioning party system. In the populist imaginary, by contrast, elections, universal adult suffrage, and majority rule stand in for and embody the doctrine of popular sovereignty in action. Elections are when the sleeping sovereigns—the people—awaken to attest to, if nothing else, their sheer existence.[15] Whereas elections are a source of anxiety for liberals because they risk mobilizing the collective agency of the people and activating their unruly collective capacities, for the populist, election time is the time of the sovereign, as evident in the electoral rhetoric of populist leaders such as Narendra Modi in India, Andrés Manuel López Obrador in Mexico, and Recep Tayyip Erdogan in Turkey.[16]

As indicated in Chapter 3, the liberal anxiety about elections and universal adult suffrage has persisted since the time of the French Revolution when a revolutionary avant garde used the name of an incarnated people to justify a reign of "virtuous terror" and purify the body politic. After the French Revolution, restricting and delaying franchise came to be seen as necessary means for deterring future aberrations of political holism.[17] Nonetheless, universal adult suffrage was on its way. The more effective alternative strategy was to devise a "liberal package" of constitutional and institutional mechanisms that promised to curb the concentration of powers in the hands of the government, especially the executive. The same package was also designed to hamper, if not nullify, the collective agency of the people.[18] The "liberal package," having evolved steadily over a long period of time, has become deeply entrenched in the daily workings of modern Western democracies. It is the default mode of our times. Not only does it steer the polity; it also sustains civil society, underwrites the market economy, and colonizes everyday life. Nevertheless, populist sentiments are never fully expunged from the liberal hegemony. Though marginalized and suppressed, the longing for "the people in their collective capacity" lingers submerged beneath the political unconscious, erupting periodically, especially around elections. It is precisely because they are ignored and dismissed as inconsequential that populist sentiments surface as fractures, marring democracy's face.

Democracy, thus deformed, gives rise to majoritarianism, a degenerate form of majority rule. Majoritarianism, like the principle of majority rule, draws its legitimacy from its claim to being a practical expression of popular sovereignty. But unlike majority rule, majoritarianism is unconstrained by liberal constitutional and institutional guardrails. It refuses the label of "deviation." Instead, such majoritarianism unabashedly embraces and endorses "illiberal democracy" for the sake of building a unified national community, as proclaimed by Hungary's Viktor Orbán.[19] The difference is structural. Political majorities, especially those assembled by political parties, are usually coalitions, even when they are led by a dominant ethnic group. Since few, if any, modern societies are homogeneous in every relevant register—class, race, ethnicity, religion, language—a political majority must be continually forged. Hence, the relationship between a majority coalition and its constituents has a dynamic metonymic (parts / whole) structure. Majoritarianism, by contrast, is performative. It springs from the perennial temptation to do away with the laborious negotiation between parts and whole characteristic of coalition building. It proclaims the metaphoric unity of a given people based on an ethnocultural identity, real or imagined.

The evils of majoritarianism—diminishing minority rights and protections, gutting the opposition, and silencing public criticism—are partly built into the very logic of majority rule, but they are also exacerbated by the exclusionary temptations and rhetorics of electoral politics. The majoritarian quest for permanently neutralizing, if not annihilating, the opposition and trying to secure an irreversible electoral majority cannot possibly succeed in the long run. Given the societal complexity and diversity of a modern democracy, one can only govern by building majority coalitions that endure for varying amounts of time, never permanently. The majoritarian temptation in electoral politics is palpable and ever present. There is a constant oscillation between the coalition politics of majority rule and the identity politics of majoritarianism, making it difficult to draw a hard and fast line between the two. Traditional political parties committed to coalition politics sometimes succumb to majoritarian lures. Similarly, majoritarian movements and parties are often forced to enter into coalitions and alliances out of necessity. Majoritarian rhetoric, often harsh, divisive, and exclusionary, might be accompanied by more conciliatory politics.

Take the case of how India's electoral politics have evolved since 1952, the year of the first national elections after independence. In the afterglow of independence, the dominant ruling Congress Party, ideologically secular and social democratic, fielded candidates without paying much attention to the caste demographics of electoral districts. In 1967, a mere fifteen years later, in the wake of the fourth elections in the lower house of Parliament, having lost its allure as the vanguard of the Indian independence movement, the Congress Party dramatically changed its electoral strategy. For the Congress Party, as well as for virtually every other party, caste demographics became the single most important criterion in selecting competitive candidates at every level of government—federal, state, and local. This shift was justified as a purely pragmatic decision rather than as a sign of ideological backsliding. Since then, the ideological basis of caste-based electoral strategies has grown stronger, and the logistics that provide its infrastructure more sophisticated (aided by big data analytics). It is customary (and to a large measure accurate) to characterize the BJP as a Hindu majoritarian party and the Congress Party as an inclusionary secular party. While their ideological positions diverge, on key "minority" issues—especially those pertaining to religion and the caste system—their electoral strategies substantially converge. The ideology, rhetoric, and logistics of the BJP are better aligned than those of the Congress Party, which appears to give the BJP an advantage. It might be an error, however, to assume that the pragmatics of misalignment are always and necessarily a disadvantage. The BJP often fields a Muslim candidate in a Muslim-majority electoral district.[20]

What does this tell us? The ethnocultural demographic unconscious, suppressed in the civil tongue of ideological discourses, continuously manifests itself in strategic thinking and data analysis. The point here is not to deconstruct the surface discourse of ideologies, be they liberal or conservative or even reactionary, to reveal that they are all complicit in yielding to ethnocultural calculations in their electoral strategies. On the contrary, the point is to recognize and acknowledge that ethnocultural demographic calculations are built into the coalition politics of majority rule itself. The historical promise that shifting and negotiable *interests* would replace enduring and nonnegotiable *identities* under the regime of capitalist modernity has not fully materialized.[21] Hence, the coalition politics of majority rule, especially in mass societies where numbers matter, is always in danger of being drawn into the politics of identities and succumbing to majoritarian temptations.[22]

Today, the BJP in India is being painted as a paradigm case of majoritarian politics. At one level, this characterization works. The BJP's ideology, rhetoric, and logistics confirm it, especially in the last two decades as the BJP has emerged as an increasingly viable national party and alternative to the Congress Party. Since its ascension to power in 2014 and its resounding victory in 2019, the BJP has pursued an audacious Hindu majoritarian agenda, marching not only through the streets but through the institutions. Yet, they don't command the majority. While India is 80 percent Hindu, the BJP has never won more than 40 percent of all eligible voters. (The same is true of Donald Trump's election.) This should not be a source of comfort to anyone who is dismayed by the BJP's political agenda. The basic political fact of representative democratic politics is that majoritarianism does not require the support of or ratification by a majority of eligible voters.

The American founding fathers promoted and endorsed a representative form of government not simply as a necessity in a large country, but as a desirable institutional formation to curb popular passions and deter the formation of tyrannous majorities. Today, the exact opposite is occurring as the electoral calculus of the representative system can easily generate majoritarian tyranny in the absence of an actual majority. In multiparty elections, a ruling party facing a fragmented opposition can win a commanding majority in the parliament without necessarily securing the majority of votes cast. This is not an uncommon phenomenon among existing democracies across the globe. This is why the fate of modern democracy cannot be tied exclusively to the representative form of government and its procedural twin, elections. Neither is capable of mastering and steering what is unleashed by the doctrine of popular sovereignty as embodied in universal adult suffrage. The liberal strategy of simultaneously invoking popular sovereignty and bridling it with constitutional norms and institutional constraints is looking exhausted and may be at its limit. One needs other means to resist and combat those majoritarian politics not grounded in actual majorities.

Each one of the three degenerations identified by Taylor has an oscillatory structure. They are not directional. They are rooted in the very structure of democracy and its representative form. They are ineliminable. Class conflicts and tensions are not going to disappear. The same is true of the politics and rhetoric of ethnonationalism and its exclusionary tendencies and temptations. "Winner-take-all" majoritarianism is imminent to the representative form of government, universal adult suffrage, and the principle of majority rule. Democracy cannot be saved simply by renovating the representative system, refining checks and balances, and cultivating liberal norms. These strategies are all necessary but not enough. The oscillatory structure demands extra-institutional pressures rooted in the demos itself. It calls for a politics of the demos, a politics of periodic direct action by the people. Democracy is a permanent struggle of the people and by the people for fairness, equity, and recognition for the people.

Rethinking Direct Action

As indicated earlier, and given the dynamism of capitalism today, "Engels's pause," the hiatus between Karl Polanyi's two movements—the great societal transformation triggered by industrial capitalism and the delayed political response to its derangements and negative externalities—keeps recurring at shorter intervals than when Polanyi recounted them in his 1944 work on *The Great Transformation*. These pauses strain democracy and call forth a distinctive mode of political response from the nonelites, the governed. That mode of politics may be broadly characterized as "direct action."

The expression "direct action" was frequently deployed by Martin Luther King Jr. during the US civil rights movement in the 1960s. In King's political imagination (which owes much to Gandhi), "direct action" implies a particular way of staging "the people" and refers to a mode of movement-based mobilization that functions as an alternative to exercising political power through elections or through parliament. "Direct action" is also regarded as an alternative to the legal route for redressing grievances when the court delays and denies social justice. For King, as well as for Gandhi, "direct action" suggests nonviolence. I will try to offer a different (not necessarily violent) genealogy of "direct action." This other genealogy takes the same agents as King and Gandhi—crowds, riots, and uprisings—but looks to the molecular rather than the molar and the local rather than the national to explore direct action's scopes, temporalities, and addressees. More than anything else, I want to invite you to rethink "direct action" (in all its ubiquity) in an age of globe-spanning rapid growth, selective abundance, asymmetrical affluence, and deepening inequality.

Since all historically known societies are marked by the unequal distribution of income and wealth—of rank and status as well as of access to resources and opportunities—there is always palpable social conflict and tension between the two broadly constituted but internally heterogeneous groups, the elites and the nonelites. It is also the case that while the nonelites are numerically vastly greater than the elites, the latter invariably control, manage, and steer the polity, economy, and culture. As David Hume perceptively observed in the mid-eighteenth century, such is the case not just under autocracies, but also under popular modes of governance:

> Nothing appears more surprising to those who consider human affairs with a philosophical eye than the easiness with which the many are governed by the few and the implicit submission with which men resign their own sentiments and passions to those of their rulers. When we inquire by what means this wonder is effected, we shall find that, as force is always on the side of the governed, the governors have nothing to support them but opinion. It is, therefore, on opinion only that government is founded, and this maxim extends to the most

despotic and most military governments as well as to the most free and most popular.[23]

While rightly claiming that the few invariably govern the many, Hume appears to have overestimated "the easiness with which the many are governed by the few." There is a constant tension as the few seek to uphold the status quo and maintain their hegemonic control over the polity by continuously defending and justifying highly stratified group formations and unequal allocations of resources and opportunities. Hume also overstates the power of opinion.

This ongoing struggle between the few and the many is not confined to the ideological or discursive planes but is constantly shifting and emerges on the extra-discursive and bodily planes of direct action. While this shift to the extra-discursive and bodily planes may occasionally be eruptive and violent, these are certainly not constitutive features. There is a tendency, especially among liberal and deliberative democrats, to view direct action as a prelude to, if not the equivalent of, violence. As poignantly and eloquently stated by King in his "Letter from Birmingham Jail," this characterization is unwarranted. In a section famously known as "Why We Cannot Wait," King explains to his "liberal" friends and supporters why he must resort to direct action (and disobedience) by marching in the streets and why he cannot, as they urge him, stick exclusively to legislative and judicial routes to seek redress and pursue racial justice.[24]

The social conflict that structures the relationship between the elites and the nonelites is also intensified and destabilized by social change. Often propelled by technoeconomic innovations and organizational changes promoted by the elites in the name of progress and prosperity, modes of social reproduction are continuously transforming. This sort of transformation, of varying intensity and scope, has been underway intermittently since the onset of the Industrial Revolution. The ensuing changes, especially when they are dramatic, can alter and destabilize existing social arrangements, straining the already unequal relation between the elites and the nonelites. Even when these changes might actually augment the wealth of a given political community, they risk accentuating the inequality between the elites and the nonelites. It might very well be the case that in the long run some of these changes—scientific and technological as well as socioeconomic—benefit the nonelites. There is hardly any question that the life expectancy of the nonelites, along with that of the elites, has steadily increased over at least the last three hundred years. The same can be said of literacy. Such an enlarged temporal horizon has little resonance, however, for those caught in Engels's pause. Dramatic changes in the modes of social reproduction hit the nonelites harder than the elites. Given their limited resources, the nonelites cannot wait indefinitely for the initiation of Polanyi's second movement—the delayed political response (or the corrective state action) to mitigate the negative externalities of opaque and distant structural changes. They must act and they do, with or without a clear agenda or a full understanding of what is to be done. They must pressure the powers that be to initiate the second movement and they do. Direct action is the objective corelative of a temporally constituted political subjectivity heralding "why we cannot wait."

Within the liberal and deliberative democratic imaginary, "direct action" is seen as an unstable and potentially dangerous "third" option available to those wishing to protest and publicize their grievances against an existing order. Further, it is assumed that in advanced Western democracies—given their mature liberal package of formal rights and rule of law, built on an inclusionary history and character and bolstered by a robust public sphere—there would be decreasing need for any aggrieved group, socioeconomically or ethnoculturally marked, to exercise this "third option." Without endorsing their tactics, liberal and deliberative democrats might understand why an aggrieved group might resort to direct action in a fledgling or corrupt democracy or in a democracy that has turned "ugly." But, in a mature and well-functioning democracy where the two legitimate and reliable options for redress—legislative and judicial—are fully available, liberal and deliberative democrats struggle to decipher the rationale behind direct action's recurrence. There is a deep historical amnesia involved in this way of thinking. What is forgotten here is the story of how each of the defining features of mature democracies, including the coveted liberal package, were fought for and secured through some type of direct action. There is a venerable tradition of reverting to direct action, time and again, both to enhance democracy and to arrest its degeneration. That tradition is alive and resurgent today. In fact, when democracy is conceived as a telic project, direct action cannot but be a constitutive feature.

While there is a deep and abiding anxiety about direct action among liberal and deliberative democrats, even they don't summarily reject and dismiss every type. They recognize that the politics of protest are an integral part of democratic tradition and struggle. Still, they retain cautious reservations.

"Direct action" is a rich and heterogeneous category made up of a broad repertoire of forms, genres, rituals and practices. Some species of it are deemed more legitimate and acceptable than others. The acceptable ones, such as petitioning, peaceful marches, and candle-light vigils, are often referred to as "civil" or "public" actions. By contrast, "sit-ins," "die-ins," "taking the knee," burning effigies, and human blockades are deemed "uncivil," disrespectful, and coercive. It is worth noting that these allegedly "uncivil" actions are by no means spontaneous. Burning an effigy is not the same as burning a public transportation bus. One must make an effigy, which takes time, talent, and planning before committing it to flame in public.

The distinction between the acceptable and unacceptable usually turns on two criteria. Any direct action associated with organized social movements with a palpable agenda and an accountable leadership is deemed acceptable and sometimes even recognized as unavoidable. The scholarly literature on social movements is extensive. It covers a wide range of historical and contemporary social movements and includes a dizzying number of causes and issues, unfolding within and across myriad national and cultural spheres. This literature shows that social movements are not reduceable to direct action; the latter is only one feature among many. Social movements often promote their agendas by legislative and judicial routes. They solicit publicity through the institutions of the public sphere; they enlist material and ideological support from civil society's figures and forces; and they align themselves with political parties, electorally as well as legislatively. Direct action is more dominant and critical in some social movements than in others, but it is never obligatory. What makes social movements credible, legitimate, and acceptable is precisely their flexible multipronged strategy for civic action.

By contrast, what is generally seen as unacceptable and undesirable is direct action associated with disorganized, leaderless, and relatively unplanned (if not wholly spontaneous) eruptions of discontent. Such eruptions are viewed as undesirable and unacceptable because they allegedly devolve into riots. There is a wide spectrum of direct actions that stretches from well-organized social movements at one end to eruptive riots at the other. Within the liberal and deliberative democratic imaginary, riots have no redeeming social value. They are seen as futile and counterproductive. Riots harm the cause that is being espoused, provided a cause is even legible amidst the mayhem; they disfigure the grievance that is being articulated. More than anything else, what fatally discredits riots is that they are destructive and violent. Here we come upon the second criterion for distinguishing between acceptable and unacceptable modes of direct action: the possibility of collective violence.

Regardless, riots are ubiquitous. People riot all the time—not every day but with alarming frequency, both in the past and in the present. People riot everywhere—across every national and cultural space, in poor countries and in rich countries alike and under authoritarian as well as democratic regimes. People riot over all sorts of things: the price of bread, oil, and onions, the publication of a book, the screening of a film, the drawing of a cartoon; they riot on account of police brutality, political corruption, and desecration of the holy places; they riot when subjected to ethnic or racial slurs (real or imagined) and when continuously deprived of basic necessities such as water, electricity, and sanitation; they riot when justice is denied and petitions are ignored; they riot after soccer games, cricket games, music concerts, and also before, during, and after elections; the list of occasions and grievances that can precipitate riots can be extended indefinitely.[25] Instead of declining and disappearing, riots appear to be multiplying, not only in the global South but also in the global North. Wikipedia lists twenty-four well-documented riot or riot-like incidents in 2019 alone, of which ten occurred in Euro-America.[26] They are an unavoidable feature of the contemporary ecology of protest. What are we to make of this?

Here again, one has to distinguish between instances of protest and riots. They are not reducible to each other. Protests come in various forms. As indicated above, direct action or protests staged by organized social movements are different from relatively spontaneous eruptions of discontent. However, a steady accumulation of eruptive moments in response to a palpable pattern of repeated injuries can coalesce and initiate a powerful social movement, as in the case of #Blacklivematter in 2013 and the subsequent founding of the Movement for Black Lives coalition in 2015. But in themselves, spontaneous eruptions might be theorized as contingent "moments," which are very different from planned protest events associated with social movements. The Chinese Academy of Social Sciences, which keeps count of such eruptive protest incidents in mainland China, euphemistically refers to them as "mass group incidents."[27] While any protest / demonstration can result in a riot, eruptive protests are seen as particularly prone to devolve into riots. This is not actually true. There are many eruptive protests all over the globe today, even in the authoritarian and highly securitized China, and most of them do not become riots leading to the destruction of public facilities and the looting of private property. There is, however, a long-standing tendency to equate them. This tendency is rooted in the fear of crowds, especially political crowds, assembled to express their grievances or to rally for a cause or a candidate/leader.

Starting with Plato's image of the demos as "a great beast," there is a persistent anti-crowd sentiment running through Western political thought. With rare exceptions, such as Machiavelli and Spinoza, there is hardly a political thinker who does not consider the bridling of the multitude an essential task for constitution-making or the art of governing.[28] In the aftermath of the French Revolution, this fear of crowds, mobs, and mass gatherings intensified—as is evident from Hippolyte Taine's hyperbolic, but highly popular, account of the French revolutionary crowds. Writing in the wake of the wreckage wrought by the Paris Commune (1871), Taine traces the susceptibility of revolutionary crowds to engage in acts of wanton destruction and bloodthirsty carnage back to their inaugural moment in the great revolution itself. According to Taine, driven by visions of emancipation and equality, ordinary French people who were once sensible and sober became unhinged and reverted to the savage ways of a "state of nature." They turned their back on the tradition that regulates desire, belief, and conduct in accordance with one's station within a stable hierarchical order. Thus, individual autonomy and social responsibility were both set aside as hordes of people looted and pillaged. Basic instincts were let loose as licentiousness, alcoholism, and gratuitous violence prevailed. Such is the orgiastic and contagious nature of crowd behavior. Hence, in Taine's account, nothing threatens civilization more than a crowd, with its egalitarian ethos and leveling impulse. The hollow republican promise of equality culminates in "spontaneous anarchy," followed by mob rule.[29]

Buttressed by the unavoidability of crowds in modern life under the sway of industrialization and urbanization, this anxiety begins to acquire a psychosocial dimension in the writings of Scipio Sighele, Gabriel Tarde, and Gustave Le Bon in the last quarter of the nineteenth century, following the tumultuous days of the Paris Commune. In their theorizations of crowds and crowd behavior, each of these three thinkers was decisively influenced by Hippolyte Taine's revisionary historical interpretation of the revolutionary crowds and mobs of the French Revolution.[30] With the coming of mass society, this tradition is further thematized and bolstered in the writings of Sigmund Freud, Ortega y Gasset, and many others, culminating in Elias Canetti's monumental *Crowds and Power* (1960).[31] Most of this literature (with the rare exception of Canetti's book) is suspicious of and hostile to crowds, comparing collective action in crowd formations to the behavior of the "drunk," the "irrational woman," and the "mentally deranged."[32]

While this is not a place to summarize the complex genealogy of the anti-crowd thesis in Western psychosocial and political thought, it should suffice to note that the proponents of liberal-deliberative democracy remain deeply fearful of crowds and mass gatherings. From that perspective, there is something intrinsically "illiberal" about the crowd to the extent it leads to the dissolution of the "individual." Within the liberal imaginary, the individual is the bedrock of social ontology, moral responsibility, and economic calculation, and the crowd jeopardizes all those invaluable assets. Every crowd is a potential mob and susceptible to rioting.[33] This way of thinking is not conducive to critically exploring one of the most striking political phenomena of our time, the return of crowds to public space. The specter that haunts Western-style liberal democracy today is no longer guerillas in the hills or generals with armored tanks, but justifiably frustrated and angry people marching in the streets and assembling in the squares. This phenomenon is often mischaracterized as the populist upsurge and gets equated with the huge political rallies of Donald Trump, Narendra Modi, Recep Tayyip Erdogan, and other authoritarian political figures, whose divisive and ethnonationalist rhetoric is distinctly "illiberal," even though it is staged on a democratic platform. But this phenomenon of the coming of the people, their embodied appearance in concrete multiplicity, in public spaces across the world, is much wider, deeper, and more consequential. This is not the first coming of the people, nor will it be the last because they have always been there, but invisible and inaudible. People becoming visible and audible, from time to time, in their collective capacity as a crowd or as an assembly, is not an orderly or a sequential process. One does not stand in a line to become visible and audible and to be hailed as a collective political subject. It happens suddenly as an event, and it is often misrecognized and dismissed by the ruling elites. This is not helpful because when people rise periodically in times of crisis, they do so to correct and renew democracy, not to disfigure and undermine it.

The Phenomenology of Political Discontent and the Imperative of Direct Action

When nonelites feel a sense of discontent, when they are aggrieved, when they are marginalized and ignored, how do they react? They may patiently endure a desperate situation for a while, but without other means of recourse, they will eventually begin to protest. To be sure, shaped by precipitating issues as well as national and cultural contexts, the scales and expressions of discontent vary. A putative phenomenology of political discontent—that is, how an aggrieved group of nonelites experiences, understands, and expresses its condition—is a temporally structured interpretive enterprise. It is imperative to recognize that the temporal horizons of elites and nonelites diverge radically; they experience the flow of time and its contingencies and urgencies differently. To dismiss the mounting number of riot-like incidents as the irrational eruptive flailing of malcontents does not advance our understanding of why, today, we are facing a veritable global protest tsunami.

One might begin by making a distinction between the expression and manifestation of discontent, on the one hand, and the organization and mobilization of that discontent toward a project for change, on the other. The latter minimally requires a set of explicit demands and an addressee (often a national, provincial, or local state) and often calls forth additional actors from the folds of political society—sympathetic NGOs, interested political parties, concerned civil servants, and sometimes, even the police. How the expression and manifestation of discontent maps onto or transforms into an organized movement for change is a critical constitutive moment in the unfolding of direct action. Two things should be noted here. First, every incident of protest does not always get organized into a movement for change, but a series of such incidents does prepare the ground for initiating a movement for change. This is why, prompted by the expressive politics of an aggrieved people, direct action often springs from the ground up—from the streets and squares. Second, direct action does not always align with electoral politics, legislative priorities, and judicial proceedings. This is because direct action tends to pursue immediate relief ahead of enduring solutions. Here, once again, dismissing the former as a band-aid tactic misses the point. The temporalities governing the exigencies of direct action undertaken by nonelites radically diverge from the temporalities of institutional governance administered by the ruling elites.

Even before a horizon limited to immediate relief, the temporalities and tactics of direct action vary significantly from case to case. For instance, the immediate relief sought during an "onion riot" is different from the elongated duration of slum-dwellers, charged with squatting, resisting eviction. These two types of direct action occur often in India. In the former case, relief arrives swiftly as state officials scramble to reduce and stabilize the market price of onions, an indispensable ingredient in the rather austere diet of Indian subalterns. In the latter case, slum-dwellers resist eviction by creating local associations and movements and soliciting support from NGOs, political parties, and sympathetic civil servants. Incidents of direct action recur as onion prices continue to fluctuate and attempts to evict squatting slum-dwellers are repeated. While government bureaucrats appear to lack the foresight to stabilize the price of basic staples—such as onions—the elites of the ruling party lack the political will to evict the squatting slum-dwellers, often considered a powerful vote-bank. Hence, there is rarely an enduring solution to such problems. Instances of direct action of this sort are a common feature of the everyday life of the lower and more precarious segments of the nonelites in India and elsewhere in the global South. For the urban poor, direct action functions, to borrow James Scott's phrase, as one of the reliable "weapons of the weak."[34] In the global North, the situation is more complicated. It is not primarily poverty and other forms of severe material duress, but powerlessness or the general lack of citizen efficacy in shaping legislative agendas and public policies that pushes people toward resorting to direct action politics. The appeal of direct action is particularly compelling when people are facing obdurate and persistent social problems such as ethnoracial discrimination, gun violence, police brutality, sexual harassment, environmental degradation, housing insecurity, job precarity, and growing social inequality and the governmental response is slow and feeble. This is evident from the direct action agenda, practices, and strategies adopted by contemporary social movements such as #BLM, #MeToo, Occupy Wall Street, March for Our Lives, and many others in the United States.

These multiple modes and variable temporalities of protest constitute a general ecology of direct action. Operating on multiple temporal layers, nonelites are remarkably resilient. As indicated before, while defending squatters' rights, slum-dwellers don't simply erupt into noisy agitation as they would in the event of an "onion riot." Instead, they organize and petition to secure access to necessities, such as drinking water and electricity and basic health services such as vaccination. They also build alliances with sympathetic outsiders in civil society whose agendas and temporalities differ from their own.[35] Sometimes, these divergent temporalities collide—for instance, when the squatters (or some other aggrieved group) shift to an agitational mode and elicit disapproval from their civil society partners. The incommensurability of temporalities evinced here is not any different than the one noted in the celebrated case of King explaining to his disapproving liberal friends that his people cannot wait any longer and must take to the streets *now*. It should be noted that the squatters switch to an eruptive mode of protest only when they are confronted with the threat of an imminent eviction or when (as is more often the case) access to basic necessities is deliberately disrupted by the authorities to harass, intimidate, or extort them. While forced to live in a state of permanent duress, the squatters and similarly disenfranchised do not live in a state of permanent rage, ready to erupt at the slightest provocation. Nor are they prisoners of time. They just happen to be more alert to its vicissitudes (than those who wear Apple Watches). Thus, to understand how expressions and manifestations of discontent evolve into organized movements for change, one has to pay close attention to the multiple temporalities motivating different groups and setting their agendas.

These temporalities, in turn, are shaped by the location and the addressee of direct action. To explicate the dynamics between location and addressee, one needs to distinguish, to borrow terminology from the French philosopher Gilles Deleuze, between two types of direct action: molecular and molar.[36] To be sure, the varied manifestations of both molar and molecular direct action share one common feature: they involve physical assembly of one sort or another.[37] But we need to think of assembly not simply as it appears in the First Amendment, as an abstract "right of people to peaceably assemble, and to petition the Government for a redress of grievances." Instead, what's required is a phenomenology of assembly capable of exploring the lived experience of people coming together, discovering hitherto unknown solidarities among strangers, and imagining common horizons. Charles Taylor believes that when they coalesce, such solidarity-inducing performative acts of mutual display occurring in distinct "topical common spaces," give rise to the "metatopical" public sphere, and hence to a reflexive understanding of "We, the people," as a collective agent.[38]

The eruptive onion riots as well as the relatively organized slum-dwellers' agitations are essentially local and molecular. The latter, however, might have national implications. Though each slum community organizes itself at a local level and, when necessary, agitates in its own defense, individual slum communities may also become a part of citywide and nationwide (and sometimes even global) slum-dwellers' organizations and movements. Despite these affiliations, slum protest and resistance remain predominantly molecular, arising most often out of local contingencies. A community of slum-dwellers might be drawn into wider spatial and longer temporal horizons when their partners in civil society and their (electorally motivated) political allies help steer their petitions and promote their causes through the legislature and the courts, but the gravitational center of their grievances is local, and the structure of their performative politics of discontent is molecular.

By contrast, even when triggered by a local case, India's anti-rape protests are quickly assimilated into a national frame and narrative. While the specificity of the transgression remains highly salient to the aggrieved (the survivor, their family, and friends), the ensuing protest is read as attesting to and bolstering the broader ongoing legislative and judicial campaigns being waged across the whole society. The same can be said of anticorruption campaigns. The provocations are usually local, but the response is often national. While the state remains a primary addressee, these protests and campaigns are also aimed more generally, as they seek to transform widespread indifference and resignation by raising societal awareness and shifting public opinion. Here, the temporal horizons extend further into the future: navigating courts and legislatures at one level and transforming culture at another require different types of organization and take time. The structure of these movements is molar rather than molecular.

We might think of molar protests and movements as phenomena of the maidan (or the square). They are national in focus and orientation. While they are often orchestrated to occur simultaneously in many places, they are bound together by agenda and addressee. The national character is also highlighted by massive rallies and demonstrations in capital city squares or similarly marked places, such as the Lincoln Memorial (the March on Washington, Washington DC, 1963), Camp Crame (People Power Revolution, Quezon City, 1986), Tiananmen Square (Beijing, 1989), Azad Square (Tehran, 1979 and 2008), Tahrir Square (Cairo, 2011), Syntagma Square (Athens, 2011), Zuccotti Park (New York, 2011), Taksim Square (Istanbul, 2013) and Maidan Nezalezhnosti (Kiev, 2013). As people of diverse backgrounds and identities assemble, these protests enact a commonly held citizenship—one recent example being the protests surrounding India's new citizenship law, which blatantly discriminates against Muslim immigrants.[39] By bridging differences, however temporarily, the enactment incarnates *the people*, a feat that established authorities are unable to accomplish. Thus, by way of a synecdoche, a series of dispersed protesting assemblies centripetally linked to a highly publicized and massive capital rally, performs the sovereign unity of the people.

Almost without exception, these molar protests brandish their disciplined, organized, and nonviolent character. Occasionally, they might devolve into riots, but that is not the way they are conceived and staged by the people and parties involved. On the contrary, considerable energy is expended to show-case their law-abiding pacifism, casting the protest as an orderly expression of grievances and the assembly as sober claimants petitioning for redress. Along these lines, one of the most extraordinary narratives to come out of the two long weeks of protest in Tahrir Square during the Arab Spring was of seg-ments of the assembly cleaning up the refuse and debris left behind every evening.[40] Lest they be mistaken for a mob, they made their message clear: the protesters were disciplined and civic-minded people.

As distinct from the maidan paradigm, the molecular mode of political protest—vastly more frequent and geographically diverse, at least in the global South—might be best characterized as a politics of the street. To be sure, the phrase the "politics of the street," deployed here to contrast and distinguish it from the "politics of the maidan," is not ideal. After all, the people who assemble to protest in a city square often march through adjoining streets to get there. (In fact, marching through the streets, to the square, is a routine occurrence in organized molar demonstrations.) One comes to a public square, however, to protest for a specific duration. One might end up occupying a public venue for an extended period of time—as in the cases of the Tahrir Square demonstrations and Occupy Wall Street at Zuccotti Park—but sooner or later the protest ends and the square reverts to its civil status and function. The maidan is a place of coming and going.

By contrast, I use "street" to signal the most common and proximate "public space" where the people—especially the nonelites—live and work. Within the paradigm of the politics of the street, protest involves a wide range of agitational forms, including rioting, that disrupt the daily flow of everyday life. These protests are not conveniently scheduled for, say, Sunday afternoons. They erupt and disrupt unexpectedly, but often. They make no normative claims to incarnate the people as a whole. Instead, they actively pressure the government to remedy a variety of intolerable conditions, ma-terial deprivations, and collective indignities in specific contexts. Numerous race riots in in the United States, often triggered by excessive and fatal po-lice violence directed at members of the Black minority community, fall into this molecular category. Similarly, those involved in periodic prison riots in the United States, Brazil, Mexico, and elsewhere in the Americas, excluded as they are from the public sphere altogether, make no claim to embody or speak for the people as a unified whole, a national body. These riots are strictly local contextually and temporally, even when they point to a larger problem and capture national attention. Eschewing transcendence, a politics of the street situates protest within multiple registers of everyday life, while remaining connected to larger geopolitical and institutional problematics. With a deep but confounding connection to everyday life, a politics of the street calls attention to an immediate dimension of the experiences of an aggrieved people, a far cry from the recurrent fictions of national unity and democratic equality.

The politics of the street does not merely refer to the fact that people pass through the street during a protest, which they certainly do, but to something more. Today, many people in the global South live either on the streets or in a nearby slum. Streets and slums are symbiotically related, with the latter proliferating at an astonishing speed. While more than two billion people live in slums or slum-like conditions today, the figure is expected to double by 2030. By then, we will certainly be living on what historian Mike Davis calls "The Planet of Slums."[41] The street and the slum have multiple functions: they serve as workshops for producing goods and services, as markets for exchanging, as theaters for self-fashioning, and, more than anything else, as schools for learning how to live under permanent duress. In the autobiographical writings of both the American Black Panthers and the Indian Dalit Panthers, the street and the slum (or ghetto) are often characterized as the primary sites of pedagogy for the oppressed. The street is where people mingle; where they size one another up; where *mutual display* occurs; where common horizons, however fleetingly, are established. According to Marx, only the industrial proletariat, not the scattered peasantry, is capable of collective revolutionary consciousness and action because they work and live together in a common space that discloses their mutual plight, their state of being exploited and oppressed by the bourgeois.[42] Today, the street has replaced the factory, and something akin to a slum consciousness has replaced class consciousness.

An exploration of the phenomenology of political discontent, be it in the global South or in the global North, must begin where the people, the nonelites, live, congregate, and resist. While the general ecology of direct action is spatially and temporally diverse, the molecular politics of street protests are an indispensable and foundational constituent of democracy. To renew the battered demos today, to arrest and reverse the democratic degenerations discussed in this volume, we must first learn to read the expressions of political discontent germinating and circulating all around us. The world is as full of signs of discontent as it is brimming with restless collective energy, ready to be tapped for productive mobilizations. The democratically mature and economically affluent countries of the Western world are also witnessing molecular manifestations of discontent. More and more protests are flaring up over simple "wallet issues" such as rising fuel prices and subway fare hikes. Not long ago, riots over rising fuel prices were the domain of countries such as Nigeria, ironically a major exporter of oil. Then, in October 2018, they came to France rather dramatically with the *mouvement des gilets jaunes*. As they decry "Les élites parlent de fin du monde, quand nous, on parle de fin du mois" (the elites talk about the end of the world, while we talk about the end of the month), we need to ask whether the temporalities governing the actions of the *gilets jaunes* in France are materially different from the temporalities propelling onion rioters in India.[43]

The *gilets jaunes* are part of a larger phenomenon of eruptive direct action that has spread across a distressed if affluent Europe and includes the Indignados in Spain, the anti-austerity Direct Democracy Now activists in Greece, and many others. Aside from the "wallet issue," nonelites all over the world share a simmering discontent over their sheer powerlessness— their voices unheard, their demands ignored, their actions scorned, and any vestige of citizen efficacy evaporated. This feeling of marginalization and abandonment might result in a withdrawal from democratic participation in any form, or it might succumb to the lures of a xenophobic exclusionary politics and the promise of an easy fix. The only way to fight these negative tendencies is to renew the demos. To do that requires embracing "direct action" and harnessing the many forms and genres of its resources and energies, rather than anxiously tolerating its fitfulness and struggling in vain to extinguish its eruptions. To secure progressive social change on both economic and cultural fronts, it is imperative for organized social movements, relevant civil society stakeholders, and electorally oriented political parties to engage with and draw on the enormous reservoir of emancipatory energy that "direct action" politics is capable of releasing and thus radically transforming the political imaginary, as in the case of the George Floyd protests in the United States recently.

7

What Is to Be Done?

CRAIG CALHOUN AND CHARLES TAYLOR

Democracy is at risk. Citizens feel disempowered. Political identity is fragmented and contested. Those who win elections seek to make their advantages permanent, manipulating laws and undermining the future of democracy as they do.

If any of this was in doubt, events of the last few years make it clear. These reveal enthusiasm for demagogues, sympathy for authoritarianism, antipathy to informed dialogue, and delusion by conspiracy theories. There has been an armed assault on the US capitol and political polarization undermining public health during a pandemic. Resurgent far-right movements declare willingness to sacrifice democracy in their campaigns to "save" Western civilization and whiteness.

We have told this story of democracy's degeneration in the neoliberal era mostly with examples from the United States and to a lesser extent Canada and Europe. Our discussion of what is to be done is even more skewed toward the United States. Potential actions are inevitably specific to national context, though we think the issues faced in the United States are exemplary for democracies more widely. Indeed, the degeneration of democracy is a broader story, shared with varying particulars by many societies around the world where democracy has seemed deeply established.

Nowhere do the challenges to democracy come just from individually iniquitous politicians or from populist movements. We have stressed erosion of democracy's social foundations. Inequality is extreme and accompanied by high levels of disruption. Instability, precarity, and loss have devastated once-prosperous middle and working classes. Institutions have deteriorated, communities have been undercut. Political parties are broken, functioning as little more than ideologically polarized fundraising machines. Elections may sometimes reassure us that countries are pulling back from the regimes most damaging to democracy. But those relieved that US voters defeated Donald Trump in 2020 have been alarmed as fanatics fought the electoral outcome to a shocking extent and as Trump retained power over the Republican Party. In any case, the problems are deeper than individuals, or even which party is in power.

The situation is only partially different in India, the world's largest democracy. The middle class is still growing, but there is also enormous volatility. As Chapters 5 and 6 reveal, new and old inequalities collide and political inclusion is far from complete. Institutions struggle to keep up, let alone progress. In India and everywhere, the future of democracy depends both on addressing problems in political institutions and processes and on renewing the underlying social conditions for democracy. Democracy will not thrive and may not even have a future without social transformation.

We need history to understand our present predicament. History reveals ways in which democracies have made progress in the past and challenges they confronted. But nostalgia is a poor guide to possible futures. We cannot just restore the kind of social democratic compromise with capitalism that shaped *les trente glorieuses*. The social democracy—or democratic socialism—of the industrial era focused on adding economic agendas to political ones. Crucially, equality was brought into better balance with liberty. Now we also need to pay attention to the social in social democracy, the search for solidarity in ever more complex and mostly very large-scale societies.

We need a new political, economic, and social vision even while we face immediate challenges. Fighting back from the economic as well as public health consequences of the devastating Covid-19 pandemic could have brought more of this than it has. There is discussion of the importance of large-scale government action, though how much there has really been a turn away from neoliberal orthodoxies remains unclear.[1] We continue to face upheavals in employment and deep inequality rooted in the economic transformation that accelerated from the 1970s. Climate change is bringing floods, fires, heat waves, and droughts. It is exacerbating the effects of other forms of environmental damage from soil erosion to polluted air and exhausted water supplies. Artificial intelligence, genetic engineering, and other new technologies demand new regulatory frameworks. Yet domestic solidarity is low in nearly every democratic country, and global cooperation is undercut by political and economic instability and declining US leadership.

We need to do a lot, all at once, and soon. This chapter doesn't lay out a whole program. It suggests some specific foci for action to empower citizens, build inclusive solidarity, and head off majoritarian efforts to capture permanent power. Then it makes a case for why we need to think big, how interconnected our needs and challenges are, what it means to reclaim commitment to the public good, and the possibility that a social movement centered on meeting environmental, economic, and social challenges can also renew democracy. First, though, we want to head off the notion that populism is an independent prime mover and that overcoming it will reverse democracy's degenerations.

Populism Is Not the Issue

It is tempting to blame democracy's problems on populism (and many analysts take this intellectual shortcut). As we discussed in Chapter 2, this is misleading and does not offer adequate paths forward.

First off, populists have long pressed for more democracy. Early populists such as the Levelers of the English Civil War helped shape the very idea of popular sovereignty and had an important impact on the founding of the United States.[2] When urban elites passed laws for their own benefit after the American Revolution, populists responded, as in Shay's Rebellion, a 1786–1787 rural revolt against taxes biased in favor of cities.[3] Jacksonian expansions of democracy in the 1820s and 1830s were populist.[4] In the late-nineteenth-century United States, agrarian insurgency gave the name "populist" to mobilizations of people who felt wronged by economic elites and established politicians and sought greater popular voice and equality. The People's Party they founded was arguably more deeply committed to democracy than the conventional political parties—including the often-racist Democratic Party that coopted parts of the populist program.[5]

These were not class mobilizations, even if class inequalities shaped them. Populist self-understanding may emphasize being workers or producers as against those who appropriate the proceeds of the people's toil. But in populism class identity is subordinated to being the "real" or authentic people.

Populists usually claim an indivisible people, not a heterogeneous public. They commonly resist evidence that they are not the whole people and perhaps do not even represent a majority. Large numbers gathered in crowds (or the social media equivalent of crowds) foster an illusion of the whole people. By comparison, survey data about the complexities of identities and opinions are unconvincing. Looking around in a crowd, populists are apt not only to feel strength in numbers but also to see mainly people like them.[6] This is especially true of physically assembled crowds, but also of electronically mediated Internet crowds. Populists may think those who do not join them simply have not been awakened to their true predicament—or true identity.

Populism does not offer an adequate overall guide for democracy, partly because democracy needs the complement of institutions and norms.[7] It is a problem when populist mobilizations (or in fact any others) pursue immediate translations of popular passions or opinions into policies rather than accepting mediation through more reflective and plural public debate. Integrating the will of the people into government is crucial to democracy; immediacy is not. Not only is it important to consider the circumstances and views of different citizens; it is important to consider future generations and social stability.

In almost all cases, populist movements incorporate not just identity claims but accusations. Politicians are corrupt. Elites ignore the needs of the people. Banks would rather force people to lose their property in bankruptcy than help them.

The accusations are often overstated, but commonly contain at least significant grains of truth. Corruption is all too real and widespread—and appears today in the form of gross profiteering, kickbacks, insider contracts, and favors for political donors. Ending these would be a major advance for democracy. But inequality and unfairness are produced not only by corruption of these sorts. As important are commitment to meritocracy and making hierarchical incorporation the only mode of membership in society, as well as relying on a global, corporate, financial capitalism that benefits elites and owners of capital while undermining the lives and livelihoods of others.

Still, populists generally do call for democracy. They seek to make government more responsive to the people. And they reveal social challenges that conventional politics commonly fails to face (or even recognize). What is problematic and potentially antidemocratic is any attempt to eliminate the plurality of popular voices. It is not populism per se that makes contemporary politics so ugly and frustrating. It is racism, sexism, nativism, and homophobia. It is the attempt to define the "real" people by excluding so many fellow citizens. It is capture by demagogues, manipulation by monied backers, and confusion by specious conspiracy theories. It is a mixture of fear, anger, and self-righteousness. It is the amplification of all of these through ideological media. These faults are too commonly displayed by populist mobilizations, but none is intrinsic to populism.

One reason that focusing on populism as such is analytically misleading is that it doesn't appear on its own. First, waves of populism arise amid great transformations and uncertainty about how the "double movement" of disruption and reaction will play out (as discussed in Chapter 2). They are not just random assertions of the importance of "the people." They are assertions that the welfare, rights, values, and self-understanding of the people are under pressure. Populism needs to be understood as part of a larger struggle to forge an effective "second movement" response to "first movement" disruption.

Second, populism is almost always part of a dialectical pair: elite self-dealing and populist response. Populism substitutes the demands and neediness of the self-styled *people* for more reflective and balanced pursuit of the *public* good. But it does this precisely (if ironically) because citizens have not been adequately engaged in controversy over the public good. The issue is not just that elites have acted on biased and often self-interested understanding of the public good. It is also that contrary views have been disqualified more than debated. Many "progressive" politicians have embraced allegedly objective, technocratic policymaking. Administrations from Clinton to Obama in the United States, Britain's New Labour, and various multiparty coalitions in Europe have all relied heavily on the expertise of unelected officials. At the same time, judges have made more and more public policy, especially in the United States. This has fanned flames of political outrage and made judicial appointments a focus of partisan controversy.[8] It has also left citizens feeling they lack efficacy.

As we have argued throughout, degeneration of democracy is manifest with disempowered citizens, lack of inclusive solidarity, and majoritarian, winner-take-all, polarized politics. These are evident not just in populism but in the conditions that produce populism.

Formulating maximally "correct" policies too often has taken precedence over engaging the public (and indeed negotiating with opponents or merely partial allies). Hillary Clinton's 1993–1994 effort to produce a new US health care policy in closed-door meetings with experts rather than open political engagement is one example. The proposed policy may have been good, but the process failed, and it made much of the public feel excluded.[9] And of course there are biases even in ostensibly objective and "evidence-based" policies.

Efforts to move "beyond politics" easily produce politicized resentment. Motivated by frustration with legislative gridlock and the power of special interests in party politics, they undermine attachments to older political parties. They make it harder for party coalitions to do some of the work of mediating differences of value, opinion, and interest. This is initially depo-liticizing, but it opens the door to populist mobilizations that may increase political participation.

Demagogues are especially successful in appealing to those who have suffered loss and disruption without the compensatory support of strong organizations. They encourage and help articulate expressions of discontent. But demagogues seldom offer viable solutions. They promote ideological fantasies and blame scapegoats—build a border wall, perhaps, while com-munities remain damaged and inequality remains extreme.

A common response from "mainstream" politicians and pundits is to chal-lenge the assertions of the demagogues, the content of their pronouncements, to treat them as though they were simply offering reasoned arguments. But demagogues don't really debate—they perform before audiences. Moreover, they don't perform persuasion, the rhetorical manipulation Plato feared from orators. They perform affirmation. They provide inclusion to people who feel elites have excluded them. When they in turn exclude others and scapegoat them for national problems, they do so in part to affirm their identity as the "real" people. In short, they speak directly to degenerations of democracy the political mainstream often ignores.

Crowds are paradigmatic for populist mobilization. Mobilizing gives a sense of efficacy to citizens frustrated by directions of change they can't con-trol. And it is important to see this not-specifically-political source for populism. Populists are not alone in repeating the lament "Everything is changing, and nothing works anymore."[10] There is a tendency to blame new media for fanning the flames of panic and generating volatile crowds. But demagogues and elites have long been able to accomplish this in low-tech ways.[11] Crowds provide a sense of occasion, of embodied participation, an experience of standing alongside like-minded fellow citizens, and a repre-sentation of scale and thus significance. In modern societies it is crucial not just that media enlarge the reach of demagogues' messages, but also that they report on the crowds. The sociologist Ruth Braunstein reports on how much validation and affirmation members of the Tea Party drew from having Rush Limbaugh take notice of their demonstrations, as in the 2009 Taxpayer March on Washington.[12]

Donald Trump was a master of this relationship. He rose to political prominence not just by staging rallies with big crowds, but by getting media coverage of these events. Trump managed to command constant media attention in many ways, but crowds were (and are) central to his specific politics of affirmation. This is why he complained when news media and official agencies suggested the crowd at his inauguration was not as "huuuge" as he claimed. His speeches commonly included both boasts about the size of crowds and complaints that the mainstream media, denigrated as "fake news," wouldn't report their true scale. His fateful speech on January 6, 2021, before the Capitol came under assault by his followers, is no exception:

> Media will not show the magnitude of this crowd. Even I, when I turned on today, I looked, and I saw thousands of people here. But you don't see hundreds of thousands of people behind you because they don't want to show that.
>
> We have hundreds of thousands of people here and I just want them to be recognized by the fake news media. Turn your cameras please and show what's really happening out here because these people are not going to take it any longer. They're not going to take it any longer. Go ahead. Turn your cameras, please. Would you show? They came from all over the world, actually, but they came from all over our country.
>
> I just really want to see what they do. I just want to see how they covered. I've never seen anything like it. But it would be really great if we could be covered fairly by the media. The media is the biggest problem we have as far as I'm concerned, single biggest problem.[13]

Implicit in Trump's speech is a distinction between the media that would celebrate the size of his crowd and the media that would ignore or deny it. Indeed, a central factor in the growing political polarization of the era leading up to and including Trump has been the reduced influence of the "mainstream" media, hobbled by financial problems and denigrated by Trump through the symbol of a supposedly dying *New York Times.* This contrasted with the rising role for what we might think of as affirmative media. In Fox News and a variety of online outlets and through amplification in social media, a sizable fraction of Americans could find confirmation of their own importance.[14] When Fox experimented with being less than affirmative, especially during the 2020 election and after January 6, Trump lashed out, and new right-wing media gained audience share.[15] Fox backed off the experiment (just as Republican senators who initially criticized the failed "coup" quickly learned they needed to be more affirmative). Thirst for affirmation helps explain why "Stop the Steal" and similar questioning of the 2020 election results has been able to last so long in the face of clear contrary evidence. Media polarization also blunts the impact of such contrary evidence, providing large audiences with reporting in which it is never mentioned. Demagogues and affirmative media join forces to conjure up alternative worldviews that amount almost to alternative realities.

Populism is chaotic, volatile, often full of resentment and anger, and sometimes dangerous. It can be a creative push for change. But amorphous populist movements also offer recruiting opportunities and a veneer of greater legitimacy to better-organized extremists—who currently come mainly from the racist far Right. But blaming populism distracts attention from identifying and dealing with the issues that give rise to it.

What is required is not just recognizing and responding to grievances, but renewing and often reimagining effective democratic politics. In recent years, however, citizens have seen erosion of organizational structures that facilitated effective popular voice and secured better material conditions. Class and other interest-based approaches to collective action are weak—and unions, local communities, and social democratic political parties have all declined over the last fifty years.

This is partly a result of the transformation of work. Though workers didn't disappear, working-class employment was undermined. Traditional social democratic parties struggled to find an effective response—partly because they were unwilling to contemplate deep changes in their own economic programs. At the same time, though, the middle and professional classes grew (for a time) and took up new political engagements. Social democratic parties embraced these concerns with environment, gender, and new politics of respect and recognition. They often found new majorities— as in the success of Clinton Democrats in the United States and New Labor in Britain. Educated professionals played bigger roles, but traditional working-class voices and values were marginalized.[16]

Political parties remain powerful fundraising machines but generate little trust. Dysfunctional political parties also contribute to legislative gridlock and block needed change.[17] They exacerbate polarization.[18] They keep electing insiders for most positions, even while they make voters crave outsiders.

Indeed, frustrations with conventional parties contribute to populist enthusiasm for demagogues—who often run against parties but then try to capture parties. Whatever the merits of Brexit, the process was prolonged and made more difficult by intraparty squabbles as well as simple partisanship. In France, Emmanuel Macron became president as an ostensible outsider running against all parties, but he was a former cabinet member and longtime insider and quickly formed a new party he could dominate unilaterally. In the United States, Donald Trump first ran against the established Republican Party, then dominated it. He continues to mobilize both fanatical supporters and cynically calculating elected officials. His attempted takeover of the US presidency, in spite of his loss at the polls, and his continuing insistence that the 2020 election was "stolen" from him may yet break the party.

In most of established democracies, demagogues have played on anxieties about immigration. There has indeed been a wave of immigration around the world, reflecting a range of different "push factors." Environmental degradation, repressive politics, religious zealotry, religious discrimination, ethnic wars, militias interested mainly in minerals and money, and lack of economic opportunities have all played roles. Democracies have also been attractive, especially where they were coupled with economic opportunity. But though the immigrants are real, political debate is unrealistic. Accusations against immigrants overstate connections to crime, welfare benefits, and competition for jobs. They understate the importance of immigrants to continued economic dynamism, especially in aging societies.

The question is how to attend to anxieties and at the same time create more effective inclusion. First, the anxieties need to be heard, not rejected out of hand. This was an important part of the work of Quebec's Commission on Reasonable Accommodation. Commissioners traversed the province listening to groups of citizens express their frustrations, anxieties, and, only sometimes, aspirations. The listening was as important as any new policy solution—and was often lacking as different countries tried to grapple with immigration and rapid social transformation.[19] Listening to fellow citizens is an important part of democracy.

Second, where immigrants are wrongly blamed for real problems, these need to be addressed. Just because immigrants didn't cause a shortage of good jobs, doesn't mean that the shortage isn't real. The right response is not so much argument about who is to blame as investment in creating enduring economic opportunities.

Third, wrenching social and cultural change has been real. Immigrants are one face of this, but hardly the prime movers. Return to some prior golden age is an illusion and often a pernicious one. But liberal individualism (neo or otherwise) is of little help. The task is to overcome fragmentation and built more integrative, solidary society and culture. Easier said than done, of course, and in what follows we will only suggest some paths not offer a comprehensive solution.

But we do make one strong assertion. While solidarity must be built at many levels, the nation (or nation-state) is a crucial one. A nation can never be found ready-made at the scale of a state, not even in the most ethnically homogeneous societies. There is always, necessarily, a project of making the nation. This is a process of literary, artistic, and cinematic productivity. It is a process of legal reform, economic integration, and social movements. It is a process of negotiated settlements and mutual recognition. It can be linked to the telos of democracy.

Solidarity within nations need not be the enemy of more global solidarity among nations nor of effectively including immigrants. On the Left as well as the Right, however, claims in the name of nation tend to embrace the preexisting majority. The challenge is greater when that majority feels beleaguered by globalization and growing diversity.[20] But in this regard as in others, majoritarianism is a degenerate form of democracy. It must be possible for immigrants to become full members in their new polities—and for them to be encouraged to do so. This does not mean they have to give up all distinguishing culture, but neither does it make sense for them to be sustained in allegedly culture-protecting but economically excluded ghettoes—as is true in much of Europe. The term "assimilation" has been rejected by advocates for immigrant rights to maintain cultural autonomy, not simply be governed by prior majorities (a problematic form of the majoritarianism we have criticized throughout). But this should not mean abandoning the notion of immigrant learning and cultural change through participation. The ideal must be balance—and better connection—between the old majority and new entrants such that both are open to change.

Democratic nations need internal diversity. This can mean differences of language, or religion, or regional sensibilities and economies. It can include differences between metropolitan cities and small local communities. But the differences need to be crosscut by a range of connections. The theme is old in political science (and indeed anthropology and other disciplines): cleavages can be managed when they don't all align with each other.[21] What is destabilizing is not difference as such, but differences with no overlaps or bridges.

It is disastrous when nationalism is invoked only by a majority trying to cling to power or privilege. It needs to embrace the full range of citizens (and often residents waiting for citizenship) to shape a better future.

Renew the Democratic Project

Since the 1970s, the stabilizing and mostly egalitarian social democratic compromise of *les trente glorieuses,* the postwar era, has deteriorated.[22] Inequality and instability have both grown; public institutions and social support systems have been weakened. Lack of solidarity is an increasingly central issue.

Democracy degenerates partly because of upheavals in social life and organization, not just from directly political causes. It is undermined by personal insecurity. Some of this comes from the contingency of jobs, some from living on credit. Neoliberal capitalism has brought the kind of precarity the poor have long suffered to once much more secure workers and members of the middle classes.

But the social issues are not all economic. Parents fear letting their children play outside. Greater freedom in forming families has not been accompanied by renewed strength and stability for families. Church attendance has declined, but far from compensating, other communal institutions have seen similar declines. Anxiety is heightened by erosion of community and feeling that problems must be faced alone. Epidemic diseases are hard to understand as well as to avoid. People live longer but are more likely to die alone in nursing homes.

This leaves society fractured, solidarity fragmented, and politics more easily hostile, especially at larger scales. It also means that citizens organized locally often lack effective voice in large-scale systems or politics. Citizens unmoored from the foundations of social solidarity—both communities and institutions—become politically unmoored and more economically vulnerable.

Americans are short not just of local community strength, but of crosscutting ties to connect people in different localities—and races, ethnicities, religions, legal statuses, and economic levels—to each other. This is true in both Canada and the United States. In each country, an effective program of national service could forge powerful connections. This need not be exclusively military.

Likewise, the United States' great state universities have long been vehicles for connections among citizens from different parts of each state, different classes, different occupational pursuits, and indeed, different politics. This has been undercut by proliferation of separate institutions organized in a competitive hierarchy and of course by cost. But the public higher education agenda could be governed more by social inclusion and public service and less by meritocracy. To some extent this is true of Canada. Everywhere, there is a tension between access and selection.[23]

To restore citizen efficacy, an inclusive demos, and commitment to a political process that bridges partisan divides requires fundamental renewal of social solidarity. We cannot retrieve a sense of efficacy without providing resources and venues for exercising it in a realistic way. Similarly, it is not enough to tolerate or even welcome diversity without building relationships that actually enable citizens to know each other. Finally, the short-term scramble for political power has corroded the representative and electoral systems from within and led to excessive polarization and the degradation of the public sphere. This disfiguration of the democratic process cannot be redressed without recuperating and renewing a shared political identity and a common destiny.

For all the reversals of previous better trends, and for all the new problems plaguing democracies today, the last fifty years have also seen real and important accomplishments. There have been major transformation in women's rights and opportunities, more places for Black Americans in elite institutions, remarkable success for Asians and some other immigrants, greater recognition and legitimacy for a variety of cultural differences and personal identities.[24] In every case the changes have advanced democracy.

Of course, each major forward step has brought backlash as well as benefit. In every case, the changes have empowered citizens—but also made some others feel they lost power at least in relative terms. In every case, the changes have advanced inclusivity in the demos—but also changed its familiar identity. In every case, the changes have followed from pursuit of better democracy—but also brought majoritarian attempts to block change.

These accomplishments have been possible in an era of extreme inequality largely because they reduced barriers to inclusion of some individuals without changing deep structures of inequality. Reduction in bias has been coupled with meritocracy and thus disproportionately benefited elites. In particular, it has disproportionately befitted professionals who have attained positions of prestige or high salaries on the basis of education.

There are more women lawyers, doctors, and executives, but this hasn't raised the pay or benefits of care workers, teachers, or most service workers. There are more Black students in Ivy League universities, but this hasn't transformed educational or employment prospects for most Black men or reduced the curse of imprisonment.[25]

The prosperity of educated professionals has, however, attracted resentment. So has the extent to which their pursuit of authentic self-expression has been coupled with a self-righteous denigration of less-educated people. Liberties and opportunities have advanced, and advances remain valuable, but a challenge today is to couple the positive side of pursuing authenticity and recognizing achievement with greater structural equality and solidarity.

Gender

Inclusion, autonomy, and equality for women are among the greatest accomplishments of the last two hundred years. They have been achieved slowly and with considerable struggle. They also remain incomplete. Much is still to be done.

As we have stressed, citizens need to be empowered not just in formal political roles but also in their capacities for "life, liberty, and the pursuit of happiness." Consider those excluded from formal political roles by the US Constitution (and in many other countries). As women and others have won the vote, they have also gained increased capacity for the pursuit of their own life projects.

Black Americans were freed from slavery, and as rocky as the road has been, gained improved work and business opportunities, standards of living, schools, housing, and personal autonomy—as well as some political power. Workers' incomes, job security, and occupational safety all improved, importantly due to unions that were empowering politically as well as economically (and that changed general conditions not just terms of employment for their members). Women gained capacity to make their own choices, despite long-standing limits and recurrent backlashes. Greater personal and occupational autonomy is also politically empowering.

Women are still underrepresented in political leadership and in top private-sector positions. They are still paid less than men for comparable work. They are still subject to physical abuse and harassment, still denied control over their own bodies, still raped. Behind material exclusion, exploitation, and violence lie constant, repetitive symbolic violence. Women are still commonly denigrated in casual conversation and comedy, even if the open grossness of Donald Trump is unusual among public figures. It is crucial that the republican legal framework guarantee women equal rights and treatment. It is imperative that those with power in all organizations make violators accountable, not laugh nervously or look the other way.

Recurrent scandals and mobilizations such as the #MeToo movement are reminders that abuse and unfair treatment affect women in the full range of occupations and at different class and income levels. But violence and discrimination are especially prevalent in the experience of less well-off women. As has long been true, the economic empowerment of women is of basic importance for their personal independence, treatment by others, and ability to form social relationships on fair bases. And the best path to this is not a case-by-case approach to fairness, valuable though that is, but a wider economic transformation.

To improve the situation of women we must dramatically increase the compensation and improve the working conditions of teachers, care workers, and service workers generally. These are the biggest categories of employment in the United States, and they are the most disproportionately female.[26] They have grown dramatically while previously well-paid and mostly male jobs have declined in sectors such as mining, manufacturing, and construction.

Of course, it is also good to make sure female computer scientists and lawyers are paid comparably to their male counterparts. But the pursuit of fairness for members of the elite will change fewer lives than greater equality. Keeping wages low in the service sector keeps wages low for women (and indeed also for Black and immigrant women). Paying wait staff living wages with benefits rather than leaving them dependent on tips would boost gender equality. A higher minimum wage would help women.[27]

There are academic debates about why the job categories with the most women are so poorly paid.[28] Resolving these has implications for whether better pay will just draw more men into those occupations rather than achieving gender equality. To some extent this seems to have happened with nursing. This pattern is a reason not to target one occupation at a time but not a reason to tolerate unequal pay. We should not just pursue higher pay for certain mostly female occupations—especially those that require advanced education or where there are labor shortages. We should act to reduce inequality across the board.

Of course, this would also benefit men—which might not be a bad thing in pursuit of equality and solidarity. Sadly, citizens who are frustrated with their status don't always call for equality. Too often, they complain about the gains of others. One dimension of recent toxic, nasty, and simply sad masculinity has been the extent to which men blame women (as well as minorities, immigrants, and others) for their career frustrations. Women do this less, whether because they expect less or for other reasons.[29]

Likewise, making high-quality childcare universally available would be a major gain for women—and indeed for families and children. Of course, men should be equally attentive to parental responsibilities, but they are not. Women are much more likely to head single-parent families (though the high rate of broken families does also affect men adversely). Women face forced choices about work and childcare that are not healthy for them, their children, or the larger society. The problem is exacerbated not just by lack of support but by lack of job security. During the pandemic, women have lost jobs faster than men—because of weaker protections against loss as well as because of competing care responsibilities.[30]

Empowerment of women has also required shifting attitudes toward sexuality. At a basic level this is about treating women not as simply sexual objects—individually or in general. Violent and forced sexuality is of course even worse. But there are less extreme issues as well—women's autonomy in sexual pleasure, the medical support of female sexuality. There has been progress; there has not been enough. Cultural change needs to continue. Recognition of political rights and achievement of economic independence matter here, too.

Men have often adjusted poorly to women's greater autonomy. Virulent displays of toxic masculinity have been a striking feature of recent right-wing populist movements. Sexual violence has increased during the pandemic. These abuses stem not just from changes that strengthen the position of women. Nor is macho resentment to gains for women the whole story.[31]

Within two generations, an old ideal of masculinity fell from favor in much of the culture. Claims to male strength and domination have come to seem abusive. Claims to male superiority are daily debunked by female success—not least in school and occupations based on educational attainment. But at the same time, some religious and other movements have tried to shore up the old ideal, to encourage men to see themselves as family breadwinners and authorities. While some cultural messages extoll greater spousal cooperation, others condemn men who fail their families.

Some of these factors have affected Black men particularly harshly. They too find it harder to stay in school than female counterparts, and harder to find good jobs without education. They too are displaced by the decline of manual—and more generally manufacturing—occupations. In addition, they face particular challenges of gangs, racist policing, and imprisonment.

Whatever the ideology, being a stereotypical male breadwinner has also become impossible for many—or at the very least an added pressure to which it is hard to measure up. New economic conditions have not supported a graceful transition to marriage as equal partnership or new understandings of self-worth. They have simply made it impossible for many working-class men—and increasingly middle-class men—to earn enough to support families.[32] Indeed, the number of hours of paid employment required to support families has increased, making the work of two parents not a path to greater economic well-being, but necessary.

The idea of being paid decently needs to be separated from notions such as a "family wage." Reducing inequality should not be dependent on reducing inequality among men and sustaining it between men and women. The best and most direct path is probably full employment—perhaps even a jobs guarantee. Income subsidies—even a Universal Basic Income—are not adequate substitutes for jobs.[33] UBI proposals seldom offer an income even close to that of employment—and employers are likely to resist such proposals just as they do the higher minimum wages because they fear having to pay employees more. Jobs are also important for self-respect and empowerment.

We have no magic solution for wounded male pride. We see too many examples of how it becomes toxic interpersonally, and problematic for democracy. Men are particularly prone to exaggerated assertions of liberty in the form of carrying guns, behaving aggressively, even flouting public health instructions to wear masks. The crowd storming the US Capitol on January 6, 2021, was overwhelmingly male, although the one protestor shot was a woman. Groups such as the Proud Boys are attractive to men; they are particularly prominent in right-wing militias and neo-Nazi groups. This needs more than condemnation. It needs recognition of the challenges before at least large segments of the male population.

Race and Voting Rights

Racial exclusion has long limited and undermined democracy in the United States. A long list of specific fixes would be desirable. Block the restriction of elections to workdays when employees must ask for time off or suffer reduced access. In particular, allow Sunday voting. End disenfranchisement of former felons. Grant the District of Columbia statehood. Abolish the electoral college with its skew toward minimally Black, minimally urban states. Apportion Senate seats by population. But it is not clear that Congress will pass even the modest but important bill now before it to secure voting rights.

From the founding of the United States, determining election procedures has been a right and responsibility assigned to the states. The drawing of districts, the certification of individual voters, and the certification of ballot results are all crucial. And all are currently hotly contested in the United States. The issues came to the fore in efforts by Donald Trump and his supporters to portray the 2020 election as fraudulent.

Trump's administration tried to block counting of mail ballots, even though Trump himself voted by mail. Then Trump and his supporters fought a massive battle to have the election results overturned by getting legitimate votes disqualified.[34] After that failed, Republicans in state legislatures around the United States began efforts to suppress more votes in the future.[35] These are not just expressions of loyalty to the defeated demagogue, nor even just efforts to secure partisan victories. They are concerted efforts to reduce voting by Blacks and other minorities. They are succeeding to a disturbing extent.

Electoral districts must recurrently be adjusted to take account of population change. In principle, they should reflect the lines of actual communities or at least population concentrations. Gerrymandering is the distortion of boundaries to try to include or exclude certain voters. This is done by incumbents and majority parties to protect their electoral advantages. It has been done to create majority Black districts and conversely to divide Black voters into different districts in order to prevent them from forming a majority anywhere. While some states have moved to depoliticize districting and reduce gerrymandering, by mid-2021 at least fourteen have enacted bills that give partisan officials more control over elections. Republicans are resisting fair districting now, but Democrats have also sometimes done so in the past. Gerrymandering for partisan or racist purposes is bad enough, but it also has the latent effect of undermining the relationship of representation to localities, making democracy seem an artificial process disconnected from the organization of ordinary life.

Voter suppression refers to efforts to prevent or inhibit voting by certain citizens. For example, insisting that elections be held on weekdays during working hours makes it harder for nonelite workers to vote—but it is common. Literacy tests were long a way to reduce voting of the less educated, including Black citizens who had been denied education. Registering to vote can be made easier or harder. Voters can be intimidated at polling places. Extra or arbitrarily complicated forms of identification can be demanded.

Voter suppression was crucial as Southern whites sought to reestablish their power after the setback of the lost Civil War and Reconstruction. It helped maintain white power for nearly a hundred years after the Civil War. It was eventually reduced (though not quite eliminated) by the 1965 Voting Rights Act. This was both a peak achievement of the civil rights movement and arguably the last major legislation grounded in the New Deal. But the advance of democracy was not linear in the United States (or anywhere else). The 1965 Civil Rights Act was gutted in 2013, when the Supreme Court ruled that there was no longer reason for close scrutiny of previously abusive states. Once again a fading majority attempted to secure its dominance by reducing the chances others—especially Black Americans—had to vote and participate in democracy.[36] A temporary majority sought antidemocratic ways to make its advantage permanent.

Struggle for renewed and expanded empowerment is underway today, but it faces both sharp opposition and internal contradictions. By 2021, Republican legislators in seventeen states had passed laws to limit ballot access.[37] Citizens need to mobilize at the state level to secure the right to vote. Deeper change is also needed. And it must overcome resistance from those who happen to be in power at any moment. Once again, the opposition commonly stems from straightforward racism, sometimes elaborated in ideologies such as white Christian nationalism. Sometimes it reflects an interest in power more than racism as such.

The United States is not unique, alas, but a leader in a bad trend; targeted voter suppression is spreading.[38] A variety of different mechanisms is used to make it harder for some citizens to vote. Polling stations are removed from minority neighborhoods. In 2020 in Texas, the Republican-controlled legislature closed 750 polling places, mainly in cities deemed more likely to vote Democratic.[39] Georgia Republicans, stung by losing both Senate seats to Democrats in 2020, have not only limited postal voting but also forbidden Sunday voting and giving a drink of water to anyone waiting in line to vote. Parties and interest groups have tried to have their potential opponents disqualified in bulk, forcing them to re-register to reduce turnout. Majorities in state legislatures have shifted the kinds of identification required, hoping that poorer voters won't have the decided-on document ready to hand.[40]

Clear legal requirements and effective enforcement could guarantee that all citizens have equal opportunities to vote and that their votes count equally. But in most countries and states those in power are allowed to set the electoral rules; challenges from those they try to keep out are difficult to sustain.[41]

Efforts to make existing advantages permanent keep stifling the advance of democracy. Selection to be a candidate commonly involves a career of participation in political parties or in ideologically focused career-builders such as the Federalist Society, which recruits lawyers to the right wing of the Republican Party in the United States. There are further mechanisms such as the provision in most US states that candidates who lose primary elections cannot run as independents in general elections—which discourages independent action among legislators.[42]

It is not just equality that is impeded, but better provision of public goods—and achievement of the public good for all. There are too many who would "drain the pool to avoid sharing."[43]

Unequal Policing and Imprisonment

Of course, racial oppression is not only maintained at the ballot box. Institutional racism is also widespread. It is intensified by increased inequality and blocked mobility. Police violence is also one of its mechanisms. In the midst of the Covid-19 pandemic severe examples of police brutality against Black Americans have been made especially visible by widely watched video recordings. These produced enormous protests, most especially in the wake of the gruesome murder of George Floyd in Minneapolis in the spring of 2020.

The protests were overwhelmingly peaceful partly because they were well organized. Some of this reflected by Black Lives Matter, which has been campaigning against racist violence since 2013.[44] But much organizing came from local communities—especially in Minneapolis's George Floyd Memorial. Impressively multiracial, the protests showed a deep desire for a more inclusive polity. Indeed, in the midst of Covid-19 pandemic and the serial crises of the Donald Trump presidency, they were an expression of solidarity that many found inspiring.

But in a deeply divided United States, the protests were met with rage, force, and sometimes hysteria. This was not all focused on race. Social media and presidential speeches alike promoted panic over "the antifa." Real but small and loosely organized networks formed to resist fascism were blown up into fearsome bogeymen. Across the United States, neighborhoods and small towns developed the paranoid notion that they were next in line for antifa attack. This was not spontaneous madness; it was misinformation and fear promoted by often obscure activists and amplified on social media. Neighborhood websites usually more focused on missing pets suddenly became obsessed with potential attacks.

Police responses to the combination of Black Lives Matter and antifascist protests were massive and harsh—far more severe than efforts to police the storming of the Capitol on January 6. Portland, Oregon, for example, saw large protests from May to September 2020. To the frustration of the main BLM organizers, there were several acts of violence and provocations from mostly white, self-styled "antifa" activists. In response, the police used force more than six thousand times over a hundred days, against mostly peaceful BLM protestors, becoming much more violent than the protestors they were was ostensibly pacifying.[45] The Trump administration made matters worse by sending in a heavily armored federal force, recruited from the Customs and Border Police. This was sent against the objections of Oregon officials and escalated the confrontation dramatically. The pretext was protecting federal buildings but the troops acted as riot police some distance from the buildings they were supposedly protecting.[46]

Tensions predictably escalated as policing used force against protestors in several cities—but not against right-wing white groups. Prefiguring the January 6 attack on the US Capitol, for example, in April of 2020 an armed crowed spilled from a rally in Michigan. Demanding an end to the governor's anti-Covid stay-at-home order.

Critics of police violence against minorities (and sympathy for right-wing groups) called to "defund the police."[47] This was a poorly chosen slogan, but it reflected a mixture of huge escalations in police budgets, spent largely on militarizing the police, and coming at the expense of needed social programs; anger at police violence and successful resistance to oversight, including paying off millions in lawsuits instead of reforming abusive practices; and anarchist arguments that society should be self-regulating. The last is a very strong position, perhaps unrealistic in a complex, large-scale society and one still sharply unequal. Previous efforts at community control of police have largely failed; taking control of the budget could greatly strengthen those efforts.[48]

Decades ago, police reform movements campaigned for greater professionalism and accountability and better relations between police and citizens. Progress was made but then reversed. Amid highly partisan and political wars on drugs and terror, police forces began to encourage their officers to think of themselves as warriors, not service providers.[49] The Pentagon supplied them with more and more heavy weapons, armored personnel carriers, even tanks. This was the analogue to high-tech medicine versus public health. It made the police more expensive, undermined efforts to strengthen ties to communities and the public, and largely failed in regard to drugs and terror. Not only nationally but in most US cities, politicians campaigned by stoking fear and presenting police as the solution. This left them beholden to police forces (and their unions) when these sought immunity against charges of abuse.

There is urgent need for democratic reform in policing—and more generally in how the goals of public security are met. It is crucial to end racism and the toleration and cover-up of racism.[50] Citizens need a well-informed democratic process to ask how public funds can best be deployed to support public security. So far, however, election results have suggested that defunding or reorganizing the police is a minority desire. Fear commands more votes.[51]

Mass incarceration is a closely related issue. Since the 1970s, the United States has seen a fivefold increase in the proportion of the population imprisoned.[52] Like high-cost policing, this tracks the neoliberal ascendancy. Neoliberal ideology may suggest reducing government cost and oppression, but this has not been the reality. This is partly because to gain power and influence, neoliberals entered into political coalitions with Evangelical Christians and others with distinct agendas. The modern right wing is a compound of neoliberalism with policies focused on abortion, drugs, personal security, and use of government to police morality.

Harsh criminalization of marijuana is an example. So are laws mandating longer prison terms and reducing judicial discretion. Increasing imprisonment not only reduces liberties; it increases government costs—by more than $80 billion a year in the United States. Prisons become even more expensive if, instead of lowering crime rates, they become part of crime's reproduction, or if they make it hard for former prisoners to find good paths in civil society. Reducing incarceration would free up funds for health care and education.

Guided by neoliberal ideas, governments contracted out much prison administration to private, for-profit companies.[53] This is a highly profitable industry, and companies are allowed to use their profits to lobby government for laws that bring more business—like the "three strikes" rule mandating long terms for repeat offenders.

This use of politics to secure protected profits is similar to the practice of pharmaceutical companies, which lobby for the United States to keep its drug prices the highest in the world.[54] The drug companies don't just stop with protecting their prices. They lobby against universal health care. So, in effect they lobby for Blacks, Latinos and Latinas, and poor rural whites to have no insurance and poor access to health care. Likewise, prison companies don't just lobby for a bigger share of the prison population. They lobby for strict laws that increase incarceration rates.

The US War on Drugs was not effective in its main official policy objectives of reducing drug use and sales. It did drive both police budgets and rates of imprisonment to unprecedented levels. They are finally tapering off. Bringing them down much further would be good for democracy.

Perhaps ironically, the failed US war on *illegal* drugs coincided with an epidemic of more or less legal drug abuse. This was driven by corporations rather than gangs (or perhaps we should say as a different form of gangs). Perdue Pharma not only manufactured but pushed drugs such as Oxy-Contin, the most famous of the opiates that have devastated lives and communities around the United States (and especially in the context of weak responses to deindustrialization).

The burden of violent policing and mass incarceration falls most heavily on Black men and Latinos (though recently it has increased for women across racial and ethnic lines). Laws banning convicted felons from voting are largely racial exclusions. Breaking the hold police and prison advocates have on government policy and funding must be a priority. Ending private prisons would be a move in favor of democracy and the public good.[55] Likewise, moving to improve public health needs to be combined with curtailing the influence of for-profit firms pushing high-profit drugs even into abusive uses.

In all these cases, the goal must be not just to put an end to acts of overt discrimination, but also to open new avenues of opportunity for those who have been blocked from full and fair participation. The continued exclusion of Black Americans is particularly glaring, but analogous fault lines also work against full justice and equality for Indigenous peoples, Latinos and Latinas, and others. While the United States may be extreme, racial division and injustice are major issues for Britain, France, and other democracies. Recurrent scandals reveal how many members of police and militaries are members or sympathizers of antidemocratic far-right groups.[56]

Money and Media

Voter suppression is not the only instance of broken political mechanisms needing repair. There is perhaps no clearer example of the disempowerment of democratic citizens than the outsize role of money in elections, lobbying, and determining who is appointed to government offices. This is directly antidemocratic and has distorted campaigns and political communication more generally—in an extreme form in the United States. The 2016 federal elections cost a staggering $6.5 billion, and at $14.4 billion the 2020 campaigns more than doubled this record amount.[57]

Costs are rising and reliance on a small number of wealthy donors becoming more significant in many of the world's democracies. Though Britain has resisted US-style money-politics, this effort has been losing ground. Fundraising is increasingly central to political parties, but much of the money comes from outside parties and contributes to their declining ability to organize political debates. Just five wealthy businessmen paid most of the costs of the successful 2016 referendum campaign for Brexit.[58]

There are straightforward remedies—such as strong limits on spending and government financing of elections. Of course, there is lack of will incumbent politicians addicted to the present system. There are complications such as the 2010 US Supreme Court decision in *Citizens United* that declared corporations could make unlimited contributions because they have the same free speech rights as human citizens. And, of course, there will be efforts to cheat, as when the Vote Leave campaign supporting Brexit illegally evaded campaign spending limits—for which it was eventually fined but after the damage was done.

Regulation of political advertising and lobbying can limit the distortion money brings to democratic politics. But even outside of elections, billionaires and corporations spend huge amounts trying to shape public opinion—to encourage continued use of coal or nuclear power, for example, or to make citizens fear public rather than private approaches to health care or other social needs. Once again, inequality is a basic issue.

The link between money and media has shifted in recent years. Instead of simply buying television time, those who would influence politics invest in social media strategies. These range from simply promoting messages on platforms such as Twitter and using Facebook to circulate information (true or false) to relying on automated systems to generate robocalls and repost messages hundreds of thousands of times, often from fake but seemingly personal accounts. They extend into mining the information collected by online platforms and using this as a basis for both campaign strategy and campaigns of disinformation.

The political consultancy Cambridge Analytica was engulfed in scandal in 2018 when it became clear that it had used a range of deceptive practices to support political campaigns. Most dramatically, it had used data from the personal accounts of millions of Facebook users, without transparency or permission, to build personality profiles for political use. Similar practices continue. Quizzes, surveys, and personality tests are presented as either research or simply information for the curious, but amount to "click bait" with the results analyzed (covertly) for political profiling. Problems arise not just from gathering new data by these tricks but also from ubiquitous surveillance.

As more and more activities and transactions are carried out online, they generate data that can be analyzed for purposes never intended or made explicit. What news articles someone reads, what entertainment they watch, what songs are their favorites, what they buy, where they travel, and what political donations they make are all tracked. Computers are then programmed not just to analyze these records but to learn from them, exploring their contents in ways not anticipated by original programmers, though still for the most part controlled by and used by them. They make it possible for stores to target new parents with ads for diapers and infant formula. They make it possible for political candidates to target messages to gun owners, pet lovers, far-right radicals, or naive patriots to trigger maximum political response or outrage.

Governments access such data to complement official sources. Sometimes they collect it covertly for law enforcement or, on an international basis, for spying. Sometimes they hack centralized data records. Doing so helps China keep track of political dissidents both at home and abroad. Other authoritarian governments do the same, deploying facial recognition software and monitoring chat rooms, credit cards, and the school enrollments of dissidents' children. The governments of democracies don't do this as much; it still causes scandal when a government agency is revealed to have breached privacy laws or programmed its computers to racially profile citizens.[59] But government monitoring has increased alongside corporate monitoring and private political surveillance. The data thus gleaned have been used to block visa requests and organize targeted assassinations. But these data exist less because of government spying than because of "surveillance capitalism."[60] This has become central to how business works, and the data collected for business can be exploited for political purposes.

This is not all new. Advertising has always been part of an "attention economy," as advertisers compete to be noticed. Why else pay millions for an ad to run during the broadcast of the Super Bowl? But there are now much more sophisticated techniques for aggregating data individual citizens commonly think of as private (if they think about data at all).[61] And there are more nefarious uses than targeted advertising. The information is used for blackmail and to apply political pressure. It is used to get candidates to drop out of elections rather than risk exposure—even false exposure.

New media structures have facilitated both actual foreign interference and consequent fears of more. This stoked the wild paranoia of Trump supporters "auditing" election results for possible fraud. Republicans in the Arizona Senate spent millions commissioning a massive audit by the inexperienced and comically named "Cyber Ninjas."[62] In the end, the honesty of the original election was affirmed; total votes for Biden even went up slightly.[63] But while Trump's angry supporters may be wrong about particular elections or about the nature of threats, they are not wrong that elections, like much of the rest of modern life, have come to be based on complex and potentially vulnerable computer and communications systems.

Societies could not exist at the scale of contemporary Britain or the United States without the support of vast infrastructures of information flow as well as transportation, water supply, and electricity. Contemplating the fragility and insecurity of such systems—and thus of our personal lives—can be disempowering for citizens. Fear turns immediately to how they contribute to authoritarian and even totalitarian government. But their manipulation for partisan political purposes is also immediately threatening.

There is no going back on the transformation of modern society by computer, communications, data, and surveillance technologies. Or at least there is none that would not involve radical collapse of large-scale social organization. The question, therefore, must be how to manage our computer-dependence. We need countervailing institutions—investigative media, consumer organizations ensuring accuracy in credit reporting, monitors for security of infrastructure, public interest law firms, and so forth. Even when accurate and used legitimately, computer systems—like many bureaucracies but even less transparently—tend to be focused on efficiency and effectiveness, not democracy and the public good.

Unfortunately, throughout the developed democracies, governments have failed to develop effective and appropriate regulation for new media. Corporations controlling social media are treated as mere conduits or platforms rather than publishers. This accordingly limits their accountability. Yet, in the absence of policies of web neutrality, providers are allowed to discriminate among content sources and users.[64] Facebook and other giant technology corporations have responded to recently publicized abuses— such as the Cambridge Analytica scandal—by introducing their own forms of censorship. These are not transparent, and it is hotly debated whether they go too far or not far enough, whether they "move fast and break things" or go slow and let disasters and disinformation accumulate.

Shifts in communications media have exacerbated problems of honesty, accurate information, and legitimacy in democratic politics. Lying is certainly not new, but has become more pervasive in many countries, with rapid am-plification through social media and less effective correction mechanisms.[65] Research has shown falsehoods to spread faster than true statements on sim-ilar topics, only partly because of sensationalism.[66] This impedes reasoned formation of public opinion, democratic debate on possible policies, electoral campaigns, and capacity to hold elected officials to account.

Government regulation inevitably plays catch-up to technological inno-vation. It is a further challenge that those with technological talent and knowledge are commonly drawn to seeking fortunes in Silicon Valley rather than to public service. Fault here lies partly with the extent to which working for the public good has lost comparative prestige to working for private profit during the neoliberal era. It lies also with governments that have not invested in capacity and therefore interesting careers for their regulators or have not made professions feel their work was valued because they failed to follow through on making it effective. Top physicians do work for the National Institutes of Health. We need top computer scientists and com-munications analysts working on how to live better and longer and more democratically with new technology.

But we also need independent, nongovernmental, and not completely profit-driven institutions. Journalism is a prime example. It has been a sup-port for modern democracy throughout its history, despite the existence of the "yellow" or "tabloid" press that anticipated some of the "fake news" in social media today. Newspapers grew from the products of single authors into newspaper organizations—mainly in the mid-twentieth century. Jour-nalism became a profession with strong (though variable) norms of objec-tive and fair reporting, reproduced in part by professional education. Both print and broadcast journalism—the "legacy media"—remain crucial to democracy, but media organizations and careers have been thrown into chaos by new technology and shifting structures of payment and profitability. This chaos has enhanced vulnerability to political attacks and created space for the emergence of what we call the "affirmative media." These amplify dominant views without critique. Yet independent journalism is key to democracy, bringing straightforward reporting, fact-checking, deeper investigation, and ensuring honesty of public officials and corporations alike. There are new models emerging for the work of journalists, often as more or less independent entrepreneurs of information and analysis. Some journalists are supported by foundations; some are reliant on marketing their work on electronic media such as Substack. None of these is yet a substitute for all that the "legacy media" offered; support is needed for continued improvement. Some of this could come from public funding, but it is crucial that media have significant independence. Funding needs to be insulated from political interference and where possible to come from multiple sources. Governments need to stand firm for press freedom and integrity.

Journalism is not the only source of investigation and analysis that check the power of governments and corporations and help citizens understand paths of social change. This is also a crucial role for universities. Academic research is important to society's knowledge base and can often provide a counterweight to claims unsupported by evidence (as for example in debates a decade ago about climate change). University education is also valuable for equipping citizens with capacity to make good judgements of both facts and possible policies. But higher education is undergoing massive restructuring. Research is increasingly harnessed to business agendas and techno-science with reduced space for critical analysis of social issues (even when such criticism is not actively attacked from outside). The worthy effort to take educational offerings to large scale has been accompanied by reductions to credentialing. Universities are not automatically democratic—they can be very hierarchical and embedded in defense of older forms of knowledge. But they are important to democracy and can potentially change in ways that make them more important rather than less.

The same goes for all the many kinds of civil society organizations. These are crucial to specific domains, of civic engagement, sustaining a plural and open society. Information is produced, analyzed, interpreted, shared, and debated in churches, unions, and nonprofit organizations dedicated to issues ranging from women's rights and racial justice to help for the homeless, environmental protection, better schools, and support for small businesses. These are important and need to be supported at a local scale. Many are also joined in national structures that do significant information gathering, analysis of public policies, and publication of their own.

Still, it is important to recognize the distinctive roles of journalism and publicly oriented academic research. These provide help in sifting through multiple claims to identify the most reliably sound knowledge. Sustained investigative reporting and research not only uncover new facts but bring together disparate information to aid in understanding of basic issues.

A vibrant public sphere is vital to democracy as the setting in which citizens establish what they regard as the public good. This means a public sphere in which communication is free and open, not managed by those with the capacity to manipulate media. It means political power should not be mobilized to stop schools from teaching both knowledge at the best current standards and the capacity for critical judgement. It means that there is genuine plurality, not either the suppression of dissent in favor of unanimity or fragmentation into separate media silos.

At large scale, it is easy for media to become vehicles of pseudo-community. People who have no other tangible relationship to each other experience joint media engagement as a form of mutuality. Such participation can be important in constructing personal and collective identity. A group defined by some similar characteristic or view can feel affirming. But it lacks the more complex relationship building, consideration of the other, and feedback on the "presentation of self" that is typical of face-to-face relationships—and sustained in electronic communication with individually known others. Because participants are not linked in multiple other ways, as they might be in a neighborhood, one dimension of similarity is exaggerated. Relationships are less undifferentiated; they are with the group more than its various members.

Given the sale of modern societies, there is no way to dispense with communications media as modes of connection among people. But it is important that people use them for differentiated and not only mass communication, that they be complemented by more directly interpersonal relations, and that they be approached with critical reflexivity.

Local Community

Investing in public institutions is necessary. But though action by the national state is crucial, it can never be the whole story. In most countries there are other levels of government. Democracy may be served by pursuing the public good in a decentralized manner, bringing provision closer to citizens in local communities.

Welfare states built in the mid-twentieth century centralized too much. During the last fifty years, markets became more radically national and global; local economies suffered. On efficiency grounds, and sometimes with claims to great quality, schools, hospitals, and other public services were consolidated. Local communities lost key institutions, often accelerating their decline.

The decline of a locality involves much more than a loss of jobs, important as this is. It also consists in a loss of local shops, of available services (for instance, a regional hospital, a community college), of transport facilities to larger centers. It is a rupture in human relations to place as well as to other people, and thus of attachment to the environment. Not least, local decline is often accompanied, both as cause and effect, by a thinning out of the associative life of the community, as churches, sports teams, pubs and cafés close and are not replaced. A recovery in the network of vigorous local and connecting associations in these declining areas is a key condition of democratic recovery in the society as a whole.

Local renewal demands not just decentralization of national government spending or service delivery. It needs limitations on colonization by large corporations and a centralized logistical economy. Above all, it needs self-organization. Changes can come about when citizens of a local community get together with the aim of improving their condition. The goals and needs can be very varied; but something important happens when potential leaders come together to clarify what the needs are, and try to define, through various kinds of consultation with their fellow citizens, how these needs can be met.

First, the very fact of coming together may shift the existential stance of the people concerned: Before, we had a sense that we as a community are hard done by, are the victims of powerful forces beyond our control: of the "globalizing elites" or "distant technocrats," or of the disloyal competition of foreigners. But now we come to see ourselves as capable of taking initiatives, of doing something to alter our own predicament.

Then, second, the fact that we have to combine and work with others, from different organizations, confessions, outlooks, races, ethnicities, even political convictions, makes us listen to each other; we now have a stake in working out something together with these others. We can't sit back and simply criticize or demonize them. Contact softens hostilities based on stereotypes. This is also one of the contributions national service can make.

Then third, if we can come up with some plan, for example, how to find new avenues of employment, or modes of retraining, or new kinds of service to the community, or whatever, we are now in a position to know what we have to demand of higher levels of government. We not only know what to demand, but in virtue of having a program based on a strong local consensus, we have inevitably some greater political clout.

We now feel empowered because we *are* empowered. Or so it might be, if local self-organization and political mobilization flourished. Enhanced capacity is the fruit of an increased density in the associational life of the community. It enables us to punch through—at least at the local level—the opacity of the representative system to ordinary voters' understanding of the mechanisms of change. John Dewey famously described publics as emerging when citizens mobilized around shared problems.[67] Mobilization itself—both debate and action—builds new social ties. This creates both solidarity and capacity for future work together. This is crucial in large, dynamic, and often fragmented societies. Communities are not just inherited and not just place-based. They are created anew in action.

It has long been a sound generalization that local communities are likely to approach issues as practical rather than partisan. Increasingly, however, political polarization has also infected local communities. Struggles over wearing masks and either closing or reopening schools during the pandemic have been succeeded by even more confrontational protests against vaccine mandates. Tensions around racial minorities and police can be very local but still very partisan. Part of the solution lies in developing organizations that simultaneously tackle policy challenges and build mutual trust.[68]

A key advantage to local communities is that social relationships can more readily be multidimensional. It helps when neighbors really know each other, of course, and when more communication is face-to-face. When people know each other in multiple contexts, their relationships are stronger. But what perhaps matters most is that people know each other in different contexts and in overlapping but not identical networks. Parents share one set of interests when they have children in the same school, though they may be of different races, go to different churches, or have different value judgments on other questions. Alas, there has been a decline in the extent to which this happens, not least because people choose private over public schools or choose neighborhoods that are racially or economically homogenous.

When neighbors go to various religious observations, places of work, sporting events, and even protests, this builds linkages and diffuses the intensity of "them / us" distinctions. Neighbors may not agree with protestors, but at least they know them. This happens less when there are fewer organizations and less dense networks—like housing developments where neighbors don't really know each other. It also happens less when all the memberships align with each other: the same people in the same neighborhoods, workplaces, churches, and voluntary organizations. That produces the local equivalent of the echo chambers found in national media.

Much of both "populism" and panic over populism has played out at national levels and in these media echo chambers. Victims of the great Downgrade may turn to the former, hoping for some kind of redress. Beneficiaries may turn to the latter, seeking more rational debate but reproducing their division from others who need to be in the same debate. This does not produce meaningful action to reverse the degenerations of democracy, restore economies, or overcome divisions. For this, local levels are crucial.

At all levels, we need more inclusive publics. But for these to flourish, we need not just media that are less siloed and polarized. We also need crosscutting social ties. Where economic interests and cultural identities divide us, we can hope schools, military service neighborhoods, workplaces or other institutions will facilitate bridge-building.

This kind of social foundation for more inclusive publics may be built best from the bottom up. But, of course, we also need crosscutting social ties, national movements, and responsive central government. In fact, to restore democracy, we need action on three levels to go forward together: creating national movements, linking them to parties (without necessarily letting them be contained by parties), and building self-organized communities at the base.[69]

Renewal of community cannot be a simple restoration of the communities of the past any more than effective trade unions today can be copies of the insurgencies of the early twentieth century or the industrial unions that were partners in postwar social democratic compromises. Place will still be important to many communities, but places have shifted and can be reimagined. Economic supports for local community are changing. Local places also have new prospects for interconnection, partly through technology. But solidarity beyond the local is crucial too. Response to disasters shows that people care about suffering at a distance. Resilience in the face of disasters—including the Covid-19 pandemic—depends very heavily on local action, but it also depends on organization of connections at other scales. If democratic government is organized importantly at national levels than we need national solidarity, and we need to make it inclusive and pluralist to work for modern societies as they really exist not as nostalgic ideologues say we should remember them.

Overcome Neoliberal Bias against the Public Good

Like a pitiless X-ray that shows the hidden pathologies in our bodies, the coronavirus pandemic has shown deep problems in the established democracies. In particular, there are weaknesses in all our social support systems, from families and local communities to large-scale public institutions.

Health care has been at once heroic and one step short of failure. Nursing homes have been among the worst centers of infection. Schools continue to face massive upheaval and hard choices.

But the problems Covid-19 has made glaringly obvious have been developing for years. Neoliberal thinking has prioritized deficit reduction and often austerity programs, especially in the wake of financial crisis. One argument was that good health care—or education or old age care—cost too much for the public budget. Another argument was that the only relevant question was efficiency, and this was best decided by markets. But most basically, neoliberal ideology one-sidedly stressed individual action empowered by private property, not the empowerment of citizens through their collective action.

The great public institutions of the welfare states have been neglected, defunded, or even closed down or sold off and privatized. This is not just a matter of economic exigency. The public good has been devalued in favor of private goods. Democratic decision-making has been sidelined in favor of market efficiency. It is crucial to reclaim citizen decision-making for democracy.

In the late twentieth century, neoliberalism brought a one-sided emphasis on private property and markets. Finance, corporate growth, new technologies, and globalization all joined in producing great wealth. But just as in the nineteenth century, this wealth went disproportionately to the very rich. Inequality increased dramatically.[70] At the same time, economic transformation upended community life and social support systems for millions of citizens. Not least, health care, education, and other institutions were cut back, privatized, and reorganized to secure revenue by charging customers rather than providing a taxpayer-funded public service.

Markets are efficient for many purposes. Through their efficiencies and incentives for productivity they provide public benefits. But they are not organized to provide the public good.[71] For one thing, markets fail to produce and allocate public goods effectively. Clean air and water and reduction of carbon consumption are well-known examples. They can be sold as ordinary consumer goods. You can go to an oxygen bar, buy a bottle of water, and pay an airline to plant a tree offsetting the environmental impact of your flight. But such private purchases cannot push production up to adequate scale. They introduce costs of their own. Above all, no sum of such private transactions provides full enjoyment of the good. Clean air, sparkling rivers, and an ocean both unpolluted and free from the warming and rising levels of climate change can be achieved only by working together. Markets fail to provide public goods because individuals either don't want to or aren't able to pay for the consumption of others. Goods that must be consumed by an indefinite public need to be paid for publicly.

The public good is not the sum of private goods, nor does it consist only of public goods in the narrow, economic sense of those that can only be enjoyed if shared and are not reduced by the sharing (such as clean air; discussed in Chapter 2). The public good also includes the equitable distribution of all goods—including access to public goods. It includes equitable distribution of public bads—like exposure to pollution or the risks from climate change. Above all, the public good is a matter of values not measured simply in higher or lower levels of consumption. Freedom, equality, and solidarity are central. Democracy itself is *a* public good. But it exists for *the* public good. Democrats share in public debate partly to determine how they should understand the public good.

Providing public services is crucial to the legitimacy of democracy. It is a matter of citizen empowerment and inclusion. It should not be undermined or held hostage by partisan political polarization. But neither should health care, education, policing, nor other public services be treated as just more consumer goods, like ice cream or cars.

Not only public institutions that were specifically part of the welfare states of *les trente glorieuses* suffered. The provision of needed services suffered much more widely. For example, in the United States, many corporations stopped providing health care and retirement benefits to their employees. Some reneged on commitments already made to retirees. Hospitals that had been founded as public charities were increasingly turned into private businesses. Private schools grew at the expense of public. Even postal services were cut back or terminated.

This new disruption was made more abrupt by severe crises in the mid-1970s and 2008–2011. In each case, the relations between government and the economy were rebuilt in ways that undercut the well-being of workers and ordinary citizens and reduced investment in the public good. In each case, there was reaction, ranging from growth in populist politics to drug use and suicide. During the same period, the state security regime was intensified both in the "War on Drugs" and then the "War on Terrorism."

Our challenge now is to produce a more positive second phase to the double movement. Proposals are commonly met with the objection that institutions to serve the public good cost too much. This has been true for years in attacks by British Conservatives (especially neoliberals among them) on the National Health Service and other public institutions. It is glaringly evident in 2021 US Senate debates that have focused on the anticipated cost of public investments rather than their anticipated benefits—with key roles played by senators with personal wealth and close industry connections. Of course, health care costs money. It is not unreasonable that there are debates about "what we can afford." But answering this question demands comparison of options. Current policies embrace high costs for the military and police—security against certain kinds of threats. But investment in public health may actually be a greater source of human security. Current policies offer massive tax breaks to wealthy investors and giant corporations—both legally and through their tolerance of tax avoidance. The crucial question is "What do we *choose* to afford?"

Health care has become expensive. High-tech medicine and intensive care near the end of life are major factors in all developed countries. But the United States spends more on health care than any other country, partly because it has failed to institute universal coverage and to use the leverage of government to hold down costs—like those of prescription drugs, which are dramatically higher in the United States than in Canada or Europe. What Americans spend, moreover, is skewed away from investments in public health, primary care and emergency rooms. Provision of public services is basic to achieving the public good. As modern societies grew large and complex, with international linkages and new technologies, it became crucial to provide these services through public institutions, not only local communities. And providing them well was one of the major legitimating foci for democracy.

So, renewing and improving delivery of public services must be at the top of any agenda for recovery from Covid-19—and collective action for a better future. This must be more than just increased funding for existing institutions, though that is vital. Reform and innovation are also needed. Ongoing action either to protect jobs or support the unemployed is urgently needed as a matter of both relief and stimulus. But even while taking stop-gap measures, it is important to initiate long-term improvements.

Care for the aged is one case in point. Provision for the elderly has greatly improved since the days when many lived in dire poverty. But though a significant fraction now live well, others find the combination of savings, pensions, and insurance inadequate. This is partly because people live longer. It is partly because many have lost the benefit of pensions as employers changed priorities (or invested pension holdings in a dishonest business that collapsed, as in the case of Enron). It is certainly because savings are inadequate, and it is clearly because too many lack insurance or their insurance covers too little. The most common immediate cause of destitution is catastrophic illness, including of course the illnesses of aging. The costs of end-of-life care are challenging for European public health systems. But the United States is out of step with both the needs of its citizens and the standard of care established by other democratic countries. Failure to focus on the public good is a reason—and it could be reversed.

Now, strikingly, care homes have been important nodes in transmission of infection. This is not just because their residents are less healthy, because they concentrate people together or because some residents find it hard to master complete compliance with preventive measures. It is also because they employ low-wage service workers who have to move back and forth between care homes and residences elsewhere. It is crucial to think at the same time about the services provided and the workers who provide them.

Too little provision and support have been provided for such vital service workers. Too often they have actually been forced to work when sick. Infection control procedures have often been lax. The culprits include lax regulation of facilities more concerned about their bottom lines than either the welfare of residents or the public good.

But even behind the issues of bad or selfish management are wider problems. The situation of the elderly is—or should be—a quintessential public concern. Indeed, this was part of the logic of Social Security from its inception. Not only would it help worthy workers in their retirement; it would create a better society in which the elderly were not poor.

Frontline health care workers became the beloved celebrities of the first months of Covid-19. Doctors and nurses were manifestly doing important work, sometimes heroically, amid long hours and personal risks. In several European countries it became a public ritual to show solidarity, banging pots from windows, singing from balconies.

But doctors and nurses are hardly the whole of health care workers. To run a hospital takes physicians' assistants, nurses' aides, physical, occupational, and psychological therapists, social workers, technicians, dieticians, orderlies, cleaners, food service workers, mechanics, computer staff, hospital administrators, and clerical staff. All have taken risks and all have played crucial roles in delivering health care during the pandemic.

There's more. Hospitals need deliveries; patients and their families need rides. Drivers are vital—just as they manifestly have been for all the people who have been receiving food and other necessities by delivery at home. The deliveries demand workers in warehouses. Hospitals need communications services, energy supplies, and waste disposal. They need their own security, and they need help from the policy. Their machinery needs repairs. They need lawyers, insurance, and financial services, and for better or worse they rely like other businesses on consultants.

Health care systems are part of a broader transformation of work and employment. As employment in manufacturing, mining, and before them farming has dwindled, new jobs have been created disproportionately in the service sector. This is a huge and internally diverse category. It includes teachers, librarians, warehouse workers, truck drivers, electricians, plumbers, wait staff in restaurants, legal aides, police and fire safety officers, prison guards, sales associates, sports stars, and the less visible workers selling tickets and cleaning the stadiums.

The impact of Covid-19 on service workers has been enormous. First, service-sector workers have been among those most exposed to infection. This includes health care workers, of course, and it is remarkable how long many had to work without proper provision of protective equipment in 2020. Many other care workers—like those in nursing homes—were also affected. Indeed, so were all those whose occupations depend on human contact. Drivers necessarily move among possible risky locations. More police officers died from Covid-19 in 2020 than from all other causes combined.[72]

Second, job losses were massive as restaurants and stores closed, events were canceled, and TV shows stopped filming. This was a huge disruption, even where unemployment benefits compensated, and not all short-term unemployment. Perhaps a fifth of all restaurants and retail businesses closed permanently and more will close as the recession continues. When the pandemic and lockdowns ease, job growth will return but without help the local businesses will not. The pandemic accelerated not only a shift to remote work but the growth of markets based on logistics not locations. Many workers are holding back, dubious about both compensation and working conditions. However, both full employment and good wages are important for democracy itself as well as for the economy narrowly conceived. They are basic to the empowerment of citizens.

Third, reorganizations of work and family balances have produced major stresses. Working from home was much easier for those with office jobs, spacious homes, and high enough incomes to order in without worry. There were different challenges for parents with children home from school—and these fell disproportionately on women, which in turn led many women to leave the work force. Parents pressed for schools to reopen, but many did not press enough for teachers to receive the protection and support they needed. Covid family care keeps many workers—especially women—out of the labor market.

Covid-19 is likely to become a more manageable, if endemic, disease. Vaccination, continued vigilance, and public health improvements are all crucial—and all have proved difficult in a polarized, hyper-partisan political context.

Quite beyond Covid, a very big part of the service sector consists of work providing care.[73] Health care includes not just direct provision of medical services but eldercare facilities, nursing homes, rehabilitation centers. Teachers and all the other employees of schools do care work. There's nonmedical care for the elderly. For the disabled. For children.

While some care workers are elite professionals like doctors, many more struggle to make ends meet at or near minimum wages. Indeed, they would be among the beneficiaries of raising the minimum wage. Care workers are more likely than most to be female, people of color, and immigrants or from immigrant families.

Failure to improve both health care and education reveal direct failure of democracy.[74] Survey after survey has made clear that citizens want better primary and emergency health care and that citizens want better schools and support for both teachers and students.[75] Distrust of government has not reduces support for government action; indeed, inadequate funding and delivery has been a reason for distrust.[76] Citizens have lacked the capacity to make their will law. Massive lobbying by the pharmaceutical industry (which profited hugely from selling drugs at higher prices than anywhere else in the world) has held back health care improvement in the United States.

Everywhere, resistance to better funding for education and health has been fueled by advertising and lobbying on behalf of corporations and the wealthy. Neoliberal thinking prioritizes deficit reduction and often austerity programs, especially in the wake of financial crisis. The public good needs a comparably strong campaign.

Citizens could demand high-quality, universal health care. Delivering this is one of the major contributions governments can make, whether they do it through direct provision or an insurance system. But, of course, this costs money, and there are debates about what we can afford. Perhaps this is a case, however, where we cannot afford to *avoid* the investment.

We can ask similar questions in every sector. Are market criteria of efficiency and profit or other systemic imperatives substituting for actual public voice in the decisions about what should count as the public good? How can we bring more democracy into basic social choices? Take higher education. Inequality and competition focus attention on outcomes for the highest elite of privileged students, not the majority (as we saw in discussing meritocracy in Chapter 4). In response to competitive pressures, universities make choices that intensify hierarchy, distract from core teaching missions, and cause the overall system to become more expensive. They too often judge research success by volume of funding not by quality, contribution to knowledge, or positive impact. They build ever-fancier facilities to impress applicants. They stick rigidly to curricular structures that are more bureaucratically convenient than helpful to students. But there is little evidence that this is what democratic publics want from their universities. One of the big post-pandemic challenges is to make high-quality university education accessible without forcing students and their families to pay high fees and commonly take on huge debts.

It is wise to ask about costs, and it is crucial to take competing priorities seriously. But it is also crucial to ask, is the tax system fair? Existing tax codes and enforcement structures allow massive tax evasion. The really large-scale tax avoidance is done by the very rich and by corporations that are disproportionately owned by the very rich. Globalization and financialization make this easier. Money is stashed in tax havens and shell companies. It is moved around fast, staying a step ahead of tax collectors. Global corporations manipulate where they pay taxes, shop for lower rates, and sometimes evade taxes altogether. All this deprives governments of the funds they need to do their work and makes other citizens pay more. Better written tax codes and better enforcement could radically cut back the abuse.[77] Tentative first steps toward a global minimum corporate tax are inadequate, but they do show that action is possible.[78]

Democracies need taxation to be transparent so that citizens can understand who pays what and what it goes for. This is also generally an argument for keeping the tax system simple. But what should be taxed and how? Wealth or income or sales? Could there be a "Tobin tax"—a tiny levy on each financial transaction above a certain scale to reduce volatility as well as produce revenue?[79] Should large inheritances or perhaps wealth generally be taxed? What should business and their corporations pay? And if there is an income tax, how progressive should it be? In almost all countries, the rich pay a bigger percentage, but how much bigger should this be? It is worth recalling that taxes rates were much higher during the postwar boom—*les trente glorieuses*—without stopping growth. In short, we have choices. Tax policy is not dictated by sheer necessity. The choices need to be made by democratic decisions with the public good in mind.

In direct opposition to democracy, the wealth of individuals and corporations has commonly been deployed in campaigns intended to starve the public sector, on the grounds that we "lack the money" to do better. It is important to rally democrats on the other side of the question, to ask how much policy should encourage the accumulation of such vast wealth rather than work to secure its redistribution for the public good. The proper business of democracy is to weigh trade-offs among different public purposes and different approaches to each.

Questions about what a country can afford are always questions of priorities. There are big questions about trade-offs among health care, education, prisons, police, and the military. It's what one chooses to pay for in each case. But there are also trade-offs between facilitating private accumulation of wealth and providing public goods. Equally important is how the decisions are made. The United States has organized health care overwhelmingly on a private and largely for-profit basis. This has given markets, financial institutions, and corporate actors control over the crucial decisions. If outsourcing all production of personal protective equipment to China seemed most efficient, this is the path they chose. High-tech medical treatments and elective surgeries became revenue streams—even bases for medical tourism. Ironically, the United States, which operates the most unequal medical system of any of the rich democracies, also pays the most for health care. The public pays a large part of the cost through expensive insurance, even though it doesn't receive the benefit of universal coverage and good public health.

Think Big

We must think big. Democracy can and should inspire and be inspired by new ideas of what is possible.

When the United States was founded, an unprecedented openness to democratic participation was exciting. The excitement reached and helped to stimulate democratic experiments in Europe, Latin America, and elsewhere.

Once established, democracies relied on recurrent experiments to continue their self-improvement. They changed the franchise and electoral rules. They experimented with different approaches to taxation, financial regulation, food safety, policing, public media, schools, and support for the unemployed. They also experimented with ways to preserve local communities and save family farms—not always successfully.

Democratic societies today confront climate change, radical transformations in work and employment, tensions between economic globalization and political nationalism, new vulnerabilities to global pandemics, new levels of threat from global crime and globalized tax evasion, and degenerations of democracy itself. As challenging as it sounds, we need to address all these issues at once. There is no point arguing over which is most basic or urgent. We can't deal with them one by one; they are too deeply entangled with each other.

We need exciting experiments in greater democracy now. Is it possible contemporary democracies could make great strides on advancing equality in a less rapacious economy, tackling environmental degradation and climate change, and renewing community and social solidarity? We think so. But to think this big, on all three fronts, we must first of all break with the constricted and impoverished social imagination that has been characteristic of the neoliberal era.

The last time the world's established democracies faced comparably severe and multidimensional crises was during the Great Depression and the coming of World War II. The stock market crashed. Overleveraged and underregulated banks failed. Workers lost their jobs. Farmers lost their land and livelihoods. Drought and dust storms brought crop failure and financial ruin to farmers throughout the plains and prairies of the central United

States and Canada. Hundreds of thousands were uprooted, virtually refugees inside their own countries. Financial globalization meant that what was initially an American crisis quickly engulfed Europe. It brought hunger and severe hardship, perhaps most of all to Central Europe. Millions were driven to emigrate, but they were only part of a wave of departures from Europe, driven by economic as well as political disaster, class as well as racism.

Democracy degenerated. Citizen efficacy was undermined by economic devastation. In much of Europe, nationalist politics embraced ideologies of ethnic purity rather than inclusion. Jews were scapegoated and attacked by anti-Semitic mobs and state policies alike. So were immigrants, gypsies, and homosexuals. Political division was extreme. There were pitched battles between communists and fascists on the streets of many European cities.

Even amid this widespread crisis, democracy was also renewed—but not everywhere. It collapsed as the Right seized power in Italy and Germany and was defeated in Spain. After Nazi invasion, France was divided between resistance and collaboration. But in much of the rest of the world, including notably the United States, response to the Great Depression itself became a democratic project, strengthening national integration and participation as well as beginning the process of stabilizing capitalism, providing for the security of citizens, and building social institutions. This would continue during and especially after the war.

Running for President in 1932, Franklin Roosevelt pledged himself to achieve a New Deal for the American People. This was nothing less than a project to save democracy.

The New Deal set out to create jobs and establish social security, restore financial stability and bring transparency to Wall Street, conserve the environment and build housing. It built energy and transportation infrastructure, public parks, and high school gymnasiums. It launched an effort to record and save traditional American music, and it brought art into the new public spaces it helped to create, such as libraries and post offices.[80]

Crucially, the New Deal was not a plan formulated in advance. Rather innovation was continuous, and it combined different programmatic ideas, many from social movements and experiments at more local levels. Some had been pursued since the Populist and Progressive movements of the late nineteenth and early twentieth centuries. They were given urgency by financial collapse and mass unemployment. But the New Deal was not just emergency response. It was an effort to build better institutions for the future. And it came with determination to think big.

Even in the midst of crisis, even alongside hardship and desperation, the New Deal showed it is possible to launch efforts to build a better society and not just to cope. And even without a master plan, diverse projects of improvement can contribute to overall progress.

Not every New Deal policy should be emulated. Partly to maintain needed political support, many were designed to benefit whites more than Blacks or indeed to exclude Blacks altogether. Some were simply poorly designed. And as they were institutionalized during World War II and the postwar era, many relied more and more on centralized bureaucracy and became less open to bottom-up creativity and initiative.

European countries also built great institutions during *les trente glorieuses*. These provided health care, education, old age support, better media, environmental protection, and regulation of banking and finance. But those who built them trusted bureaucracy—rules, hierarchy, formal procedures—more than they trusted ordinary people and social relationships. They empowered central governments more than they strengthened local and intermediate-level society.

Neoliberals responded to the problems of bureaucracy and centralized decision-making with attacks on almost all institutions—even while they allowed or encouraged continued erosion of community and intermediate associations. It is now a crucial task to restore associational life at all scales and balance it better with needed state structures.

Capitalism has changed with the rise of giant global corporations, the ascendancy of finance, globalization, and transformative new technologies. It will inevitably change further. Communities are again being disrupted by economic transformations. There has been a failure of social solidarity. Not nearly enough has been done to provide support for those bearing the brunt of deindustrialization and those for whom globalization is a challenge rather than a boon. But this is not just a matter of helping those who might otherwise be left behind and it is not just a matter of the last wave of economic changes. It is also a matter of supporting those who play crucial roles in our new economic and social formations but often without much power or enough compensation: care workers, logistics workers, educators, and others.

The Covid-19 pandemic has called attention to all these service and care workers but hasn't yet brought them fairer compensation. This may change as labor shortages develop. But a basic factor is that service workers are much less unionized than industrial workers were when that sector dominated. Collective representation is a basic right and a practical need for workers, and the greater the asymmetries between them and their employers, the more they need it. Indeed, it is precisely because of unions that steelworkers, autoworkers, and machinists long had good pay and good benefits. But for the last fifty years unions have declined. This is partly because of deindustrialization, which hit traditionally unionized industries hard. It is also because neoliberal campaigners and politicians introduced policies designed to weaken unions. But it is also because unions have not reached service workers effectively enough. And that is partly because service workers are disproportionately female, minority, and immigrant.

There is no escape from wrenching transformations of work and employment. There is no easy answer to climate change and environmental degradation. But perhaps there are ways to work on both together—build a sustainable society with good jobs, and advance justice in the transition.[81] This is the premise behind calls for a "Green New Deal." Making this happen would require large-scale investment, social transformation, and lots of creativity. But it could also renew democracy.

Recognizing that the phrase "Green New Deal" triggers opposition—and also evokes a program associated with his rivals in the Democratic primaries—US President Biden avoids the phrase. He has settled on the slogan "Build Back Better," which doesn't do justice to the strong initiatives he has launched—more than his critics on the Left expected. The slogan sounds too much like repair and restoration and not enough like the innovation needed to renew democracy—and social life in America.

Correcting faults and failings is a start. Degenerations of democracy both reflect and produce innumerable procedural problems, broken mechanisms, damages to institutions. We face immediate challenges from the Covid-19 disaster and accompanying recession. But we need more than a quick fix.

Whatever the slogan, the first response of many critics is to try to deflate optimism, to undermine any "can do" spirit. The costs are too high; they will fuel too much inflation. The promises won't be fulfilled. Can't we just rebuild roads without building a better Internet? Do we have to provide better care for children at the same time? Will enough of the benefits come to my people? Will too many go to *those* people (who by implication don't really deserve them)?

Of course, proposals for trillions of dollars in federal investment demand scrutiny. Passing legislation often does require compromises and the bundling together of projects in ways that make proposals opaque. But picking potentially promising proposals apart has become— like hyper-partisanship and polarization—a primary mode of public engagement.

Europe has developed skepticism into cynicism and a certain amount of depression. In most European countries, voters seem weary of all the old stripes of politicians: Social Democrats, Conservatives, and Liberals. Social Democrats have perhaps lost the most (so far), but pretty much all the conventional political parties are broken. They are seen mainly as mechanisms for some people to seek power and sectional benefits; no one really expects exciting proposals. And they are all losing power.

We need to be able to approach projects like this with optimism and shared effort. This is perhaps the most important lesson the original New Deal offers to a Green New Deal today.

It Takes a Movement

Perhaps the most striking thing about contemporary politics is that there is no large-scale movement for building a better society. There is discontent. There are mobilizations. There are many protests, but only rarely do these coalesce into larger movements. Most remain just moments.[82] But from Occupy Wall Street to the Indignados to the protests in Turkey's Zeki Square and France's Yellow Vests, they are more or less ephemeral. Anarchist direct action is widespread, and anarchists are prominent in a range of mobilizations. But their loose-knit networks do not easily scale up for sustained or larger-scale mobilization.

Black Lives Matters did scale up dramatically, at least for a time. It also connected a range of different kinds of collective action in the United States—including community development projects, public art, and environmental justice, as well as the protests against police violence that have been its most visible face. BLM has sparked international resonance. But it hasn't yet reached critical mass for a general transformation of society.

The women's movement was genuinely transformative in the peak years of "second-wave feminism." Its issues remain significant, but the movement is fragmented—not least by resistance of many young women to the frame or label "feminist." Successful mobilizations such as #MeToo are oriented more to media than to membership; it remains to be seen whether strong connections will be forged across issues and whether response to abuses will extend to an agenda of social transformation.

It's been years since social democracy was really a movement. Over the last five decades it was downgraded into just a set of political parties, mostly on the center left. New parties, like the Greens, are rising. But most offer fresher faces and cleaner hands more than they offer transformative visions. Nationalist parties have grown more by embracing old ethnic prejudices, racism, and anxiety about cultural change than by offering practical proposals for national cohesion and improvement. The same goes for Bexit.

The labor movement has been in decline for decades, but the current crisis of work has brought new energy. New ideas and approaches are important; it can't succeed simply as an extension of the old labor movement based in nineteenth- and early twentieth-century industries. To grow it will need to be much more creative. Without deserting commitments to jobs and economic security, it will need to develop new visions beyond the workplace narrowly understood. Centrally, these will need to be visions of renewed democracy. Goals that can't readily be met by actions on (disappearing) shop floors will need to be pursued through community organizing, elections, and quasi-political mechanisms such as ballot initiatives.

All these things are connected. We need to pay attention to how different change projects affect each other but not imagine we can or should control all the connections. After all, if these are truly creative, transformative projects, they will generate new outcomes and new possibilities for more action.

Climate activism is perhaps the largest and most dynamic social movement in the world today. It has attracted a huge base of participants, especially among young people. It resonates with a still wider range of sympathizers. So far, its focus has been mostly on averting apocalypse—an obviously worthy goal! This demands a sense of urgency and need for action to reduce carbon emissions. Mitigating the damage already done is increasingly crucial. In both regards, the climate movement faces the challenge of generating commitment from national governments that also face competing and sometimes more immediate political pressures. This is where a Green New Deal (or something like it) comes in.

The premise, in a nutshell, is that we can tackle climate change and improve economic livelihoods at the same time. Shifting to electricity over fossil fuel will generate jobs in manufacturing and installing a new green infrastructure. This means not just new technologies but also better urban development: reduced commuting, better housing near public transport, less waste, less loss of water supplies, and so forth. Transforming industrial production, shipping, and logistics can also be basic to an economy at once less carbon-intensive and more oriented to human needs. Not only material production and infrastructure are important. Health care, education, and other services are crucial sectors for jobs and for meeting societal and human needs.

Most Green New Deal proposals seek large-scale growth to achieve to achieve a transformation adequate to the scale of both climate change and social need. So far, change at local levels has not received enough attention, though it is crucial. Thinking big can include reconceiving how place and community fit into large-scale structures, bringing both environmental and social gains.

Interconnected problems with interconnected solutions. This is not only a matter of thinking at planetary scale. It is necessarily also a matter of forging strong connections of people to places, of localities to each other, and among all different scales from local through national, global, and planetary.

We say with emphasis "a" Green New Deal, not "the" Green New Deal. We mean to signal that there is not yet any single, authoritative articulation of the relevant movement goals or potential policies. Discussion moved to the forefront in 2019 when Congresswoman Alexandra Ocasio-Cortez and Senator Ed Markey introduced bills to make it official policy.[83] These US efforts have echoes around the world, including both movement-organizing and proposed legislation in all the established democracies.[84] There is an increasingly rich discussion of the agenda for such a program, but this remains a work in progress.[85] This is not a flaw. It means that democratic engagement can shape a Green New Deal and the movement that might bring it into place. The US debate has been changed by the Biden administration, as it has adopted some proposals but resisted the overall frame of the project. It has been changed also by political polarization, an evenly split Senate, anxieties over inflation, and the uncertainties of Covid. Major infrastructural renewal is gathering momentum. But the question of just how transformational efforts will be remains squarely on the table.

Engagements in projects like a Green New Deal differ with national contexts and even vary among states and cities in the United States. Though climate change is among the most global of challenges, it does not affect every country or community or cultural category of people in the same way. Equally, there is variation in the other issues any Green New Deal must address, the resources it can bring into mobilization, and the opposition it will face.

We also say "a" Green New Deal because the needed movement must be at once more ambitious and more modest. It must be more ambitious because it is not enough to bring together action on climate change and economic futures (including jobs). As both Black Lives Matter and the coronavirus pandemic remind us, there are other crucial, connected issues from education to health care and public security. Either some version of a Green New Deal needs to be broader, or it needs to be part of a more general movement for social transformation.

It must also be more modest because it needs to be open to democratic participation and continual reshaping of the agenda. Some existing proposals are worryingly technocratic and centralized. They imply that figuring out precisely the right techno-economic actions and getting governments to finance and implement them will be enough. Even if this were possible, it would make achieving a Green New Deal a project for experts and officials, not popular action.

It is not enough to find technical solutions to these issues and call for them to be implemented by experts, governments, and businesses. In the first place, technical solutions from carbon capture to reoxygenation of oceans around coral reefs may be all to the good, but they do not add up to an overall resolution to the crisis. This can only come with societal transformation, changes in the way we live, work, produce, trade, build housing and transportation systems, and indeed manage our relations with others. It is crucial to develop a broad, democratic movement to join citizens together in guiding transformation and securing a better future. This is no doubt necessary for political will, but equally such a movement can renew solidarity and citizen empowerment, nationally, as well as in local communities and intermediate associations. Such mobilization can provide a positive completion to the current phase of double movement, responding to the damage of the last fifty years. Fighting for a sustainable future, for a just economy, and for effective and fair social institutions can be at the same time a fight to renew democracy.

Social transformation will take resources. But thinking big is more than committing a lot of money to financial stimulus or relief after the Covid-19 pandemic. Each of these may be crucial, but such money can be invested in ways too close to business as usual—renewing polluting industries, for example, producing more low-paying jobs in high-profit companies, or further militarizing the police. Transformation demands not just resources but reaching beyond established ways of doing things and changing not just personal habits but both place-specific communities and powerful large-scale systems. This is a task for democratic, not technocratic change.

The challenge today is to knit response to disruptions and building for a better future together in an effective, positive movement. Such a movement needs to engage people in the effort to renew democracy and build a better society as well as to solve practical problems. This is what social democratic parties accomplished in the middle of the twentieth centuries. Their success was only partial, and the same formulae cannot in any case be repeated. We can build on what was learned, but a twenty-first-century movement for democracy and social solidarity will need to be different.

Action from central governments is absolutely essential to a Green New Deal. Such action will include large-scale investment, but it cannot be limited to stimulus spending. There must be an equal focus on reorganization of economies to reduce climate damage and on renewal of solidarity and on reversal of the degenerations of democracy. New institutions will need to be created and old ones renewed. We should make sure they are dynamic, nimble, and responsive. But it is also important to facilitate and engage with decentralized social organization among ordinary citizens—and indeed residents who are not yet citizens. There will be different worthwhile projects in different communities and states. These should be interconnected but need not be uniform. A Green New Deal should be a bottom-up project, not only top down.

More generally, governments pursuing Green New Deal restructuring of national economies would do well to fund ways to support small and medium-sized businesses located throughout their countries. Businesses are not all large corporations and not all driven by capital accumulation. Liberals and the Left need to get over a specious equation lumping of small business into large-scale capitalism and consequent hostility to all business. Right-wing ideologues have seized on the same specious equation to convince small business owners that their interests are similar to those of large corporations. They are not, and local business organization could help to reverse or mitigate the centralizing tendencies of the capitalist economy. To be sure, global logistical systems are convenient, but carbon-intensive delivery of goods to far-flung individuals need not be the entire future.

Because many problems are global—from climate change to corporate power, financial crises, and illicit trafficking in money, weapons, drugs, and people—it is tempting to say social movements should also be global. Global mobilizations are already reshaping understanding of themes from feminism to climate change to alternative economies. Cultural change is a basic dimension of effective mobilization for large-scale social change. So global connections must be part of addressing contemporary problems and seeking a better future.

But movements and change are organized not only globally, but also at the levels of nation-states and local communities and a variety of scales in between. This variety is important to the effectiveness of action. States, provinces, cities, and regions all need to play a positive role and doing so demands changing the politics that drive central governments and international agreements. Organizing at multiple levels is also crucial to achieving truly democratic, solidaristic results. For change to be democractic, we need to empower citizens, achieve inclusive understandings of what makes our body politic whole, and reduce polarization. For that to happen, we need to renew communities, strengthen intermediate associations, and build national solidarity—as well as to link the democratic projects of different countries together.

It has been hard to achieve unity in the face of a global pandemic; this does not bode well for facing the even more massive and frightening challenge of climate change. We must think and act globally, but we cannot simply resume globalization as we have known it. In the first place, equality matters very basically to achieving good levels of health. As we have already seen in the Covid-19 pandemic, the impressive success of science—sometimes corporate science—in developing vaccines is not enough. Distribution and public health systems are crucial. There is a basic and troubling political economy to what polities and localities have the vaccine and which must beg.

There are lessons in the social organization of administering the vaccine or other treatment. Responses are sometimes centralized and top-down; they work through a bureaucratic hierarchy to reach nodes of actual care provision. This is certainly better than nothing, but it is not as effective as decentralized engagement from a variety of often more local actors. For all the challenges it faced, public health response to AIDS went better than response to tuberculosis precisely because of this distributed engagement.[86]

Could we do away with poverty, improve schooling, ensuring adequate health care, and reduce regional imbalances? Yes. But we won't if we don't recover both solidarity and a sense of citizen efficacy. A Green New Deal would be a good start, but only a start.

The full restoration of democracy will require a full return to the rule of law, both in its letter, but also in the spirit of republicanism in its historic form. This entails, among other things, that no individual, or group, or faction has a right to claim permanent power. Free and fair public exchange and debate must flourish and be effective in shaping policy. This is of course easier said than achieved, especially in our new reality of polarized and siloed media. Proposals such as better fact-checking and regulation of intentional distortion and promotion of violence can be helpful. But much more basically we need better connections among citizens across lines of division and distinction. This is a key reason to seek more equal educational structures, to consider mandatory national service, and to build both local communities and intermediate, crosscutting associations. Not least, though, it is important to nurture citizens' knowledge of their countries and each other, the republican spirit of civic virtue, and an orientation to the public good. We need connections and we need commitment.

Democracy is not simply a set of formal procedures to be established. It is a project. It is made and remade and advanced in the course of solving problems. Real *democratic* renewal means politics that addresses the full range of issues in citizens' lives. There is no solution in trying to reform political processes separate from economic and social issues.

Current challenges are enormous, but taking action can be a path to democratic renewal. If we join with each other in great national—and local—projects, in building institutions, in providing mutual support, then we can renew solidarity and democracy. Essential as repair is, it is not enough. We need new democratic experiments. We need to imagine new possibilities and test these in innumerable experiments—sometimes in local government not national, in social movements rather than enduring institutions, and in policies that will be improved by repeated revisions not delayed in search of perfection.

Despite all the difficulties of existing democratic institutions and practices, we need more democracy not less.

Conclusion

The wave of democratic transitions and consolidation that seemed so promising and spread so swiftly across the globe in the final quarter of the last century is now in serious disarray, troubled and turbulent.

That wave began in 1974 with the retreat of authoritarian governments in southern Europe (Portugal, Spain, and Greece) and arrived in Latin America in the 1980s (Brazil, Argentina, and Chile). It continued with the recuperation and restoration of democracies in Asia and Africa. Throughout the postcolonial world, democratic governments had withered and broken down, confronted with massive poverty and economic hardship, ethnic and religious conflicts, and machinations of corrupt and self-serving elites. India and Senegal were exceptions, with their democratic regimes enjoying continuity, though not without challenges.

The authoritarian regimes that took over democracies with the promise of mitigating poverty, corruption, and internal conflict only exacerbated these problems. Most were eventually forced to relinquish power to popular movements and elected governments. Finally, in the early 1990s, in the aftermath of an abrupt collapse of communist regimes in the Soviet Union and its satellite states, the great wave crested. Democratization came to Eastern Europe and Russia. At almost the same moment, South Africa's apartheid regime also gave way to democracy. It seemed as if a new era of democracy was dawning, another springtime of the people was at hand.

During that euphoric period, numerous democratic constitutions were written and ratified; elections were held all over the world (though they were not always free and fair, and occasionally were violent). People marched, and dictators fell. Blueprints for republican institutions were drafted and debated and plans for nation-building were devised and circulated. Scholars spoke and wrote excitedly about the importance of a robust public sphere and a pluralistic civil society for nurturing democratic culture and subjectivity. Social movements dedicated to promoting social justice on multiple fronts proliferated. Human rights discourse grew louder and could no longer be ignored. Nongovernmental organizations, self-appointed champions of the weak and dispossessed, emerged as an influential and ubiquitous force on the political scene, both nationally and globally.

This great democratic wave seemed unstoppable. Political scientists celebrated it as the "Third Wave" and developed a specialty in the comparative study of democratic transitions. Dubbed "transitology," this line of research focused on mechanisms and variations in what was understood to be almost an inexorable march of progress. Francis Fukuyama, invoking Hegel, proclaimed the final triumph of the liberal-capitalist democracy—the best way to structure and govern political economy—and declared the end of history. At long last, the two grand Enlightenment narratives of reason and of freedom had coalesced. Even for those less ebullient than Fukuyama, it seemed as if there were no viable and legitimate alternatives to the democratic mode of governance, liberal-capitalist or otherwise.

That great promise of the "end of history," however, and the institution of a "new world order" never materialized. It turned out to be a mirage, a "false dawn."

What happened? Did we miss something? Was there something else that was afoot during that tumultuous quarter-century? So certain of the brighter days ahead, what didn't we see in the half-light?

In this book, three of us address these questions, both individually and collaboratively. Perplexed and dismayed, we have been mulling over these questions for some time. The diagnosis we offer is not exhaustive, but it suggests new ways of thinking about democracy today. To be more precise, in the context of democracy's ongoing crisis and what it has disclosed, we have sought to rethink the democratic project in terms of its intrinsic strengths and vulnerabilities and ask how it might contend with the challenges posed by the changing social world within which it is embedded. Charles Taylor and Craig Calhoun have been more determined to be optimistic and suggest paths forward. Dilip Gaonkar has been more tempted to think the Greeks were right—that democracy is inherently unstable and that change is frequently not progressive.

Waves and Cycles and Predictions of the End

Democracy is under duress, not just here and there, but across the globe. Its decay has touched all the world's regions. Larry Diamond, a comparative political scientist who assiduously tracks and maps democratic waves, has unambiguously stated that we have now moved into a precipitously recessionary phase of the third wave.[1] He might be right, but we need to ask how predictable and internally consistent the wave pattern is. Can we be confident this is only a temporary setback? How much do the individual cases of democratic crisis within a larger "wave" differ? What distinguishes this recessionary phase from the previous two? Is there a deeper crisis?

It is tempting to think of democracy's present troubles as precipitated by the same set of recurring conditions and causes that corroded and undermined democracies in the previous recessionary phases. Such an interpretation also conveniently assimilates the "wave theory" with Aristotle's famous account of how the three forms of rule—monarchy, aristocracy, and democracy—are caught in a perpetual cycle propelled by tyranny and oligarchy (monarchy and aristocracy's degenerate twins). According to Aristotle, the vicious cycle can be arrested only by the founding of a *politeia* (the fairer twin of democracy), a delicately balanced and assiduously cultivated form of "mixed government" that, while drawing on the virtues of previous forms of rule, avoids some of their most dangerous vulnerabilities.[2] The founders of modern democratic republics, with the United States as the inaugural and paradigmatic case, appear to have partly heeded Aristotle's advice. The redacted model of *politeia* provides the conceptual and normative nucleus for the modern republican imaginary of a constitutionally bound and institutionally fortified political order sustained by virtuous citizenry with a shared vision of public good.

There's the rub. In our view, this very republican imaginary is now under severe duress. It has guided modern Western democracies since their inception and partially succeeded in attenuating, if not arresting, the cyclical dialectic of expansion and recession. It has helped idealized versions of a few of the world's strongest democracies stand as models for democracies elsewhere. But there is now degeneration even in those previous exemplars.

Taylor and Calhoun, in Chapter 1 and Chapter 2, respectively, provide accounts of how that imaginary has lost some of its traction today: declining citizen efficacy, weakening local communities, fraying intergenerational bonds, evaporating small-scale economic opportunity, and eroding social ties that had once knit citizens together across lines of difference and fostered solidarity.

This leads us to conclude that there is something new, different, and paradoxical about the present difficulties democracies face all over the world. There is certainly a recession, but not just that. This crisis of degeneration has disclosed and dramatized a set of vulnerabilities intrinsic to the democratic project of which we have been dimly aware, but slow to acknowledge. Our reluctance to acknowledge these vulnerabilities has generally taken one of two forms: we exaggerate the crisis by proclaiming that democracy is dying everywhere, or we downplay the crisis by suggesting that it is confined mostly to poor and developing countries in the global South, where fledgling democracies are seen as being especially prone to authoritarian temptations. Hyperbolic pronouncements about the impending death of democracy are not particularly helpful. A series of books with provocative and catchy titles, some by distinguished scholars, often of liberal persuasion, hint at the imminent demise of democracy.[3] The portentous titles often shape public discussion more than the more cautious and nuanced analyses found inside the books. There is also a great deal of loose chatter about the tell-tale signs of the coming tyranny and forced analogies between our troubled times and situation with the much-discussed interwar years of political turmoil in Europe, especially with the beleaguered Weimar Republic and its eventual collapse. Through this comparison, the fascist consequences of the Weimar Republic's disintegration lend ahistorical desperation to these analytic accounts of democracy's present crisis.

Tantalizing as that analogy is for those anxiously watching the resurgence of authoritarian ethnonationalism under the banner of populism, it is a distorting and distant mirror. It fails to capture what is really ailing and undermining democracies today. In this book, we have dwelt at length on two defining features of the current phase of democratic crisis and recession.

First, as Gaonkar notes in Chapter 5, while democracies are under severe duress, they are not dying. They are not being overthrown by quasi-military movements. Though polarized, they are not divided by clashes between revolutionary communists and fascists as they were in the 1930s. Democratic regimes are not being summarily overthrown and dismantled by the armed forces, as was often the case during the second recessionary wave that ran from the late 1950s to the early 1970s, of which the Chilean coup d'état of September 11, 1973, deposing the socialist president Salvador Allende, is the paradigmatic example. Instead, as we argue in this book, democracies today are being corrupted and undermined from within.

Second, unlike in the previous recessions, the weakening and undermining of democracy is no longer confined either to recently established democracies like Weimar Germany or to the poor and developing countries of the global South, which have swung back and forth between democratic and nondemocratic modes of governance. Debilitating internal decay and corruption have now reached the shores of mature western democracies. Even the United Kingdom and the United States have not escaped this blight. This is evident from Britain's ordeal over Brexit, including not just a contentious and divisive campaign, but a long parliamentary impasse and difficulty reestablishing solidarity in its wake. And it is evident in the long four years of Donald Trump's tragicomic US presidency that culminated in an insurrectionary assault by his diehard followers on Congress as it sat in session to certify the election of his successor on January 6, 2021. This was at once alarming—the defeated president himself incited the mob—and altogether inadequate as a would-be revolutionary mobilization. The threat to democracy lay less in what happened that day, than in what preceded that assault and what has followed since. True believers circulated endless lies and misinformation about a "stolen election." Republicans who were initially aghast fell into line with the Trumpite message; many mobilized to restrict voting rights. There has been continued and often armed organizing on the far Right. The teaching of American history has become a minefield of distorted narratives and political controversy.

To be sure, the military overthrow of democratically elected governments has not altogether ceased, as the brutal recent coup d'état in Myanmar demonstrates. There have been coups in Mali, the Central African Republic, Zimbabwe, Sudan, and Thailand. Egypt's democratically elected government was overthrown by the army in 2013—a revealing example since it came in the wake of the "Arab Spring," itself a movement for greater democracy. There have been many cases of military suppression of such movements. Violence has been used to sway elections. But there has not been a wave of replacements of relatively well-institutionalized democracies by military rule. In this context, the case of Pakistan is instructive. Since its independence in 1947, the military has been the most dominant institution and force in the country. On several occasions in the past, in times of strife and turmoil, the Pakistani military has overthrown the elected civilian governments and seized power. In so doing, it has invariably portrayed itself as the guardian of national integrity and the country's Islamic republican constitution, defending the citizenry against the fragmentation and corruption allegedly fomented by opportunistic politicians and their parties. But while Pakistan has gone through a series of deep and devastating political crises in the last two decades, providing ready grounds for a military takeover, there has been no military coup since 1999. Increasingly, the most acute threats to democracy come from within.

Corrosion from Within

Such is the paradox of democracy today. Authoritarianism is resurgent all over the world and threatens democracies old and new alike, but militaries, the most potent agents of authoritarianism, remain in their barracks. In the established democracies, the conviction remains strong that the military should be an institution standing apart from politics. There are anxieties about contrary tendencies, but actual military interventions into the political process are rare. Neither military nor other external attacks are destabilizing democracies. The sources of the current democratic crisis are internal. We must look to vulnerabilities intrinsic to the democratic project itself, as Taylor argues in Chapter 1 and Gaonkar in Chapter 5. And we must look to weaknesses in democratic responses to radical and disturbing transformations in the social foundations of democracy, as Calhoun shows in Chapter 2 and Chapter 3.

Contemporary democracies are being corrupted and eroded from within rather than being suspended and dismantled from without. For the most part, today's populists, nationalists, authoritarians, religious zealots, and racists do not disavow and denounce democracy (or even bourgeois democracy), as fascist and communist ideologues did during the interwar period. Today's antidemocratic forces, including their overtly authoritarian variants, retain at least a democratic facade and often many of the practices of formal democracy.

Leaders with little or no commitment to democracy seize the reins of government and the state apparatus by succeeding in elections—as indeed fascists and Nazis did in the 1930s. Of course, thumbs are put on the electoral scales by manipulation of media and by both intimidation and more nuanced legal vote suppression. Constitutions are not suspended or scrapped; instead, they are amended and rewritten in an anti-republican / anti-liberal vein, weakening both the autonomy of institutions and the rights of citizens. Hungary, Poland, and Turkey all offer examples. At least the appearance of democracy and perhaps some of the substance remain important to countries such as Iran, Russia, and many of their Eurasian neighbors that hold tightly controlled elections, often undemocratically "disqualifying" certain candidates from running for higher offices. Their judiciaries may remain technically independent, but be packed by the ruling party. The press, media, and the public sphere remain open, often cacophonous, even commercially vibrant, but they are muzzled and intimidated in multiple ways, ranging from the cruder methods of imprisoning and assassinating investigative reporters to the subtler methods associated with new surveillance technologies.

Still, not without irony, the would-be democratic people—singular and plural—continue to call attention to its / their existence. Citizens march in the streets and assemble in squares, expressing specific grievances and generalized discontent.[4] In some countries, public demonstrations have become predictable Sunday morning rituals. Instead of suspending and dispersing the assembled protesters, which happens occasionally, ruling powers let the disarrayed opposition openly vent their frustrations. As is common in India and Turkey, in order to show that they, not the protesting rabble, truly represent and incarnate the people, the ruling powers mount their own counter-demonstrations and assemblies.

All of this is part of the democratic theater today and makes for an unusual and vexing situation. The antidemocratic elements—Gaonkar's "ugly democrats"—are doing just fine within the rubric of electoral democracy. They have realized that democracy can be a means to gaining and maintain political power, not a barrier. Moreover, winning elections confers a degree of legitimacy they would not otherwise enjoy. Hence, the paradox: even as the ugly democrats increasingly employ antidemocratic practices and rhetoric, democratic processes and institutions continue to grant legitimacy. That paradox is further complicated by the fact that democracy itself has lost much of its luster and political legitimacy in recent years. Under seemingly constant duress, democracy is no longer seen as the wave of the future. As the paradoxes pile up, the crisis of legitimacy deepens.

Confronted with this extraordinary situation, many democratic theorists (especially the more liberally minded) dismiss these subverted "ugly democracies" as pseudo-democracies or, more generously, as "illiberal democracies." The implication of this dismissal is clear: "ugly democracies" are democracies in name only and cannot tell us anything about the true nature of democracy. Hence, how they come to power and what they do once they have it are questions about the dynamics of authoritarianism, not about how to cultivate and protect democratic agendas. "Ugly democrats" do not possess the proper democratic subjectivity. They refuse to internalize democratic norms, they subvert republican institutions, they ignore republican rituals, and they resent democratic culture. While bent on exploiting its legitimizing forms, institutions, and rhetoric, they are agnostic toward the normative thrust of the democratic project. This kind of dismissive account focuses on the ugliness at the expense of the democracy. By refusing to contend with the many ways that "ugly democrats" are very much still agents of democracy, we overlook democracy's constitutive vulnerabilities. By focusing on the machinations of "ugly democrats," we overlook how democracy's more liberal defenders might also be contributing to its erosion. As Calhoun and Taylor argue in Chapter 4, meritocracy and identity politics, historically associated with the emancipatory discourse of equal liberty (opportunity) and equal standing (recognition), respectively, might be undermining democratic culture and democratic subjectivity under the present capitalist mode of socioeconomic reproduction.

Why Not Blame Populism?

Three culprits are routinely identified as prime movers in the current democratic crisis, especially in the advanced and mature democracies: populism, neoliberal capitalism, and transformed communications, especially new social media. In each case, there are real issues, but most characterizations are faulty. In particular, they render the latest versions of long-standing issues as new, and they exaggerate the extent to which the threats are external to democracy rather than shaped by democratic engagements.

The most commonly cited is in fact the most misleading: populism. The term "populism" is usually used as a loose characterization of demands in the name of "the people," especially as voiced by demagogues. Defenders of democracy are especially worried by its right-wing ethnonationalist variants. We share some of the worry, but find the usual conceptualizations and analyses inadequate.

Most accounts of populism are highly selective—or arbitrary—in their choices of historical cases. They may focus on Italy and Germany but leave out Argentina, for example, or forget the late-nineteenth-century People's Party of the United States, which gave birth to the term. The last is signifi-cant not least because it is an example of activists embracing the label *pop-ulist* rather than having it hurled at them as an accusation. The story of populism in the United States runs from Shays' Rebellion through Jackso-nian democracy in the 1820s and 1830s, the anti-immigrant "Know Noth-ings" and the American Party in the 1850s, late-nineteenth-century agrarian populists and the mostly urban Knights of Labor, the 1896 "cross of gold" presidential campaign of William Jennings Bryan, the early-twentieth-century redistributive demagoguery of Huey Long and proto-fascism of Father Coughlin, the segregationist rhetoric of George Wallace in the 1960s, the quasi-libertarian Tea Party movement launched in 2009, the 2011 as-sertion by Occupy Wall Street that "we are the 99 percent," to both the 2016 ascendancy and ongoing veneration of Donald Trump and the con-temporary "democratic socialist" campaigns of Bernie Sanders. To equate populism with Trumpism and the current domination of the Republican Party by his anti-immigrant "Make America Great Again" movement / fol-lowers, is not just to slight history but to get the phenomenon wrong.

First, populism is reactive. It is poorly understood as a matter of enduring ideology. Rather, populist mobilizations respond to perceived violations, outrages, and failures of more conventional politics. They adopt ideologies in response to these "provocations" and as they are influenced by dema-gogues, more serious leaders, and internal circulation of ideas. Populists tend to blame individual politicians and bear generalized resentments against elites. But populist movements are commonly occasioned by social transformations and upheavals even if they don't analyze them clearly. Karl Polanyi's account of the "double movement" is apt. A first movement of radical disruption and sometimes dispossession—in Polanyi's example the Industrial Revolution was exacerbated by liberal refusals of support for the displaced—triggers a chaotic second movement of responses. Populist pro-test is an important dimension of this and can help to tilt the balance between authoritarianism and building institutions for the public good. Borrowing a phrase from the economic historian Robert Allen, Calhoun in Chapter 2 characterizes the hiatus between the radical disruption and potential insti-tutional reconstruction as "Engels's pause," a time of severe stress, strife, and turmoil, a time of social movements and political mobilizations, and a time rife with emancipatory possibilities as well as reactionary rage and exclusionary nationalism. This is also the time of the resurgence of populism, the revolt of the nonelites both on the Left and the Right.

Second, and relatedly, populism can appear in "left" or "right" or ambiguous versions. American populism has long included and vacillated between egalitarian and inclusive agendas and ethnonationalist, racist, and exclusionary politics. Many of the key leaders and idealogues associated with the populist movements have uneasily combined contradictory political agendas, both progressive and reactionary, on different issues. Though eventually harnessed to a mostly hard right-wing agenda, Donald Trump himself was a confounding ideological chameleon.

Third, populism can be a force for political innovation. It often develops outside of party structures or demands change from parties. It can move quickly, partly because of weak commitments to either ideological consistency or the careers of politicians. Even seemingly "failed" populist projects can change political ecology and conventional parties. In the 1890s, financial interests and local political establishments succeeded in defeating the People's Party by driving wedges between Black and White farmers and between farmers and urban workers who were often immigrants. Nonetheless, the movement exerted sustained pressure on the traditional political parties to enact progressive legislation on subjects such as the regulation of banks and railroads, farm credits, the progressive income tax, the direct election of senators, and much else in the early decades of the twentieth century.[5]

Fourth, as both Gaonkar and Calhoun have argued in preceding chapters, populism is intrinsic to the democratic project itself. It draws its basic rationale and appeal from the same source as democracy—namely, the doctrine of popular sovereignty. Neither populism nor democracy is possible or viable without a prior commitment to the proposition that "the people" is the ultimate source of political authority and legitimacy, whether it acts directly, or through representatives, or only gives its often tacit consent.

However, modern democracy has evolved well beyond the direct and unmediated expression of the people's collective power and authority. It has become embedded in a liberal / republican imaginary that enables and stabilizes representative government. Underwritten by the Constitution, this institutionalization provides for separation of powers, rule of law, and a suite of individual rights, all sustained by autonomous institutions, especially an independent judiciary. By contrast, populism remains, especially in agitation, the raw expression of the doctrine of popular sovereignty, insistent on reiterating the power and authority of the people in the last instance.

Republican institutions and the liberal theory of rights can never fully succeed in bridling the force of populism, especially since the doctrine of popular sovereignty found its own institutional expression in universal adult franchise coupled with regular, periodic elections and majority rule. This results in recurrent tension, such as that over minority rights, for example. Nor have democratic elections ended rule by elites, though they have changed selection mechanisms and introduced some measure of account-ability. Consent of the governed and its periodic electoral ratification need not be mere formalities, as in autocratic simulacra of democracy. They can change the democratic equation dramatically.

To preserve and protect democracy requires meeting twin threats stem-ming from the volatility of masses on the one hand and the oligarchic ten-dencies of elites on the other. It is customary to think of republican norms and institutions as guardrails against assault by the former. In a similar vein, one should think of populism and its periodic eruptions as an indispensable mechanism to curb the transgressions of the latter. Jefferson, echoing Ma-chiavelli, notably claimed that the well-being of a republic depends on peri-odic revolutionary outbursts by the people to deter the predatory elites. "What country can preserve its liberties," Jefferson wrote from Paris in 1787, "if rulers are not warned time to time that their people preserve the spirit of resistance?"[6] The people are always standing in reserve.

Systemic Compromises

Neither republican governments nor projects to advance democracy dic-tate the structure of democratic societies. Politics may have an influence, but societies are shaped also by history, geography, demography, and a range of other factors. Two of the most important for modern democratic socie-ties are capitalism—basic to the economies of all contemporary democratic states—and sociotechnical systems of communications and other infrastruc-ture. These have been long enough entwined with democracy and repub-lican governments that each has shaped the other. When analysts of con-temporary democratic decline point to neoliberal economic policies and rapid, minimally regulated globalization, they are partly correct but their analysis and concerns need to be put in the context of the long struggles to achieve a compromise between democracy and capitalism. As Chapter 3 details, one such compromise was produced in the mid-twentieth century in the form of "organized capitalism." It was achieved not just by negotiations between government on the one hand and banks and businesses on the other. The compromise was also shaped by democratic pressures "from below": trade unions and social movements, local experiments in business regulation, popular demand for social security. When that compromise unraveled, it was partly because capitalists found ways to evade the responsibilities and costs imposed by democratic governments. It was partly because of popular as well as business frustrations with welfare state institutions. And it was partly because of the allure of two ideologies of freedom: neoliberalism and expressive individualism.

Democrats have compromised with capitalism for two hundred years (or more). There have been calls for democracy too radical to coexist with capitalism, but these have stayed mostly at the margins. Compromise enabled politicians to deliver prosperity to a public that eagerly demanded it (though that public was perhaps only a fraction of the citizens, let alone residents, in each partially democratic country). It is not new for capitalism at once to deliver some of what democrats want and to pursue structural rearrangements antithetical to the stability of democracy. Deindustrialization and finance-driven globalization coexisted with a transition to private home ownership (on credit), new jobs in sunbelt cities, the production of a host of consumer technologies, and a rise in opiate addiction.

So, yes, neoliberalism is genuinely a culprit in the crisis of democracy. But no, it isn't all new, and it isn't a blow from outside the long history of democratic compromises with capitalism. It is an extreme position in the long-standing struggle to balance freedom, equality, and solidarity. It is crucial to recognize that neoliberalism was initially articulated by Friedrich Hayek not just as an economic doctrine but as a political defense of liberty in the face of fascism (and less immediately of communism).

Part of the problem with neoliberalism, globalization, deregulation, and deindustrialization since the 1970s is simply that they came so fast. Some Americans could move to the sunbelt; some British workers could leave the deindustrializing parts of the North and Midlands for relatively prosperous cities such as Manchester and Reading. Workers, however, can never move as easily as capital. Disruption to families, local communities, and individual life prospects was, and continues to be, sharply destabilizing. In this (as Calhoun suggests in Chapter 3), the great transformation of the last five decades echoes precisely the great transformation analyzed by Karl Polanyi. Disruptions invariably undermine the social foundations for democracy even if, in the long term, economic growth provides seeming compensation to the grandchildren of those whose lives were disrupted.

Something similar goes for the game-changing transformation of technologies of information and communication. This has upended the dynamics of the traditional bourgeois public sphere, but not for the first time. Modern democracy depended on newspapers as it grew; they provided a crucial basis for the democratic public sphere in which policy was debated and collective identity established. Broadcast media upended a print-based understanding of democratic will-formation by means of discursive deliberation and decision-making. Before social media and ubiquitous information technology, there was a phase of destination internet sites and slower messaging through email and chat rooms. The phases overlap, and the media are not the same, but they are all part of a long history of opportunities and challenges for the democratic endeavor.

Democracy has grown in relationship with communications media through different phases of technology and different structures of ownership and production. Now democrats mourn the decline and financial difficulties of the "legacy media." But, of course, these had to be built. There was a time when newspapers were new and literacy uncommon. There was a time when journalism schools did not exist. There was a time before the waves of consolidation that created giant media corporations. Democracy had to contend with all these evolving shifts and turns in media ecology, as it continues to do today.

It is a basic truth of modern media that even at their most democratic, they have flourished mainly as profit-making business enterprises. States have complemented these with public media, some splendid, especially in broadcasting. But the transformation of media is a matter not just of technology, but also of business structures.

Not least, for all the many problems of media today, there are democratic attractions. It was a false hope to think the internet would be more empowering for the global masses than for corporations and states. It was a false hope to imagine social media would be a utopia of large-scale linkages among individuals, rather than subject to the distortions of robots, hacking, and the profit-seeking agendas of platform providers. But the false hopes were nonetheless democratic hopes. There is democratic potential in a media ecology with more independent producers, if enough can make a living.

Part of the challenge of new media is simply that they are new. They are abruptly, destabilizingly new. We have not developed adequate democratic practices, institutions, and regulations. But this does not mean we cannot.

Insofar as the new media are implicitly part of new structures of surveillance and data aggregation, it is hard to imagine how this can be "good" for democracy—though it can certainly make valuable state projects (as well as malign, repressive ones) more efficient. But it is not hard to see the democratic attractions of social media. Whether or not we meet the challenge of adequately regulating and institutionalizing them—not much progress so far—we can see that uptake is not some separate phenomenon of consumerism or personal pleasure—though it is both of these. It is also a reflection of the democratic urge to engage.

Here we need to think of media history as part of a broader history of infrastructural technologies that enable very large-scale social structures—and economies and democracies. As Calhoun discusses in Chapter 2, there are qualitative differences in scale between ancient and early modern democracies and democracies today. Cities are of a scale unimaginable a hundred years ago, let alone to the ancients. Radically new capacities for communications and for transfers of goods and information knit together the citizens of modern countries and enable large-scale often bureaucratized government. Not least, physical things and information flow across national borders in ways that make the regulation of early modern smuggling seem easy—and yet it was hard at the time.

So, in short, it is true that we must worry about the implications of new media and new structures for the control of media and both the spread and siloed limitation of messages. But it is also true that this has been an issue at least partly internal to democracy throughout the modern era.

Compromises have a price. Even when they seem to leave the constitution, republican institutions, the rule of law, and the liberal suite of individual rights intact, they commonly disturb the delicate balance among democracy's three guiding norms—liberty, equality, and solidarity. The compromises of the last fifty years have all reflected a paradox. On the one hand, they have been made attractive by privileging liberty over equality and solidarity. On the other, they have destabilized democracy accordingly. They have undermined collective commitment to a common good and shared future, both essential to democracy's flourishing. Further, they have been an integral part of new systems of control that are anything but simple projects of freedom.

It's not just that privacy vanishes before new technologies of surveillance. It is that at least partially automated, increasingly abstract systems govern large aspects of our lives.[7] New technologies are not just mechanisms of power, either supporting or opposing democracy. They are mechanisms of very large-scale social organization achieved by more or less impersonal and even automated means. Many of the biggest challenges for democracy concern coping with this new technological landscape.

Short of revolutionary overthrow of capitalism—a very tall order—democrats have little choice but to pursue better compromises. This has been the historical mission of social democracy and much of democratic socialism. As Calhoun argues in Chapter 3, the struggles have had some success, especially during *les trente glorieuses.*

The Great Unraveling

During the decades of relatively successful compromise, the rich continued to get richer, but not too fast and not, as is the case today, by radically disrupting the prosperity of the middle and working classes. The expansion of the welfare state and a Fordist model of industrial production built on a regime of cooperation between capital (large corporations along with their investors and creditors), labor (represented by unions), and government. Together they ensured that class conflict took the form of collective bargaining more than insurrection. Moreover, as Calhoun points out, democracy's social foundations were strengthened not only by welfare state policies of redistribution and equity, but by the vitality of civil society and associational life (including political parties). Social ties frequently cut across lines of difference on both local and national planes.

To be sure, the social order that emerged during this time was rife with contradictions. It was still unequal in important ways, excessively bureaucratic, and pervasively disciplinary. Conformity commonly reigned over embrace of difference. Women and many racial and ethnic minorities were largely left out of the bargain. The struggle to include those groups and accord them equal standing has faced constant resistance and remains only partially realized today. *Les trente glorieuses* don't offer a model of perfection; they offer proof that democratic political choices can temper and shape social conditions and the way capitalism works.

With the onset of "stagflation" (stagnant economic growth that combined high inflation and high unemployment) in the mid-1970s, and accompanying economic recession, organized capitalism and *les trente glorieuses* began to unravel. Governments cut spending on welfare and social institutions. Big corporations reneged on their obligations to workers, even those seemingly guaranteed by contracts. Neoliberalism became the ascendant economic and political ideology.

Under this new compromise, the three democratic ideals—liberty, equality, and solidarity—were adversely reconfigured.[8] The onset of neoliberalism folded liberty, private property, and remarkable ingenuity together to funnel the benefits of capitalist production upward. It came with soaring inequality and a refusal to moderate or compensate for the ravages of deindustrialization in the interest of solidarity. There was hypertrophy of acquisitiveness, reinforced and even celebrated in the name of meritocracy.

Intoxicated by free-market fundamentalism, neoliberals cast aside traditional constraints and the lessons of history. While they appropriated the political label "conservative," they abandoned its long-standing commitments to place, nation, and solidarity. And, of course, they were no socialists. They sought to privatize the public goods and affordances necessary for preserving citizen autonomy and for cultivating a shared sense of collective future. They embraced globalization without any regard for how place-based communities might suffer, for how intergenerational bonds might disintegrate, or for how national solidarities might fall apart. Ultimately, neoliberals sought to subject every sphere of human life, every fraction of time and ounce of labor, to economization and its distinctive rationality. They promoted a *homo economicus* who stood for private gain against social equality and political solidarity.[9]

At the same time, ironically, these individualists built giant corporations. Following Milton Friedman, they denied that these had any obligations to be "socially responsible" and asserted that they existed only to create value for their shareholders. Of course, this didn't stop them from having massive social effects. Neoliberal "market fundamentalism" was oddly coupled not just to the rise of enormous, powerful, and largely unregulated corporations but also to the production of a new level of abstract, impersonal, systems connecting people around the world without any pretense of consulting their will or seeking their consent. The new capitalism is in important senses even more "organized" than that of the postwar boom, but the organization is not open to democratic participation. As Calhoun notes in Chapter 3, automation, globalization, and financialization are built into the very logic of the neoliberal order. They have brought wealth and concentrated ownership of that wealth. They have also wrecked lives, destroyed communities, and generated staggering inequalities. None of this bodes well for a democratic way of life.

But now the neoliberal order is unravelling, though the ideology is still powerful. Its financial architecture nearly failed a decade ago in a crisis from which the West has never fully recovered. Populism challenges "prudent" government policy. Global religious and civilizational divisions, made prominent by the 9/11 attacks among others, reveal that culture and loyalties still matter in what was supposed to be the era of individualistic *homo economicus*. Neoliberalism in the West ironically hastened the rise of China (and perhaps even its authoritarianism). But neoliberals are poorly prepared to deal with the corresponding decline in US hegemony and shakeup in geopolitics. The recent pandemic reveals the fragility of global structures, including both international cooperation and long supply chains.

We have the chance to make new choices today. Of course, they are still choices constrained by material conditions—climate change, the mismatch between the pay of most jobs and the cost of living, the power of corporations, the reality of pandemics. But then *les trente glorieuses* were achieved in the wake of the unprecedented destruction wrought by World War II, alongside the Cold War and its potentially disastrous arms race.

How did this happen? How did we miss the extraordinary transformation of modes of social reproduction that was unfolding before us? How did we countenance, if not endorse, this "dirty realist" view of the human subject as a *homo economicus* bereft of any impulses other than self-investment and monetization? Are these the wages of capitalist realism?[10] Why were we blindsided?

First, the neoliberal compromise emerged alongside the third wave of democratic transitions and consolidations that began in the mid-1970s with la Transición in Spain, the Revolução dos Cravos in Portugal, and Metapolitefsi in Greece. In those euphoric days of democratic triumph, one took little notice of the stealth threat this new compromise represented.[11] As the threat mounted, the streets and squares remained empty. Academics and policymakers pushed neoliberal economics as the cure to the stalled growth, stagflation, and recessions of the 1970s. Neoliberals quietly tested their methods and refined their theories in Chile, with the full cooperation of Pinochet's junta, and then, at the behest of governments led by dominant political parties from the Right (Reagan and Thatcher) and from the Left (Clinton and Blair), they brought their ideas home. It was a revolution from above in the name of growth and prosperity, not an attack on democracy.

Second, the bleak future that *homo economicus* promises has been obscured by its loose alignment with two other emergent social and ideological forces, both regarded as honorable and emancipatory: the ethic of authenticity and the call of meritocracy.

An Ethic of Authenticity

Rooting ethics in authenticity can be traced back to Romantic era ideals: be true to oneself, follow one's inner spirit and desires, and never lose sight of one's unique individuality amid demands for conformity imposed by one's family, friend, religious, and communitarian affiliations.[12] The ethic of authenticity's appeal was originally confined to a small circle of poets, artists, and self-styled bohemians. It was attractive to many as a counterweight to Enlightenment rationalism and gained adherents in recurrent waves into a kind of apotheosis in the 1960s. Today, its sweep is wide and deep, influencing modern conceptions of identity and belonging, and driving emancipatory movements for recognition, especially among individuals and groups historically stigmatized and discriminated against on account of race, ethnicity, gender, sexual preference, disability, and much else.

In the early 1960s, a host of "direct action" mobilizations—the US civil rights movement, second-wave feminism, the gay rights movement—mounted a powerful and largely successful struggle for recognition and equal standing. As Black Lives Matter, #MeToo, ACT UP, and numerous others attest, the spirit behind those mobilizations remains active and influential, albeit in different versions and incarnations. In this regard, the ethic of authenticity is an integral part of democracy's telic project, widening and deepening its inclusionary scope.

As Calhoun and Taylor argue in Chapter 4, while the ethic of authenticity and identity-based political movements have certainly mobilized solidarity within various groups, they have not fostered the kinds of connections across lines of difference that are essential to any flourishing democratic way of life. Instead, in some cases, cultural tensions have escalated and polarization of public discourse has intensified. Of course, identity-based political movements and mobilizations representing historically marginalized groups are not to blame for the current state of public discord and acrimony—the new "culture wars." The forces of social and cultural conservatism remain strong and entrenched as they deny past atrocities, ignore ongoing injustices, and refuse to accord various groups the full recognition and equal standing they demand.

The terrain of these culture wars, where values and lifestyles are pitted against each other and identity differences become hard and fast, is the result of complex sociological factors. The most consequential of these is how the ethic of authenticity's *expressive cultural individualism* has become deeply entangled with neoliberalism's *possessive economic individualism*. Unlike their predecessors and given their focus on political recognition, the new identity-based social movements have been less concerned with problems of socioeconomic inequality and the politics of redistribution. This cultural focus on identity and lifestyle, "to just be yourself," blends smoothly with neoliberalism's libertarian and entrepreneurial ethos. Thanks to the degree of social mobility modern large-scale societies afford, self-investment can be seen as a universally available solution to discrimination: once individuals acquire marketable skills, they are free to pursue their preferred lifestyle wherever they choose. This notion obviates unpleasant confrontations as well as productive dialogues. Thus, the old sociological distinction between the "locals" and the "cosmopolitans" has become rigidly reconfigured into a distinction between, in David Goodhart's terminology, "Somewheres" and "Anywheres."[13] For Calhoun and Taylor, the bifurcation between the beliefs, behaviors, and lifestyles of "Somewheres" and "Anywheres" makes fostering a sense of common purpose and shared futures all but impossible; it is nonetheless perfectly compatible with the neoliberal dispensation.

The Call of Meritocracy

Like the ethic of authenticity, the call of meritocracy has its roots in an emancipatory project, namely, a rising bourgeoisie's struggle against aristocratic rank, status, and blood in society's economic and professional spheres. Among other things, the bourgeois revolution demanded the progressive equalization of opportunities to better one's material conditions. Wealth and success, the bourgeoisie believed, should not be the result of inherited social status, but based on merit—talent, hard work, and resilience. Although this epochal revolution was successful, it did not lessen, let alone eradicate, social inequality. The stratification of bourgeois society was no less unequal than that of the societies that preceded it. In fact, as the productivity and affluence of bourgeois society surpassed even the greediest aristocratic fantasies, inequality increased. The bourgeoisie, like the ruling elites of today, devised a rationale to justify inequality's persistence: merit. In the ensuing "opportunity society," success would depend strictly on one's talent and hard work, and everyone would have a fair chance at prosperity. Those who possess talent or acquire skills through prudent self-investment and perseverance should be appropriately rewarded. Failure in such a society may be exacerbated by a lack of talent, but it is caused by a lack of effort. This is how meritocracy explains inequality. Once deployed to dismantle privileges based on rank, status, and blood, the meritocratic argument came to justify inequalities allegedly arising from the uneven distribution of talent, hard work, and perseverance among free people. This simplistic ideology blithely confuses formal equality with substantive equality and defers the "social question" altogether. It has also become highly resonant in times of neoliberalism.

Historically, meritocratic ideology has been associated with liberal professional classes and institutions.[14] Its appeal is stronger among those engaged in mental labor, artistic work, and cultural production than it is among those engaged in physical labor, service work, and industrial production. In cultivating meritorious competence, one must set aside the highly elusive concept of natural "talent"—as well as its more grandiose cousins "genius" and "giftedness"—and focus on individual capacity building and skill acquisition through education and training regimes. Once they have been cultivated, effectively leveraging this kind of self-enrichment requires extensive planning and the investment of yet more time and resources. The rewards and compensation for those who succeed in professions involving mental, artistic, and cultural enterprises is staggeringly greater than for those engaged in blue-collar, physical, industrial, and low-wage service work.[15]

The bourgeoisie defeated their aristocratic masters not by force of arms but through persuasive theories about political economy, not by mobilizing in the streets and squares but by transforming trading and manufacturing with new technologies and business models. This revolution continues to this day as modes of social reproduction continue to transform under the sway of capital's shifts and accelerations. In its current phase, an increasingly financialized capital concentrates wealth creation and growth within a technocentric knowledge economy that spans finance, marketing, technology, health care, pharmaceuticals, communication, information, media, entertainment, design, and other forms of culturally coded work. Across these sectors, a class of highly paid and massively sought after "knowledge workers"—the "creative class"—generate unprecedented returns.[16] Although there is wide variation in compensation among these workers, they make more money, receive better benefits, and enjoy greater job security relative to those engaged in physical, industrial, and low-end service work. During the financial crisis of 2008 as well as amid the economic turmoil of the Covid-19 crisis, knowledge workers have remained well positioned (many have even grown richer), while other workers have been pushed into the rapidly growing "gig economy." With the illusory freedom to work if and when they choose, these members of the "precariat" slip in and out of the workforce with neither benefits nor security.

The meritocratic ideology of spurious "equal opportunity" and entrepreneurial individualism is repeatedly mobilized by neoliberals to justify staggering inequality in the name of growth and prosperity, no matter the consequences for social harmony and democratic flourishing. Nonetheless, the full weight of this meritocratic ideology's destructiveness remains obscured by its rhetorical hold and appeal, even among its victims. This is an untenable situation.

New Technologies of Captivation

The third and final clue as to how and why we failed to fully grasp the baleful trajectory of the neoliberal economic order has to do with its alignment with the spectacular changes in communication and information technologies that began in the mid-1970s. Along with resurgent populism and the worldwide implementation of neoliberal economic policies, this technological revolution is also one of the three culprits commonly identified as responsible for the current democratic crisis. Especially in the advanced and mature democracies, it is held responsible for upending the dynamics of the traditional bourgeois public sphere, long seen as the prerequisite for democratic will-formation by means of discursive deliberation and decision-making.

Not without a touch of historical irony, the beginning of this great technological transformation, which was destined to transform the way we live and work irrespective of race, gender, religion, and national belonging, perfectly coincided with the beginning of the "third wave" of democratic transitions. It started with the founding of Microsoft in 1975 and Apple in 1976, continued with the founding of AOL in 1985 and Amazon in 1994, and accelerated with the founding of Google in 1998, Facebook in 2004, and Twitter in 2006. Along with similar companies the world over (too numerous to mention), these American technology giants have changed just about every facet of everyday life. One does not have to be a technological determinist to acknowledge that they are the engines of the great transformation afoot today. With a remarkable degree of efficiency and reliability (and, to be sure, with many glitches), they serve as the nervous system of the complex market societies in which we all live and work and a critical part of the infrastructure that sustains the integrated global order.

These companies unfailingly present themselves as providers of "technologies of freedom" and as agents of individual empowerment. Given the proliferation of smart phones and the endless ingenuity of those using them in the slums of Mumbai and Lagos, in the favelas of Rio, in *gecekondular* of Istanbul, and in shantytowns all over the world, one must concede that there is an element of truth in this emancipatory narrative. Similarly, with some important qualifications, the benefits of these technological innovations are widely accessible to individual users irrespective of race, gender, age, sexual preference, nationality, and, to an extent, even class. Unlike earlier technologies of connectivity such as air transportation, these innovations of information and communication have become available to a vast number of people in a very short period. If there was any doubt before, the Covid-19 pandemic has made the importance and influence of these technology companies abundantly clear.

What is less legible is that these technology companies share, promote, and deploy the same ideology as the proponents of the neoliberal economic order, their libertarian and egalitarian rhetoric camouflaging the negative externalities that come with how they operate and profit. They create jobs, many of which are high paying, but, compared with companies in other sectors, the number of workers they directly employ is very low.[17] By dominating their fields of specialization—Google and search, Facebook and social media, Amazon and e-commerce—they function as monopolies. Together, Google and Facebook command more than 80 percent of web-based ad revenue in the United States. Print media, once the backbone of the public sphere and default home of democratic dialogue and deliberation, cannot compete. The mega-companies gobble up potential competitors with exorbitant buyouts and accrue mountains of cash. They are the prime agents of disruptive innovations not only in technology, but in business, and they pride themselves on their ability to "move fast and break things." Much of this is known. There is a vast and growing literature, celebratory as well as critical, about these big tech titans and how they operate.

Much concern has been focused on a "digital divide" between those with the resources to participate fully in increasingly computer-mediated culture and those who are excluded for lack of equipment, connectivity, or know-how. Such inequality is important, but the discussion misses key points. First, techno-capitalist corporations thrive by including as many people as possible in the use of their products and services, not by excluding them. Second, money can buy "influencers," both human and nonhuman—from algorithms to bots—so there is a divide in influence despite dispersal of sources. Third, inequality is organized less in terms of having or lacking access and more in terms of differences of quality of access and magnitude of use. In other words, the tendency is for all citizens to be included, but not on equal terms. This makes the media another setting for what Calhoun (in Chapter 4) calls "hierarchical incorporation." Fourth, the dominant feature of today's media ecology is not restricted access, though that exists, but segmentation. This is a severe impediment to cultivating the civility, transparency, dialogue, and mutual understanding necessary for public accord and democratic culture. Segments link the unfiltered voices of the "masses" with the partisan agendas of political elites and business interests. Media optimists long hoped that rapid and ubiquitous communication would help the public sphere thrive. Instead, it has degraded the public sphere and compromised civil society's key institutions—university, church, legacy media, and other cultural industries. The jury is out on whether this will be overcome and whether instant but problematic messages must drown out reflection.

Civility has been hard hit. With little or no regard for how others may be affected by vituperative or hate speech, one can say whatever one pleases. As Taylor notes in Chapter 1, there are neither repercussions for breaking the codes of civility, nor mutual engagement and dialogue. Opponents shout at each other or huddle in echo chambers with like-minded partisans. The second casualty is truth. A deluge of misinformation, "alternative facts," and outright lies circulate without contestation. Attempts at fact-checking or unmasking the sinister interests behind disinformation campaigns have little discernible impact, not on Trump's "Stop the Steal" election fraud lie, not on Tucker Carlson's anti-vaccination disinformation on Fox News. The third casualty is transparency. For an average citizen, the operational logic of large-scale modern society is already too complex and opaque to comprehend. The same is increasingly true of the representative system of government and its deliberative and decision-making processes. Without the mediating and filtering functions once discharged by the traditional fourth estate, information becomes noise, and a disoriented citizenry becomes susceptible to bias, prejudice, fearmongering, exclusionary xenophobia, conspiracy theories, and much else. At this moment, as Calhoun and Taylor point out in Chapter 7, big money pounces and colonizes the mediascape. It not only buys bulk television time to broadcast partisan political messages; it also saturates social media platforms such as Twitter and Facebook with tendentious content designed to further disorient the citizenry and pull them into biased and prejudiced opinions that align with its economic agenda. With that, the open society shrivels. The prospect of democracy dims. And the backlash begins.

Solidarity after the Backlash

The backlash today is subsumed under the sign of populism. We have argued throughout this book, however, that populism is not the real issue and is by no means the sole culprit responsible for democracy's degenerations. Moreover, the backlash is not without redeeming features. In the dark shadows of populist rage and resentment, we might be able to discern what we failed to see in the blinding, euphoric glare of democracy's "third wave" and new dawn. In a state of disquiet, with no other legitimate political game in town, what precisely is the nature of the democratic project that we so adamantly pursue? Under the signs of populist unrest, can we re-politicize the democratic endeavor?

In our extended meditations on the shape and sources of democratic degenerations, we have sought to draw out the critical implications of three interrelated propositions: (1) Democracy is a telic project (Taylor). (2) As a socially embedded human endeavor, democracy requires social foundations it cannot completely control (Calhoun). (3) Democratic regeneration requires more than remedial legislative and executive action. It takes the consorted direct action of the people, the sleeping sovereign, in its multiple incarnations (Gaonkar).

Democracy is conceived as a telic project, seeking continual improvement. But it will never deliver perfection, a political order that enables a people to live together peacefully and harmoniously in perpetuity. Moreover, democracy's trajectory is not necessarily progressive. Democratic regimes can widen and deepen their promise of inclusive self-rule, but they can also stagnate, decline, and even collapse. Over time, all democracies—ancient and modern alike—move unevenly, progressing on some counts while regressing on others. From Solon (594 B.C.E.) to Callisthenes (508 B.C.E.) to Ephialtes (460 B.C.E.), Athenian democracy went through a series of critical transformations, often billed as reforms. In many ways, these reforms broadened and enhanced citizen efficacy and participation (from the abolition of debt slavery among citizens to providing a daily allowance so that citizens could attend the deliberative assembly when in session), but they also imposed severe restrictions on who could count as a citizen.

Since the great democratic revolutions in the United States and France, modern democracies have displayed a similar pattern of uneven progress, periodic backsliding, and selective exclusions. In the very first year after its full ratification, the US Constitution, designed with so much care in a deliberate effort to avoid the shortcomings of the ancient models of Athens and Rome, would be subjected to ten amendments through the Bill of Rights.[18] More amendments would follow, all in accordance with what the preamble to the Constitution identifies as its foremost objective: to build solidarity in support of "a more perfect union." The very existence of the provision for amending the Constitution, however complex and onerous the process, attests to the fact that democracy is an open and living project, its pursuit of perfection always unfinished. The telic commitment to form "a more perfect union" would be tested time and again; during the fratricidal years of the Civil War, the Union itself teetered on the brink of collapse. And yet the Union has endured by constantly adapting—through progressive reforms as well as reactionary compromises—to the ever-changing social world within which it is embedded.

Thus, while there is a broadly conceived democratic repertoire of constitutional norms and principles, institutional procedures and practices, modes of political conduct and subjectivity, and an egalitarian public culture that distinguishes political regimes as democratic across history and geography, none of them is perfect and none is complete. Democracy is always and everywhere a work in progress, an open-ended collective journey, and the self-fashioning of a people through history's vicissitudes. Its telic character beckons us to the unending task of fortifying republican institutions and cultivating republican virtues and culture.

Despite the telic drive to better realize democracy's ideals, actual change is shaped by broader social patterns. Work to strengthen republican institutions and to deepen democracy is not simply internally propelled but linked to efforts to address social problems. Throughout this book, we have reiterated that democracy, as a socially embedded human endeavor, does not fully control its own destiny. We have shown how democracy must contend with exogenous forces rooted in history, culture, geography, and economy that continually challenge its normative promise and disrupt its trajectory. More importantly, we have discussed at length how modern democracy, whose career has been deeply entangled with modern capitalism, responds to the societal accelerations and transformations wrought by the ever-changing dynamics of the capitalist mode of production. These transformations continually scramble the composition of populations and reconfigure the ledgers of social stratification. As a result, class conflict can only ever be partially and temporarily tamed.

Thus, the problem of inequality remains a permanent challenge for democracy. While doctrinally committed to political equality and to equal standing before the law, democracy is neither equipped nor designed to deliver other forms of equality. Political equality cannot protect public solidarity from the devastating effects of material inequalities of wealth, income, rank, status, resource, and opportunity. Democracy must constantly build and rebuild social foundations to provide the public goods and affordances that balance the competing claims of the three republican ideals—liberty, equality, and solidarity.

There is no sure recipe, however, for the mixture of public goods and affordances that will maintain social harmony and keep class conflict and other divisive forces under check. What worked once—say, the social democratic compromise with capitalism during *les trente glorieuses*—will not work today, even though history's lessons remain invaluable.

What we have before us, to borrow a phrase from Walter Benjamin, is a "dialectical image" of democracy.[19] The telic project to fortify autonomous republican institutions and inclusionary democratic culture is constantly undercut by capitalism's ever-changing modes of social reproduction. There is no permanent resolution to this dialectic. But there is an impermanent one: continuously rethink the democratic project and rebuild its social foundations. In times like these, when the democratic crisis is deepest, the task of democracy's regeneration cannot be left to legislative actions and executive programs. It will take a movement. The people must awaken.

Populist movements are only one part of a whole field of mobilization and protest. Perhaps we are entering one of the eras of heightened movement activity that have come to the United States every few decades. Perhaps the many disparate actions will never coalesce. But it is important to see that throughout the era considered here—the period of the "the third wave," of neoliberalism, of globalization, of information and communication revolution—there have been countless mobilizations, protests, and riots. They come in multiple forms and performative genres—marches and assemblies, demonstrations and rallies, vigils, boycotts, human blockades, labor strikes, picket lines, hunger strikes, and even suicides. They have occurred all over the world and are led by different groups—Black Lives Matter and Occupy Wall Street activists in the United States (and elsewhere), Movimento Passe Livre (Free Fare Movement) advocates in Brazil, the Indignados in Spain, the Umbrella Movement protestors in Hong Kong, the Taksim Gezi Park protesters in Turkey, the Yellow Vests in France, and the Dilli Chalo farmers in India. The list goes on.

Protest, in planned actions as well as spontaneous eruptions, is an inescapable feature of our times, especially in the urban areas of the global South but also in the North. But a protest is not in itself a movement. It is a moment that can be part of a larger, more sustained, and cumulative movement, or not.

Most protests are localized and ephemeral, rarely reported on regionally, let alone in national and global news media. Some political analysts and commentators treat them as an unavoidable nuisance, dismissing them as exercises in futility, and, when protests deteriorate into riots and looting, accusing them of self-sabotage. In Chapter 6, Gaonkar challenges this dismissal. He argues that the sheer ubiquity of protests and riots is a sign of deeper discord, a warning that our social contract is under duress. Their repeated occurrence, even in the highly controlled cities of authoritarian China, is an expression of how frustrated the governed are with their governors. As Martin Luther King Jr. insisted, "A riot is the language of the unheard."[20] The people are speaking, and what they are saying goes beyond a mere expression of immediate grievances. The moment, not yet a movement for sure, is one of politicization and engagement. However faintly, theirs is a claim of popular sovereignty. Rigged elections and engineered consent do not return democratic legitimacy, and the people know that the government's legitimacy depends on their consent.

As Calhoun and Taylor argue in Chapter 7, however, these countless moments of protest are not up to the task of orchestrating democracy's renewal. While the micropolitics of specific grievances and targeted anger prepare the ground for consorted political action, it takes a movement to channel the people's democratic energies toward constructive change. But it also takes a government to integrate dispersed agendas into meaningful policy.

It is perhaps a moot point whether we need one single movement knitting together a range of different themes or a field of semiautonomous movements that inform each other and sometimes cooperate. The New Deal of the 1930s offers a compelling example of government action to formulate policies in response to many different mobilizations and arguments. There was no "New Deal movement." There were larger and broad movements such as socialism and progressivism. There were movements in specific arenas such as trade unions. There was activism without exactly the breadth of mobilization usually associated with the term "movement"— like that on behalf of farmers. And there were calls for action on issues such as social security and pensions or transparency in securities markets. It was the work of government to turn these into a larger agenda under the label "New Deal"—and it was relative success in that agenda that gave history the notion of an integrated policy (though it is sometimes pointed out that many strands of New Deal policy were only realized in World War II).

Proposals for a Green New Deal promise similarly dramatic action today. At their heart is the proposition that climate activism and labor activism need to be joined. They have seemed opposed and failure to cooperate has hurt them politically. But there are no separate solutions to the problems of endangered economic futures and endangered planetary futures. It's not enough that building green infrastructure can both generate jobs and reduce carbon emissions. They need to be embedded in a wider transformation of society. This should not be something dictated centrally and imposed on citizens, but something citizens can embrace as their choice. For this to happen requires social movements not just good policy. Of course, a movement to bring about such transformation could also propose improvements in health care, not least with pandemics in mind; in education, and in racial justice. Action on all of these is needed, but a lesson from the original New Deal is that a master plan is not crucial. Action is crucial, and multiple social movements can converge.

Movement activity can be empowering in itself, can build solidarity and inclusion. It is also crucial as pressure on government and on parties and candidates in elections. We have argued throughout this book that democracy develops and sometimes flourishes in the relationship of popular mobilization and cultural innovation to republican legal structures and state institutions. It degenerates when such "formal democracy" fails to respond effectively to changes in citizens' lives and self-understanding. Movements are crucial in making what matters to ordinary people politically effective.

Democracy, we have argued, is self-transforming. It consists partly in the telic pursuit of ideals that are important even if never fully realized. It is the project of trying to ensure not just that the current wants of "the people" are met but that together the people increase their liberty, equality, and solidarity.

Democracy depends not just on formal political procedures but on social conditions. These are conditions for effective citizen participation in governance, or at least in elections and the consent of the governed. They are also conditions for citizens' solidarity with each other, and for collective recognition of the inclusive polity. They are conditions for citizens' empowerment in all aspects of their lives. Indeed, if democracy gives freedom, it is not just freedom to engage in politics, but freedom in the "pursuit of happiness."

But social conditions are recurrently disrupted. Sometimes changes are modest and impacts local, but occasionally there is a more radical and general transformation. Great transformations open new possibilities, but they also upend jobs and livelihoods, communities, and institutions. Challenges come not just to the material conditions of life but also to the realization of what citizens regard as morality and virtue in their lives together.

The results can be chaotic, ranging from depression and withdrawal to populist protest to violent confrontations to social movements trying to guide society's transformation. There is no way to renew democracy solely within the bounds of formal democratic processes. Extra-parliamentary action is vital. Some will amount to pressures for state action, and states will likely be crucial to integrating disparate demands. Some will bypass the state to work directly on social conditions or culture. Movements may try to package a comprehensive alternative or make many separate proposals. The crucial task for democrats is to channel all this into constructive action.

We offer this book as a plea for democracy, renewing the French Revolution's great call for *liberty, equality, and solidarity*. This entails political action in the strongest and best senses. Instead of narrowing ideas of democracy to fit into formal politics, we should expand our ideas of politics to take up citizen empowerment, social and cultural inclusion, and pursuing the public good rather than temporary victories for polarized factions. Politics must be *poiesis*, working together to make and remake not just government but also society itself.

NOTES
ACKNOWLEDGMENTS
INDEX

Notes

Introduction

1. Our focus in this book is on democracy inside states, not on prospects for transnational democracy. The latter may be desirable, but o achieve it would require not just new legal arrangements, nor respect for universal rights, but social foundations that do not currently exist. State capacities are challenged by global pressures today, but states are still important to democratic projects.

2. To follow Pierre Bourdieu, one might note that university professors, journalists, and some other professionals constitute a dominated fraction of this dominant class. They are privileged, have elite educations, and have capacities for voice and influence denied to most citizens. But they generally do not have either economic or political power. Pierre Bourdieu, *Distinction: A Social Critique of the Judgement of Taste* (Cambridge, MA: Harvard University Press, 1984).

3. As the former Yugoslavia was breaking up, ethnic realignment was encouraged by asking, as a common saying had it, "Why should I be in a minority in your country when you can be a minority in mine?" So reports political scientist Ivan Krastev in Ezra Klein, "The Rest of the World Is Worried about America," *New York Times,* July 1, 2021.

4. Robert P. Jones, *The End of White Christian America* (New York: Simon and Schuster, 2017).

5. Ezra Klein, *Why We're Polarized* (New York: Simon and Schuster, 2021).

6. Amid political polarization, it is commonly remarked that facts do not change opinions. It would be more accurate to say that the ways facts are taken on board reflects unconscious efforts to maintain commitments to preexisting ways of thinking and feeling. In a famous study, the social psychologist Leon Festinger and colleagues examined how members of a cult whose leader predicted apocalypse responded when the disaster did not materialize. The short answer is that while some dropped out of the cult, most found ways to minimize the implications of the uncomfortable fact, to explain it as merely an error of calculation, and to sustain their commitments to both their belief system and their community. They acted to reduce "cognitive dissonance," which is an emotional state as well as a problem of thinking. Leon Festinger, Henry W. Riecken, and Stanley Schachter, *When Prophecy Fails* (New York:

Harper, 1956); see also David Heise, *Expressive Order: Confirming Sentiments in Social Actions* (New York: Springer 2007). One might begin along these lines to explain the willingness of many of Donald Trump's followers to interpret his electoral defeat as theft. Obviously, encouragement from siloed media and conspiracy theorists helped. But we should apply the same sort of analysis to the dominant liberal elite that for years has had such difficulty even seeing the "fact" of the popular discontents that shaped support for Trump.

7. Karl Polanyi, *The Great Transformation* (New York: Farrar and Rinehart, 1944).

8. For "possessive individualism" see C. B. Macpherson, *The Political Theory of Possessive Individualism* (Oxford: Oxford University Press, 1962). For the "expressive" tradition see Charles Taylor, *Sources of the Self* (Cambridge, MA: Harvard University Press, 1989). Almost all the terms in debates about democracy are ambiguous and contested, but none more so than the words "liberal" and "liberalism." These share an obvious reference to the idea of liberty, or freedom, but can emphasize (1) freedom of economic action from government restriction, (2) freedom of individuals to develop their own identities and pursue their own goals, (3) the institutional framework intended to guarantee freedom, especially by articulating rights, or (4) free formation of the voluntary associations of civil society. The first sense has been more prominent in Europe, and the second sense in North America, where it informed both the emphasis on religious freedom in the era of the country's founding and the more recent proliferation of claims for recognition of different identities. The third sense is common in phrases such as "liberal democracy," meaning that which is coupled with guarantees of civil rights. In this book, we include this third sense in our use of the term "republican," both to reduce confusion with the first two senses of liberalism and to recognize the important republican tradition in political thought that was basic to the development of constitutional government. Republicanism also emphasizes associational life among citizens, though often either as inherited community or personal moral commitment to the whole. Liberalism in the fourth sense crucially contributed the emphasis on *voluntary* associations. In this, it was reinforced by Scottish moral philosophy, with its ideas of civil society, sympathy, and common sense. There are further complexities, such as whether groups have liberties (or rights) that do not reduce to the liberties of their individual members. For example, is freedom of religion entirely grasped by freedom of individual conscience, or is there an additional dimension of freedom for religions as socially organized or culturally integrated groups with authority structures other than individual conscience?

9. There is an analogy to the international project of human rights which flourished, especially since the 1970s, in place of projects of political transformation. See Sam Moyn, *The Last Utopia* (Cambridge, MA: Harvard University Press, 2010). To really achieve the equal rights claimed by all domestic "identity" groups or the human rights promised by the proliferation of activism in the last fifty years would require large-scale political and economic change. But it is possible to separate the utopian and necessarily collective dimension of each from the less radical project of protecting the rights of individuals without transforming political or economic regimes.

10. It is a dirty and seldom recognized secret that the triumph of neoliberalism, financialization, and a new cluster of giant corporations brought not only the deindustrialization of the United States, Great Britain, and other Western countries, but also their decline in the face of a rising China.

11. Amartya Sen, *Poverty and Famines: An Essay on Food Supply and Distribution* (Oxford: Oxford University Press, 1983).

12. In both the Soviet Union and China, disastrous famines were evidence that, without democracy, communism failed to live up to its own ideals and to keep citizens alive. In the Soviet Holodomor—death by hunger—of 1932–1933 some six million people perished.

Forced collectivization was a major factor but hunger was also deployed politically against peasants resisting change, especially in the Ukraine. A classic source on the long-denied famine is Robert Conquest, *The Harvest of Sorrow: Soviet Collectivisation and the Terror-Famine* (London: Pimlico, 2000; orig. 1986). Bad agricultural policy, botched central planning, and politically driven willingness to accept deaths cost more than fifteen million lives in China's Great Famine of 1959–1961; this was also denied. See Frank Dikötter, *Mao's Great Famine: The History of China's Most Devastating Catastrophe, 1958–1962* (London: Bloomsbury Publishing, 2010).

13. See Jan Bremen, Kevan Harris, Ching Kwan Lee, and Marcel van der Linden, eds., *The Social Question in the Twenty-First Century* (Berkeley: University of California Press, 2019).

14. This decline in social associations is the central theme of Robert Putnam, *Bowling Alone* (New York: Simon and Schuster 2000). In *Upswing* (New York: Simon and Schuster, 2020, with Shaylyn Romney), he charts some reasons to hope for renewal.

15. The collapse of German democracy in the 1930s is hardly the only example. See the cases addressed by Steven Levitsky and Daniel Ziblatt in *How Democracies Die* (New York: Crown Penguin, 2018) and Adam Przeworski, *Crises of Democracy* (Cambridge, UK: Cambridge University Press, 2019).

1. Degenerations of Democracy

1. It should be clear that the institutions and constitutional arrangements required to realize this condition will be very different in different societies and eras, depending on the role of government, the sources of power, the types of parties and social movements, and a host of other factors. What the *telos* requires is constantly changing in history.

2. Joseph A. Schumpeter, *Capitalism, Socialism, and Democracy* (New York: Harper and Brothers, 1942).

3. It is a remarkable fact that these links between social ranking and the level of voting do not hold universally. Mukulika Banerjee shows in *Why India Votes?* (New Delhi: Routledge India, 2017) how these relationships are reversed in that country so that, for instance, the poor and lower caste vote more than the rich and upper caste. Her research shows that rituals of the day of voting, when the multiple, severe hierarchies of the society seem to be at least temporarily set aside and the realm of the people seems on the same level as that of those in power, create a sense of the power of democracy and feed what is called here "enthusiasm" around an experience of forward movement. Whether an election-day "high" can survive the many daily experiences of spectacular elite power remains to be seen.

4. See Thomas Piketty, *Le capital au XXIe siècle* (Paris: Seuil, 2013), chaps. 8 and 9.

5. For discussion of the "skyboxification" of American leisure activities, see Michael J. Sandel, *What Money Can't Buy: The Moral Limits of Markets* (New York: Farrar, Straus and Giroux, 2012), 163–203.

6. The reference here is to the (in)famous remark by Mitt Romney during the 2012 presidential election season to the effect that 47 percent of the population was drawing from, rather than contributing to, the wealth of the country and that the protagonists of a return to austere self-reliance start off in any election with a handicap.

7. Joan C. Williams, *White Working Class: Overcoming Class Cluelessness in America* (Boston: Harvard Business Review Press, 2017), 100.

8. See Alana Samuels, "The End of Welfare as We Know It," *Atlantic,* April 1, 2016.

9. The quotation is from a personal conversation. Michael Warner makes similar comments in his lecture "Fake Publics," a transcript of which is so far regrettably unpublished,

though a precis of which can be found at https://www.jfki.fu-berlin.de/en/v/dgfa2018/program/keynotes/warner_abstract/index.html.

10. Luke Bretherton, *Resurrecting Democracy: Faith, Citizenship, and the Politics of a Common Life* (Cambridge, UK: Cambridge University Press, 2015).

11. I owe this latter point and much of the above discussion to Dan Carpenter.

12. Craig Calhoun, *Nationalism* (Minneapolis: University of Minnesota Press, 1997); Craig Calhoun, *Nations Matter: Culture, History and the Cosmopolitan Dream* (Oxford: Routledge, 2007).

13. Jeffrey C. Alexander, *The Civic Sphere* (Oxford: Oxford University Press, 2006). See also Michael Mann, *The Dark Side of Democracy* (Cambridge, UK: Cambridge University Press, 2005).

14. Habermas, *Inclusion of the Other* (Cambridge, MA: MIT Press, 1996).

15. See Sasha Polakow-Suransky, *Go Back to Where You Came From* (New York: Nation Books, 2017), chap. 2.

16. Polakow-Suransky, *Go Back to Where You Came From,* chap. 3.

17. Polakow-Suransky, *Go Back to Where You Came From,* chap. 8. Fears of this kind also play a role in the United States, as discussed in later chapters of this book. Remember the slogan of white supremacists at the Charlottesville demonstration in 2017: "Jews will not replace us," quoting Renaud Camus. The deranged man behind the 2019 El Paso mass shooting produced a manifesto expressing the same sentiments, as described in John Eligon, "The El Paso Screed, and the Racist Doctrine Behind It," *New York Times,* August 7, 2019.

18. The outlook is described by W. E. B. Du Bois in his description of the perspective of American white men: "They are filled with Good Will for all men, provided these men are in their places," and they "aim to treat others as they want to be treated themselves, so far as this is consistent with their necessarily exclusive position" (quoted by Robert Gooding-Williams in the *Bulletin of the American Academy of Arts and Sciences* (Winter 2019), 28. Of course, these assumptions of precedence can motivate very different actions, all the way from a simple feeling of "we come first" to fascist-style white supremacy militias. They all have to be opposed, but with very different methods.

19. For a fuller discussion of the scapegoat mechanism, see the work of René Girard, particularly *Le bouc émissaire* (1984), translated as *The Scapegoat,* trans. Yvonne Freccero (Baltimore, MD: Johns Hopkins University Press, 1986).

20. See Williams, *White Working Class.*

21. See J. D. Vance, *Hillbilly Elegy: A Memoir of a Family and Culture in Crisis* (New York: Harper, 2016).

22. See Johannes Hillje, "Return to the Politically Abandoned: Conversations in Right-Wing Populist Strongholds in Germany and France," report, Das Progressive Zentrum, 2018, https://www.progressives-zentrum.org/wp-content/uploads/2018/10/Return-to-the-politically-abandoned-Conversations-in-right-wing-populist-strongholds-in-Germany-and-France_Das-Progressive-Zentrum_Johannes-Hillje.pdf. In addition, Germany has not altogether escaped the ravages of neoliberalism. A milder version has increased the precariousness of employment and the widening of social inequality (and has even more damaging consequences for other countries of the Eurozone). See Oliver Nachtwey, *Germany's Hidden Crisis: Social Decline in the Heart of Europe,* trans. Loren Balhorn and David Fernbach (London: Verso, 2019); for an incisive review of this work, see Hans Kundnani, "Downwardly Mobile Society: Unseen Problems in the German Economy," *Times Literary Supplement,* February 8, 2019. Something of the same sense of being downgraded seems to underlie the rebellion of the *gilets jaunes* in France, responding to the decline of *la France profonde,* the emptying of smaller centers, and the hyper-concentration in Paris at their ex-

pense, as well as the threat to a precariously maintained standard of living. See Christophe Guilluy, *Twilight of the Elites: Prosperity, the Periphery, and the Future of France,* trans. Malcolm DeBevoise (New Haven, CT: Yale University Press, 2019).

23. "As an open advocate of "illiberal democracy"—his country is the first and only EU member state to be considered just "partly free" by the think tank Freedom House—Orbán has never tried to sugarcoat his autocratic aims, and has justified them by invoking national sovereignty and national security." Yasmeen Serhan, "The EU Watches as Hungary Kills Democracy," *Atlantic,* April 2, 2020.

24. "Populist" rule in East European societies has to be understood in light of the special conditions attending their transition from communism and their fraught relations with the longer-established democracies of Western Europe. See the interesting discussion in Ivan Krastev and Stephen Holmes, *The Light That Failed: Why the West Is Losing the Fight for Democracy* (London: Allen Lane, 2019), especially chap. 1.

25. See the interesting description of the outlook in the early 1930s in the West in Ira Katznelson, *Fear Itself: The New Deal and the Origins of Our Time* (New York: Liverwright, 2013).

26. Hannah Arendt, *The Human Condition* (Chicago: University of Chicago Press, 1958).

27. Pierre Rosanvallon, *La contre-démocratie: La politique à l'âge de la défiance* (Paris: Seuil, 2006).

28. For further detail on this, see the interesting discussion in Steven Levitsky and Daniel Ziblatt, *How Democracies Die* (New York: Penguin Random House, 2018).

2. Contradictions and Double Movements

1. To be sure, a few of the world's democracies are still officially kingdoms; this is one of the ways democracy can be incomplete. But these are *constitutional* monarchies—which means, in effect, monarchy tempered by republicanism. The will of the monarch is limited by rules and by provision for others to exercise power. The government exists for the public good not simply the benefit of its monarch. Neither it nor the country can be owned like private property. Public good was rendered as "commonwealth" in seventeenth-century England. The word lives on, almost unnoticed, in the official names of several American states and a few countries such as Australia and the Bahamas. Finally, several countries are formally named "Democratic Republic" to signify the importance of both sets of ideas, although, ironically, many of these, like the People's Democratic Republic of (North) Korea, display little republican freedom, rule of law, or democratic voice.

2. The US Pledge of Allegiance is a very distinctively American articulation of ideals and commitments. It was not formally adopted by government until the Second World War and the phrase "under God" was only inserted during the anti-communist movement of the early 1950s. But its roots lie in seeking national unity after the Civil War. It was formulated by Francis Bellamy, an activist and entrepreneur trying to sell magazine subscriptions on the four-hundredth anniversary of Columbus's landing in the New World. A Baptist minister, Christian socialist, and racist opponent of immigration, Bellamy incorporates into one person many of the contradictions of American patriotism and pursuit of progress. See Richard J. Ellis, *To the Flag: The Unlikely History of the US Pledge of Allegiance* (Lawrence: University Press of Kansas, 2005). Kevin Kruse, *One Nation under God: How Corporate American Invented Christian America* (New York: Basic Books, 2015).

3. See Thomas E. Ricks, *First Principles: What America's Founders Learned from the Greeks and Romans and How That Shaped Our Country* (New York: Harper, 2020).

4. The Roman historian Sallust was widely read and wrote of the transition to empire: "Riches became the epidemic passion; and where honours, imperial sway, and power, followed in their train, virtue lost her influence, poverty was deemed the meanest disgrace, and innocence was thought to be no better than a mark for malignity of heart. In this manner riches engendered luxury, avarice, and pride; and by those vices the Roman youth were enslaved. Rapacity and profusion went on increasing; regardless of their own property, and eager to seize that of their neighbours, all rushed forward without shame or remorse, confounding every thing sacred and profane, and scorning the restraint of moderation and justice" (Arthur Murphy, ed., *The Works of Sallust* [New York: J. Carpenter, 1807], 17).

5. John Adams's wrote *A Defence of the Constitutions of Government of the United States of America* (1787) in response to French criticism that Americans too slavishly followed the English idea of a mixed constitution full of checks and balances.

6. The phrase *Liberté, Egalité, Fraternité* was articulated by Robespierre in a speech of 1790, spread widely on posters and was painted on walls. *Fraternité* is the hardest idea to translate. "Solidarity" is a less sexist alternative to the word "fraternity." But it does not fully incorporate all important lineages of *fraternité*. Brotherhood invokes not just family relations but also Christianity and the traditions and institutions of artisans. See William H. Sewell, Jr. *Work and Revolution in France: The Language of Labor from the Old Regime to 1848* (Cambridge, UK: Cambridge University Press, 1980). Though connotations have shifted, the idea of fraternity was long a basic political theme in America. See Wilson Carey McWilliams, *The Idea of Fraternity in America* (Berkeley: University of California Press, 1973).

7. This was true throughout early modernity and such experience of distinctive social conditions and ways of life is enduringly significant. Thinking about freedom, like thinking about much else, was changed by the rise of industry, cities, large-scale markets, and national integration. Among other distinctions of the preindustrial United States from Europe was the greater distance between farms and between towns—which favored a strong ethos of self-reliance.

8. Philip Pettit, *Republicanism: A Theory of Freedom and Government* (Oxford: Oxford University Press, 1997); Philip Pettit, *Just Freedom: A Moral Compass for a Complex World* (New York: W. W. Norton, 2014).

9. Ideas of negative versus positive liberty are long standing. See Isaiah Berlin, "Two Concepts of Liberty," in Isaiah Berlin, *Four Essays on Liberty* (London: Oxford University Press, 1969); Charles Taylor, "What's Wrong with Negative Liberty," in Alan Ryan, ed., *The Idea of Freedom: Essays in Honour of Isaiah Berlin* (Oxford: Oxford University Press, 1979); Amartya Sen, *Development as Freedom* (Oxford: Oxford University Press, 1999); Martha Nussbaum, *Creating Capabilities: The Human Development Approach* (Cambridge, MA: Harvard University Press, 2011); Elizabeth Anderson, "What Is the Point of Equality?" *Ethics* 109:2 (1999), 287–337.

10. Charles Taylor has discussed of horizons of evaluation and qualitative discussions among goods in many works, including *Sources of the Self* (Cambridge, MA: Harvard University Press, 1989). See also Michiel Meijer, *Charles Taylor's Doctrine of Strong Evaluation* (Lantham, MD: Rowman and Littlefield, 2018).

11. Orlando Patterson has argued that the ancient birth of the very idea of freedom was linked to the unfreedom of slavery; see *Freedom, Vol. 1: Freedom in the Making of Western Culture* (New York: Basic Books, 1991). He links slavery to the dehumanizing condition Franz Fanon calls "social death;" see *Slavery and Social Death: A Comparative Study* (Cambridge, MA: Harvard University Press, 1982).

12. As many commentators have observed, the Declaration complains that the King of England is reducing Americans nearly to the status of slaves without considering the justice of slavery as practiced in America. The authors, including Thomas Jefferson, seem to have had a remarkable capacity for blocking this issue out of their thought. See Danielle Allen, *Our Declaration: A Reading of the Declaration of Independence in Defense of Equality* (New York: W. W. Norton, 2014). Simply extending the right to vote to a majority of its citizens took the United States over 130 years. In France, universal male suffrage was declared in 1792, but swiftly abandoned; French women didn't gain the vote until the last days of World War II. Delays were similarly long in other "democracies." Sanford Lakoff sees the progressive overcoming of such limits as basic to democracy; see Sanford Lakoff, *Democracy: History, Theory, Practice* (Boulder, CO: Westview, 1996).

13. Carol Anderson, *The Second: Race and Guns in a Fatally Unequal America* (London: Bloomsbury, 2021). These issues have not gone away. Fear of Blacks is a major factor in both opposition to gun control and severe, often fatal, policing of Blacks with guns.

14. I here borrow the phrase Hannah Arendt famously used to describe the condition of stateless people such as refugees fleeing the Holocaust. See *The Origins of Totalitarianism* (New York: Harcourt, Brace, Jovanovich, 1951). Like refugees, slaves were without political community.

15. Judgment in the US Supreme Court Case *Dred Scott v. John F. A. Sanford*, March 6, 1857, Case Files 1792–1995, Record Group 267, Records of the Supreme Court of the United States, National Archives, Washington, DC. The transcript of the majority decision read out by Chief Justice Roger B. Taney can be viewed at https://www.ourdocuments.gov/doc.php?flash=false&doc=29&page=transcript.

16. In 2019, the *New York Times* initiated fierce debate with the publication of a set of essays and literary works intended to put slavery and racism at the center of American self-understanding. The device was to memorialize the 1619 arrival of a slave ship and the sale of these transported Africans to American colonists. This, the authors suggested, constituted the start of the country as much or more than many familiar dates and events, including the Declaration of Independence. "Our founding ideals of liberty and equality were false when they were written," the introductory essay by Nikole Hannah Jones asserts; "Black Americans have fought to make them true." Nikole Hannah Jones, "America Wasn't a Democracy, Until Black Americans Made It One," *New York Times*, August 14, 2019. The binary rhetoric of true and false is misleading, and the account contained overstatements that helped fan controversy even among otherwise sympathetic historians. But the new national original story did call attention to a basic structuring contradiction in American history and pursuit of democracy.

17. Preston Brooks battered Sumner with a heavy cane, stopping only when the cane snapped. This cemented a Northern image of Southern brutality but was widely celebrated in the South as a justified defense of honor. Efforts to remove Brooks from Congress failed and indeed he was reelected. Two Southern towns renamed themselves in his honor. See Williamjames Hull Hoffer, *The Caning of Charles Sumner: Honor, Idealism, and the Origins of the Civil War* (Baltimore, MD: Johns Hopkins University Press, 2010). See also Harlan Joel Gradin, "Losing Control: The Caning of Charles Sumner and the Breakdown of Antebellum Political Culture," PhD Diss., University of North Carolina, Chapel Hill, 1991, especially for its thoughtful account of the degeneration and divergence of American political cultures.

18. I do not mean that there were no laws or policies from which Blacks and others benefited or none that tried to reduce discrimination. The New Deal was in many ways a

boon to Black Americans even though it incorporated deep inequality. Rather, I mean that, in that more than seventy-five-year gap, there was no legislation at the federal level specifically empowering Blacks as democratic citizens.

19. To be precise, Lincoln never used the word "democracy" in the speech. He described the United States as a country conceived in liberty and dedicated to equality, said that it should have a "new birth of freedom," and declared that government of, by, and for the people would not perish. Garry Wills, *Lincoln at Gettysburg: The Words that Remade America* (New York: Simon and Schuster, 1992) sees the address as giving equality new emphasis; James T. Kloppenberg, in *Toward Democracy: The Struggle for Self-Rule in European and American Thought* (Oxford: Oxford University Press, 2012), chap. 14, sees solidarity and unity as the core message, additional to earlier articulations of equality.

20. After Lincoln was assassinated, Senator Charles Sumner gave a eulogy, aptly linking Lincoln's speech to the Declaration of Independence. In it, he also rightly recognized how words as well as deeds matter in history. Lincoln's address spoke of the heroism of those who fought at Gettysburg, and included this prediction: "The world will little note, nor long remember what we say here, but it can never forget what they did here." But, of course, as Sumner indicated, Lincoln was wrong about this. The speech itself was "a monumental act," he asserted: "The world noted at once what he said, and will never cease to remember it. The battle itself was less important than the speech." Charles Sumner, *Promises of the Declaration of Independence: Eulogy on Abraham Lincoln, June 1, 1865* (Boston: Ticknor & Fields, 1865).

21. Similar contradictions beset other "advanced" democracies. In Germany, a conspiracy of silence accompanied the maintenance of ex-Nazis in positions of power. In many European countries, contradictions were inherited from the simultaneous formation of nation-states at home and colonies abroad. France, for example, fought Algerian independence from 1954 to 1962, and had fought for nearly a decade before that to maintain its hold on Vietnam.

22. Republican thought emphasized the virtues of politics, seeking resolution to problems in debate and agreement with fellow citizens. Arguably, rights thinking encouraged too much reliance on the judiciary rather than pursuit of political solutions. One of the problems for the civil rights movement was the extent to which its victories depended on courts and were resisted in legislatures—and in communities, voluntary associations, and businesses.

23. Business corporations and governments both built bureaucracies to address the issue of coordinating action at large scale; see Max Weber, *Economy and Society* [1922], ed. Guenther Roth and Claus Wittich (Berkeley: University of California Press, 1978), chap. 11. It is instructive to note the close links to transportation and communications infrastructure in, for example, the development of continental railroads shaped the rise of the modern corporation in the United States; see Alfred Chandler: *The Visible Hand* (Cambridge, MA: Harvard University Press, 1977). See also Craig Calhoun, "The Infrastructure of Modernity: Indirect Relationships, Information Technology, and Social Integration," in H. Haferkamp and N. J. Smelser, eds., *Social Change and Modernity* (Berkeley: University of California Press, 1992), 205–236.

24. With original legislation passed in 1944, this combined earlier New Deal agendas with an effort to create opportunities for returning World War II veterans. See Glenn Altschuler and Stuart Blumin, *The GI Bill: The New Deal for Veterans* (Oxford: Oxford University Press, 2009).

25. See Ira Katznelson, *When Affirmative Action Was White* (New York: W. W. Norton, 2006); Sarah Turner and John Bound, "Closing the Gap or Widening the Divide: The Effects of the G. I. Bill and World War II on the Educational Outcomes of Black Americans,"

NBER Working Paper No. 9044, July 2002; Erin Blakemore, "How the GI Bill's Promise Was Denied to a Million Black WWII Veterans," *History Today,* September 30, 2019.

26. In 1940, 5.5 percent of men and 3.8 percent of women had completed four years of college. By 1964, the gap was 11.7 percent to 6.8 percent—and it kept growing until the 1980s, when it began to narrow again. In 2014, the number of women passed the number of men. A chart of data collected by the US Census Bureau can be viewed at Statista, "Percentage of the US Population Who Have Completed Four Years of College or More from 1940 to 2020, by Gender," published by Erin Duffin, June 11, 2021, https://www.statista.com /statistics/184272/educational-attainment-of-college-diploma-or-higher-by-gender/.

27. Nancy Felice Gabin, *Feminism in the Labor Movement: Women and the United Auto Workers, 1935–1975* (Ithaca, NY: Cornell University Press, 1990).

28. Leah Platt Boustan and William J. Collins, "The Origins and Persistence of Black–White Differences in Women's Labor Force Participation," NBER Working Paper No. 19040, May 2013; see also Claudia Goldin, "Female Labor Force Participation: The Origin of Black and White Differences, 1870 and 1880," *Journal of Economic History* 37:1 (March 1977), 87–108.

29. This is partly due to lower pay rates but also to differences in rates of employment, which in turn reflect a variety of factors, from education, to the kinds and locations of jobs on offer, to direct discrimination, and to indirect discrimination such as bias against the formerly imprisoned (and bias in who gets imprisoned). See summary and references in Olibenga Ajilore, "On the Persistence of the Black–White Unemployment Gap," Center for American Progress, February 24, 2020, https://cdn.americanprogress.org/content/uploads /2020/02/20113909/Unemployment-Gap-1.pdf?_ga=2.130885647.1246435009.1614528832 -1612283697.1614528832.

30. Indeed, the Declaration says that this people in North America is separating from another people—by implication the English or perhaps British people (not just the British Empire, a political structure, not a people). England was an old kingdom and old identity, with a long-evoked but not unproblematic sense of common "peoplehood." The recurrently contested notion of a British people, inclusive of English, Scots, and Welsh, was new to this era. See Linda Colley, *Britons: Forging the Nation 1707–1832* (New Haven, CT: Yale University Press, 1992).

31. A large literature opposes "ethnic" to "civic" nationalism, but misleadingly implies a sharp contrast of types and maps them onto other contrasts such as traditional and modern and simply bad and good. It is more helpful to see a variety of ways to forge "peoplehood," overlapping in different combinations in different settings. Some of the relevant literature is addressed in Craig Calhoun, *Nations Matter: Culture, History and the Cosmopolitan Dream* (London: Routledge, 2007).

32. J. G. A. Pocock, *The Machiavellian Moment: Florentine Political Thought and the Atlantic Republican Tradition* (Princeton, NJ: Princeton University Press, 1975) traces republicanism from Florence through seventeenth-century England to America. For a philosophical account of the relationship of republicanism to democracy, see Philip Pettit, *On the People's Terms: A Republican Theory and Model of Democracy* (Cambridge, UK: Cambridge University Press, 2012).

33. Hannah Arendt, *On Revolution* (London: Penguin, 1963). See also Calhoun, "The Democratic Integration of Europe: Interests, Identity, and the Public Sphere," in Mabel Berezin and Martin Schain, eds., *Europe without Borders: Remapping Territory, Citizenship, and Identity in a Transnational Age* (Baltimore: Johns Hopkins University Press, 2003), 243–274.

34. Arendt was almost hostile to the other social dimensions of cohesion, deeming them at best lesser forms of integration, intrusions of necessity and interest where the emphasis should be on choice and the public good. See Arendt, *The Origins of Totalitarianism.*

35. This is discussed in *Federalist* 10 (in C. Rossiter, ed., *The Federalist Papers* [New York: New American Library, 1961], 77–84), where Madison moves away from thinking of parties as factions—a term of abuse among republicans because they split the polity for personal advantage. There is always risk that partisanship will move in that direction, if parties or partisans lose willingness or capacity to negotiate and instead seek simply to win at all costs.

36. Craig Calhoun, "Plurality, Promises, and Public Spaces," in Craig Calhoun and John McGowan, eds., *Hannah Arendt and the Meaning of Politics* (Minneapolis: University of Minnesota Press), 232–259.

37. Madison quoted in James T. Kloppenberg, *The Virtues of Liberalism* (Oxford: Oxford University Press, 1998), 178.

38. Rousseau grappled with related questions when he distinguished a majority from unanimity or the will of all individuals, and both from the *general* will as the expression of what people shared as members of a community. This is close to the idea of public good, though not quite the same. Speaking of "will" rather than "interests" emphasizes commitment and choice, whereas the term "interests" suggests potential benefits which citizens may recognize, or not, and may act to secure, or not.

39. Recently, some members of the Republican Party have taken to asserting that the US Constitution establishes a republic, not a democracy—rather than government combining the two. This is both mistaken and pernicious. See the discussion in George Thomas, "'America Is a Republic Not a Democracy' Is a Dangerous—and Wrong—Argument," *Atlantic,* November 2, 2020.

40. Dennis C. Rasmussen, *Fears of a Setting Sun: The Disillusionment of America's Founders* (Princeton, NJ: Princeton University Press, 2021), may overstate its case but is salutary.

41. For eloquent writing on the centrality of equality, see Danielle Allen, *Our Declaration: A Reading of the Declaration of Independence in Defense of Equality* (New York: W. W. Norton, 2014).

42. For economists (following Paul Samuelson), goods are naturally public (a) if they cannot be consumed by any without making them available to many more, though not necessarily all (say, clean air); and / or (b) if consumption by one does not diminish availability to all (they are "non-rivalrous"). Paul A. Samuelson, "The Theory of Public Expenditure," *Review of Economics and Statistics* 36 (1954), 386–389. What I have called "interdependent" goods are similar, but there are distinctions, too. Clean air is good whether others participate or not; it is public only in the sense that restricting who gets it is hard (though not entirely impossible, as different prices for houses built just by the freeway or the polluting factory suggest). But with equality and solidarity, the issue is not just how they are distributed or consumed. Interdependence is built into what they are.

43. Quoted in Ricks, *First Principles,* 287–288.

44. Alexis de Tocqueville, *Democracy in America* [1835–1840], in *Democracy in America and Two Essays on America,* ed. Isaac Kramnick, trans. Gerald Bevan (London: Penguin Classics, 2003).

45. Madison's main concern is to show that direct democracy cannot work at such scale and that representative democracy is necessary. In addition to *Federalist* 10, see *Federalist* 14 (in C. Rossiter, ed., *The Federalist Papers* [New York: New American Library, 1961]): "In a democracy, the people meet and exercise the government in person; in a republic, they assemble and administer it by their representatives and agents. A democracy, consequently, will be confined to a small spot. A republic may be extended over a large region." But the key distinction here is direct exercise of government versus mediation or management through representatives. Being able to work at larger scale was one advantage to republican

political structures; other mechanisms were also important for keeping the focus on longer-term public good. But this was not a simple opposition of democracy to republicanism. It was an effort to combine them.

46. Tocqueville, *Democracy in America,* vol. 1, includes an entire section on "How the Americans Combat Individualism by the Principle of Interest Rightly Understood." Volume 2 returns to the theme with more fine-grained social and cultural analysis.

47. Michael J. Sandel, *Democracy's Discontents: America in Search of a Public Philosophy* (Cambridge, MA: Belknap Press of Harvard University Press, 1998).

48. Tocqueville saw equality as the defining feature of democracy—and yet he mostly ignored slavery. His English contemporary Harriet Martineau was clearer about the contradiction and its implications for the future of the United States (not surprisingly, she also saw gender issues more clearly). See her *Society in America* (London: Saunders and Otley, 1937).

49. Robert Putnam, *Bowling Alone: The Collapse and Revival of American Community* (New York: Simon and Schuster, 2000).

50. John Dewey, *Democracy and Education* [1919] (New York: Free Press, 1997); John Dewey, *The Public and Its Problems* [1927] (Columbus: Ohio University Press, 1994).

51. This is a significant backdrop to Dewey's famous debate with Walter Lippmann. Lippmann was not only more politically conservative and less optimistic; he was a journalist more attentive to the transformations that scale was bringing. He wrote of a "phantom public" in which most people engaged with public affairs very little unless mobilized by leaders, who often produced public opinion by manipulation rather than debate. See Walter Lippmann, *The Phantom Public* [1925] (Piscataway, NJ: Transaction, 2006). Confronted with fascism and disillusioned with democracy, Lippman called for a focus on simply making government efficient and relying on elite definitions of the public good. Dewey argued that democratic publics were merely in eclipse and could be renewed. The authors of this book share that hope, however chastened by yet another round of the kind of mediated manipulation of publics that disillusioned Lippmann.

52. Tocqueville, *Democracy in America,* vol. 2, chap. 6.

53. Tocqueville, *Democracy in America,* vol. 2, chap. 6.

54. There are numerous studies of this history. For the United States, see Paul Starr, *The Creation of the Media: Political Origins of Modern Communications* (New York: Basic Books, 2005). In this, as in so much else, the 1970s marked a turning point. US newspaper circulation peaked in 1973 and has since fallen by nearly two-thirds. Pew Research Center, "Newspapers Fact Sheet," June 29, 2021, https://www.journalism.org/fact-sheet/newspapers/.

55. Tim Wu, *The Attention Merchants: From the Daily Newspaper to Social Media, How Our Time and Attention Is Harvested and Sold* (London: Atlantic Books, 2017).

56. Current systems correctly identify the gender of white men nearly 100 percent of the time—but get that of Black women wrong more than 30 percent of the time. Controversially, Google has forced out women who point to the problem. Cade Metz, "Who Is Making Sure the AI Machines Aren't Racist?" *New York Times,* March 15, 2021.

57. See Shoshana Zuboff, *The Age of Surveillance Capitalism: The Fight for a Human Future at the New Frontier of Power* (New York: PublicAffairs, 2019).

58. Nicole Cobie, "The Complicated Truth about China's Social Credit System," *Wired,* June 7, 2019.

59. There is great contestation over names today. In this book we refer to those who inhabited the United States before colonization and remain important members of the country as "American Indians." The name obviously reflects a historical error—yet it has also become part of historical reality. Our decision to use this rather than "Native American" or

other locutions is based mainly on what seem to be the primary choices of the people concerned (when they are referring to a wider category and not their distinct peoples). In Canada the term is First Nations. We use "indigenous" when we refer to the more global range of peoples who have confronted settlement, imperialism, and national expansion as encroachments on their territories and ways of life. There are obvious wrongs in abuse and expropriation. There is no simple right answer in nomenclature.

60. Tensions between imperialism and democracy appear not only in dominated territories. Europe's first colonial powers, Spain and Portugal, were among its last democracies.

61. Lawrence Goodwyn, *Democratic Promise: The Populist Moment in America* (Oxford: Oxford University Press, 1976).

62. Mark Twain and Charles Dudley Warner, *The Gilded Age: A Tale of Today* [1873] (London: Penguin, 2001).

63. See Christophe Guilluy, *Twilight of the Elites: Prosperity, the Periphery, and the Future of France,* trans. Malcolm DeBevoise (New Haven, CT: Yale University Press, 2019).

64. The sentiment helped to drive Brexit, the move to end British membership of the European Union. See Craig Calhoun, "Populism, Nationalism, and Brexit," in William Outhwaite, ed., *Brexit: Sociological Responses* (London: Anthem Press, 1976), 57–76. It continues to shape renewed English nationalism. See Alisa Henderson and Richard Wyn Jones, *Englishness: The Political Force Transforming Britain* (Oxford: Oxford University Press, 2021).

65. See Michael McQuarrie, "The Revolt of the Rust Belt: Place and Politics in the Age of Anger," *British Journal of Sociology,* 68 (2017), S120–S152, and his still unpublished comparative research on England and the United States.

66. Tracing the decline of employment in automotive manufacturing is complicated. Do you count just car making, or also the manufacturing of tires, glass, and paint? But the trend is clear and part of a sharp overall decline. US manufacturing jobs peaked at about 20 million in 1979, fell to less than 17 million by 1982, and, after recovering slightly, fell to 11 million between 1999 and 2011. For a chart of US Bureau of Labor Statistics created by the Federal Reserve Bank of St. Louis (FRED), see https://fred.stlouisfed.org/series/MANEMP. Alongside the decline in numbers came a decline in the proportion of unionized and average wages.

67. See the moving reportage in George Packer, *The Unwinding: An Inner History of the New America* (New York: Farrar, Strauss, Giroux, 2014) and the analysis in Michael McQuarrie, "The Revolt of the Rust Belt: Place and Politics in the Age of Anger," *British Journal of Sociology* 68 (2017), S120–S152.

68. The experience noted here is a theme of Georg Simmel's classic "The Metropolis and Mental Life," in Georg Simmel, *On Individuality and Social Forms: Selected Writings,* ed. Donald N. Levine (Chicago: University of Chicago Press, 1971), chap. 20.

69. Karl Polanyi, *The Great Transformation* (New York: Farrar & Rinehart, 1944). See the helpful discussion in Fred Block and Margaret R. Somers, *The Power of Market Fundamentalism: Karl Polanyi's Critique* (Cambridge, MA: Harvard University Press, 2014); and Kurtuluş Gemici, "Karl Polanyi and the Antinomies of Embeddedness," *Socio-Economic Review* 6:1 (2008), 5–33.

70. See Craig Calhoun, "Indirect Relationships and Imagined Communities: Large-Scale Social Integration and the Transformation of Everyday Life," in Pierre Bourdieu and James S. Coleman, eds., *Social Theory for a Changing Society* (Boulder, CO: Westview Press,1991); Craig Calhoun, "The Infrastructure of Modernity: Indirect Relationships, Information Technology, and Social Integration," in Hans Haferkamp and Neil J. Smelser, eds., *Social Change and Modernity* (Berkeley: University of California Press, 1992), 205–236.

71. Anselm Strauss, *Images of the American City* (New York: Free Press, 1961); Lyn Lofland, *A World of Strangers: Order and Action in Urban Public Space* (New York: Basic Books, 1974); Harvey Molotch, William Freudenburg, and Krista E. Paulsen, "History Repeats Itself, But How?: City Character, Urban Tradition, and the Accomplishment of Place," *American Sociological Review* 65:6 (2000), 791–823; Gary Fine, "The Sociology of the Local," *Sociological Theory*, 28:4 (2010), 355–376.

72. Corporate actors are characterized by more than just hierarchy or even scale. They are empowered by laws that recognize them as wielding concerted agency, with a separation between the will and legal responsibility of the corporation as such and either its owners or employees. Corporations can own property, enter into contracts, or litigate in the courts even though they are not persons in an ordinary sense. A disturbing 2010 US Supreme Court decision in the case of *Citizens United v. Federal Election Commission* even declared that corporations are protected by the Bill of Rights in the same way as other "citizens"—at least insofar as their free speech cannot be infringed by limits on their political campaign contributions. This asymmetry is surprisingly little considered in political theory. For a sociological perspective, see James S. Coleman, *The Asymmetric Society* (Syracuse, NY: Syracuse University Press, 1982).

73. For one summary among many, see Mariana Mazzucato, *The Entrepreneurial State: Debunking Public vs. Private Sector Myths* (New York: PublicAffairs, 2015).

74. Venkatesh Rao suggests that an increasingly critical class distinction is whether or not you work "above the API"—that is, above the "application programming interface" that allows two software systems to talk to one another. (He attributes the coinage of the phrase "below the API" in this sense to technology sector executive Peter Reinhardt.) In other words: Do you issue commands to the digital networks that shape our lives, or do they issue commands to you? See Venkatesh Rao, "The Premium Mediocre Life of Maya Millennial," blog post, August 17, 2017, https://www.ribbonfarm.com/2017/08/17/the-premium-mediocre-life -of-maya-millennial/. See also Peter Reinhardt, "Replacing Middle Management with APIs," blog post, February 3, 2015, https://rein.pk/replacing-middle-management-with-apis.

75. Cited in Kloppenberg, *Toward Democracy*, 633.

76. Craig Calhoun, "The Class Consciousness of Frequent Travelers: Toward a Critique of Actually Existing Cosmopolitanism," *South Atlantic Quarterly* 101:4 (2002), 869–897.

77. Trying to mitigate this concern, Appiah has argued for a more "rooted" cosmopolitanism. See Kwame Anthony Appiah, *Cosmopolitanism: Ethics in a World of Strangers* (New York: W.W Norton, 2007).

78. For one of the first and best reports on the local lives that cosmopolitan elites so often fail to notice, see Sarah Kendzior, *The View from Flyover Country: Dispatches from the Forgotten America* (New York: Flatiron Books, 2018).

79. Karl Marx and Friedrich Engels, *The Communist Manifesto* [1848], ed. Jeffrey C. Isaac (New Haven, CT: Yale University Press, 2012), 77.

80. The phrase is famously associated with Facebook's founder, Mark Zuckerberg. See Jonathan Taplin, *Move Fast and Break Things* (Boston: Little Brown, 2017). For the encouraging hope that business is turning away from this ideology, see Hemant Taneja, "The Era of 'Move Fast and Break Things' Is Over," *Harvard Business Review*, January 22, 2019.

81. The term "disruptive technologies" was popularized by innovation theorist Clayton Christensen. See, for example, Joseph L. Bower and Clayton M. Christensen, "Disruptive Technologies: Catching the Wave," *Harvard Business Review*, 73 (January–February 1995), 43–53.

82. In *The Condition of the Working Class in England in 1844* (Oxford: Oxford University Press 2009), Friedrich Engels reports: "I once went into Manchester with such a bourgeois,

and spoke to him of the bad, unwholesome method of building, the frightful condition of the working-peoples quarters, and asserted that I had never seen so ill-built a city. The man listened quietly to the end, and said at the corner where we parted: 'And yet there is a great deal of money made here, good morning, sir'" (276).

83. They are called "Luddites" because many proclaimed themselves followers of a (probably mythical) leader named Ned Ludd. Two classic accounts are Eric J. Hobsbawm, "The Machine Breakers," *Past and Present* 1 (February 1952), 57–70; and E. P. Thompson, *The Making of the English Working Class* (London: Victor Gollancz, 1965). See also Craig Calhoun, *The Question of Class Struggle: Social Foundations of Popular Radicalism During the Industrial Revolution* (Chicago: University of Chicago Press, 1982).

84. The full passage: "But this *long run* is a misleading guide to current affairs. In the long run we are all dead. Economists set themselves too easy, too useless a task if in tempestuous seasons they can only tell us that when the storm is long past the ocean is flat again" (John Maynard Keynes, *A Tract on Monetary Reform* [London: Macmillan, 1923], 80). This foreshadowed the emphasis on countercyclical government investment in Keynes's later work.

85. This strange misreading—perhaps sometimes a willful distortion—is often repeated, including infamously by Niall Ferguson; see Simon Taylor, "The True Meaning of 'In the Long Run We Are All Dead,'" blog post, May 5, 2013, https://www.simontaylorsblog.com /2013/05/05/the-true-meaning-of-in-the-long-run-we-are-all-dead/.

86. Robert C. Allen, "Engels' Pause: Technical Change, Capital Accumulation, and Inequality in the British Industrial Revolution," *Explorations in Economic History,* 46:4 (2009), 418–435.

87. In *The Question of Class Struggle* and *Roots of Radicalism* (Chicago: University of Chicago Press, 2011), I argue that facing this kind of obliteration of communities as well as livelihoods produces greater radicalism than being part of a growing working class able to strike compromises with capitalism.

88. The pioneering supermarket chain A&P was founded in direct response to the completion of the transcontinental railroad in 1869, initially specializing in prepackaged tea and going on to scale up its logistics to offer lower prices. It was thus disruptive to small groceries. See Marc Levinson, *The Great A&P and the Struggle for Small Business in America* (New York: Hill and Wang, 2011); James R. Beniger, *The Control Revolution: Technological and Economic Origins of the Information Society* (Cambridge, MA: Harvard University Press, 1986). John Kenneth Galbraith, *American Capitalism* [1952] (London: Penguin, 1963), makes A&P a prime example in presenting the large firm as an alternative to both government price controls and the ideology of perfect competition. By 2010, A&P itself was bankrupt, a victim of further disruptive change.

89. W. Fred Cottrell, "Death by Dieselization: A Case Study in the Reaction to Technological Change," *American Sociological Review* 16:3 (1951), 358–365.

90. See Alfred D. Chandler Jr., *The Visible Hand: The Managerial Revolution in American Business* (Cambridge, MA: Harvard University Press, 1977).

91. See Block and Somers, *The Power of Market Fundamentalism,* chap. 5, on the "old poor law" associated with Speenhamland and social policy.

92. Friedrich Engels, *The Condition of the Working Class in England* [1845], trans. Florence Kelley Wischnewetzky (New York: John W. Lovell, 1887).

93. Polanyi, *The Great Transformation.*

94. Our discussion is about domestic politics, but democracy is also affected by international upheavals, including shifting global hegemony, as in the Thirty Years War, when the Dutch and then the British consolidated hegemony in struggles with the Hapsburg Em-

pires. During the conflicts from 1918 to 1945, which included struggles with new imperial powers, Britain passed hegemony to the United States. See Immanuel Wallerstein, *The Modern World-System*, 4 vols. (Berkeley: University of California Press, 1974–2011); Giovanni Arrighi and Beverly J. Silver, *Chaos and Governance in the Modern World System* (Minneapolis: University of Minnesota Press, 1999).

3. Compromises with Capitalism

1. This changed in the 1970s with the rise of "Eurocommunism" and the commitment of communist parties in Italy, Spain, and elsewhere to electoral democracy. See Santiago Carrillo, *Eurocommunism and the State* (London: Lawrence and Wishart, 1977); Ernest Mandel, *From Stalinism to Eurocommunism* (London: New Left Books, 1979).

2. See Daniel Ziblatt, *Conservative Parties and the Birth of Democracy* (Cambridge, UK: Cambridge University Press, 2017). On how democratic transitions often leave elites in power, see Michael Albertys and Victor Menaldo, *Authoritarianism and the Elite Origins of Democracy* (Cambridge, UK: Cambridge University Press, 2018). On the possible end of elite support for democracy, see Anne Applebaum, *Twilight of Democracy: The Seductive Lure of Authoritarianism* (New York: Doubleday, 2020).

3. Membership organizations could be integral to local community; where it eroded they could not quite replace it. They declined precipitously in the new neoliberal era. This is the central theme of Robert Putnam, *Bowling Alone: The Collapse and Revival of American Community* (New York: Simon and Schuster, 2000). In a later book, Putnam charts some reasons to hope for renewal: Robert D. Putnam with Shaylyn Romney Garrett, *The Upswing: How America Came Together a Century Ago and How We Can Do It Again* (New York: Simon and Schuster, 2020).

4. Karl Polanyi's *The Great Transformation* (New York: Farrar & Rinehart, 1944) is a particularly informative account.

5. Jean Fourastié, *Les Trente Glorieuses, ou la révolution invisible de 1946 à 1975* [1975] (Paris: Hachette, 2004).

6. Public health had improved through the twentieth century in most developed countries. Trends commonly accelerated during *les trente glorieuses;* that for maternal mortality is especially focused in this period. For the British example, see Geoffrey Chamberlain, "British Maternal Mortality in the 19th and Early 20th Centuries," *Journal of the Royal Society of Medicine* 99:11 (2006), 559–563.

7. John Kenneth Galbraith, *The Affluent Society* [1958] (New York: Houghton-Mifflin, 1984).

8. Thomas D. Snyder, ed., *120 Years of American Educational Statistics* (Washington, DC: Center for Educational Statistics, 1993). As the previous chapter stressed, rates of overall improvement masked racial disparities.

9. Louis Menand's exciting general account appeared just as this book was going to press: *The Free World: Art and Thought in the Cold War* (New York: Farrar, Strauss, and Giroux, 2021).

10. See Menand, *The Free World*.

11. "Modernization theory" produced an enormous literature, and its critical evaluation is nearly as voluminous. At the center of debates are how much it exercised Western power in proportion to benevolence, even after the end of formal colonial rule, and whether commitment to capitalism blocked the smooth growth it envisaged. On the political and social theory, see Nils Gilman, *Mandarins of the Future* (Baltimore, MD: Johns Hopkins University

Press, 2003). Early and influential economic critiques include Walter Rodney, *How Europe Underdeveloped Africa* [1972] (London: Verso, 2018); Samir Amin, *Unequal Development* (New York: Monthly Review Press, 1976); Fernando Henrique Cardoso and Ernesto Faletto, *Dependency and Development in Latin America* (Berkeley: University of California Press, 1979). On continuing economic limits imposed not just by capitalism but by the self-interested approach the Western capitalist powers exercised individually and through the World Bank and the International Monetary Fund, see Ha-Joon Chang, *Kicking Away the Ladder: Development Strategy in Historical Perspective* (London: Anthem Press, 2002).

12. On the utopian dimensions of the postwar and Cold War–era in the United States, see Menand, *The Free World.*

13. Sadly, from about the same time that the EU reached its peak enlargement, it began to lose its ability to look forward in solidarity. Enlargement itself exacerbated other sources of inequality and tensions over the financial contributions and benefits of member states. In 2005, elites sought backing for tighter integration and suffered defeats in ill-considered referenda. The financial crisis of 2008–2009 hit Europe especially hard and was made worse by policy responses that favored financial institutions and investors while imposing austerity on citizens. Tensions over Islam and immigration festered until they shaped the catastrophic failures of 2015. Financial and migration policies brought clashes within countries as much as among them. Indeed, domestic discontents and polarized politics drove Brexit—both the 2016 referendum and the years of largely bungled implementation that followed—and continue to drive upheavals and threats to leave the EU in different countries.

14. The Philippines had actually declared independence from Spain in 1898, seeking to establish a constitutional democratic republic, only to find Spanish rule replaced by American. On the United States' never quite explicit empire, see Julian Go, *American Empire and the Politics of Meaning* (Durham, NC: Duke University Press, 2008) and Daniel Immerwahr, *How to Hide an Empire* (New York: Farrar, Straus and Giroux, 2019).

15. To be sure, democracy has had an uneven history in Ghana and Africa more generally. Among many, see Nic Cheeseman, *Democracy in Africa* (Cambridge: Cambridge University Press, 2015); Claude Ake, *Democracy and Development in Africa* (Washington, DC: Brookings Institution, 1996).

16. Martin Luther King Jr., Foreword, *A Freedom Budget for All Americans* (New York: A. Philip Randolph Institute, 1967).

17. Alan Brinkley, "Great Society," in Eric Foner and John A. Garraty, eds., *The Reader's Companion to American History* (Boston: Houghton Mifflin, 1991), 42; Alan Brinkley, *The End of Reform: New Deal Liberalism in Recession and War* (New York: Knopf, 1995); Steve Fraser and Gary Gerstle, eds., *The Rise and Fall of the New Deal Order, 1930–1980* (Princeton, NJ: Princeton University Press, 1989).

18. This was a core theme for Jane Jacobs's popular and influential *Life and Death of Great American Cities* (New York: Vintage, 1961), though she focused on urban neighborhoods rather than suburbs (which she tended to consider lost causes).

19. On the nature of such transformations in the modern world system, see Giovanni Arrighi and Beverly J. Silver, *Chaos and Governance in the Modern World System* (Minneapolis: University of Minnesota Press, 1999); Craig Calhoun and Georgi Derluguian, eds., *Aftermath: A New Global Economic Order?*, vol. 3 of *Possible Futures* (New York: New York University Press, 2011).

20. The term has a history going back to Rudolf Hilferding who in the early twentieth century drew a contrast to extreme, nineteenth-century economic liberalism. It became prominent as organization was unravelling and neoliberalism being asserted. See Claus Offe:

Disorganized Capitalism: Contemporary Transformations of Work and Politics (Cambridge: Polity, 1985); Scott Lash and John Urry: *The End of Organized Capitalism* (Cambridge: Polity, 1987); Martin Höpner, "Coordination and Organization: The Two Dimensions of Nonliberal Capitalism," MPIfG Discussion Paper, No. 07/12 (Cologne: Max Planck Institute for the Study of Societies, 2007); Wolfgang Streeck and Kozo Yamamura, eds.: *The Origins of Nonliberal Capitalism: Germany and Japan in Comparison* (Ithaca, NY: Cornell University Press, 2001).

21. The term "Fordist" comes from Antonio Gramsci. It clarifies that asymmetrical power shaped the bargains that produced organized capitalism. See Michel Aglietta, *Theory of Capitalist Regulation* (London: Verso, 1976); Bob Jessop and Ngai-Ling Sum, *Beyond the Regulation Approach* (Northampton, MA: Edward Elgar, 2006).

22. As Danielle Allen has argued, what democracy demands may be less actual equality than a sense of justice—which is achieved partly by continuous movement in the direction of justice. Danielle Allen, *Education and Equality* (Chicago: University of Chicago Press, 2016).

23. See data summarized in Thomas Piketty, *Capital in the Twenty-First Century*, trans. Arthur Goldhammer (Cambridge, MA: Harvard University Press, 2015). See also David M. Kotz, *Rise and Fall of Neoliberal Capitalism* (Cambridge, MA: Harvard University Press, 2015).

24. This had enduring consequences, as Roberto Frega emphasizes in "The Fourth Stage of Social Democracy," *Theory and Society* 50:6 (2021), 489–513.

25. To be precise, these "groups" are categories of people who suffered inequality. Within the category identified by each label, experiences varied partly on the basis of webs of social relations. Active participation in churches and communities linked to certain historically Black colleges and universities partially counterbalanced the effects of belonging to the larger category subject to discrimination. See discussion in Charles Tilly, *Durable Inequality* (Berkeley: University of California Press, 1999).

26. For an insightful review of the political science literature, making the important point that we should be concerned not only with aggregate levels of trust, but also with how trustworthy the objects of trust are, see Margaret Levi and Laura Stoker, "Political Trust and Trustworthiness," *Annual Review of Political Science* 3:1 (2000), 475–507. See also Lee Rainie and Andrew Perrin, "Key Findings about Americans' Declining Trust in Government and Each Other," Pew Research Center, July 22, 2019, https://www.pewresearch.org/fact-tank/2019/07/22/key-findings-about-americans-declining-trust-in-government-and-each-other/.

27. Max Weber, *Economy and Society* [1922], ed. Guenther Roth and Claus Wittich (Berkeley: University of California Press, 1978). This passage comes in the context of (a) extensive discussion of the connection between bureaucracy and advancement of material infrastructure for connectivity and communication, and (b) development of Weber's ideas about self-government not only in local communities but in "collegial" settings where relations among colleagues could replace or reduce top-down control.

28. Luc Boltanski and Eve Chiapello have persuasively argued that business became increasingly attractive in the late twentieth century precisely because it projected a "coolness," dynamism, and expressive freedom absent from government bureaucracy. Luc Boltanski and Eve Chiapello, *The New Spirit of Capitalism* [1999], trans. Gregory Elliott (London: Verso, 2018).

29. David Garland, *Punishment and Modern Society: A Study in Social Theory* (Chicago: University of Chicago Press, 1993).

30. See Henry Giroux and David Purpel, eds., *The Hidden Curriculum and Moral Education: Deception or Discovery?* (Berkeley: McCutchan, 1983); Samuel Bowles and Herbert

Gintis, *Schooling in Capitalist America: Educational Reform and the Contradictions of Economic Life* (New York: Basic Books, 1976).

31. See Richard H. Thaler and Cass R. Sunstein, *Nudge: Improving Decisions about Health, Wealth, and Happiness* (New Haven, CT: Yale University Press, 2008). To say that discipline is a dimension of projects of behavior change (or social engineering) does not mean that they do not produce real benefits. It does mean that decisions—and behavioral compliance—are produced on bases other than informed choice, and as Foucault would suggest, that the human being, the person subjected to the discipline, is being remade in the process.

32. See David Lyon, *The Culture of Surveillance: Watching as a Way of Life* (Cambridge, UK: Polity, 2018); Shoshana Zuboff, *The Age of Surveillance Capitalism: The Fight for a Human Future at the New Frontier of Power* (New York: PublicAffairs, 2019); and brief discussion in Chapter 2 of this book.

33. The phrase was printed on the punch cards used by computers that were growing increasingly prominent. It neatly aligned student protest against bureaucracy in the mass university—registration, for example—with criticism of disciplinary trends in the wider society. See Steven Lubar, "'Do Not Fold, Spindle or Mutilate': A Cultural History of the Punch Card," *Journal of American Culture,* 15:4 (Winter 1992), 43–55..

34. Pierre Bourdieu and Jean-Claude Passeron, *The Inheritors: French Students and Their Relations to Culture* (Chicago: University of Chicago Press, 1979); Randall Collins, *The Credential Society: An Historical Sociology of Education and Stratification* (New York: Academic Press, 1979).

35. Richard Sennett and Jonathan Cobb, *The Hidden Injuries of Class* (New York: W. W. Norton, 1972).

36. Among the many challenges for each category of subordinated or marginalized Americans have been identifying terms. There were not only insulting, pejorative terms. There were also paternalistic efforts to add dignity. There have been improvements proposed by intellectuals and activists. There is likely no perfection. We have settled on saying Black, American Indian, and Latino or Latina, which are perhaps the most common self-identifications.

37. There is by now a huge literature on neoliberalism. The term was coined in 1938 to describe arguments advanced especially by Friedrich Hayek and Ludwig von Mises (Angus Burgin, *The Great Persuasion* [Cambridge, MA: Harvard University Press 2015], 38–52). It was then developed into ideology and communicated effectively and widely by Milton Friedman, among others. It was a network and social movement as much as a specific set of ideas. Hayek, Friedman, and colleagues created the Mont Pèlerin Society to support their new movement. For accounts of neoliberal economics and its political engagements, see Angus Burgin, *The Great Persuasion;* Philip Mirowski and Dieter Plehwe, eds., *The Road from Mont Pelerin: The Making of the Neoliberal Thought Collective* (Cambridge, MA: Harvard University Press, 2009); Binyamin Applebaum, *The Economists' Hour* (New York: Little Brown, 2019); Daniel Stedman Jones, *Masters of the Universe: Hayek, Friedman, and the Birth of Neoliberal Politics* (Princeton: Princeton University Press, 2014). For a critical examination informed by Marxism, see David Harvey, *A Brief History of Neoliberalism* (Oxford: Oxford University Press, 2007). For an intellectual history of neoliberalism's relationship to globalism, see Quinn Slobodian, *The Globalists: The End of Empire and the Birth of Neoliberalism* (Cambridge, MA: Harvard University Press, 2018).

38. The argument that "neoliberalism is not a suitable analytical category because it changes or because it has multiple and sometimes contradictory meanings amounts to self-

defeating denialism, expressing a desire for a neat and simple singular ideology with an ahistorical essence to replace the messy world of competing worldviews. Marxism, liberalism, and conservatism have experienced kaleidoscopic refraction, splintering, and recombination over the decades. We see no reason why neoliberalism would not exhibit the same diversity" (Dieter Plehwe, Quinn Slobodian, and Philip Mirowski, eds., *Nine Lives of Neoliberalism* [London: Verso, 2020], Kindle Edition, 3).

39. Paradoxically, economics became more pervasively influential at the same time that it became more abstractly mathematical. Perhaps understanding the formal models gave practitioners extra authority; certainly, there was a demand for experts to explain them.

40. Friedrich Hayek, *The Road to Serfdom* [1944] (Chicago: University of Chicago Press, 1994), 16. Hayek's book is exactly contemporary to Karl Polanyi's *The Great Transformation* (1944), discussed in the previous chapter. Both fled Nazism to spend the war years in London, and the rise of fascism was influential on each of their great works, though they offered contrasting analyses. Hayek feared state domination and saw socialism as all too similar to Nazism (which had indeed called itself "national socialism"). Polanyi saw Nazism as a failed response to social disruption and social democracy as a better one.

41. Of course, there were economists deeply influenced by neoliberalism who advocated different policies, including more active government interventions. The founders of neoliberalism offered not only policy prescriptions but conceptual tools that could be used by other economists who reached different conclusions. And though it is hard to map, there is a difference between neoliberalism as a mode of economic analysis and as a more rigid ideology taken up in business policy debates.

42. Dean Baker, "This Is What Minimum Wage Would Be If It Kept Pace with Productivity," Center for Economic and Policy Research, January 21, 2020, https://www.cepr.net /this-is-what-minimum-wage-would-be-if-it-kept-pace-with-productivity/.

43. Republicans have resisted raising the minimum wage for decades and continue to resist this as a component of stimulus packages—even for health workers in response to the current pandemic. The reasoning is partly that higher minimum wages would discourage creation of jobs, but mostly that, if higher wages are warranted, markets will bring them about.

44. Adam Smith was frequently claimed as an iconic forebear, but neoliberalism did not clearly reflect his views on markets in *The Wealth of Nations*. Smith's emphasis on sympathy and virtues in *Theory of Moral Sentiments* was even more distant from neoliberalism.

45. See discussion in the previous chapter. James S. Coleman, *The Asymmetric Society* (Syracuse, NY: Syracuse University Press, 1982), is one of the few works to address this asymmetry systematically. It is also interesting because it comes from a methodological individualist in many ways sympathetic to neoliberal economics, but serious in following Adam Smith's lead on this dimension.

46. To be clear, the state is itself a kind of corporation, developed out of a venerable doctrine distinguishing individual human rulers from the office of kingship and, by extension, the organizational apparatus reporting to them. See Ernst Kantorowicz, *The King's Two Bodies* (Princeton, NJ: Princeton University Press, 1957). A similar line of reasoning distinguished the church and formal positions such as bishop and pope from those persons who might hold any such position. The distinction was poorly observed by corrupt kings and bishops, but played an important role in the development of the idea of sovereignty. This asserted not just autonomy from external interference, but also the right to determine internal arrangements and law. Republics likewise claimed sovereignty and were particularly concerned with protection against office-holders interested in personal gain rather than the public good.

47. *Dartmouth v. Woodward* 17 US (4 Wheat.), 518.

48. See Coleman, *The Asymmetric Society;* Meir Dan-Cohen, *Rights, Persons, and Organizations: A Legal Theory for Bureaucratic Society* (Berkeley: University of California Press, 1986); Craig Calhoun, "The Infrastructure of Modernity," in Hans Haferkamp and Neil J. Smelser, eds., *Social Change and Modernity* (Berkeley: University of California Press, 1992), 205–236.

49. The quotation is from a *New York Times* article in which Friedman popularized ideas from his 1962 book *Capitalism and Freedom* (Chicago: University of Chicago Press, 2002). Milton Friedman, "A Friedman Doctrine: The Social Responsibility of Business Is to Increase Its Profits," *New York Times,* September 13, 1970.

50. See discussion in Julio H. Cole, "Milton Friedman on Income Inequality," *Journal of Markets and Morality,* 11:2 (2008), 239–253.

51. Milton Friedman, *Capitalism and Freedom* (Chicago: University of Chicago Press, 1962), 161–162.

52. See Klaus Schwab and Peter Vanham, *What Is Stakeholder Capitalism? The Davos Agenda 2021,* https://www.weforum.org/agenda/2021/01/klaus-schwab-on-what-is-stakeholder-capitalism-history-relevance/.

53. The term comes from John Ruskin, who noticed in nineteenth-century England that focus seemed to fall always on what was new and added, not on what was lost and damaged—or indeed made ugly. See John Ruskin, *Unto These Last* [1862] (London: Penguin, 1986).

54. For a summary of neoliberalism's impact, see Harvey, *A Brief History of Neoliberalism.*

55. The rise of finance was shaped not only economics but also by politics. See Greta Krippner, *Capitalizing on Crisis* (Cambridge, MA: Harvard University Press, 2011).

56. On the way neoliberalism came to inform US Federal Reserve efforts to address inflation in the 1970s and pave the way for unregulated financialization, see Timo Walter and Leo Wansleben, "How Central Bankers Learned to Love Financialization: The Fed, the Bank, and the Enlisting of Unfettered Markets in the Conduct of Monetary Policy," *Socio-Economic Review,* March 21, 2019.

57. The term comes from Rudolf Hilferding's *Finance Capital: A Study of the Latest Phase of Capitalist Development* [1910] (London: Taylor and Francis, 2011).

58. Tom Wolfe, *The Bonfire of the Vanities* (New York: Farrar Straus Giroux, 1987).

59. On how this informed the crisis of 2008–2009, see Craig Calhoun, "From the Current Crisis to Possible Futures," in Craig Calhoun and Georgi Derluguian, eds., *Business as Usual: The Roots of the Global Financial Meltdown* (New York: New York University Press, 2011), 9–42. There is, of course, an enormous literature on the crisis itself.

60. See Alfred Rappaport, *Creating Shareholder Value: The New Standard for Business Performance* (New York: Free Press, 1986). General Electric CEO Jack Welch was an influential emissary for the notion. For a more critical analysis, see Frank Dobbin and Dirk Zorn, "Corporate Malfeasance and the Myth of Shareholder Value," *Political Power and Social Theory* 17 (2006), 179–198.

61. See Claus Offe, *Disorganized Capitalism* (Cambridge, MA: MIT Press, 1985); Scott Lash and John Urry, *The End of Organized Capitalism* (Madison: University of Wisconsin Press, 1987).

62. This number comes from "Riding the Storm: Market Turbulence Accelerates Diverging Fortunes," a study released by Swiss bank UBS and accounting firm PwC on October 7, 2020; https://www.ubs.com/content/dam/static/noindex/wealth-management/ubs-billionaires-report-2020-spread.pdf.

63. Martin Neil Baily, William Bekker, and Sarah E. Holmes, "The Big Four Banks: The Evolution of the Financial Sector, Part I," Brookings Institute report, May 2015, https://www

.brookings.edu/wp-content/uploads/2016/06/big_four_banks_evolution_financial_sector
_pt1_final.pdf. Bank consolidation, along with financialization generally, was an international trend.

64. These were major factors in the financial crisis. See Joseph Stiglitz, *Freefall: America, Free Markets, and the Sinking of the World Economy* (New York: W. W. Norton, 2010); Craig Calhoun, "From the Current Crisis to Possible Futures..

65. The seductive glamor is nicely evoked by Boltanski and Chiapello in *The New Spirit of Capitalism.*

66. Stiglitz, *Freefall.*

67. China alone lifted some 500 million people out of poverty; see Branko Milanovich, *Global Inequality: A New Approach for the Age of Globalization* (Cambridge, MA: Harvard University Press, 2016). Neoliberalism facilitated transfer of economic leadership from the United States and the West to China and Asia and thus the decline of American hegemony. The onset of this decline encouraged Richard Nixon's opening to China. See Orville Schell, "The Road to Beijing," *The Wire: China,* July 11, 2021. But the extent of geopolitical churn still seemed new when it shaped Donald Trump's appeal to "Make America Great Again." When Ronald Reagan used a nearly identical phrase, in the context of a deindustrializing America, the international referent was still Cold War competition. When Trump appropriated it, after deindustrialization was nearly complete, the rise of China was the central international concern.

68. See Mariana Mazzucato, *The Entrepreneurial State* (New York: PublicAffairs, 2015), on whether wise policy might enable renewed public investments and greater public returns on them.

69. There are exceptions such as doctors and lawyers. But it is worth noting that even their work has been subject to reorganization. A variety of less well-paid jobs have been created in a division of labor intended to reduce the costs of the most expensive professionals.

70. Years after many citizens' lives were devastated by addiction, courts are recognizing the liability of once-respected corporations such as Johnson and Johnson. For a more detailed account of one particular firm and the Sackler family that ran and profited from it, see Patrick Radden Keefe, "The Family That Built an Empire of Pain," *New Yorker,* October 23, 2017. The Sacklers also offer an example of how the "recycling" of wealth through philanthropy in fact takes resources away from some communities—workers and the towns they lived in—and delivers it to others; in the Sackler case, the big recipients were Israel and museums in several major cities. See Anand Giridharadas, *The Elite Charade of Changing the World* (New York: Vintage, 2018).

71. See Barry Meier, "A Nun, a Doctor, and a Lawyer—and Deep Regret over the Nation's Handling of Opioids," *New York Times,* August 18, 2019.

72. See Figure 3. See also Tommy Beer, "Top 1% of U.S. Households Hold 15 Times More Wealth than Bottom 50% Combined," *Forbes,* October 8, 2020. Globally, about half of the world's wealth is owned by the richest one percent. Credit Suisse Global Wealth Report, 2018, https://www.credit-suisse.com/about-us/en/reports-research/global-wealth-report.html.

73. Kerry A. Dolan, Jennifer Wang, and Chase Peterson-Withorn, "Billionaires," *Forbes,* March 5, 2019; Institute for Policy Studies, "Billionaire Bonanza 2017," November 8, 2017, https://ips-dc.org/report-billionaire-bonanza-2017/.

74. Ben Steverman and Alexandre Tanzi, "The 50 Richest Americans Are Worth as Much as the Poorest 165 Million," Bloomberg, October 8, 2020.

75. Information on the taxes paid—or avoided—by the very rich became available in 2021 when IRS records were leaked to the public interest journalism group ProPublica. See Jesse

Eisinger, Jeff Ernsthausen, and Paul Kiel, "The Secret IRS Files: Trove of Never-Before-Seen Records Reveal How the Wealthiest Avoid Income Tax," ProPublica, June 8, 2021, https://www .propublica.org/article/the-secret-irs-files-trove-of-never-before-seen-records-reveal-how -the-wealthiest-avoid-income-tax. For deeper analysis of tax evasion, see Emmanuel Saez and Gabriel Zucman, *The Triumph of Injustice: How the Rich Dodge Taxes and How to Make Them Pay* (New York: W. W. Norton, 2019); John Guyton, Patrick Langetieg, Daniel Reck, Max Risch, and Gabriel Zucman, "Tax Evasion at the Top of the Income Distribution: Theory and Evidence," NBER working paper 28542, March 2021, https://www .nber.org/papers/w28542.

76. See Gabriel Zucman, *The Hidden Wealth of Nations* (Chicago: University of Chicago Press, 2015); Saez and Zucman, *The Triumph of Injustice*.

77. Carter Coudriet, "These Billionaires Want the Ultra-Wealthy to Pay More in Taxes," *Forbes,* October 15, 2019.

78. R. Lachmann, *First Class Passengers on a Sinking Ship: Elite Politics and the Decline of Great Powers* (London: Verso, 2020).

79. Raj Chetty, John Friedman, Emmanuel Saez, Nicholas Turner, Danny Yagan, "Income Segregation and Intergenerational Mobility across Colleges in the United States," *Quarterly Journal of Economics* 135 (2020), 1567–1633.

80. Rick Seltzer, "A Gulf in the Earnings Gap," *Inside Higher Ed,* September 6, 2018..

81. Lisa J. Dettling, Joanne W. Hsu, Lindsay Jacobs, Kevin B. Moore, and Jeffrey P. Thompson, "Recent Trends in Wealth-Holding by Race and Ethnicity: Evidence from the Survey of Consumer Finances," *FEDS Notes,* September 27, 2017, https://www.federalreserve .gov/econres/notes/feds-notes/recent-trends-in-wealth-holding-by-race-and-ethnicity -evidence-from-the-survey-of-consumer-finances-20170927.htm. This dataset does not give data for Asians. Overall, Asians have more wealth than other minorities and less than whites, but this masks complexity. For example, Japanese Americans have twenty times the wealth of Korean Americans. See Dedrick Asante-Muhammad and Sally Sim, "Racial Wealth Snapshot: Asian Americans and the Racial Wealth Divide," National Community Reinvestment Coalition, May 14, 2020, https://ncrc.org/racial-wealth-snapshot-asian-americans-and-the -racial-wealth-divide/.

82. See data and analysis by the Inequality.org project of the Institute for Policy Studies, https://inequality.org/facts/gender-inequality/; and the website of the advocacy group Closing the Women's Wealth Gap, https://womenswealthgap.org.

83. For access to the report "OECD Regions at a Glance 2016," see OECD, "Regional Inequalities Worsening in Many Countries," press release, June 16, 2016, https://www.oecd .org/regional/regional-inequalities-worsening-in-many-countries.htm.

84. Mary Harrington nicely discusses personal paths to lack of ownership and liquidity in "In Defence of the Woke Lefts," *UnHerd,* May 13, 2021. See also Zygmunt Bauman, *Liquid Modernity* (Cambridge: Polity, 2000).

85. Polanyi, *The Great Transformation.*

86. Hastie's words have been quoted widely, and as far back as news articles in the 1940s. I have not been able to find its original source.

4. Authenticity and Meritocracy

1. Of course, there were precursors. The autocratic Otto von Bismarck introduced elements of a welfare state as early as the 1870s to secure support as he worked to unify Germany and make sure it stayed capitalist rather than socialist.

2. C. B. Macpherson, *The Political Theory of Possessive Individualism* (Oxford: Oxford University Press, 1962).

3. The phrase comes from a 1970 song by Janis Joplin (written in collaboration with Bob Neuwirth and Michael McClure). Prosperity theology has older roots, including in the teachings of Oral Roberts and other American Evangelists, but has been prominently promoted in the era of neoliberalism. It has also become global; see Simon Coleman, *The Globalization of Charismatic Christianity: Spreading the Gospel of Prosperity* (Cambridge: Cambridge University Press, 1970); Simon Coleman, "The Prosperity Gospel: Debating Charisma, Controversy and Capitalism," in S. Hunt, ed., *The Brill Handbook of Contemporary Christianity: Movements, Institutions and Allegiance* (Leiden: Brill, 2016), 276–296.

4. David Goodhart, *The Road to Somewhere: The Populist Revolt and the Future of Politics* (London: Hurst, 2017).

5. Goodhart, *The Road to Somewhere*, 3–4.

6. Goodhart, *The Road to Somewhere*, 9.

7. Goodhart, *The Road to Somewhere*, 11.

8. Margaret O'Mara, *The Code: Silicon Valley and the Remaking of America* (London: Penguin, 2019); Fred Turner, *From Counterculture to Cyberculture: Stewart Brand, the Whole Earth Network, and the Rise of Digital Utopianism* (Chicago: University of Chicago Press, 2006); John Markoff, *What the Dormouse Said: How the Sixties Counterculture Shaped the Personal Computer Industry* (New York: Viking Penguin, 2005).

9. Of course, giant corporations exert pervasive control over their employees and are driven by profit and the accumulation of capital. The same tech industry is also behind an unprecedented level of surveillance of what once was called private life. See David Lyon, *The Culture of Surveillance: Watching as a Way of Life* (Cambridge, UK: Polity, 2018); Shoshana Zuboff, *The Age of Surveillance Capitalism: The Fight for a Human Future at the New Frontier of Power* (New York: PublicAffairs, 2019).

10. Alexis de Tocqueville, *Democracy in America*, [1835–1840], in *Democracy in America and Two Essays on America,* ed. Isaac Kramnick, trans. Gerald Bevan (London: Penguin, 2003), vol. 2, chap. 13; Richard Sennett and Jonathan Cobb, *The Hidden Injuries of Class* (New York: W. W. Norton, 1993), 257.

11. Joe Biden, Tweet of November 28, 2020, https://twitter.com/joebiden/status /1332783824716009472.

12. Charlene Pempe, "He's Sending a Taste of Joy to Your Door," *Financial Times,* May 13, 2021.

13. Charles Taylor, *The Ethics of Authenticity* (Cambridge, MA: Harvard University Press, 1991); Charles Taylor, *Multiculturalism and the Politics of Recognition* (Princeton, NJ: Princeton University Press, 1992).

14. Paul Embery describes why many English workers are angry at Left and Right alike: "Both hitch their wagon to every minority crusade and then afford to it an undue level of prominence. Both are largely ignorant—and often contemptuous—of the lives and priorities of those in small-town Britain, of their communitarian impulse, traditional values, desire for belonging and sense of national pride" ("Labour Isn't Working," *UnHerd,* May 8, 2021).

15. A website under the banner of #SayTheirNames maintains a list of Black people who lost their lives to acts of racism and excessive force, https://sayevery.name/#2021.

16. Jonathan Dunn, Sheldon Lyn, Nony Onyeador, and Ammanuel Zegeye, "Black Representation in Film and TV: The Challenges and Impact of Increasing Diversity" (New York: McKinsey and Co., March 11, 2021), https://www.mckinsey.com/featured-insights /diversity-and-inclusion/black-representation-in-film-and-tv-the-challenges-and-impact -of-increasing-diversity.

17. Richard Alba, *The Great Demographic Illusion: Majority, Minority, and the Expanding American Mainstream* (Princeton, NJ: Princeton University Press, 2020).

18. This resulted in sociological differences over analyses of "class" and "stratification." Class analysis emphasized breaks between classes and commonalities within each. Stratification analysis emphasizes potentially innumerable layers and individual mobility among them. Marxists sought to overturn the class system; non-Marxist socialists more often campaigned just to reduce the inequalities among classes. In the United States, explicit socialists were fewer, and "progressives" often sought not to reduce inequality but to increase opportunity and fairness. For one of the few studies of downward mobility, see Katherine S. Newman, *Falling from Grace: Downward Mobility in the Age of Affluence* [1988] (Berkeley: University of California Press, 1999).

19. George Bernard Shaw, *Pygmalion* [1912] (New York, Doubleday 2014), 29. The speech is preserved almost intact in George Cukor's film adaptation, *My Fair Lady* (1964), though that film takes other liberties such as introducing Hollywood's notion of a happy ending.

20. Michael Young coined the term in the satirical novel *The Rise of the Meritocracy* (London: Penguin, 1961).

21. See Daniel Markovits, *The Meritocracy Trap: How America's Foundational Myth Feeds Inequality, Dismantles the Middle Class, and Devours the Elite* (London: Penguin 2019).

22. Pierre Bourdieu and Jean-Claude Passeron, *The Inheritors: French Students and Their Relation to Culture* [1964] (Chicago: University of Chicago Press, 1973).

23. See his somewhat disgusted complaint in Michael Young, "Down with Meritocracy," *Guardian,* June 28, 2001.

24. Michael J. Sandel, *The Tyranny of Merit: What's Become of the Common Good?* (New York: Farrar, Straus and Giroux, 2020), 14. This point also applies to nations. None is entirely self-made or self-sufficient. Yet some nationalists persist in thinking this way. The Republican former US Senator Rick Santorum combined insult and absurdity in a speech denigrating American Indians that, while extreme, reflected attitudes that have been widespread. "We birthed a nation from nothing—I mean, there was nothing here," he said to an audience of right-wing Young Americans for Freedom. "I mean, yes, we have Native Americans, but candidly, there isn't much Native American culture in American culture" (John L. Dorman, "CNN Drops Rick Santorum after Dismissive Comments about Native Americans," *New York Times,* May 5, 2021).

25. Alison Bashford and Philippa Levine, eds., *Oxford Handbook of the History of Eugenics* (Oxford: Oxford University Press, 2010).

26. Here it is important to remember growing capacities to alter human biology and development—starting with genetic engineering. In addition to all the social and ethical risks these pose, they challenge the notion that human beings are natural and that variations among them result from chance, evolution, or divine will. For the reflections of one leading scientist, see Jennifer Doudna, *A Crack in Evolution: Gene Editing and the Unthinkable Power to Control Evolution* (Boston: Houghton Mifflin 2017). And among the growing number of studies of related social issues, see John H. Evans, *The Human Gene-Editing Debate* (Oxford: Oxford University Press, 2020); and Michael J. Sandel, *The Case against Perfection: Ethics in the Age of Genetic Engineering* (Cambridge, MA: Harvard University Press, 2009).

27. By always emphasizing achievement rather than simply being, Byung-Chul Han suggests we have created a "burnout society." Byung-Chul Han, *The Burnout Society* (Palo Alto, CA: Stanford University Press, 2015).

28. The question was posed by Jon Boeckenstedt, vice provost for enrollment management at Oregon State University, in a since-deleted tweet, April 3, 2021.

29. Thorstein Veblen, *The Theory of the Leisure Class* [1899] (Oxford: Oxford University Press, 2009).

30. Our high-status publisher, Harvard University Press, uses a style guide that indicates its preference for "Latinx" over "Latina" and "Latino" which are both gendered and less friendly to trans people. We think Harvard is motivated by trying to do what is right and to reduce gender bias. We also think efforts to change habitual language can play a positive role in social change. But we note that correcting for one bias can introduce others. Inclusion in the elite community of those who know the new, right words is still the reproduction of an elite even if positive in other ways. And construction of new terms can also be in tension with using identity terms that people choose for themselves.

31. Conservatives have been quicker to challenge new jargon, partly because they are invested in old cultural categories and hierarchies. This makes it hard to distinguish the critique of tacit elitism from defense against more substantive challenge. See Nicholas Clairmont, "The Language of Privilege," *Tablet,* September 28, 2020; David Brooks, "This Is How Wokeness Ends," *New York Times,* May 13, 2021. Similar arguments are also made by self-styled progressives such as Todd Gitlin, who objects to the vocabulary as well as the substance of identity politics in *The Twilight of Common Dreams: Why America Is Wracked by Culture Wars* (New York: Henry Holt, 1995); Eleanor Robertson, "Intersectional-What? Feminism's Problem with Jargon Is that Any Idiot Can Pick It Up and Have a Go," *Guardian,* September 30, 2017; Ben Andrew, "The Language of the Left—And How It Alienates Progressives from Their Own Causes," *Liberal Democratic Voice,* November 14, 2016.

32. Harry Brighouse, "On the Meaning of Merit," keynote address, USC Rossier Center for Enrollment Research, Policy, and Practice Annual Conference, January 16, 2014. Brighouse's slide deck can be viewed at https://drive.google.com/file/d/17hqMrilDfvUHHABu3KW16d _ookwYhoh/view. A summary was created for the event's blog: https://www.dropbox.com/s /acrtni4bu39z8e6/USC%20Rossier%20Brighouse%20Merit%20Achievement%20CERPP .pdf?dl=o. The critique of tacit elitism has a point, but this should not obscure the importance of contesting cultural categories.

33. In the United States, more and more students attend schools with some manner of private selection system and usually private funding, whether these are simply private market ventures or linked to churches or organized as "charter" schools. By comparison, France retains a strong, centralized, and basically universalistic system of public education. It is highly selective internally, but it is the same system for almost all students. In England, private, fee-based, and selective schools have long histories. Comprehensive schools open to all potential students were set up after World War II and expanded under Labour in the 1960s. Since then, during the neoliberal era, private and selective schools have grown more prominent—and are widely seen as key factors perpetuating or even increasing inequality. See David Kynaston and Francis Green, *Engines of Privilege: Britain's Private School Problem* (London: Bloomsbury, 2019), though note that England relies more on private schools than other parts of Britain.

34. We refer to credentialed, institutionally consecrated, and market-recognized higher education. As a remarkable history of autodidacts demonstrates, people can learn a lot without universities or colleges.

35. Paul Bolton, "Education: Historical Statistics," House of Commons Library Standard Note SN/SG/4252, updated November 27, 2012, https://dera.ioe.ac.uk/22771/1/SN04252.pdf.

36. This argument was decisively answered by extensive empirical research associated with the Robbins Report of 1963: *Higher Education: Report of the Committee appointed by the Prime Minister under the Chairmanship of Lord Robbins* (London: Her Majesty's Stationery

Office 1963). See also Nicholas Barr, ed., *Shaping Higher Education: Fifty Years After Robbins* (London: London School of Economics and Political Science, 2014).

37. It is worth noting that countries that have historically benefited from relatively egalitarian university systems, such as Canada and Germany, have recently been introducing more hierarchy, largely to try to move up in global rankings. This is not just a part of university strategy; countries also compete over rankings—say, as destinations for investment.

38. Zhao "Molly" Yusi, quoted in Laurie Chen, "Hard Work Got Me into Stanford University, Says Chinese Student in Viral Video after Parents Paid US$6.5 Million to Get Her Accepted," *South China Morning Post,* May 3, 2019.

39. Sara Goldrick Rabb, *Paying the Price: College Costs, Financial Aid, and the Betrayal of the American Dream* (Chicago: University of Chicago Press, 2016). This is also an enormous burden on families. See also Caitlin Zaloom, *Indebted: How Families Make College Work at Any Cost* (Princeton, NJ: Princeton University Press, 2019).

40. Tressie McMillan Cottom, *Lower Ed: The Troubling Rise of For-Profit Colleges in the New Economy* (New York: New Press, 2017).

41. Capital takes multiple forms, according to Bourdieu, and is convertible among them. Converting financial wealth into educational credentials or markers of cultural taste is, among other things, a way of legitimating inequality. But it is also possible to convert social connections and cultural standing into economic opportunities and resources. See Pierre Bourdieu, "The Forms of Capital," in John G. Richardson, ed., *Handbook of Theory and Research for the Sociology of Education* (New York: Greenwood, 1986), 243.

42. Jason DeParle, "Harder for Americans to Rise from Lower Rungs," *New York Times,* January 4, 2012.

43. Alexis de Tocqueville made a similar point in *Democracy in America,* where he noted that in a society that rejects inheritance and confidently proclaims itself open to social mobility, those who fail to advance are implicitly encouraged to blame themselves. Sennett and Cobb showed this indeed to be still the pattern in *The Hidden Injuries of Class.* Social mobility and its absence have many explanations, and individual talent and effort are only part of the mix. Possession of various kinds of capital typically matters more.

44. Sandel, *The Tyranny of Merit,* 17.

45. Bourdieu develops an analysis of symbolic violence as the exercise of power in how people are categorized in *Outline of a Theory of Practice* [1972] (Cambridge: Cambridge University Press, 1977) and many subsequent works. See also Michael Burawoy, *Symbolic Violence: Conversations with Bourdieu* (Durham, NC: Duke University Press, 2019).

46. Clinton supporters have suggested that her comment, made in the heat of an ugly campaign, was misinterpreted and intentionally distorted. See Domenico Montenaro, "Hillary Clinton's 'Basket of Deplorables,' in Full Context of This Ugly Campaign," *National Public Radio,* September 10, 2016.

5. Making the Demos Safe for Democracy?

1. Aside from numerous invaluable conversations with my coauthors, Craig Calhoun and Charles Taylor, I have profited from my discussions with Sally Ewing, Robert Hariman, Benjamin Lee, and Liam Mayes while writing this chapter. I am especially indebted to Liam Mayes for his assistance in editing the final draft and providing suggestions for many constructive revisions and refinements.

2. The oligarchic tendencies of democracy, presciently identified and analyzed by Robert Michaels in 1911, might require some updating, but that phenomenon itself is his-

torically unmistakable and sociologically unavoidable. Robert Michaels, *Political Parties: A Sociological Study of the Oligarchic Tendencies of Modern Democracy,* trans. Eden and Cedar Paul (New York: Free Press, 1962).

3. Peter Sloterdijk, *Rage and Time,* trans. Mario Wenning (New York: Columbia University Press, 2010).

4. My point is that in the framework of democratic politics, class conflict, especially in modern highly stratified societies, has limited interpretive value. While one might be able to offer a rigorous Marxist or sociological analysis of class conflicts and either how they undermine the democratic project or how democracies contain and deflect them—class conflict itself tends to be removed from the vocabulary of practical democratic politics. Moreover, progressive candidates or movements are likely avoid invoking the idea of class conflict lest they be accused of fomenting class conflict by their opponents, a potent negative charge in bourgeois electoral democracies. Thus, to dwell on the social conflict unavoidable in any given society, one needs to recast it in the language of the elites and the non-elites. Although such a recasting might be analytically even more nebulous than a traditional class analysis, the opposition between elites and nonelites has far more resonance in the daily language of politics, especially democratic politics since time of the ancient Athenian democracy. See Josiah Ober, *Mass and Elite in Democratic Athens: Rhetoric, Ideology, and the Power of the People* (Princeton, NJ: Princeton University Press, 1989).

5. Samuel P. Huntington, *The Third Wave: Democratization in the Late Twentieth Century* (Norman: University of Oklahoma Press, 1991), 15.

6. Larry Diamond, "Is the Third Wave Over?," *Journal of Democracy* 7:3 (1996), 20–37; Larry Diamond, "Facing Up to the Democratic Recession," *Journal of Democracy* 26:1 (2015), 141–155.

7. Steven Levitsky and Daniel Ziblatt, *How Democracies Die* (New York: Crown Penguin, 2018), 3.

8. Larry Diamond, *Ill Winds: Saving Democracy from Russian Rage, Chinese Ambition, and American Complacency* (New York: Penguin, 2019); David Runciman, *How Democracy Ends* (New York: Basic Books, 2018); Timothy Snyder, *The Road to Unfreedom: Russia-Europe-America* (New York: Penguin Random House, 2018); Astra Taylor, *Democracy May Not Exist, But We'll Miss It When It's Gone* (New York: Henry Holt, 2019).

9. Francis Fukuyama, "The End of History," *National Interest* 16 (Summer 1989), 3–18; Francis Fukuyama, *The End of History and The Last Man* (New York: Free Press, 1992).

10. See Daniel A. Bell, *The China Model: Political Meritocracy and the Limits of Democracy* (Princeton, NJ: Princeton University Press, 2015).

11. Michael Ignatieff, "Democracy against Democracy: The Electoral Crisis of Liberal Constitutionalism," keynote address delivered at *Popular Sovereignty, Majority Rule, and Electoral Politics,* a conference hosted by the Institute for Human Sciences (IWM), Vienna, Austria, May 30, 2019.

12. Levitsky and Ziblatt, *How Democracies Die,* 5.

13. The name of the principle derives from Leo Tolstoy's 1877 novel *Anna Karenina,* which begins: "All happy families are alike; each unhappy family is unhappy in its own way."

14. See, for instance, what Larry Diamond calls "the autocrats' twelve-step program," in *Ill Winds,* 64–65.

15. Roger Cohen, "Steve Bannon Is a Fan of Italy's Donald Trump," *New York Times,* May 18, 2019.

16. For an excellent case study, See Prashant Jha, *How BJP Wins: Inside India's Greatest Election Machine* (New Delhi: Juggernaut Books, 2017).

17. It was peaceful, but not exactly civil. The incumbent, John Adams, did not stay for the inauguration and, on the last day of his presidency, appointed a host of judges aligned with his Federalist Party. In retirement, however, Jefferson and Adams did reconcile. Today, their massive correspondence stands as a monument to the lost art of political friendship.

18. With a commanding parliamentary majority, Prime Minister Indira Gandhi persuaded President Fakhruddin Ali Ahmed to impose the "Emergency" (rule by decree), ostensibly to quell mounting incidents of "internal disturbances." The emergency was in effect for a twenty-one-month period from June 25, 1975, to March 21, 1977, during which, among other things, civil liberties were curbed, the press was censored, and a large number of political opponents were imprisoned. On January 18, 1977, Indira Gandhi abruptly called for new parliamentary elections for March and released all political prisoners on the obvious assumption that she would be returned to power with an overwhelming majority and thus vindicate her decision to declare the "Emergency." Instead, her Congress Party was decisively defeated, including Indira Gandhi's losing her own seat in the Lok Sabha (lower house). In the Indian political imaginary, the election of 1977 has acquired a hallowed status of attesting to the wisdom of the Indian electorate, largely poor and illiterate.

19. Similarly, Erdogan's party recently lost municipal elections in Istanbul, a stronghold of his party. Erdogan accepted the results. This does not mean Erdogan and his party will stop transgressing constitutional constraints and institutional guardrails. Rather, it suggests that the only way to push back against majoritarian democracy is to defeat it electorally.

20. Joseph A. Schumpeter, *Capitalism, Socialism and Democracy*, 2nd ed. (New York: Harper, 1947), 269, cited in Huntington, *The Third Wave*, 6.

21. Huntington, *The Third Wave*, 7.

22. Huntington, *The Third Wave*, 9–10.

23. Robert A. Dahl, *A Preface to Democratic Theory* (Chicago: University of Chicago Press, 1956), 3.

24. Carole Pateman, *Participation and Democratic Theory* (New York: Cambridge University Press, 1970), 9.

25. It is ironic that the "election," unlike the "lot," was historically regarded as the preferred aristocratic mechanism within the republican tradition, both ancient and modern, that ensured rule by the elite rather than by the multitude. In our age of mass democracy, even though the elites (perhaps not the right kind of traditional elites) continue to rule, the election is viewed as a populist / majoritarian mechanism prone to trample liberal values and republican institutions. See Bernard Manin, *The Principles of Representative Government* (New York: Cambridge University Press, 1997).

26. Pateman, *Participation and Democratic Theory*, 10

27. Josiah Ober, *Political Dissent in Democratic Athens: Intellectual Critics of Popular Rule* (Princeton, NJ: Princeton University Press, 1988).

28. It is worth noting that in Athenian democracy, the privilege of citizenship (and therefore, the right to political participation) was severely restricted. Further, within that restricted group, an ethos of meaningful equality was created by artfully separating the political realm of equals from the *oikoi*, the economic realm of unequals within and across households. Moreover, Athens was a relatively homogeneous political community, bound together by common ancestry, religion, language, cultural tradition, shared memories, and other bands of solidarity. Despite so many things in its favor for the optimal functioning of political equality in public assemblies, it was deemed and declared impractical and dangerous by the critics of democracy, Plato being the most penetrating and influential of all such critics.

29. Jacques Rancière, *The Philosopher and His Poor* [1983], trans. John Drury, Corinne Oster, and Andrew Parker (Durham, NC: Duke University Press, 2004).

30. Plato, *Protagoras,* in *The Collected Dialogues of Plato,* ed. Edith Hamilton and Huntington Cairns (Princeton: Princeton University Press, 1961), 320d–328d.

31. Plato, *Protagoras,* 322b–d.

32. John Dewey, *The Public and Its Problems* (New York: Henry Holt, 1927); Walter Lippmann, *The Phantom Public* (New York: Macmillan, 1927). For the contemporary relevance of the Dewey-Lippmann debate, see Mark Whipple, "The Dewey-Lippmann Debate Today: Communication Distortions, Reflective Agency, and Participatory Democracy," *Sociological Theory* 23:2 (2005), 156–178.

33. Pateman, "Rousseau, John Stuart Mill and G. D. H. Cole: A Participatory Theory of Democracy," in *Participation and Democratic Theory,* 22–44; Michael Walzer, "The Civil Society Argument," in Ronald Beiner, ed., *Theorizing Citizenship* (Albany: State University of New York Press, 1995), 153–174.

34. Plato, *Republic,* book 6, 492–493d in John M. Cooper, ed., *Plato Complete Works* (Indianapolis: Hackett, 1997), 1114–1115.

35. Aristotle, *Politics,* book III, chap.11: "The principle that the multitude ought to be supreme rather than the best . . . , though not free from difficulty, yet seems to contain an element of truth. For the many, of whom each individual is but an ordinary person, when they meet together may very likely be better than the few good, if regarded not individually but collectively" (Richard McKeon, ed., *Basic Works of Aristotle* [New York: Random House, 1941], 1190, 1280a.40–1281b.5).

36. While discussing his alternative to democracy, the *poletia,* the mixed government that would artfully balance the claims (and strengths) of monarchic, aristocratic / oligarchic, and democratic elements in a community, Aristotle singles out the democratic element as an indispensable source of legitimacy. Note that *demos* here refers to the poor, the nonelite, a distinct part of the political whole, not the whole itself as in the case of the "national people," which masks the reality of class differences and stratification, and thus elides the social question.

37. This is one of the daunting challenges facing the so-called China Model as the Chinese Communist Party tries to disentangle the historically complex braiding of political legitimacy and popular sovereignty. The Chinese project to delink the two might be no more successful than Habermas's attempt to ascertain and posit the elective affinities between popular sovereignty and public law. See Bell, *The China Model;* Jürgen Habermas, "Popular Sovereignty as Procedure" [1988]," in *Between Facts and Norms: Contributions to a Discourse Theory of Law and Democracy,* trans. William Rehg (Cambridge, MA: MIT Press, 1996), 463–490.

38. Alexis de Tocqueville, *Democracy in America* [1835, 1840], trans. Gerald Bevan (New York: Penguin, 2003), 583–587.

39. For the idea of people as "fiction," see Edmund Morgan, *Inventing the People: The Rise of Popular Sovereignty in England and America* (New York: W. W. Norton, 1988). For the idea of people as "empty signifier," see Claude LeFort, "The Question of Democracy," in *Democracy and Political Theory,* trans. David Macey (Minneapolis: University of Minnesota Press, 1988), 9–20; Ernesto Laclau, "The 'People' and the Discursive Production of Emptiness," in *On Populist Reason* (London: Verso, 2005), 67–128.

40. Aristotle, *Politics,* book III, chap. VIII, 1280a.5, in McKeon *Basic Works of Aristotle,* 1187.

41. Jacques Rancière, *Disagreement: Politics and Philosophy,* trans. Julie Rose (Minneapolis: University of Minnesota Press, 1999).

42. Benedict Anderson, *Imagined Communities: Reflections on the Origin and Spread of Nationalism* (London: Verso, 1983); Craig Calhoun, *Nationalism* (Minneapolis: University of Minnesota Press, 1997).

43. On "constitutive exclusion," see Ernesto Laclau and Chantal Mouffe, *Hegemony and Socialist Strategy: Towards a Radical Democratic Politics* (New York: Verso, 1985).

44. Hannah Arendt, *On Revolution* (New York: Penguin, 1963), 126–135.

45. C. B. Macpherson, *The Political Theory of Possessive Individualism: Hobbes to Locke* (New York: Oxford University Press, 1962).

46. Gerald N. Rosenberg, *The Hollow Hope: Can Court Bring About Social Change?* (Chicago: University of Chicago Press, 2008).

47. Terry Lynn Karl, "Imposing Consent? Electoralism versus Democratization in El Salvador," in Paul Drake and Eduardo Silva, eds., *Elections and Democratization in Latin America, 1980–1985* (San Diego: Center for Iberian and Latin American Studies and Center for US-Mexican Studies, University of California at San Diego, 1986), 9–36, cited in Diamond, "Is the Third Wave Over?," 21–22.

48. John Adams enshrined the concept of "a government of laws, not of men" in the 1780 Massachusetts state constitution.

49. Levitsky and Ziblatt, *How Democracies Die,* 7–8.

50. Diamond, *Ill Winds,* 39.

6. The Structure of Democratic Degenerations and the Imperative of Direct Action

1. Aside from numerous invaluable conversations with my coauthors, Craig Calhoun and Charles Taylor, I have profited from my discussions with Sally Ewing, Robert Hariman, Benjamin Lee, and Liam Mayes while writing this chapter. I am especially indebted to Liam Mayes for his assistance in editing the final draft and providing suggestions for many constructive revisions and refinements.

2. J. G. A. Pocock, *The Machiavellian Moment: Florentine Political Thought and the Atlantic Political Tradition* (Princeton, NJ: Princeton University Press, 1975).

3. See Richard Hofstadter, "John C. Calhoun: The Master of the Master Class," in his *The American Political Tradition and the Men Who Made It* [1948] (New York: Vintage, 1989), 87–118. Hofstadter cites a series of passages from the writing of Calhoun, an indefatigable pro-slavery exponent, on the unavoidability of class conflict. Here is one: "There never has existed a wealthy and civilized society in which one portion of community did not, in point of fact, live on the labor of the other." It would be too difficult "to trace out the various devices by which the wealth of all civilized communities has been so unequally divided, and to show by what means so small a share has been allotted to those by whose labor it was produced, and so large a share to the non-producing classes" (104).

4. In 2019, the incomes of the lowest quintile and of the second-lowest quintile were 3.1 percent and 8.3 percent of the national income, respectively. By contrast, the income of the highest quintile was 51.9 percent and that of the top five percent was 23 percent. US Census Bureau, "Income Distribution Measures Using Money Income and Equivalence-Adjusted Income: 2018 and 2019," in *Income and Poverty in the United States: 2019,* table A-3, https://www.census.gov/library/publications/2020/demo/p60-270.html.

5. For a conceptually rich discussion about the elites, especially the distinction between the ruling elite and the nonruling elite, see Gaetano Mosca, *The Ruling Class* (New York:

McGraw-Hill, 1939); Vilfredo Pareto, *The Rise and Fall of the Elites: An Application of Theoretical Sociology* [1901] (New York: Routledge, 2017). See also T. B. Bottomore, *Elites and Society* (Middlesex, UK: Penguin, 1966).

6. See Guy Standing, *The Precariat: The New Dangerous Class* (New York: Bloomsbury, 2011). There has been a rapidly growing body of scholarly literature on the precariat phenomenon in the last decade.

7. Alexis de Tocqueville, *Democracy in America* [1835, 1840], trans. Gerald Bevan (New York: Penguin, 2003), 583–587.

8. Walt Whitman, *Democratic Vistas* (Washington, DC: 1871); Jawaharlal Nehru, *The Discovery of India* (Calcutta: Signet, 1946).

9. For the idea of people as "empty signifier," see Claude Lefort, "The Question of Democracy," in *Democracy and Political Theory,* trans. David Macey (Minneapolis: University of Minnesota Press, 1988), 9–20; Ernesto Laclau, "The 'People' and the Discursive Production of Emptiness," in *On Populist Reason* (London: Verso, 2005), 67–128. For the idea of people as "fiction," see Edmund Morgan, *Inventing the People: The Rise of Popular Sovereignty in England and America* (New York: W. W. Norton, 1988).

10. For the recurrent idea of "heartlanders" in populist discourse, see Paul Taggart, *Populism* (Birmingham: Open University Press, 2000).

11. On the idea of "constitutional patriotism" in the European context, see Jürgen Habermas, *The New Conservatism: Cultural Criticism and the Historian's Debate,* ed. Sherry Weber Nicholsen (Cambridge, MA: MIT Press, 1989); Jürgen Habermas, *The Postnational Constellation: Political Essays,* trans. and ed. Max Pensky (Cambridge, MA: MIT Press, 2001).

12. David A. Hollinger, *Postethnic America: Beyond Multiculturalism* (New York: Basic Books, 2006).

13. Craig Calhoun, *Nations Matter: Culture, History, and the Cosmopolitan Dream* (New York: Routledge, 2007).

14. James Madison, *Federalist 10,* in Alexander Hamilton, John Jay, and James Madison, *The Federalist: A Commentary of the Constitution of the United States, Being a Collection of Essays Written in Support of the Constitution Agreed Upon September 17, 1787, by the Federal Convention* [1787–1788] (New York: Modern Library, Random House, 1937).

15. For an interesting discussion of Thomas Hobbes's idea of the "sleeping sovereign," see Richard Tuck, "Democratic Sovereignty and Democratic Government: The Sleeping Sovereign," in Richard Bourke and Quentin Skinner, eds., *Popular Sovereignty in Historical Perspective* (New York: Cambridge University Press, 2016), 115–141.

16. For an insightful account of Modi's ethnonational populist rhetoric, see Christophe Jaffrelot, *Modi's India: Hindu Nationalism and the Rise of Ethnic Democracy,* trans. Cynthia Schoch (Princeton, NJ: Princeton University Press, 2021), especially 112–147.

17. Charles S. Maier, "Democracy since the French Revolution," in John Dunn, ed., *Democracy: the Unfinished Journey 508 BC to AD 1993* (New York: Oxford University Press, 1992), 125–154.

18. This second dimension is particularly evident in the US Constitution. While noting that "the principle of representation was neither unknown to the ancients nor wholly overlooked in their political constitutions," Madison in *Federalist 63* claims, "The true distinction between these and the American governments, lies IN THE TOTAL EXCLUSION OF THE PEOPLE, IN THEIR COLLECTIVE CAPACITY, from any share in the LATTER, and not in the TOTAL EXCLUSION OF THE REPRESENTATIVES OF THE PEOPLE from the administration of the FORMER" (413).

19. Marc F. Plattner, "Illiberal Democracy and the Struggle on the Right," *Journal of Democracy* 30:1 (2019), 5–19.

20. This is not unique to India. The ethnoracial considerations appear to be ubiquitous in the strategic thinking and discourse surrounding electoral campaigns in the United States. Here are some media headlines about the electoral campaigns for the US presidency in 2020: "Why Is Kamala Harris Struggling with Black Voters So Much?" *New York Magazine,* August 13, 2019; "Pete Buttigieg Is in Bad Shape with Black Democrats. Here's Why," *New York Times,* November 21, 2019; "Buttigieg Has a Serious Latino Problem Too," *Politico,* November 27, 2019; "Understanding Trump's White Working Class Support," *American Prospect,* September 3, 2019; "Can Elizabeth Warren Fix Her Problem with Black Voters?" *Guardian,* November 21, 2019; "Joe Biden Refocuses on White Working-Class Voters," *Time,* October 23, 2019.

21. In designing and defending a mixed or balanced government as an antidote to majoritarianism, James Madison and Edmund Burke speak the language of interests rather than of identities, although the Irish question was already vexing Burke. See Hanna Fenichel Pitkin, *The Concept of Representation* (Berkeley: University of California Press, 1967), 168–208.

22. It should be noted that the majoritarian politics of identity rarely commands the numerical majority. This is the complex legacy of representative government. In a small country such as Hungary, which is deemed relatively homogeneous in terms of race / ethnicity, religion, and language, one might foresee how the coalition politics of majority rule can imperceptibly and possibly irreversibly slide into the majoritarian politics of identity. This is simply not the case, however, in big and diverse countries such as India and the United States.

23. David Hume, "Of the First Principles of Government," Essay 5, in *Essays and Treatises on Several Subjects* (London: Printed for A. Millar; A. Kincaid, and A. Donaldson, 1758), 20.

24. Martin Luther King, Jr., "Letter from Birmingham Jail" (April 16, 1963), in his *Why We Can't Wait* (New York: Harper and Row, 1964), 77–100.

25. For more on this, see Dilip Gaonkar, "After the Fictions: Notes Towards a Phenomenology of the Multitude," *e-flux journal* 58 (October 2014).

26. List of Riots, Wikipedia, n.d.

27. "Protest and Dissent in China," Wikipedia, July 2019.

28. The impressive extent to which the US founding fathers were preoccupied with a fear of the mob while drafting and subsequently ratifying the constitution is copiously documented in *The Federalist.*

29. Hippolyte A. Taine, *The French Revolution,* vol. 2 of *Les origines de la France contemporaine,* 6 vols. (Paris: Hachette, 1876–1894). *The French Revolution* was published in French in 1878 and translated into English by John Durand in 1880. The first book of this volume, titled "Spontaneous Anarchy," contains Taine's fearful and hyperbolic account of revolutionary crowds and rioting mobs.

30. For an excellent account of crowd theory from a psychosocial perspective, see Susanna Barrows, *Distorting Mirrors: Visions of the Crowd in Late Nineteenth-Century France* (New Haven, CT: Yale University Press, 1981). See also Jaap van Ginneken, *Crowds, Psychology, and Politics, 1871–1899* (Cambridge: Cambridge University Press, 1992).

31. Elias Canetti, *Crowds and Power* [1960], trans. Carol Stewart (New York: Viking, 1963). See also Sigmund Freud, *Group Psychology and the Analysis of the Ego* [1922], trans. James Strachey (New York: Liveright Publishing,1959); José Ortega y Gasset, *The Revolt of the Masses* [1930], trans. Teresa Carey (New York: W. W. Norton, 1932).

32. I have developed this point in two previous essays: Dilip Gaonkar, "After the Fictions" and "Demos Noir: Riot After Riot," in Natasha Ginwala, Gal Kirn, and Niloufar Tajeri, eds., *Nights of the Dispossessed: Riots Unbound* (New York, Columbia University Press, 2021), 30–54.

33. For more on this, see Gaonkar, "After the Fictions."

34. James C. Scott, *Weapons of the Weak: Everyday Forms of Peasant Resistance* (New Haven, CT: Yale University Press, 1985).

35. For an excellent account of the temporalities and tactics of the slum-dwellers in Mumbai, see Arjun Appadurai, "Deep Democracy: Urban Governmentality and the Horizon of Politics," *Public Culture* 14:1 (Winter 2002), 21–48. See also Partha Chatterjee, "The Politics of the Governed," in his *The Politics of the Governed* (New York: Columbia University Press, 2004), 53–78.

36. Gilles Deleuze and Felix Guattari, *A Thousand Plateaus: Capitalism and Schizophrenia* [1980], trans. and forward by Brian Massumi (Minneapolis: University of Minnesota Press, 1987).

37. For a recent theorization of the centrality of assembly in "direct action" politics, see Judith Butler, "We, the People: Thoughts on Freedom of Assembly," in her *Notes Toward a Performative Theory of Assembly* (Cambridge, MA: Harvard University Press, 2015), 154–192.

38. Charles Taylor, *Modern Social Imaginaries* (Durham, NC: Duke University Press, 2004), 84–85.

39. For a short discussion of the Citizenship (Amendment) Act passed by India's parliament on December 11, 2019, see Anupama Roy, "Citizens / Non-Citizens: The Constitutive and the Dialogical," *Social Change* 50:2 (2020), 278–284.

40. Jessica Winegar, "A Civilized Revolution: Aesthetics and Political Action in Egypt," *American Ethnologist* 43:4 (2016), 609–622.

41. Mike Davis, *Planet of Slums* (New York: Verso, 2006).

42. Karl Marx and Friedrich Engels, *The Communist Manifesto* [1848], trans. Samuel Moore, ed. Gareth Stedman Jones (New York: Penguin Books, 1967). See the section on "Bourgeois and Proletarians," 219–233.

43. Raphaëlle Rérolle, "Gilets jaunes: 'Les élites parlent de fin du monde, quand nous, on parle de fin du mois,'" *Le Monde,* November 24, 2018. An American news report translated: "'Macron is concerned with the end of the world,' one Yellow Vest slogan put it. 'We are concerned with the end of the month'" (Peter S. Goodman, "Inequality Fuels Rage of 'Yellow Vests' in Equality-Obsessed France," *New York Times,* April 15, 2019).

7. What Is to Be Done?

1. See Adam Tooze, *Shutdown: How Covid Shook the World's Economy* (New York: Viking, 2021).

2. Edmund Morgan, *Inventing the People: The Rise of Popular Sovereignty in England and America* (New York: W. W. Norton, 1988); Rachel Foxley, *The Levellers: Radical Political Thought in the English Revolution* (Oxford: Oxford University Press, 2013).

3. See David Szatmary, *Shay's Rebellion: The Making of an Agrarian Insurrection* (Amherst: University of Massachusetts Press, 1980); Leonard Richards, *Shay's Rebellion: The American Revolution's Final Battle* (Philadelphia: University of Pennsylvania Press, 2003); Sean Condon, *Shay's Rebellion: Authority and Distress in Post-Revolutionary America* (Baltimore, MD: Johns Hopkins University Press, 2015).

4. See Marvin Meyers, *The Jacksonian Persuasion* (Palo Alto, CA: Stanford University Press, 1957); David and Jeanne Heidler, *The Rise of Andrew Jackson: Myth, Manipulation, and the Rise of Modern Politics* (New York: Basic Books, 2018). For deeper context of the campaigns, see Harry Watson, *Jacksonian America* (New York: Hill and Wang, 2006).

5. See Lawrence Goodwyn, *Democratic Promise: The Populist Movement in America* (Oxford: Oxford University Press, 1976). Urban-rural and especially cross-race alliances were directly targeted by anti-populist—and antidemocratic—divide-and-conquer tactics. Thomas Frank is right to suggest, in *The People, No: A Brief History of Anti-Populism* (New York: Metropolitan, 2020), that understanding of populists is much too widely based on the slurs of anti-populist elites and lumping of other kinds of less democratic mobilizations in with "true" populists.

6. For many populists, it is important that crowds be orderly and disciplined—thus revealing that they represent a people—or public—capable of self-government. Mobs, like the one that stormed the US Capitol on January 6, 2021, communicate disorder (even if there are underlying organizational networks). See discussion in Craig Calhoun and Michael McQuarrie, "The Reluctant Counterpublic," in Craig Calhoun, *Roots of Radicalism* (Chicago: University of Chicago Press, 2012).

7. In contemporary democracies, these come crucially from republicanism, but that is not the only possible source of stability, adequate recognition of minorities, and protections for individual conscience and public debate. Visions of radical populism are helpful antidotes to politics as usual and often more democratic, but they are insufficient. See Chantal Mouffe, *For a Left Populism* (London: Verso, 2018).

8. In the United States, decisions are especially likely to be based on identifying and discriminating among absolute rights rather than mediating multiple rights or negotiating competing interests. For example, in *Roe v. Wade,* the US Supreme Court held that a right to privacy guaranteed access to abortions. It did not say that "this is a hard choice because multiple rights and interests are involved, and we think on balance that this is the best decision." It in effect declared that the losing position(s) lost completely. The result was to dramatically increase partisan political polarization around abortion—and also violence—from those who felt they had no other recourse. It encouraged anti-abortion activists to campaign to change the members of the Supreme Court. Ironically, in the long run, the court decision has made abortion a less readily available option. See Jamal Greene, *How Rights Went Wrong: Why Our Obsession with Rights Is Tearing America Apart* (New York: Houghton Mifflin, 2021); Guido Calabrese, *Ideals, Beliefs, Attitudes, and the Law* (Syracuse, NY: Syracuse University Press, 1990); Drew Halfmann, *Doctors and Demonstrators: How Political Institutions Shape Abortion Law in the United States, Britain, and Canada* (Chicago: University of Chicago Press, 2011).

9. There are also efforts to combine populism and technocracy, mostly in campaign appeals. Technocratic populism can win—witness Macron in France—but it translates poorly into actual governance or policy. See Christopher J. Bickerton and Carlo Inverzizzi Accetti, *Technopopulism: The New Logic of Democratic Politics* (Oxford: Oxford University Press, 2021).

10. Jürgen Habermas quotes this phrase from the great systems theorist Niklas Luhmann, in Stuart Jeffries, "A Rare Interview with Jürgen Habermas," *Financial Times,* April 30 2010. Luhmann saw it as a characteristic attitude of those faced with systems so complex that not only could they not be consciously managed, but they could not relate all their parts to each other. This meant contingency and unpredictability necessarily increased. See *Social Systems* [1984] (Stanford, CA: Stanford University Press, 1996).

11. Arguably the Florentine Friar Savonarola was a pioneer of populism with his mass protests and "bonfires of the vanities." See Craig Calhoun, "Populism and Democracy: The Long View," in B. Vormann and M. Weiman, eds., *The Emergence of Illiberalism: Understanding a Global Phenomenon* (London: Routledge, 2020), 227–246.

12. Ruth Braunstein, *Prophets and Patriots: Faith in Democracy across the Political Divide* (Oakland: University of California Press, 2017).

13. Bryan Naylor, "Read Trump's Jan. 6 Speech, A Key Part of Impeachment Trial," National Public Radio, February 10, 2021, https://www.npr.org/2021/02/10/966396848 /read-trumps-jan-6-speech-a-key-part-of-impeachment-trial.

14. The US media ecology is distinctive, not least in the rise of Fox News and what we have called "affirmative media." Other media controlled by Rupert Murdoch, such as Sky News, are similar. These have many precursors, but have become large-scale and in that sense mainstream media. But affirmative messaging is prominent throughout the world's democracies.

15. New media sources such as OAN (One America News) and Newsmax benefited from Fox's introduction of more critical perspective. See Adam Gabbatt, "The Fall of Fox?" *Guardian,* January 2, 2021. In competition and conflict with each other, Fox, OAN, and Newsmax are all searching for the right balance of affirmation and credibility as news media. See Brian Stetler, "How Right-Wing Networks Covered the January 6 Hearing after Months of Soft-Pedalling the Capitol Attack," *CNN Business,* July 27, 2021: https://www .cnn.com/2021/07/27/media/fox-news-oan-newsmax-january-6-hearing/index.html

16. See Joan C. Williams, *White Working Class: Overcoming Class Cluelessness in America* (Boston: Harvard Business Review Press, 2017); David Goodhart, *The Road to Somewhere* (London: Hurst, 2017); Justin Gest, *The New Minority: White Working-Class Politics in an Age of Immigration and Inequality* (Oxford: Oxford University Press, 2016). One prominent Labour activist in Britain goes so far as to suggest that "the modern Left loathes the working class" (Paul Embery, *Despised: Why the Modern Left Loathes the Working Class* [London: Polity, 2021]). Embery is sympathetic to the Blue Labour agenda introduced by Maurice Glassman, which tries to combine socialism with socially conservative values; see I. Geary and A. Pabst, eds., *Blue Labour: Forging a New Politics* (London: I. B. Taurus, 2015). This challenges the domination of Labour by highly educated professionals who find the themes of family, religious faith, patriotism, and local community largely anathema.

17. For a global view, see Patrick Liddard, "What Can Be Done about the Problem of Political Parties," Wilson Center, September 2019, https://www.wilsoncenter.org/publication /what-can-be-done-about-the-problem-political-parties.

18. This is so especially when divisions over major issues such as race and immigration coincide strongly with party preferences. In the past, parties have been internally divided, on these and other major national fault lines, which led them to do more moderating work themselves. See James A. Morone, *Republic of Wrath: How American Politics Turned Tribal, from George Washington to Donald Trump* (New York: Basic Books, 2020).

19. G. Bouchard and C. Taylor, *Building the Future: A Time for Reconciliation* (Quebec: Gouvernement du Québec, 2008).

20. The challenge—and the tyranny of old habits of thought—is particularly evident in left-nationalist struggles. In Catalonia, for example, investments of even radical political leaders are typically in an older ethnonational understanding of being Catalan. This excludes (or only very tepidly welcomes) half the people of Catalonia. See Eunice Romero, "La República Que Farem: Emerging Imaginaries of Migrantness and Nationhood in the Catalan Independence Movement," XIX ISA World Congress of Sociology, Toronto 2018.

21. See M. Taylor and D. Rea, "An Analysis of Cross-Cutting between Political Cleavages," *Comparative Politics* 1:4 (1969), 534–547. The idea is applied to both individual voters and party systems. For one classic, see S. M. Lipset and S. Rokkan, "Cleavage Structures, Party Systems, and Voter Alignments: An Introduction," in S. M. Lipset and S. Rokkan, eds. *Party Systems and Voter Alignments: Cross-National Perspectives* (New York: Free Press), 1–64. But it applies also to how people maintain or change beliefs, as argued by Leon Festinger, *A Theory of Cognitive Dissonance* (Palo Alto, CA: Stanford University Press, 1957). And it applies to dispute resolution in many contexts, including feuds; see Max Gluckman, "The Peace in the Feud," *Past and Present* 8:1 (1955), 1–14.

22. Robert Frega observes that Social Democratic parties have suffered even more than others in this period and argues that the old social democratic compromise with capitalism needs to be rethought for social democracy to be renewed as a force for emancipation. See Roberto Frega, "The Fourth Stage of Social Democracy," *Theory and Society* 50.3 (2021), 489–513.

23. Public funding of higher education is skewed toward elite and selective institutions rather than those providing the widest access. This is partly because the former produce major research. But public funding also supports the privilege of small classes and plush campuses in private universities—not least (but not only) through tax exemption. And public funders are not immune to the allure of competitive prestige.

24. Again, to varying degrees, the same can be said for Britain and most of continental Europe—though in some places such as Poland and Hungary greater pluralism was quickly countered by authoritarian leaders.

25. Though Black women face the double challenge of racism and sexism, they have benefited more from new opportunities than Black men. Why this is so is a complex question, with partial answers ranging from educational attainment to employment, violence, and mass incarceration.

26. One-fifth of all American employees work in health care and social assistance, and about 15 percent work in retail trade and accommodation and food services. See census data at https://www.census.gov/library/stories/2020/10/manufacturing-still-among-top-five-united-states-employers.html. https://www.bls.gov/cps/cpsaat11.htm.

27. D. Boesch, R. Bleiweis, and A. Haider, "Raising the Minimum Wage Would Be Transformative for Women," Center for American Progress, February 23, 2021, https://www.americanprogress.org/issues/women/news/2021/02/23/496221/raising-minimum-wage-transformative-women/.

28. See, among many, Paula England, "The Gender Revolution: Uneven and Stalled," *Gender and Society* 24:2 (2010), 149–166, and the provocative argument that the current level of gender inequality can't last in Robert Max Jackson, *Destined for Equality* (Cambridge, MA: Harvard University Press, 1998).

29. This may be one reason for the persistently greater male voter support for right-wing "populist" candidates like Donald Trump. Among many popular discussions for a phenomenon not yet adequately understood, see E. Levitz, "Men and Women Have Never Been More Politically Divided," *New York,* October 19, 2020.

30. D. Boesch and S. Phadke, "When Women Lose All the Jobs: Essential Actions for a Gender-Equitable Recovery," Center for American Progress, February 1, 2021, https://www.americanprogress.org/issues/women/reports/2021/02/01/495209/women-lose-jobs-essential-actions-gender-equitable-recovery/. For a broader perspectives, see S. L. Averett, L. M. Argyris, and S. D. Hoffman, eds., *The Oxford Handbook of Women and the Economy* (Oxford: Oxford University Press, 2018), especially the chapter on "Women, Work, and Family" by Francine D. Blau and Anne E. Winkler. In our era of "culture wars" and po-

litical polarization, an ideological illusion has been encouraged by focusing on "family values" rather than the extent to which strong families and good childhoods depend on material social and economic conditions. See Kathleen Gerson, *The Unfinished Revolution: Coming of Age in a New Era of Gender, Work, and Family* (Oxford: Oxford University Press, 2011).

31. Indeed, similar factors are among the sources of homophobia and violent attacks on LGBTQ Americans. Gains in both freedom and equal treatment for gay men and lesbians have been impressive. They are still contested. Rights for trans men and women are more controversial, but recognition has grown. But as LGBTQ rights and identities have been more widely recognized and protected, backlash has also grown. The causes are not mainly economic, but male disempowerment and contradictory messages about masculinity—and gender more widely—are among them.

32. See Chapter 3. This is not just a question of whether men could earn enough for women to stay out of the labor market. It is also a matter of whether men can earn enough to provide the increasingly expensive goods that media and cultural norms suggest families need. And it is complicated by status asymmetry as women attain more education and different kinds of job options.

33. Running for president of the United States in 2020, for example, the technology entrepreneur Andrew Yang proposed to pay each citizen $1,000 a month. This income would, of course, be welcomed, but it is hardly a substitute for a $50,000-a-year job. It could be nice as an extra or added security net, but it is not really a solution to transformations of work unless it is high enough to truly raise workers' standard of living and empower workers to deal collectively with capital. This would require a much more significant transfer of wealth than rich advocates of a universal basic income seem to be contemplating. See critical analysis in Aaron Benanov, *Automation and the Future of Work* (London: Verso, 2020).

34. William Cummings, Joey Garrison, and Jim Sergent, "By the Numbers: President Donald Trump's Failed Efforts to Overturn the Election," *USA Today*, January 6, 2021.

35. See Sue Halpern, "The Republicans' Wild Assault on Voting Rights in Texas and Arizona," *New Yorker*, June 8, 2021. The nonpartisan Brennan Center for Justice publishes and updates a list of state bills to reshape elections: https://www.brennancenter.org/our -work/research-reports/state-voting-bills-tracker-2021. See also https://www.politico.com /news/2021/03/15/voting-restrictions-states-475732; https://www.motherjones.com/politics /2021/02/voting-rights-republicans-trump-georgia/.

36. The literature on voting rights is large because it is such a basic—and current—concern. See S. Abrams, C. Anderson, K. M. Kruse, H. C. Richardson, and H. C. Thompson, *Voter Suppression in US Elections* (Athens: University of Georgia Press, 2020); Carol Anderson, *One Person, No Vote* (London: Bloomsbury, 2019); Gilda Daniels, *Uncounted* (New York: New York University Press, 2020). On the role of courts, see L. Goldstone, *On Account of Race* (Berkeley, CA: Counterpoint, 2020). For an account of the problems and the struggle by the most important voting rights campaigner today, Stacey Abrams, *Our Time Is Now* (New York: Holt, 2020).

37. Brennan Center for Justice, "Voting Rights Roundup, May 2021," https://www .brennancenter.org/our-work/research-reports/voting-laws-roundup-may-2021?campaign_id =9&emc=edit_nn_20210713&instance_id=35184&nl=the-morning&regi_id=39283977 &segment_id=63295&te=1&user_id=cf9c1c42af53919bb3f4eefbb7085f6e.

38. See "The Spreading Scourge of Voter Suppression," *The Economist*, October 10, 2020. On the comparative integrity of elections more generally see the website of the Electoral Integrity Project (www.electoralintegrityproject.com) and multiple volumes by its founding director, Pippa Norris, including *Strengthening Electoral Integrity* (Cambridge, UK: Cambridge University Press, 2017).

39. Michael Barajas and the *Texas Observer,* "Texas and the Long Tail of Voter Suppression," *The Nation,* October 16, 2020.

40. This practice was imported from the United States to the United Kingdom by the Conservative government, ostensibly to reduce voter fraud—though in fact there was little evidence of any fraud. See Caroline Davies, "Conservatives Accused of Suppressing Voters' Rights over Leaked Photo ID Plans," *The Guardian,* October 13, 2019. See also Pippa Norris, "The UK Scores Worst in Electoral Integrity in Western Europe. Here's Why," Democratic Audit, March 30, 2016, www.democraticaudit.com/2016/03/30/the-uk-scores-worst-in-electoral-integrity-in-western-europe-heres-why.

41. When votes cannot be suppressed, other approaches to subverting democracy are common. Majorities in partisan state legislatures have sought to maintain their grip by denying funds and power to popularly elected governors. See Richard Fausset and Trip Gabriel, "North Carolina's Partisan Rift Widens in Fight Over Governor's Powers," *New York Times,* December 15, 2016.

42. This situation has been getting worse for years. See Jonathan Rauch, "How American Politics Went Insane," *The Atlantic,* July 2016; T. E. Mann and N. J. Ornstein, *It's Even Worse than It Looks* (New York: Basic Books, 2016); P. Norris, S. Cameron, and T. Wynter, eds., *Electoral Integrity in America: Securing Democracy* (Oxford: Oxford University Press, 2018). And, on the still more extreme situation since the 2020 election, see Lee Drutman, "America Is Now the Divided Republic the Framers Feared," *The Atlantic,* January 2, 2020; P. Trubowitz and P. Harris, "The End of the American Century? Slow Erosion of the Domestic Sources of Usable Power," *International Affairs* 95:3 (May 2019), 619–639. For an academic review of consequences for Congress, see S. Binder, "The Dysfunctional Congress," *Annual Review of Political Science* 18 (2015), 85–101.

43. Heather McGhee, *The Sum of Us: What Racism Costs Everyone and How We Can Prosper Together* (London: One World, 2021).

44. The BLM movement had been started in response to the 2013 killing of Trayvon Martin by George Zimmerman—and Zimmerman's acquittal. Christopher J. LeBron, *The Making of Black Lives Matter* (Oxford: Oxford University Press, 2018).

45. For a journalistic summary of the findings of attorneys for the US Department of Justice, see Tyler Sonnemaker, "Portland Police Officers Used Force More Than 6,000 Times against Protesters Last year," *Business Insider,* March 20, 2021.

46. See Mike Baker, Thomas Fuller, and Sergio Olmos, "Federal Agents Push into Portland Streets, Stretching Limits of Their Authority," *New York Times,* July 25, 2020.

47. For a useful review, see Jessica M. Eaglin, "To 'Defund' the Police," *Stanford Law Review* 73 (June 2021).

48. The prominence of calls to defund is in one sense ironic. Black Americans have been disproportionate victims not only of police violence but of police neglect. That is, police budgets have placed a much greater priority or securing the safety of central business districts and well-off, mostly White, residential areas. Black Americans, and in varying degrees other minorities, suffer constant insecurity as a result.

49. Radley Balko, *Rise of the Warrior Cop: The Militarization of America's Police Forces* (New York: PublicAffairs, 2013); Abigail R. Hall and Christopher Coyne, *Tyranny Comes Home: The Domestic Fate of U.S. Militarism* (Palo Alto, CA: Stanford University Press, 2018); Elizabeth Hinton, *From the War on Poverty to the War on Crime: The Making of Mass Incarceration in America* (Cambridge, MA: Harvard University Press, 2016.)

50. Police work is one of the few areas of service work that provides good wages and job security to the kinds of workers who might previously have had more options in manufac-

turing. Police benefit from strong unions. But these sometimes unwisely (and often at public expense) protect racist and violent officers. Noam Scheiber, Farah Stockman and J. David Goodman, "How Police Unions Became Such Powerful Opponents to Reform Efforts," *New York Times,* June 6, 2020; Samantha Michael, "The Infuriating History of Why Police Unions Have So Much Power," *Mother Jones,* September / October 2020.

51. A proposal was brought in the wake of George Floyd's murder to replace the Minneapolis Police Department with a Department of Public Safety. It failed in the 2021 election. Likewise, New York City voters elected a former police officer as mayor, defeating advocates of police reform or defunding. See Mitch Smith and Tim Arango, "'We Need Policemen': Even in Liberal Cities Voters Reject Scaled-Back Policing," *New York Times,* November 3, 2021.

52. Angela Davis has been an early and persistent critic; see *Are Prisons Obsolete?* (New York: Seven Stories, 2003). Among many studies, see Heather Ann Thompson, "Why Mass Incarceration Matters: Rethinking Crisis, Decline, and Transformation in Postwar American History," *Journal of American History,* 97.3 (December 2010), 703–734; Peter Enns, *Incarceration Nation: How the United States Became the Most Punitive Democracy in the World* (Cambridge, UK: Cambridge University Press, 2016); Hinton, *From the War on Poverty to the War on Crime;* Franklin E. Zimmring, *The Insidious Momentum of American Mass Incarceration* (Oxford: Oxford University Press, 2020).

53. Lauren-Brooke Eisen, *Inside Private Prisons* (New York: Columbia University Press, 2019); Shane Bauer, *American Prison* (London: Penguin, 2019). On putting privatization of prisons in the context of wider privatization of public institutions during the neoliberal era, see Lawrence Baines, *The Privatization of America's Institutions* (Bern: Peter Lang, 2019).

54. Indeed, rates of incarceration and the high costs of medicine are the two areas in which the United States most clearly leads the world. On the latter, see Andrew W. Mulcahy, Christopher M. Whaley, Mahlet Gizaw, Daniel Schwam, Nathaniel Edenfield, and Alejandro U. Becerra-Ornelas, International Prescription Drug Price Comparisons: Current Empirical Estimates and Comparisons with Previous Studies (Santa Monica, CA: RAND Corporation, RR-2956-ASPEC, 2021). RAND found identical drugs cost on average 2.56 times more in the United States than elsewhere.

55. Elizabeth Warren has been a prominent advocate of ending private prisons. See the work of the nonprofit organization Abolish Private Prisons at its website: https://www .abolishprivateprisons.org. In January 2021, President Biden signed an executive order phasing out federal use of private prisons, though this leaves in place the much larger reliance of states on private contractors. Executive Office of the President, "Reforming Our Incarceration System To Eliminate the Use of Privately Operated Criminal Detention Facilities," January 29, 2021, https://www.federalregister.gov/documents/2021/01/29/2021 -02070/reforming-our-incarceration-system-to-eliminate-the-use-of-privately-operated -criminal-detention.

56. Anne Höhn and Nina Werkhäuser, "Bundeswehr Remains under Fire for Far-Right Extremism," *Deutsche Welle (DW),* March 23, 2021. Penetration of the police is significant but less organized. See Rob Schmitz, "With Far-Right Extremism on the Rise, Germany Investigates Its Police," *Morning Edition,* National Public Radio, December 10, 2020, https://www.npr.org/2020/12/10/943823021/with-far-right-extremism-on-the-rise-germany -investigates-its-police; https://www.dw.com/en/german-state-police-declared-free-of-far -right-networks/a-56844972. French soldiers have published multiple anonymous letters making thinly veiled threats of civil war as France grapples with reactions to Muslims and its president moves to the right. See Leo Pierrard, "Deuxième lettre ouverte signée par des militaires," *La Presse,* May 10, 2021; Elise Vincent, "Tribunes de militaires: Le Général Lecointre

en appelle à la 'cohésion' face aux 'tentatives d'instrumentalisation," *Le Monde,* May 12, 2021; Constant Méheut, "New Military Letter Warning of 'Brewing' Civil War Prompts Outrage in France," *New York Times,* May 12, 2021. Britain considered its police to be immune until recently; see Kevin Rawlinson, "Warning That Police Grasp of Far-Right Threat Is Decade out of Date," *Guardian,* April 2, 2021.

57. Karl Evers-Hillstrom, "Most Expensive Ever: 2020 Election Cost $14.4 Billion," *Open Secrets,* February 11, 2021, https://www.opensecrets.org/news/2021/02/2020-cycle-cost-14p4-billion-doubling-16/; W. C. R. Horncastle, "The Scale of US Election Spending Explained in Five Graphs," *The Conversation,* October 15, 2020, https://theconversation.com/the-scale-of-us-election-spending-explained-in-five-graphs-130651; Shane Goldmacher and Rachel Shorey, "Trump Raised $255.4 Million in Eight Weeks as He Sought to Overturn Election Result," *New York Times,* January 31, 2021.

58. Adam Payne and Will Martin, "The 21 Biggest Donors to the Brexit Campaign," *Business Insider,* May 8, 2017.

59. Catie Edmondson, "'Rogue' U.S. Agency Used Racial Profiling to Investigate Commerce Dept. Employees, Report Says," *New York Times,* July 16, 2021.

60. Shoshana Zuboff, *The Age of Surveillance Capitalism: The Fight for a Human Future at the New Frontier of Power* (New York: PublicAffairs, 2019).

61. For an affirmative account of this "new" mode of business, see Thomas Davenport and John Beck, *The Attention Economy: Understanding the New Currency of Business* (Boston: Harvard Business School Press, 2001). For critical reflections, see Tim Wu, *The Attention Merchants: From the Daily Newspaper to Social Media, How Our Time and Attention Is Harvested and Sold* (London: Atlantic Books, 2017); Matthew B. Crawford, *The World beyond Your Head: On Becoming an Individual in an Age of Distraction* (New York: Farrar, Straus and Giroux, 2015); John Lanchester, "You Are the Product," *London Review of Books* 39 (August 2017), 16–17.

62. Arizona Republicans also embraced a rumor that Chinese interference could be spotted by traces of bamboo in ballots. Sam Levine, "Arizona Republicans Hunt for Bamboo-Laced China Ballots in 2020 'Audit' Effort," *The Guardian,* May 6, 2021; Zacchary Petrizzio, "Bamboo Ballots Don't Exist, Manufacturer Says, as Arizona Auditors Search for 'Watermarks,'" *Salon,* June 23, 2021.

63. Nicholas Reimann, "Arizona Audit Cost Trump Supporters Nearly $6 Million—Only to Assert Biden Won by Even More," *Forbes,* September 24, 2021.

64. Siva Vaidhyanathan, *Antisocial Media* (Oxford: Oxford University Press, 2018).

65. Nathaniel Persily and Joshua A. Tucker, *Social Media and Democracy: The State of the Field, Prospects for Reform* (Cambridge, UK: Cambridge University Press, 2020); Jay David Bolter, "Social Media Are Ruining Political Discourse," *The Atlantic,* May 2019.

66. For research on Twitter, see Soroush Vosoughi, Deb Roy, and Sinan Aral, "The Spread of True and False News Online," *Science* 359:6380 (2018), 1146–1151.

67. John Dewey, *The Public and Its Problems* (New York: Holt, 1927),

68. For a fuller discussion of the advantages of such local organization, as well as a discussion of examples of this local action or consultation in the United States and the European Union, see Charles Taylor, Patrizia Nanz, and Madeleine Beaubien Taylor, *Reconstructing Democracy: How Citizens Are Building from the Bottom Up* (Cambridge, MA: Harvard University Press, 2020). See also Peter Plastrik, Madeleine Taylor, and John Cleveland, *Connecting to Change the World* (Washington DC: Island Press, 2014). For a discussion of local projects in the style of Saul Alinsky, see Luke Bretherton, *Resurrecting Democracy* (Cambridge, UK: Cambridge University Press, 2015).

69. See James and Deborah Fallows's interesting and informative book, *Our Towns: A 100,000-Mile Journey into the Heart of America* (New York: Pantheon, 2018), which documents the rich fund of ideas and entrepreneurial initiatives that exist in a large number of local communities in the United States. They regret the fact that these are not complemented by supportive action on the part of the federal government. We very much agree that some synergy between the two is essential to the rebuilding of American democracy.

Mention might also be made of direct action, such as the projects initiated among Indignados in Spain, which acted to prevent the repossession of homes by banks after those living there had defaulted on their mortgages. Many of these efforts were highly successful, and one of the leaders involved was subsequently elected mayor of Barcelona. This kind of "extralegal" action can help the formation of effective political parties, like Podemos.

70. To be precise, inequality inside countries increased. Inequality among countries was reduced somewhat, mainly by advancing economies in Asia. Even though inequality went up in China, too, the country's overall growth meant that millions of people could escape poverty. See Branko Milanovich, *Global Inequality: A New Approach for the Age of Globalization* (Cambridge, MA: Harvard University Press, 2016).

71. For a discussion of the ways that one-sided emphasis on markets undermined and changed provision of public goods, see LaDawn Haglund, *Limiting Resources: Market Led Reform and the Transformation of Public Goods* (University Park: Penn State University Press, 2010).

72. Christopher Ingraham, "Covid-19 Has Killed More Police Officers This Year than All Other Causes Combined, Data Shows," *Washington Post,* September 2, 2020.

73. See Paula England, "Emerging Theories of Care Work," *Annual Review of Sociology* 31 (2005), 381–399; Mignon Duffy, *Making Care Count:: A Century of Gender, Race, and Paid Care Work* (New Brunswick, NJ: Rutgers University Press, 2011).

74. Vicente Navarro, "Consequences of the Privatized Funding of Medical Care and of the Privatized Electoral Process," *American Journal of Public Health* 100:3 (2010), 399–402.

75. Bianca Quilantan, "New Poll Finds Majority of Voters Support Public Education," *Politico,* February 3, 2020; Jocelyn Kiley, "Most Continue to Say Ensuring Health Care Coverage Is Government's Responsibility," Pew Research, October 3, 2018, https://www.pewresearch.org/fact-tank/2018/10/03/most-continue-to-say-ensuring-health-care-coverage-is-governments-responsibility/.

76. Pew Research, "Little Public Support for Reductions in Federal Spending," April 11, 2019, https://www.pewresearch.org/politics/2019/04/11/little-public-support-for-reductions-in-federal-spending/.

77. For one influential set of proposals, see Emmanuel Saez and Gabriel Zucman, *The Triumph of Injustice: How the Rich Dodge Taxes and How to Make Them Pay* (New York: W. W. Norton, 2019). A related issue, too complex to discuss here, is how mechanisms for tax avoidance fuel a much wider illicit capitalist economy on a global scale, mixing funds off the books for tax reasons with the finance of trafficking in drugs, weapons, and people.

78. Alan Rappeport, "Finance Leaders Reach Global Tax Deal Aimed at Ending Profit Shifting," *New York Times,* June 5, 2021.

79. See James Tobin, "A Proposal for International Monetary Reform," *Eastern Economic Journal* 4:3–4 (July–October 1978), 153–159.

80. There is a large literature on the New Deal, but also a superb and accessible online introduction curated by UC Berkeley geography professor Richard Walker: https://livingnewdeal.org.

81. Craig Calhoun and Benjamin Y. Fong, eds., *The Green New Deal and the Future of Work* (New York: Columbia University Press, 2022).

82. Craig Calhoun, "Occupy Wall Street in Perspective," *British Journal of Sociology,* 64:1 (2013), 26–38.

83. See "House Resolution Recognizing the Duty of the Federal Government to Create a Green New Deal," 116th Congress, 1st Session, February 7, 2019, https://ocasio-cortez .house.gov/sites/ocasio-cortez.house.gov/files/Resolution%20on%20a%20Green%20 New%20Deal.pdf. Their work is closely related to the a range of activist organizations and networks, including especially the Sunrise Movement. See "What Is the Green New Deal?," an introduction posted on the movement's website, https://www.sunrisemovement.org/green -new-deal/?ms=WhatistheGreenNewDeal%3F; Osita Nwanevu, "A Decisive Year for the Sunrise Movement," *New Yorker,* May 14, 2019.. A Green New Deal Task Force created by the Green Party offered a US plan as early as 2006. Without directly referencing it, the *New York Times* columnist Thomas Friedman used the phrase in a 2007 article, "A Warning from the Garden," *New York Times,* January 19, 2007..

84. The Green New Deal Group at Britain's New Economics Foundation issued its own report in 2008: Andrew Simms, Ann Pettifor, Caroline Lucas, Charles Secrett, Colin Hines, Jeremy Legget, Larry Elliott, Richard Murphy, and Tony Juniper, "A Green New Deal," July 20, 2008, https://neweconomics.org/2008/07/green-new-deal. See also Mark Lynas, "A Green New Deal," *New Statesman,* July 17, 2008; there and elsewhere, a range of specific programs with local and national sources are grouped together under the new name.

85. More books and articles are being published every day. Some of the most important are Naomi Klein, *On Fire: The (Burning) Case for a Green New Deal* (New York: Simon and Schuster, 2020); Jeremy Rifkin, *The Green New Deal: Why the Fossil Fuel Civilization Will Collapse by 2028, and the Bold Economic Plan to Save Life on Earth* (New York: St. Martins, 2019); Larry Jordan, *The Green New Deal: Why We Need It And Can't Live Without It—And No, It's Not Socialism!* (Chula Vista, CA: PageTurner Books, 2019); Kate Aronoff, Alyssa Battistoni, Daniel Aldana Cohen, and Thea Riofrancos, *A Planet to Win* (London: Verso 2020). Some authors, it should be said, focus more on the image of having a new war to win against climate—echoing the top-down mobilization of World War II more than the broad combination of forces in the New Deal.

86. See Eugene T. Richardson, *Epidemic Illusions: On the Coloniality of Global Public Health* (Cambridge, MA: MIT Press, 2020); Paul Farmer, *Infections and Inequalities* (Berkeley: University of California Press, 2001) and *Fevers, Feuds, and Diamonds* (New York: Farrar, Strauss Giroux, 2020).

Conclusion

1. Larry Diamond, "Democratic Regression in Comparative Perspective: Scope, Methods, and Causes," *Democratization* 28:1 (2020).

2. By virtue of its inherently precarious balance, *politeia* unfortunately remains susceptible to corruption over time.

3. For example, Anne Applebaum, *Twilight of Democracy: The Seductive Lure of Authoritarianism* (New York: Doubleday, 2020); Larry Diamond, *Ill Winds: Saving Democracy from Russian Rage, Chinese Ambition, and American Complacency* (New York: Penguin, 2019); Steven Levitsky and Daniel Ziblatt, *How Democracies Die* (New York: Penguin Random House, 2019); David Runciman, *How Democracy Ends* (New York: Basic Books, 2018); Astra Taylor, *Democracy May Not Exist, But We'll Miss It When It's Gone* (New York: Henry Holt & Company, 2019).

4. With every country fixated on the immeasurable benefits of the "knowledge economy," the centrality of universities has never been greater. But their campuses are not the prominent sites of protest they were in the past. Universities are indispensable as sites of research, training, and credentialing. But they are largely harnessed to serve as the nexus between business and techno-science. The traditional role of universities as the protected space of social critique and emancipatory discourse has been radically diminished.

5. Charles Postel, *The Populist Vision* (New York: Oxford University Press, 2007).

6. Letter of Thomas Jefferson to William Stephens Smith, Paris, November 13, 1787, accessible at Founders Archives, https://founders.archives.gov/documents/Jefferson/01-12 -02-0348.

7. This was the great theme of Niklas Luhmann; see, among many works, his *Social Systems* (Palo Alto, CA: Stanford University Press, 1995) and *Theory of Society* (Palo Alto, CA: Stanford University Press, 2013). Jürgen Habermas offered an account of modernity—and the potential for democracy—as necessarily accepting the separation of systemic management by "nonlinguistic steering media" from lived experience, including that of political freedom, in the "lifeworld." See his *Theory of Communication Action* (Boston: Beacon, 1987), esp. vol. 2, part 6.

8. For an extensive account of the relationship between democracy and the emergence of the neoliberal order, see Chapter 3.

9. Wendy Brown, *Undoing the Demos: Neoliberalism's Stealth Revolution* (New York: Zone Books, 2015).

10. Mark Fisher, *Capitalist Realism: Is There an Alternative?* (Winchester, UK: Zero Books, 2009).

11. Wendy Brown, *Undoing the Demos: Neoliberalism's Stealth Revolution* (New York: Zone Books, 2015).

12. Charles Taylor, *The Ethics of Authenticity* (Cambridge, MA: Harvard University Press, 1992).

13. David Goodhart, *The Road to Somewhere: The New Tribes Shaping British Politics* (London: C. Hurst, 2017).

14. The asymmetrical social status between mental work and physical work has been in existence in some form or other for a very long time—likely since the division of labor reached a certain level of complexity in the earliest settled agricultural communities. Its ideological justification can be found in philosophy as well as theology in every civilization. The Brahmins of ancient India are a perfect social embodiment of this ideology in operation. With the onset of the bourgeois revolution and the changes in the modes of social reproduction it wrought, mental labor came to enjoy not only higher social status relative to physical work, but increasingly disproportionate material rewards as well.

15. When one examines these social factors, education, with the credentials it confers, stands out as primary and preeminent. For instance, self-investment often entails acquiring appropriate skills and training through educational institutions that confer credentials. Further, educational institutions themselves are hierarchically ranked and the credentials they bestow are differentially valued. Thus, education has been transformed from a primary social good to which all citizens should have reasonable access to a competitive positional good to rank, value, and differentiate individuals and groups from each other.

16. Richard Florida, *The Rise of the Creative Class: And How It's Transforming Work, Leisure, Community, and Everyday Life* (New York: Basic Books, 2002).

17. For instance, in 2019, Apple directly employed 147,000 people and reported a revenue of $275 billion compared with Walmart's 2.2 million direct employees with a revenue

of $524 billion. The more revealing figures, however, pertain to revenue and profitability per employee: while Apple workers each generated $1.9 million in revenue and $403,328 in profit, their Walmart counterparts each generated only $246,415 in revenue and $8,752 in profit.

18. The ratification process of the US Constitution went from September 1787 to May 1790, and the Bill of Rights was ratified in December 1791.

19. Walter Benjamin, *The Arcade Project,* trans. Howard Eiland and Kevin McLaughlin (Cambridge, MA: Harvard University Press, 1999), 473.

20. Martin Luther King Jr., "The Other America," speech at Grosse Pointe High School, March 14, 1968; transcript at https://www.gphistorical.org/mlk/mlkspeech/. King's speech has had renewed currency in the wake of recent police murders, including especially that of George Floyd.

Acknowledgments

This book focuses on political deterioration and crisis, so it is not altogether cheerful. The process of writing it, however, has been much happier—despite the frustrations of the daily news and the need to eliminate large sections, whole chapters, and favorite sentences to keep the length manageable. We must acknowledge first the enormous value of friendship.

The idea for the book was born when the three of us presented interestingly intersecting papers at a conference organized by Shalini Randeria at the Albert Hirschman Center on Democracy at Geneva's International Graduate Institute at the end of 2017. We were in the midst of a "populist" political wave headlined by Brexit and the election of Donald Trump. This included European rightists from Viktor Orbán to Marine Le Pen and "left" populists in Greece and Spain. Farther afield, populism tangled with democracy in India's election of Narendra Modi, lip service to democracy in Vladimir Putin's Russia, and anti-democracy in Xi Jinping's China.

We initially planned a shorter, quicker, and more abstract volume consisting of the three original papers. As we talked with each other and as we worked, our understanding grew deeper and the book longer. We tried to attend to more actual cases, at least in the world's established democracies. The book grew longer and less finished. Eventually, we reached the compromise of looking at the general and more global issues largely through consideration of the United States, with some attention to Canada and Europe (and Britain if it still counts as Europe) more sustained comparison to India. Our delay meant the book could not appear before the 2020 US presidential election, as we once hoped. Predictably, the issues remain current.

We have discussed every aspect of the book together, learning from each other, debating, being surprised sometimes by our agreements and sometimes by what we saw differently. We come from different countries and different academic disciplines. We share a great deal, but not everything (appropriately enough for a book on democracy).

We have maintained and acknowledged our distinct voices. All chapters emerged from dialogue, however, and in many cases have been improved by questions from other members of the authorial team. While it is necessary to bring any book to an end, we hope these conversations and collaborations will continue. And it is fitting for a book on democracy that there seems always so much more work to do.

Like all authors, we have received intellectual gifts and incurred debts while writing. Our slower than anticipated progress gave us the chance to accumulate more. After the Geneva event that set this project in motion, we made similar intersecting presentations at conferences organized by Claudio Lomnitz at Centro de Investigacón y Docencia Económica (CIDE), Mexico City, in 2018; by Nilufer Gole of PublicDemos Project at EHESS, Paris, in 2019; and by Dilip Gaonkar and Shalini Randeria at Institute für die Wissenschaften vom Menschen, Vienna, in 2019. We have also rehearsed these ideas and arguments at numerous conferences and workshops organized by the Democratic Agendas Network sponsored by the Center for Global Culture and Communication (CGCC) at Northwestern University for the last four years. We have also spoken individually at too many symposia to mention, learning from the questions and criticisms of many colleagues. We are grateful to all the organizers and the attentive audiences they assembled.

Our friendship and collaboration have been nurtured by the Center for Transcultural Studies. Founded nearly fifty years ago in Chicago by the late (and wonderful) Bernard Weissbourd, the center is no longer a place. It is a network of far-flung participants in conversations about the transformations of culture, society, and politics. Since the 1980s, the center has been literally central to our intellectual growth and efforts to think through challenging public questions. It reminds us that our individual achievements—such as they may be—are possible only in social relationships.

We are grateful to too many other members of the center network to list them all. Jianying Zha, Ben Lee, and Michael Warner were particularly influential as we developed this project. Our partners, Pamela DeLargy, Sally Ewing, and Aube Billard, have been drawn into this network and these discussions. They are indispensable to our lives as well as to our thinking.

Liam Mayes provided sustained research and editorial support. Elizabeth Whiteman provided further valuable editorial suggestions. Dale Whittington and Boris Vormann read and offered helpful suggestions on a draft manuscript. We have also benefited from the supportive management of the editorial process by Ian Malcolm, Lindsay Waters and anonymous copyeditors and proofreaders at Harvard University Press.

Index

Page numbers in *italics* indicate figures.

abandonment, 207. *See also* neglect
acclamation, 168
achievement, possibility of, 12
Adams, John, 63, 178
Adenaue, Konrad, 91
advertising, 232
AfD (Alternative für Deutschland), 39–40
affirmation, 213–215
affirmative action, 145
affluent society, 91
Affordable Care Act, 23
Africa, 258. *See also individual countries*
African Americans. *See* Black Americans
aged, care for, 241–242
agency. *See* efficacy, citizen
AIDS, public health response to, 256
Alcibiades, 173
Alexander, Jeff, 34
Algeria, 93
all, definition of, 129
Allen, Robert, 85, 266
Allende, Salvador, 108, 163, 262
Alternative für Deutschland (AfD), 39–40
Amazon, 122, 278. *See also* information and communication transformation
American dream, 157. *See also* meritocracy
American Indian Movement, 56, 127
American Indians, 54, 69, 106, 116, 126. *See also* indigenous populations
anarchists, 251

anger bank, 161
anti-elitism, 123
antifa, 227
anti-intellectualism, 102
antitrust law, 71
Anywheres, 135–136, 276
AOL, 278
Apple, 278
Arab Spring, 20, 162–163, 205, 262
Arendt, Hannah, 42, 59, 176
arete, 173
Argentina, 258
aristocratic inheritance, 144
Aristophanes, 170
Aristotle, 18, 21, 171, 173, 175, 260
Asia, 42, 258. *See also* China
assembly, 203. *See also* crowds; riots
associations, 80, 89, 99, 272; civil society organizations, 234–235; climate action and, 256; erosion of, 236, 249; importance of, 65; neoliberalism and, 117; newspapers and, 66; road travel and, 95. *See also* community; connections; organizations; social support; solidarity; unions
attention economy, 232
austerity programs, 32, 40, 131, 245. *See also* euro crisis
authenticity, 24, 105, 129–130, 131–142, 175, 220, 275–276; appeal of, 130; as form of individualism, 133; meritocracy and, 147; neglect of less fortunate, 139; Silicon Valley and, 137. *See also* autonomy; identity; individualism; self-sufficiency

authoritarian democracy, 166
authoritarianism, 22, 44, 179, 208, 258, 263;
    dynamics of, 265; information flow and, 232;
    nationalism and, 22; resurgence of, 261; surveil-
    lance by, 231. *See also* China; Soviet Union
authoritarian populism, 165
automation, 26, 31, 121, 136, 273–274. *See also*
    technology; work, transformation of
autonomy, 130. *See also* authenticity

backsliding, 20, 23, 38, 165. *See also* degenerations
    of democracy
banks, 120
Bannon, Steve, 166
Belgium, 93
benefits: demands for, 107; loss of, 101; retirement,
    71, 90, 101, 119, 240, 242; in *les trente glorieuses*,
    100. *See also* health insurance; retirement
Benioff, Mark, 125
Benjamin, Walter, 283
Bezos, Jeff, 123, 124, 125
Bharatiya Janata Party (BJP), 166, 169, 179, 188, 192
Biden, Joe, 110, 138, 232, 244, 250
billionaires, 120, 123–124. *See also* elites
Bill of Rights, 52, 282
BJP (Bharatiya Janata Party), 166, 169, 179, 188, 192
Black Americans, 220, 222–223, 229; citizenship
    of, 53; Constitution and, 52–53; demands for
    equality of, 106; discrimination against, 57, 58;
    economic exclusion of, 100; empowerment
    and, 220; eugenics and, 148; exclusion of in New
    Deal, 249; GI Bill and, 57; great migration,
    75; illth and, 116; mass incarceration and, 220,
    228–229; police violence against, 37, 141–142,
    205, 207, 226–227; recognition of, 140;
    veterans, 57, 58; wealth of, 126. *See also* civil
    rights movement; exclusion; slavery; voter
    suppression; voting rights
Black Lives Matter, 37, 142, 198, 207, 226, 251
Black men, 222–223, 229. *See also* Black
    Americans
Black Panthers, 206
Blair, Tony, 146, 274
Bolshevism, 46
Bolsonaro, Jair, 166, 168
Bourdieu, Pierre, 104, 146, 157
Bourdieu catch, 104–105, 106, 146, 185–186
bourgeois revolution, 276–278
Braunstein, Ruth, 213
Brazil, 166, 258
Bretton Woods, 92
Brexit, 1, 3, 4, 38, 103, 136, 157, 216, 230, 252, 262
Brighouse, Harry, 151

Britain: Brexit, 1, 3, 4, 38, 103, 136, 157, 216, 230,
    262; collective identity in, 4; Conservatives
    against Labour, 36; Covid-19 response in, 14;
    democracy's endurance in, 160; education in,
    153; historical context and, 48; institutions in,
    240; internal decay and corruption in, 262;
    money-politics in, 230; Reform Acts, 54;
    undemocratic institutions in, 160; voting rights
    in, 54. *See also* England
Brown v. Board of Education, 178
Bryan, William Jennings, 70, 119, 266
Buffett, Warren, 123, 124
"Build Back Better," 250
bureaucracy, 25, 103–104, 106, 249
Burke, Edmund, 117
Bush, George H. W., 164
Bush, George W., 27
business: government economic engagement
    and, 99. *See also* companies; corporations
businesses, small and medium-sized, 255

Cambridge Analytica, 231, 233
campaigns, 26, 167, 169. *See also* elections
Canada, 4, 48, 218, 219. *See also* Quebec
Canetti, Elias, 199
capitalism, 9, 182, 268; changes in, 184, 249;
    compromise with democracy, 88, 97–102, 106,
    268–269, 283 (See also *trente glorieuses, les*);
    disruption by, 82–87, 185
capitalism, crony, 26
capitalism, organized, 98–102, 121, 269, 273.
    See also *trente glorieuses, les*
capitalism, stakeholder, 113–114
capitalism, surveillance, 231
capital markets, 76
Capitol, assault on, 1, 208, 214–215, 223, 227,
    262
care homes, 241–242
Carlson, Tucker, 280
cars, 95–96
censorship, 233
Census, US, 64
centralization, 74, 80, 236, 244, 249, 255, 256.
    See also decentralization
CEO compensation, 115
change, movements for, 203. *See also* social
    movements
changes, social, 7, 10, 85, 86, 87, 185–186, 195, 209,
    217, 286. *See also* institutions; transformation;
    trente glorieuses, les
Chávez, Hugo, 166, 168
childcare, 101, 222. *See also* institutions
Chile, 108, 163, 258, 262, 274

China, 46, 130; authoritarian governance of, 14–15; Covid-19 and, 14–15; loss of, 93; Mandarin elite, 144; mass group incidents in, 198; model of government, 1–2, 164–165; predictions of democracy in, 22; rise of, 274; surveillance in, 231; totalitarian rule in, 42

Christensen, Clayton, 82

Christians, Evangelical, 228

cities, 70, 72, 75. *See also* cosmopolitanism

citizens, 49; corporations as, 114; disempowerment of (*See* disempowerment of citizens; efficacy, citizen). *See also* demos; "people"

citizenship: of Black Americans, 52–53; equal, decline of, 24–26; in India, 204; removing restrictions on, 53–58. *See also* equality; inclusion

Citizens United, 112, 114, 230

Civic Sphere, The (Alexander), 34

civic virtue, 2. *See also* social foundations of democracy

civility, 280

civil rights, 90. *See also* voting rights

Civil Rights Act of 1875, 54–55

Civil Rights Act of 1957, 55

Civil Rights Act of 1964, 97

civil rights movement, 56, 58, 94–95, 127, 176, 178, 194, 225. *See also* social movements

civil society, 272

Civil War, US, 54–55, 56–57, 225, 282

class, socioeconomic, 100. *See also* elites; inequality; middle class; nonelites; working class

class conflict, 24, 174, 182–186, 283

class consciousness of frequent flyers, 81–82

climate action, 128, 253

climate change, 10, 42, 209, 249. *See also* Green New Deal

Clinton, Bill, 28, 274

Clinton, Hillary, 157, 167, 212

coalitions, majority, 190–191. *See also* majoritarianism

cohesion, 15, 59, 60–61; achieving, 59; democracy's need for, 134; loss of, 128; neoliberalism and, 117; in *les trente glorieuses*, 100. *See also* identity; public good; solidarity

Cold War, 89, 92, 93, 106, 274. See also *trente glorieuses, les*

collectivities: political capacity of, 173. *See also* demos; nonelites; "people"

college. *See* education, higher

colonialism, 93

colonialism, internal, 70

communication, 268. *See also* information and communication transformation; media

communism, 88, 91, 92, 134, 258, 269. *See also* China; Soviet Union

community, 16, 89; Anywheres, 135–136, 276; building new, 76; climate action and, 256; deindustrialization and, 122; erosion of, 2, 74, 96, 128, 209, 215, 218, 236, 239, 249; loss of young people, 74; neoliberalism and, 117; polarization in, 237–238; renewing, 85, 235–239; self-organized, 236, 238; Somewheres, 135–136, 276. *See also* associations; connections; mobility, geographic; relationships; solidarity; support systems

community, deliberative, 42–43

community, imagined, 176. *See also* "people"

companies. *See* business; corporations; employment; jobs; work

complacency, 8, 23

compromises, 271–272. See also *trente glorieuses, les*

conflict: between classes, 13, 24, 123, 161, 174, 181, 182–186, 283; culture wars, 275–276; social change and, 195. *See also* social tension

conformity, 272

Congo, 93

connections: democracy and, 81; economic ideology and, 78–79; erosion of, 2; media and, 235; national service and, 218, 236; need for, 217; renewal of democracy and, 257; republicanism and, 81. *See also* community; social connections; solidarity; support systems

connectivity, technologies of, 279. *See also* information and communication transformation

conservatism, 109

conservative label, 273. *See also* neoliberalism

conservatives, classical, 117

conspiracy theories, 208

Constitution, US, 21, 49, 50; amendments to, 281; Bill of Rights, 52, 282; Black Americans and, 52–53; contradictions in, 51–53, 57; discrimination in, 146–147; exclusion in, 51–52; First Amendment, 112, 114; Nineteenth Amendment, 53; overcoming contradictions in, 53–58; removing restrictions on citizenship in, 54–58; revision of, 52; Second Amendment, 52; task of, 62

constitutional-institutional strategy, 177

constitutions: erosion of democracy and, 264; republican, 50; undermining, 178–179

consumerism, 24, 91, 98

consumption, conspicuous, 151

coronavirus pandemic. *See* Covid-19 pandemic

corporate social responsibility, 112–114

corporations, 77–78, 111–118, 230, 273. *See also* business; employment; jobs; work

corruption, 2, 26, 154–156, 204, 211
cosmopolitanism, 81–82. *See also* cities
Cottom, Tressie McMillan, 155
Coughlin, Charles, 266
counter-powers, 44
coups d'état, 108, 163, 261–263
Covid-19 pandemic, 37, 123, 209; democracies and, 14–15; disempowerment of citizens and, 80; elites during, 81–82, 120, 139; health care workers and, 243; job losses and, 243–244; knowledge workers during, 278; polarization and, 208; recovery from, 10, 241, 244, 254; resilience and, 238; response to, 14–15; revelation of weaknesses by, 30, 239; service workers and, 243–244; technological transformation and, 279; vaccines and, 15, 244, 256, 280
creative class, 278
creativity, 121
crime, reproduction of, 228
crises: elites during, 123; euro crisis, 32, 40; financial crisis (2008–2009), 119, 120, 123, 131, 240, 274, 278; financialization and, 118–127; Great Depression, 90, 99, 247–249; neoliberalism and, 108–111; of 1970s, 106–127, 241, 272–273. *See also* climate change; Covid-19 pandemic
crowds, 194, 199–200, 211, 213–214. *See also* protests; riots
Crowds and Power (Canetti), 199
cultural capital, 104, 146, 156
cultural change, 217. *See also* social change
cultural fear, 40–41
culture, 41, 179. *See also* identity
culture wars, 275–276
cynicism, 12, 251

Dahl, Robert, 170
Dalit Panthers, 206
data collection, 67–69, 104, 230–233
Davis, Mike, 206
debt, student, 126, 155
decentralization, 236, 244
Declaration of Independence, 51–52, 58–63, 94
decolonization, 93
de Gaulle, Charles, 91
degenerations of democracy, 1–2, 16, 20, 31, 33–41, 193, 208–209, 218, 261
deindustrialization, 13, 87, 98, 113, 119, 121, 122, 249, 269. *See also* job loss
Deleuze, Gilles, 203
demagogues, 208, 213–216. *See also* populism; Trump, Donald J.
democracy, 18–19, 88, 126; adaptability of, 282; backsliding, 20, 23, 38, 165; compromise with

capitalism, 88, 97–102, 106, 268–269, 283 (See also *trente glorieuses, les*); confidence in, 7–8; contradictions in, 53–58; excluding from economics, 110 (*See also* neoliberalism); expanding capitalism and, 182; failure of, 244; future of, 1, 209; goal of, 38; historical contexts and, 48; identifying, 19–20; legitimacy of, 240; maintaining appearance of, 264; modern vs. ancient, 30; moving toward, 20; need for social transformation, 209; as only legitimate form of government, 164 (*See also* legitimacy); as permanent struggle, 193; predictions of end of, 164; as process, 128; as project, 8–9, 17, 48; resistances to, 160, 162; as self-transforming, 286; survival of, 161; telic character of, 19–22, 27, 31, 32, 48, 128, 160, 186, 281–283; undermined from within, 165, 262, 263–265; uneven progress by, 282; versions of, 159 (*See also* democracy, ugly); views of, 18–19, 21, 61–62; vulnerabilities of, 261, 265. *See also* degenerations of democracy; renewal of democracy; social foundations of democracy
democracy, Athenian, 170–172, 282
democracy, authoritarian, 166
democracy, direct, 61
democracy, failed, 17, 178–179, 244
democracy, illegitimate, 165
democracy, illiberal, 41, 166, 190, 265
democracy, representative, 26–28, 192–193
democracy, rigged, 41, 46. *See also* Iran; Russia; Turkey
democracy, social. *See* social democracy
democracy, ugly, 11, 165, 166–167, 178, 196, 264–265
Democracy in America (Tocqueville), 174
democratic breakdowns, 162, 163. *See also* degenerations of democracy
democratic crisis, 265
democratic method, 169
democratic recessions, 163. *See also* degenerations of democracy
democratic regeneration. *See* renewal of democracy
democratic socialism, 90, 209. *See also* social democracy
democratic theater, 264
democratic transitions, 7–8, 162–164, 258–259, 274, 278
Democratic Vistas (Whitman), 186
demonstrations, 204. *See also* direct action; protests
demos, 18, 49, 60; capacity for participation, 172; liberal anxiety about, 170–174; loss of cohesion, 128; Plato's image of, 199; recalling and remaking, 161–162, 178–180 (*See also* renewal of democracy); redescribed, 37 (*See also* exclusion;

populism); taming, 172, 176–178; translation of, 19. *See also* citizens; nonelites; "people"

Denmark, 36

depersonalization, 76

deprivation, 31–33. *See also* job loss; unemployment

deregulation, 115, 120, 269. *See also* neoliberalism

deskilling, 121

DeVos, Betsy, 155

Dewey, John, 65, 172, 237

dialectical image of democracy, 283

Diamond, Larry, 162, 179, 260

differences, accepting, 133

digital divide, 280

direct action, 182, 194–200, 201, 275; acceptable vs. unacceptable, 197–198; anxiety about, 196; appeal of, 202; in Europe, 207; in India, 201–202; location and addressee of, 203–204; molar, 203, 204–205; molecular, 203–204, 205–206, 207; temporal horizons of, 202–203, 204; violence and, 195. *See also* crowds; mobilization; protests; riots; social movements

disabilities, citizens with, 133, 140

discipline, 28, 104, 105, 106

discontent, 197–198, 201, 203, 207. *See also* direct action; frustration; protests; riots

Discovery of India, The (Nehru), 186

discrimination: authenticity and, 132; in Constitution, 146–147; loss of efficacy and, 185. *See also* inequality

disembedding, 49, 74–77. *See also* mobility, geographic

disempowerment of citizens, 3, 6, 9, 13, 126–127, 128; information flow and, 232; markets and, 79; meritocracy and, 150, 157; systemic organization of social life and, 80. *See also* efficacy, citizen; empowerment; inequality; voter suppression

disengagement from political system, 28, 180. *See also* efficacy, citizen

disinformation, 280

display, mutual, 206

disruption: by capitalism, 82–87; by Industrial Revolution, 74, 83–84, 89–90; responses to, 90 (*See also* movement, double); solutions to in *les trente glorieuses*, 128

dissent, suppression of, 235

distancing from politics, 180. *See also* efficacy, citizen

diversity, 217. *See also* inclusion

double movement. *See* movement, double

Dred Scott, 52

drug abuse, 228, 229, 269

drug prices, 228–229

Duterte, Rodrigo, 166, 168

ecological responsibility, 32, 128. *See also* climate action

economic relations, organization of, 79

economics, voodoo, 27

economy, stagnant, 118, 272–273

education, 50, 101, 240; artificial scarcity and, 149–150; capacity for participation and, 172; climate action and, 253; democracy and, 65; discrimination in, 146–147; expansion of opportunities, 146; failure to improve, 244; hidden curriculum, 104; investment in, 148; meritocracy and, 144, 145–147, 148–150; mobility and, 135; neoliberalism and, 118, 240–241; during postwar boom, 153; racial restrictions on, 94; reproduction of inequalities by, 104–105; required for work, 105; service to public, 245; sorting and, 105, 152. *See also* institutions

education, higher: academic research by, 234; access to, 219; admissions scandal, 154–155; competition for rankings, 153–154; cost of, 153–154; GI Bill, 57, 101, 153; hierarchy in, 152, 153–154, 155–156; importance to democracy, 234; inequality of, 150; less rich students in, 155; necessity of, 155; paying for, 126, 155; prestige and, 149; for-profit institutions, 126, 155; prosperity and, 219–220; public support for, 151; renewal of democracy and, 245; restructuring, 234; tuition, 154

educational attainment, 91

efficacy, citizen: decline of, 22–33, 37, 38–39, 45, 47, 136, 180, 182, 202, 248 (*See also* disempowerment of citizens); deprivation and, 31–33; dual tracks of, 184–185; enhancing, 180; during Great Depression, 247–249; loss of confidence in representative system, 26–28; nonparticipation and, 31; opacity and, 29; restoring, 185, 219; sense of, 184–185

efficiency, 14, 246. *See also* neoliberalism

Egypt, 163, 204, 205, 262

Eisenhower, Dwight, 95

elderly, provision for, 241–242

election fraud, claims of, 215, 224, 232, 262, 280

elections, 21, 193, 209; access to, 223, 224–225; centrality of, 170; erosion of democracy and, 263–264; fear of, 168; identifying democracy and, 19; improving, 223–226; liberal anxiety about, 190; media and, 230–231, 232; money and, 230; questioning of, 215; rigged, 41–42, 284; ugly democracies and, 166–167; views of, 189–190. *See also* campaigns; participation; Trump, Donald J.; voter turnout; voting rights

Index

electoral college, 168

electoral districts, 224

electoral fallacy, 178

electoral method, 169

electorates. *See* citizens; "people"

electrification, 95

elites, 25, 82; billionaires, 120, 123–124; conspicuous consumption by, 151; control exercised by, 177; during Covid-19 pandemic, 81–82, 120, 139; during crises, 123; distorted views of social reality, 141; dominance of newly emergent democracies, 160; globalization and, 10; justification of inequailty by, 156; meritocracy and, 150–151; mobility of, 81–82; relation with nonelites, 13, 123, 161, 181 (*See also* inequality; populism); rule by, 20–21; self-dealing by, 212

employment: full, 223; reliance on benefits from, 101; secondary benefits of, 98; service sector, 122; tax reduction and, 32; transformation of, 243, 249-250. *See also* jobs; wages; work

empowerment, 3, 237; freedoms and, 51; technology and, 279; of women, 221–222. *See also* disempowerment of citizens

engagement, 179, 180. *See also* participation

Engels, Friedrich, 82, 85

Engels's pause, 85, 86, 122, 182, 193–194, 196, 266. *See also* movement, double

England: democracy's emergence in, 160; Midlands, 73. *See also* Britain

English Civil War, 210

Enron, 242

environmental degradation, 106, 249. *See also* climate change; Green New Deal

environmentalists, 253

environmental movement, 32, 128. *See also* climate action

equality, 21, 32, 90, 271, 286; critiques of, 171; as democratic goal, 142–143; drive toward, 174–175; freedom and, 134–135; vs. inclusion, 140; maintaining established privilege and, 97; of opportunity, 138; public good and, 240; sharing, 62; solidarity and, 133; in *les trente glorieuses*, 100, 102. *See also* citizenship; inclusion; participation; social justice; social movements

equality, gender, 35, 106, 221

equality, racial, 95. *See also* civil rights movement

equals, society of, 171

Erdogan, Recep Tayyip, 166, 168, 190, 200. *See also* Turkey

essentialism, 130. *See also* authenticity

estate tax, 124–125

ethnonationalism, 186–189, 261. *See also* exclusion; "people"; populism

EU (European Union), 92–93, 103. *See also* Brexit

eugenics movement, 147–148

euro crisis, 32, 40. *See also* austerity programs

Europe: cynicism in, 251; direct action in, 207; exclusion in, 39–40, 248; housing in, 96; integrated economic development, 92; interwar years, 261; nativism in, 39–40; populism in, 45; reconstruction of, 95; during *les trente glorieuses*, 249; xenophobia in, 41. *See also individual countries*

Europe, Eastern, 20, 93, 162, 258

European Union (EU), 92–93, 103. *See also* Brexit

eviction, resisting, 202

exceptions, 146

exclusion, 6, 40–41, 129, 229; attempt to define "real" people by, 211; in Constitution, 51–52; digital divide, 280; in Europe, 39–40; false moralization and, 34; GI Bill and, 101; higher education and, 150; in housing, 96; idea of national people and, 176; moral reason and, 35; in New Deal, 249; during *les trente glorieuses*, 272; unions and, 86; waves of, 33–41, 45; in workplace, 100. *See also* Black Americans; immigrants; meritocracy; "people"; populism; racism; voting rights; women; xenophobia

expectations, democracy and, 8

experimentation: cultural / personal, 91; in greater democracy, 247–250

externalities, 116–118, 185

Facebook, 231, 233, 279. *See also* information and communication transformation; media

Fair Housing Act of 1968, 96

fairness, 21. *See also* inclusion

false dawn, 259

families, 239. *See also* community; relationships

family structure, 96–97

family wage, 101, 223

famines, 15

Fanon, Franz, 51

Farm Aid, 71

farmers' movements, 70, 119

fascism, 263, 269

Federalist Society, 226

Federal Reserve Bank, 118–119

feminism, 32, 251. *See also* women

film production, racial bias in, 142

financial crisis (2009–2011), 119, 120, 123, 131, 241, 274, 278 financial institutions, 120, 121

financialization, 12, 25, 118–127, 130, 245, 249, 273–274

Financial Times (London), 139

First Amendment, 112, 114

Five Star movement (Italy), 27

Floyd, George, 37, 141, 207, 226

Fordism, 98, 118, 272

Fortuyn, Pym, 35

fossil fuels, dependence on, 95

Foucault, Michel, 104

Foucault catch, 104–105

foundations for democracy. *See* social foundations of democracy

founders, US, 21, 50, 61–62

Fox News, 28, 214–215, 280

fragmentation, 24. *See also* partisanship; polarization

France: colonies of, 93; Covid-19 response in, 14; democracy's emergence in, 160; French identity, 72; Front National / Rassemblement National, 36, 38, 45; historical context and, 48; Macron, 216; republics in, 50–51, 160; rural life in, 72–73; voting rights in, 54; welfare state, 73; xenophobia in, 36; Yellow Vest protests / *gilets jaunes*, 72, 207

franchise. *See* suffrage, universal; voting rights

freedom, 129, 286; citizen empowerment and, 51; democracy's need for, 134; economic goals as, 92; as equal freedom of all, 129; equality and, 134–135; expressive, 105; individual, 12, 13; public good and, 240

Freedom House, 129

French Revolution, 50, 62, 190, 199, 286

Freud, Sigmund, 199

Friedman, Milton, 112–113, 273

Front National, 36, 45

frustration: blame for, 222; with bureaucracies, 103; inequality and, 134; limits to democracy and, 9; meritocracy and, 157. *See also* opacity; protests; social movements

fuel prices, 72, 207

Fukuyama, Francis, 164, 259

Galbraith, John Kenneth, 91

Gandhi, Indira, 169

Gandhi, Mohandas, 194

Gates, Bill, 76, 123

gay rights movement. *See* LGBTQ community

GDP. *See* gross domestic product

gender, renewal of democracy and, 220–223. *See also* equality

gender norms, 57–58

gender roles, 97, 104

Germany: AfD, 39–40; Covid-19 response in, 14; democracy in, 17; exclusion in, 39–40; historical context and, 48; nativism in, 39–40; populism in, 40; Social Democratic Party, 101; Weimar Republic, 261, 262

Germany, Nazi, 17, 148, 263

gerrymandering, 44, 224. *See also* voter suppression

Gettysburg Address, 55, 56, 58, 81, 181

Ghana, 93

GI Bill, 57, 101, 153

gig economy, 278. *See also* precarity; Uber

Gilded Age, 20, 71

gilets jaunes (Yellow Vest protests), 72, 207

Glass-Steagall Act, 120

globalization, 10, 13, 25, 26, 30, 87, 122, 130, 245, 249, 268, 269, 273–274, 284; beginning of, 92; job loss and, 31; people left behind by, 136. *See also* neoliberalism

global warming. *See* climate change

good, public. *See* public good

Goodhart, David, 135, 136, 276

Google, 279. *See also* information and communication transformation

Gorbachev, Mikhail, 164

governance, good, 164

government: distrust of, 102, 244; investment in capitalist growth, 98–99; lack of regulation by, 115; markets and, 79–80; neoliberal policies implemented by, 118; responsibility for conditions for democracy, 115; unions and, 99; wellbeing as object of, 102

government, minimalist, 108–109, 117. *See also* neoliberalism

government, mixed, 173–174, 260

Great Britain. *See* Britain

Great Depression, 90, 99, 247–249. *See also* New Deal

Great Downgrade, 23, 32, 33, 37, 47. *See also* backsliding; efficacy, citizen; 1970s

Great Transformation, The (Polanyi), 85, 194

Greece, 40, 93, 160, 162, 207, 258, 274

greed, 106, 130. *See also* neoliberalism

Green New Deal, 250–251, 252–255, 285

gross domestic product (GDP), 115–116

growth, economic, 270; after Second World War (See *trente glorieuses, les*); climate action and, 253; end of, 107 (*See also* 1970s); environmental damage caused by, 106; free markets and, 29; government investment in, 98–99; return to after pandemic, 244; social transformation and, 97. *See also* neoliberalism

Index

Habermas, Jürgen, 34
happiness, pursuit of, 62, 286
Harper, Stephen, 34
Hastie, William, 128
have-nots, 136
Hayek, Friedrich, 109, 110, 131, 269
health, public, 90, 101, 228–229, 241, 256
health care, 23, 98, 101, 150, 212, 230, 240, 244;
    access to, 228–229; climate action and, 253;
    control over crucial decisions, 246; during
    Covid-19 pandemic, 239, 243, 244; cuts to,
    119; efficiency in, 14; employment and, 98;
    failure to improve, 244; failure to invest in,
    241–242; neoliberalism and, 109, 239, 241–242;
    universal, 229, 241, 245; workers needed by,
    243. See also institutions; public good; public
    health; service workers
health insurance, 89, 90, 101, 109, 247. See also
    institutions; welfare, social
hedge funds, 120
Hegel, G. W. F., 259
heteronormativity, 151
hierarchy, 149, 151, 152, 153, 155–156, 280–281.
    See also inequality
Hispanic populations: exclusion of, 229; illth and,
    116; police violence and, 229; wealth and, 126
history, end of, 259
Hochschild, Arlie, 36
Hollinger, David, 188
Hollywood, racial bias in, 142
home ownership, 96
homo economicus, 273, 274, 275. See also
    neoliberalism
homosexuality: as identity, 132–133. See also
    LGBTQ community
housing, 94, 96
How Democracies Die (Levitsky and Ziblatt),
    163, 164
human capital, 83
Hume, David, 194–195
Hungary, 41, 45, 46, 165, 166, 190, 264. See also
    Orbán, Viktor
Huntington, Samuel P., 162, 170
hyper-partisanship, 3, 5, 126. See also polarization

ideals, 56
identity, 24, 33–35, 130, 132, 175, 186, 187, 211,
    235. See also authenticity; cohesion; exclusion;
    inclusion; "people"
identity, American, 4, 55
identity, British, 4
identity, French, 72
identity, mixed-race, 142

identity, political, 45, 60. See also polarization;
    populism
identity, shared, 2, 4, 60. See also cohesion;
    "people"; social foundations of democracy
identity politics, 140, 265, 275
Ignatieff, Michael, 165
illth, 115–116
IMF (International Monetary Fund), 92
immigrants, 12, 40, 217; accusations against, 216;
    economic exclusion of, 100; eugenics and,
    148; hostility to, 13; illth and, 116; as threat to
    "people," 187. See also exclusion
immigration, 71, 75–76, 216. See also migration
imperialism, 70, 160. See also settler societies
incarceration, mass, 62, 220, 228–229
inclusion, 4, 11, 32, 97; backlash against, 219;
    connections and, 219, 238; demands for, 107;
    vs. economic equality, 140; failures of, 3, 6,
    126, 212–213; hierarchical incorporation,
    280–281; informal, 4; media and, 238; move-
    ment activity and, 285; politics of recognition
    and, 140–142; problems of, 127; progress in,
    219; social foundation for, 238; socioeconomic,
    88; solidarity and, 129; as telic concept, 21;
    without changing structures of inequality, 219.
    See also equality; fairness; social movements;
    solidarity; voting rights
income subsidies, 223
India, 2, 11, 93, 209; anticorruption campaigns,
    204; anti-rape protests, 204; BJP, 166, 169,
    179, 188, 192; citizenship law, 204; Congress
    Party, 191, 192; Covid-19 response in, 14;
    democratization in, 258; election system in,
    169; electoral politics in, 191–192; ethnonational
    pull in, 188; Hindu majoritarian agenda in,
    192; liberals in, 169; Modi, 166, 168, 169, 190,
    200; population of, 64; slums in, 201–204;
    struggle over meaning of "We, the people" in,
    188–189
Indian Removal Act, 54
indigenous populations, 69, 93, 229. See also
    American Indians
individual, vs. crowd, 200
individualism: authenticity as form of, 133; entre-
    preneurial, 278; expressive, 132, 137, 269, 276;
    forms of, 132; increase in, 24; liberal, 217;
    possessive, 12, 132, 177, 276. See also authen-
    ticity; liberalism, expressive
Indo-Chinese peninsula, 42
Indonesia, 93
Industrial Revolution, 74, 83–84, 89–90
industry, 84, 121, 122. See also deindustrialization;
    job loss; work, transformation of

inequality, 2, 3, 6, 19, 30, 47, 79, 123–124, 125–126, 183, 184, 209; addressing, 185; authenticity and, 132; Covid-19 and, 14, 15; as desirable, 113; digital divide, 280; distribution of, 130, 140; education and, 149–150, 152; as fair, 105; in Gilded Age, 71; inclusion and, 219; increase in, 23, 26, 31, 128, 129, 218, 240; justification of, 156; loss of efficacy and, 185; meritocracy and, 143–145, 148; neoliberalism and, 14, 106, 138–139, 239; as permanent challenge for democracy, 283; perpetuation of, 104–105, 148; populism and, 210; problems with, 122; reducing, 89; struggle against, 186; technology and, 280; under Trump presidency, 23. *See also* class conflict; elites; meritocracy; nonelites; poor

inflation, 118–119, 272–273

information, 29. *See also* media; social media

information and communication transformation, 78, 233–235, 270–271, 284; blamed for democratic crisis, 265; empowerment and, 279; journalism and, 233–235; lack of regulation and, 232–233; neoliberalism's alignment with, 278–281. *See also* social media

information flow, 232

infrastructure, 95–96, 268

innovation, 91. *See also* information and communication transformation

insecurity, personal, 218

instability, 210, 218

institutions, 101, 209, 244; anger at, 105; biases in, 58; changes in, 29; declining trust in, 102; democracy's need for, 211; emphasis on, 178–179; functions of, 89; loss of, 209, 218, 235–236, 239; neoliberalism and, 106, 240–241, 249; New Deal and, 248–249; undermining of, 167, 178–179. *See also* centralization; decentralization; health care; support systems; welfare, social

institutions, counter-majoritarian, 177–178. *See also* Supreme Court, US

insurance, 120. *See also* health insurance

integration, 73–74, 77–78. *See also* inclusion

International Monetary Fund (IMF), 92

Interstate Highway System, 95

interwar years, 261

investment banking, 120, 146

investors, 115, 120

invisibility, 141

Iran, 41–42, 161, 188, 264

isegoria, 170–171, 184

Italy, 27

Jackson, Andrew, 53, 54

Jacksonian Revolution, 20

Jamaica, 93

Japan, 92

Jefferson, Thomas, 69, 73, 168, 268

job loss, 26–27, 30, 39, 58, 84, 90, 243–244

jobs: crisis of, 32; education required for, 105; importance of, 223; knowledge workers, 278; racial restrictions on, 94; reliance on benefits from, 101; service sector, 122, 242–243, 244, 249–250; supporting families and, 223; transitional occupations, 83. *See also* employment; wages; work

job security, 222

job shortage, 216

journalism, 66, 233–235

judiciary: denial of social justice by, 194, 195; packed by ruling party, 264; policymaking by, 212; voting rights and, 225. *See also* Supreme Court, US

justice, 151

Kaczyński, Jarosław, 166

Kennedy, John F., 56, 61

Keynes, John Maynard, 83

King, Martin Luther, Jr., 56, 94, 176, 194, 195, 203, 284

Klein, Ezra, 5

knowledge workers, 278

Koch Brothers, 32

Korea, 93

Korea, North, 42

Kurds, 46

labor movement, 251

Lachman, Richard, 125

Laclau, Ernesto, 187

Lafort, Claude, 187

laissez-faire, 111

Latin America, 162, 163, 258. *See also individual countries*

Latinos / Latinas. *See* Hispanic populations

law, rule of, 22, 49, 178, 257. *See also* stability

leadership, US, 210

Le Bon, Gustave, 199

Left, political, 101. *See also* communism

Left Behind, 135–136

legitimacy, 164, 165, 172, 173, 174–175, 264

Le Pen, Marine, 36, 38

Levitsky, Steven, 163, 165, 178

LGBTQ community, 32, 35, 127, 140. *See also* homosexuality; social movements

liability, limited, 111, 112

liberalism, classical, 12

liberalism, double, 136

liberalism, expressive, 12, 13, 130. *See also* individualism, expressive
liberal package, 190
liberals, 168, 169, 170–174, 190
liberty, 51, 271, 286
Libya, 163
life expectancy, 195
Limbaugh, Rush, 214
Lincoln, Abraham, 55, 56, 58, 81, 181
Lippmann, Walter, 172
literacy, 153, 196
loans, 120. *See also* debt, student
lobbying, 245
local, 82. *See also* community; rural life
Long, Huey, 266
López Obrador, Andrés Manuel, 190
Loughlin, Lori, 154
loyalty, 60
Luddites, 83, 122
luxury goods, 139, 154

Machiavelli, Niccolò, 181, 199, 268
Macpherson, C. B., 132, 177
Macron, Emmanuel, 216
Madison, James, 61, 65, 189
Maduro, Nicolás, 166
maidan, phenomena of, 204–205
majoritarianism, 3, 166, 169, 179, 181, 189–193, 212, 217; desire for permanence, 43–44, 191, 225, 257 (*See also* polarization; populism); evils of, 191; vs. majority rule, 190–191; republics and, 62
majorities, national, 4
majority, 42, 43, 61
majority rule, 43–44, 46, 190–191
majority status, 4
males, white, 100–101
manufacturing, 84, 121, 122. *See also* deindustrialization; job loss; work, transformation of
Marcos, Ferdinand, 168
marginalized communities, 178, 207. *See also* Black Americans; efficacy, citizen; Hispanic populations; immigrants; LGBTQ community; women
market failures, 110
market fundamentalism, 109–111, 117, 273. *See also* neoliberalism
market logic, 182. *See also* capitalism
markets, 16, 29–30, 240; disembedded, 76, 77; disempowerment of citizens and, 79; government and, 79–80; in neoliberalism, 109–111; public good and, 239–240; re-embedding, 76; as socially organized systems, 80; unthinking faith in, 30. *See also* deregulation; neoliberalism

markets, capital, 76
Markey, Ed, 253
Marshall, John, 111
Marshall Plan, 92
Marx, Karl, 82, 174, 183, 206
masculinity, 222
masses. *See* demos; nonelites; "people"
mass gatherings, 200. *See also* crowds
mass group incidents, 198
McCarthy, Joseph, 91
McKinsey & Company, 142
media, 212, 270–271, 279; affirmative, 234; changes in, 68; control of, 28–29; Fox News, 28, 32, 214–215, 280; hierarchical incorporation and, 280–281; inclusion and, 238; independence of, 234; invisibility of Black people in, 142; new, 17, 232–233; old/legacy, 16–17, 69, 233–234, 270; populism and, 32, 213; siloed, 5–6; Tocqueville on, 66; transformation of, 270 (*See also* information and communication transformation); Trump and, 28, 214–215; in ugly democracy, 167; as vehicles of pseudocommunity, 235. *See also* information and communication transformation; social media
membership, 129. *See also* inclusion
men, 221–222, 223
men, Black, 62, 220, 222–223. *See also* Black Americans
meritocracy, 105, 106, 137, 143, 175, 219, 245, 265, 276–278; as antidemocratic, 157; appeal of, 130; corruption and, 152, 154; defined, 130, 144; disempowerment by, 150, 157; education and, 144, 145–147, 148–150; elite and, 150–151; eugenics and, 148; inequality and, 143–145, 148; public good and, 150–152; resentment and, 157; *The Rise of the Meritocracy*, 158; Silicon Valley and, 137; solidarity undermined by, 151
#MeToo movement, 141, 221, 251
Mexico, 190
Microsoft, 278
middle class: erosion of, 123; growth of, 100; in India, 209; meritocracy and, 144; during *les trente glorieuses*, 91
migration, 10, 85. *See also* immigrants; mobility, geographic
military rule, 262–263
military service, 16
minimalist government, 108–109, 117. *See also* neoliberalism
minimum wage, 110, 221
minorities: demands for inclusion, 107; Supreme Court and, 178; as threat to "people," 187; voter suppression and, 224–225. *See also* Black

Americans; Hispanic populations; immigrants; women

misinformation, 227, 280

mobility, geographic, 74, 75, 81–82, 96, 134, 156. *See also* disembedding

mobility, social, 32, 135, 156–157

mobilization, 167–168, 251, 275; around problems, 237; climate action and, 253–254; of disaffected nonvoters, 180; ephemeral, 251; global, 255–256; vs. persuasion, 167–168. *See also* direct action

Modi, Narendra, 166, 168, 169, 190, 200

money: politics and, 230; power and, 122

monitoring, 67–69, 231. *See also* surveillance

monopolies, 71, 279

moralization, false, 34, 39

Morgan, Edmund, 187

mortgage and loan industry, 120

movement, double, 49, 85–87, 100, 127, 193, 212, 254, 266. *See also* Engels's pause

Movement for Black Lives, 198

movements, national, 238

movements, social. *See* social movements

moving, 75, 134. *See also* disembedding; mobility, geographic

Mubarak, Hosni, 168

Mugabe, Robert, 168

Musk, Elon, 124, 125

Muslims, 35

myths, 72

narrative, 186, 187

National Association for Advancement of Colored People (NAACP), 178

nationalism, 10, 22, 134, 188

national service, 218, 236

Native Americans, 54, 69, 106, 116, 126

Native peoples, 69, 93, 229

nativism, 39–40, 45. *See also* immigrants; immigration; xenophobia

Nazis, 17, 148, 263

neglect, 7, 38, 39–40. *See also* efficacy, citizen

Nehru, Jawaharlal, 186

neoliberal dispensation, 183

neoliberalism, 12–13, 26, 28, 131–142, 217, 269, 284; connections among people and, 78; corporations in, 111–116; crises and, 108–111; deindustrialization and, 113; externalities and, 116–118; inequality and, 14, 106, 138–139; insecurity and, 218; institutions and, 106, 240–241, 249–250; market fundamentalism of, 109–111, 273; mass incarceration and, 228; meritocracy and, 130; mythology of, 32; property rights and, 109, 117, 138; prosperity gospel of, 135;

public good and, 113, 117, 239–246; response to financial crises and, 131; spread of, 30; technological transformation and, 278–281; true costs of, 30 (*See also* health care; inequality)

Netherlands, 35, 93

New Deal, 88, 90, 95, 97, 110, 248–249, 285

newspapers, 66, 270. *See also* media

new world order, 259

New York Times, 214

New Zealand, 15

9 / 11 attacks, 274

1970s, 106–127, 241, 272–273. *See also* financialization

1960s, 103, 104, 106

Nixon, Richard, 107

nonelites, 174; ability of system to help, 28; relation with elites, 13, 123, 161, 181 (*See also* inequality; populism)

nonparticipation, 31

nonviolence, 194

normative, 186, 187

norms, 53, 179, 211

nostalgia, 209

nuclear disarmament, 93

Obama, Barack, 31, 44, 167

Ocasio-Cortez, Alexandra, 253

Occupy Wall Street, 27, 205, 266

oil crisis, 107

1 percent, 116, *125*. *See also* elites

opacity, 27–30, 280–281

OPEC (Organization of Petroleum Exporting Countries), 107

opiate epidemic, 122, 269

opinion, power of, 195

opportunity, 156, 229, 265; disembedding and, 75; equality of, 138, 276; restrictions on, 145; in *les trente glorieuses*, 100; wealth and, 125–126. *See also* meritocracy

opposition, in ugly democracy, 167

optimism, 94, 103, 251

Orbán, Viktor, 41, 45, 165, 166, 168, 190. *See also* Hungary

organization, social, 74–77

Organization of Petroleum Exporting Countries (OPEC), 107

organizations, 89. *See also* associations

Ortega y Gasset, José, 199

other, 27, 36. *See also* exclusion; immigrants

outsiders, 47. *See also* exclusion; immigrants

Pakistan, 262–263

Paris Commune, 199

participation, 64, 179; anxiety over, 170; capacity for, 171–172; decline in, 23, 25; of disaffected nonvoters, 180; learning, 65; by welfare recipients, 28. *See also* disengagement from political system; elections; equality; voter turnout; voting rights

parties, political. *See* political parties

partisanship, 3, 5–6, 60, 126. *See also* polarization

Pateman, Carole, 170, 172

patriotism, constitutional, 34

Patterson, Orlando, 51

peace, 97, 127

pensions, 71, 90, 101, 119, 242. *See also* institutions; welfare, social

"people," 19, 181, 186–189; cohesion of, 60–61 (*See also* cohesion; public good); in Declaration of Independence, 58; definitions of, 27; degenerative tendencies and, 187–189; direct action and, 204; disaggregating, 177; dumbing down, 27; as equals, 20; renewal of democracy and, 281; understandings of, 175–177, 187. *See also* demos; identity; nonelites; populism; solidarity

People's Party, 267

performance, 150, 213–215. *See also* meritocracy

personal protective equipment, 246

persuasion, vs. mobilization, 167–168

Pettit , Philip, 51

pharmaceutical industry, 228–229, 245

Philippines, 93, 166

Pinochet, Augusto, 108, 163, 274

place. *See* community

Plato, 18, 170, 171–173, 183, 199, 213

poiesis, 286

Poland, 41, 46–47, 166, 264

Polanyi, Karl, 9, 49, 74, 76–77, 85, 100, 127, 182, 193–194, 196, 269

polarization, 5–6, 10, 23, 24, 42–47, 127, 188, 209, 212, 215, 253, 275; Covid-19 pandemic and, 208; in local communities, 237–238; media and, 214–215; populism and, 136. *See also* majority; partisanship

police reform movements, 227–228

policing, unequal, 37, 141–142, 198, 205, 207, 226–229. *See also* Black Lives Matter

politeia, 18, 173, 260. *See also* government, mixed

political integration, 92–93. *See also* European Union (EU)

political parties, 238; in Europe, 216; frustrations with, 216; loss of power, 251; nationalist, 251; polarization of, 215; populism and, 213; social democratic, 27, 215, 251, 255

politicians, 5

politics: money and, 230; purpose of, 117–118

poor, 25, 148. *See also* inequality; nonelites

Poor People's Campaign, 94

popular classes. *See* demos; nonelites

popular sovereignty, 174, 175, 189, 193, 267, 284

populism, 3, 6–7, 13, 23, 44, 119, 128, 131, 210–217, 261, 274, 283; accusations by, 211; authoritarian, 165; backlash and, 281; crowds and, 200; demagogues and, 216; democracy's problems blamed on, 210, 265–268; effects of, 27; ethnonationalism and, 189; in Europe, 45; in Germany, 40; historical, 53, 55, 70, 210, 266, 267; identifying and dealing with issues of, 215–217; identity claims in, 211; ideology and, 267; inclusion vs. exclusion in, 38; intrinsic to democratic project, 267–268; Jackson, 20, 54; in low-density areas, 73; political implications of, 38; political parties and, 213, 216; as reactive, 212, 266; surge of, 32; susceptibility to, 33; in United States, 39. *See also* Brexit; exclusion; Trump, Donald J.

populist democracy, 166

Portland, Oregon, 226–227

Portugal, 93, 162, 258, 274

postwar era, 88. See also *trente glorieuses, les*

poverty, 130. *See also* nonelites; poor

poverty reduction, 89, 99, 113

power: constitutions and, 49–50; corporations organized for, 112; economic relations organized by, 79; money and, 122; peaceful transition of, 168; permanent, 257; sources of, 22–23

power, balance of, 18, 50

powerlessness, 25, 42, 202, 207. *See also* disempowerment of citizens; efficacy, citizen; exclusion

precarity, 126, 184, 202, 209, 218, 279

precedence, assumptions of, 36–37, 38

press, free, 50

priorities, 246

prisons, 62, 228–229

privilege, 130, 144, 145, 147

production, relocation of, 74, 84. *See also* deindustrialization

progress, 83–84

Progressives, 20

property, freedom of, 90

property, private, 108, 109, 117–118, 138, 240. *See also* corporations; neoliberalism

prosperity gospel, 135. *See also* meritocracy

protests, 27, 201, 251, 284; antifascist, 227; Black Lives Matter, 37, 198, 207, 226–227, 251; discipline and, 205; ephemeral, 284; of 1960s, 103, 104; response to, 226–227, 264; vs. riots,

198; temporalities of, 202–203. *See also* crowds; direct action; social movements

pseudo-democracy, 166

public, idea of, 49

public good, 2, 50, 59–61, 63, 235; commitment to, 15; democracy and, 240; idea of, 49; inclusion and, 141; majority's neglect of, 61; meritocracy and, 150–152; neoliberalism and, 113, 117, 239–246; prioritizing, 61; provision of public services and, 241–242; working for, 233. *See also* cohesion; health care; social foundations of democracy

public goods, 63. *See also* equality; solidarity

public health, 90, 101, 228–229, 241, 256

public services. *See* institutions; public good

public sphere, 235

public transit, 96

Putin, Vladimir, 166

Putnam, Robert, 65

Pygmalion (Shaw), 143

QAnon, 29

Quebec, 33, 35, 40, 216. *See also* Canada

race riots, 205

racial exclusion, 223. *See also* exclusion; voting rights

racial oppression, 226

racial purity, 148

racism, 13, 53, 58, 94, 141, 142, 228. *See also* civil rights movement; exclusion; inclusion; social movements

railroads, 95–96, 118

rallies, 204. *See also* direct action

Rand, Ayn, 45

rape, 204

Rassemblement National, 36, 38, 45

Rawls, John, 183

Reagan, Ronald, 27, 108, 274

recognition, 140–142, 265

Reconstruction, 54, 225

redress, options for, 196. *See also* direct action; judiciary

Red Scare, 91

re-embedding, 76–77

reform, 88, 248. *See also* social foundations of democracy

refugees, 40

regulations, 88, 99, 114, 115. *See also* deregulation; social foundations of democracy

relationships, 77, 80, 85; climate change and, 254; in communities, 237–238; companies and, 98; media and, 235; neoliberalism and,

117. *See also* associations; community; connections; solidarity; support systems

relief, immediate, 201

religion, 16, 35, 132, 145, 222, 228

relocation of production, 74, 84, 121. *See also* deindustrialization

renewal of democracy, 2, 218–246; communities, 235–239; experiments in greater democracy, 247–250; gender and, 219–223; higher education and, 245; money and media, 230–235; money and politics, 230; overcoming neoliberal bias against public good, 239–246; "people" and, 281; policing and, 226–229; protests and, 284; recalling and remaking demos, 161–162; rule of law and, 257; social change and, 10; taxation and, 245–246; voting rights, 223–226. *See also* direct action; Green New Deal

repetition, 168

repression, 89, 94. *See also* voter suppression; voting rights

Republic, The (Plato), 18

republican government, 49, 50, 59, 81. *See also* Constitution, US

republican imaginary, 260–261, 267

Republicans, 44. *See also* Right, American

republics, 18, 50–51, 60, 63–66, 165

research, academic, 235

resilience, 238

responsibility, personal, 132. *See also* individualism

retirement, 71, 90, 101, 119, 240, 241–242

rhetors, 173

Right, American, 34. *See also* Republicans

rights, individual, 177

rights, political, 88

right wing, 34, 228

riots, 194, 197–199, 201–202, 203, 284. *See also* Capitol assault; crowds

road building, 95

Road to Serfdom, The (Hayek), 109

Roman Republic, 50, 160

Romney, Mitt, 34

Roosevelt, Franklin, 248

Roosevelt, Theodore, 20

Rosanvallon, Pierre, 44

Rousseau, Jean-Jacques, 183

rule of law, 22, 49, 178, 257. *See also* stability

rules. *See* bureaucracy

rural life, 70–74. *See also* local

Russia, 41, 46, 166, 264. *See also* Soviet Union

Rustin, Bayard, 94

safety nets, 89. *See also* welfare, social

Sandel, Michael, 65, 147, 157

Sanders, Bernie, 38, 266. *See also* populism
scale, 63–66, 81, 103, 271
Scandinavia, 97, 131
scarcity, artificial, 149, 153, 157
Scholastic Aptitude Test (SAT), 156
schools. *See* education
Schumpeter, Joseph, 20, 169, 170
Schumpeterian model, 22
Scott, James, 202
Second World War, 92, 247, 274
segregation, 142, 152
selectivity. *See* inequality
self-definition, 129, 142. *See also* authenticity
selfishness, 63
self-realization, 130. *See also* authenticity
self-reliance, 26, 39
self-sufficiency, 130. *See also* authenticity
Sen, Amartya, 15
Senegal, 258
services, centralization of, 74. *See also* centralization
service workers, 122, 241–243, 244, 249–250. *See also* health care
settler societies, 37, 93. *See also* imperialism
sexism, 141
sexual aggression / violence, 141
sexuality, attitudes toward, 222
Shaw, George Bernard, 143
Sherman Act, 71
short termism, 5, 119
Sighele, Scipio, 199
Sikhs, 35
Silicon Valley, 82, 137, 146
Sky News, 32
slavery, 51–53, 160. *See also* Black Americans; Civil War , US; exclusion
Sloterdijk, Peter, 161
slums, 201–204, 206, 279
small and medium-sized businesses, 255
Smith, Adam, 78, 111, 112
social change, 7, 10, 80, 85, 86, 87, 185–186, 195, 209, 216, 217, 286. *See also* institutions; transformation; *trente glorieuses, les*
social cohesion. *See* cohesion
social connections. *See* connections
social contract, 99
social democracy, 30, 90, 165, 209; as mainstream, 101; as movement, 252; in Scandinavia, 131; during *les trente glorieuses*, 98–102; US version of, 101
social democratic political parties, 27, 215, 251, 254
social foundations of democracy, 2, 49, 88, 89, 159, 181; disruption to, 70–74; erosion of, 16, 208; importance of, 281, 286; renewing, 127

(*See also* renewal of democracy; *trente glorieuses, les*); responsibility for, 115; welfare state and, 272. *See also* identity; public good; regulations; solidarity
social issues, 218
social justice, 194. *See also* equality; protests; social movements
social media, 29, 67, 230, 232–233, 265, 270, 279. *See also* information and communication transformation
social movements, 30, 57, 86, 203, 275–276, 284, 285–286; after *les trente glorieuses*, 106, 127–128; Black Lives Matter, 37, 198, 207, 226–227, 251; Black Lives Movement, 142; ephemeral, 251; global, 255–256; #MeToo, 141, 221, 251; opacity and, 29; protests of late 1960s, 103; rise of, 32; solidarity and, 100; strategies of, 197. *See also* Black Lives Matter; civil rights movement; direct action; ecological responsibility; equality; inclusion; LGBTQ community; protests; women
social question, 15. *See also* inequality
social reproduction, 195, 277
social responsibility, 112–114, 273
Social Security, 242
social support. *See* support systems; welfare, social
social tension, 161, 173, 275. *See also* conflict
social transformation, 7, 10, 86, 87, 185–186, 195, 209, 217, 286. *See also* institutions; transformation; *trente glorieuses, les*
solidarity, 2, 4, 90, 99–100, 133–136, 187, 203, 271, 286; beyond local, 238–239; Black Lives Matter, 226; building, 134, 184, 237; climate action and, 256; equality and, 133; erosion of, 130, 131, 210, 249; global, 217; inclusion and, 129; lack of, 212, 218; meritocracy and, 157; movements and, 285; at national level, 217, 239; national people idea and, 176; need for, 134, 188, 239; polarization and, 10; public good and, 240; renewal of, 219; republics and, 50–51; sharing, 62; sources of, 16; in *les trente glorieuses*, 100; undermining of, 122, 128, 129, 133, 151; welfare states and, 131. *See also* associations; cohesion; community; connections; inclusion; "people"; social foundations of democracy; support systems
Somewheres, 135–136, 276
Sophists, 173
Soros, George, 125
South, global, 206
South Africa, 8, 93, 258
Soviet successor states, 162, 258. *See also* Europe
Soviet Union, 161, 162, 258

Spain, 31, 93, 162, 207, 258, 274
Spencer, Herbert, 109
Spinoza, Baruch, 199
square, public, 204–205
squatters, 201–203. *See also* slums
stability, 21–22, 115; end of (*See* 1970s); during postwar era, 86 (See also *trente glorieuses, les*); value of, 62. *See also* rule of law; *trente glorieuses, les*
stagflation, 118, 272–273
stakeholder capitalism, 113–114
standards of living, 91, 97
status quo, affirmation of, 141
Strangers in Their Own Land (Hochschild), 36
street, politics of, 205–206
suburbanization, 96
suffrage, universal, 19, 21, 168, 170, 181, 189; fear of, 169, 190; vs. individual rights, 177; legitimacy and, 174–175; popular sovereignty and, 268. *See also* majoritarianism; voting rights
Sumner, Charles, 54
supply chains, 14
support systems, 75; democracy and, 126; erosion of, 85, 218, 239; standardized tests and, 156. *See also* community; connections; disembedding; institutions; welfare, social
Supreme Court, US: *Citizens United*, 112, 114, 230; on corporations, 111–112; *Dred Scott*, 52; marginalized communities and, 178; voting rights and, 225
surveillance, 67–69, 165, 231, 272
suspicion, 161
Syria, 163

Taine, Hippolyte, 199
Tarde, Gabriel, 199
taxes, 245–246; estate tax, 124–125; fuel tax, 72; in postwar era, 89; reducing, employment and, 32; very rich and, 27, 123
tax evasion / avoidance, 124, 245
Taylor, Breanna, 141
Tea Party, 213–214, 266
technology, 68–69, 87, 121, 122, 130, 137, 149. *See also* automation; information and communication transformation; media, new
telic character of democracy, 19–22, 48, 128, 160, 186, 281–283
telos of democracy, 22, 27, 31, 32, 48. *See also* degenerations of democracy
Tennessee Valley Authority, 95
tests, 148, 156
Thatcher, Margaret, 108, 109, 274
thinking big, 254

Thucydides, 170
time, passage of, 182
Tobin tax, 246
Tocqueville, Alexis de, 64, 65, 67, 142–143, 174, 184
totalitarianism, 42, 232
towns, small, 135. *See also* community
transfer payments, 99
transformation, 9, 130, 270; climate action and, 254–255; by Industrial Revolution, 74, 83–84, 89–90; need for, 10–11; reproduction of inequalities and, 105; during *les trente glorieuses*, 94–97. *See also* civil rights movement; disruption; financialization; globalization; information and communication transformation; social change; technology; *trente glorieuses, les*; welfare, social
transitional occupations, 83
transitology, 259
transparency, 29, 50, 245–246, 280–281. *See also* opacity
travel, 92
trente glorieuses, les, 55, 90–97, 127, 183, 209, 272, 283; contradictions in, 94; decolonization during, 93; democracy's compromise with capitalism and, 86; end of, 106–107 (*See also* 1970s); Europe during, 249; exclusion during, 272; focus on needs of white males in, 100–101; optimism of, 94, 103; social transformation during, 94–97; taxation during, 246; unraveling of, 273. *See also* stability; welfare, social
Trinidad and Tobago, 93
Trump, Donald J., 22, 36, 178, 179, 262; assumptions of precedence and, 37, 40; Capitol assault and, 1, 208, 214–215, 223, 227, 262; claims of election fraud, 215, 224, 232, 262, 280; Covid-19 response and, 15; crowds and, 214; defeat of, 209; economics and, 27; election of, 157, 168, 192; father of, 76; followers of, 141; ideology of, 267; inequality and, 23; media and, 28, 214–215; polarization and, 44–45; political parties and, 216; populism of, 38; rallies, 200; response to protests, 227; veneration of, 266; women and, 221. *See also* populism
Trumpism, 3. *See also* populism
Turkey, 41, 46, 166, 190, 264. *See also* Erdogan, Recep Tayyip
Twain, Mark, 71
Twitter, 279

Uber, 81, 95
UK (United Kingdom). *See* Britain
unemployment. *See* job loss

unemployment benefits, 90. *See also* institutions; welfare, social

unions, 76, 77, 83, 89; bargains and, 99; decline of, 215, 249–250; exclusion and, 86; in Gilded Age, 71; right to organize, 84; suppression of, 55; during *les trente glorieuses*, 99; undermining of, 119. *See also* associations; workers

United Kingdom (UK). *See* Britain

United Nations, 91–92

United States, 11; Capitol assault, 1, 208, 214–215, 223, 227, 262; Declaration of Independence, 51–52, 58–63, 94; declining leadership of, 209; declining trust in government, 102; democracy founded in, 49; democracy's emergence in, 49, 160; democracy's endurance in, 160; educational system, 146–147 (*See also* education, higher); ethnonational pull in, 188; expansion of, 69–70; fear of Left in, 101; founders, 21, 50, 61–62; historical context and, 48; immigration to, 75–76; infrastructure in, 95–96; institutions in, 101; interest in rest of world, 92; internal decay and corruption in, 262; interventions against democracy, 93, 161; polarization in, 45 (*See also* polarization; Trump, Donald J.); population of, 64, 70; rural life in, 70–72; social vision of, 72; suburbanization in, 96; during *les trente glorieuses*, 94; undemocratic institutions in, 160. *See also* Constitution, US

Universal Basic Income (UBI), 223

upper-middle class, 123

uprisings, 194

utopianism, 91–92, 94

vaccines, 15, 244, 256, 280

Veblen, Thorstein, 151

Venezuela, 166

Vietnam War, 56, 93, 94, 107

violence: against Black Americans (*See* policing, unequal); direct action and, 195; against women, 204, 220–221, 222. *See also* crowds; riots

violence, collective, 198. *See also* riots

violence, symbolic, 157

virtue, public, 59, 64–65, 67

visibility, 141

voter suppression, 26, 34, 44, 62, 179, 224–225, 262, 264

voter turnout, 1, 25, 26, 170, 179. *See also* participation

voting rights, 4, 53–54, 94, 95, 223–226. *See also* civil rights; inclusion; participation; suffrage, universal

Voting Rights Act (1965), 97, 225

vulnerabilities, 181, 182. *See also* degenerations of democracy; exclusion; majoritarianism; "people"

wages: for care workers, 244; CEO compensation, 115; demands for increase in, 107; family wage, 101, 223; of knowledge workers, 278; minimum wage, 110, 221; in neoliberal era, 115, *116*; recovery from pandemic and, 244; supporting families and, 223; in *les trente glorieuses*, 100; for women, 221

Wallace, George, 266

wallet issues, 207

Wall Street (film), 130

Walzer, Michael, 172

war, 16

Warner, Charles Dudley, 71

Warner, Michael, 29

wave theory, 260

"We, the people." *See* "people"

wealth: distribution of, 115, 184; lack of, 126; opportunity and, 125–126; opposition to democracy, 246; shares of, 123

wealth gap, 98, 125–126. *See also* inequality

Weber, Max, 103

Weber catch, 103–104, 105

Weimar Republic, 261, 262

welfare, social, 131, 272; after Second World War, 86, 88, 95 (See also *trente glorieuses, les*); bureaucracy and, 103–104; catches, 103–106, 185–186; centralization in, 236; critics of, 157; disciplinary dimension of, 28, 104, 106; erosion of, 28; false moralization and, 34, 39; in France, 73; ideologies of unworthiness and, 26; under neoliberalism, 240–241; social foundations of democracy and, 272. *See also* institutions; social support; *trente glorieuses, les*

welfare reforms, 106

wellbeing, 102

Whitman, Walt, 186

Wilders, Geert, 35, 38

winner-take-all majoritarianism. *See* majoritarianism

women: economic exclusion of, 100; effects of pandemic on, 244; empowerment of, 221–222; equality of, 35, 106, 221–222; exclusion of, 51; gender norms and, 57–58; inclusion and, 107, 133; isolation of, 97; #MeToo movement, 141, 221, 251; recognition of, 140; violence against, 204, 220–221, 222, 229; voting rights for, 53; wages for, 221; wealth and, 126 women's movement, 54, 127, 251. *See also* social movements

work: crisis of, 251; exclusion in, 100; from home, 244; job shortage, 216; mobility and, 135; reliance on benefits from, 101; transformation of, 215, 243, 249–250, 273–274 (*See also* information and communication transformation)

workers: competition among, 74; displacement of, 85 (*See also* deindustrialization); empowerment and, 220; knowledge workers, 278; migrant, 101; mobility of, 269; neoliberalism and, 111, 113, 117; parties representing, 97; regulations and, 99; service workers, 122, 242–243, 244, 249–250 (*See also* health care)

working class, 100, 123, 215

World Bank, 92
World Economic Forum, 113
World War II, 92, 247, 274
Wright, Daunte, 141

xenophobia, 35, 36, 41, 43, 44, 207. *See also* exclusion; immigrants; immigration
Xi Jinping, 46

Yellow Vest protests, 72, 207
Yom Kippur War, 107
Young, Michael, 143–144, 146, 153, 157, 158

Zhao, Yusi, 154
Ziblatt, Daniel, 163, 165, 178
Zuckerberg, Mark, 124